The West Indian

A History of the West Indies

Jack B. Watson, M.A.

Senior Lecturer in History, Preston Polytechnic

John Murray 50 Albemarle Street London

Acknowledgements

Among those to whom this book owes a debt, I would particularly wish to thank Errol Carbon, who has influenced my thinking more than he knows. My debt to the writers of published works is acknowledged in the pages of this book and in the Further Reading. I owe a special debt of gratitude to Ed Rayner for his tireless efforts to improve the book while it has been in preparation, and for so generously making available to me both his knowledge as a historian and his expertise as a teacher. I would particularly like to thank Tessa Tulk-Hart and Dorothy Couzens at John Murray for their help, and also David Mandell, who drew the illustration on page 80. Finally, I must mention my wife whose interest in small islands is part of her own heritage, and whose assistance in the preparation of the book has been invaluable.

Thanks are due to the following for their kind permission to reproduce copyright illustrations:

Pages 35, 37, 48, 50, 60, 96, American History Picture Library; 9, 26, 98, 129 (bottom), 139, 144, 173, 181, Camera Press; 79 (bottom), Educational Productions Ltd, 0950/2 (1966); 49, 106, 156, Jamaican Tourist Board; 136, 145 (both), 165, Keystone Press; 79 (top), from *The Making of the West Indies* (p. 240) by F. R. Augier, S. C. Gordon, D. G. Hall and M. Record (Longmans); 85, The Mansell Collection; 2, 15, 20, 25, 33, 55, 69, 72, 75, 81, 99, 110, 112, 120, 124 (both), 153, Mary Evans Picture Library; 171, 187, 190, 192 (bottom), Popperfoto; 135, 154 (top), 'Punch'; 8, The Stamp Magazine (March 1978); all stamps are by permission of the Post Office and obtainable from Stanley Gibbons Ltd.

Printed in Great Britain by
Cox and Wyman Ltd, London, Fakenham and Reading

0 7195 3541 7

Preface

This book has been written primarily for West Indian readers who wish to know something of their heritage. It is concerned with the development of the West Indies from the late fifteenth century to the present day, and it attempts to draw together the many and varied threads which make up the heritage of the twentieth-century West Indian. Most of the West Indian islands and some of the adjacent mainland areas are considered but, since the book is written for the English-speaking reader, there is particular emphasis on the English-speaking islands and on Guyana.

The West Indian heritage is a rich one. The Caribbean communities descend from many varied peoples who came to the West Indies in past centuries. Successive European powers imposed on them their own culture and languages. But the age of colonial empires has passed, and West Indians are today building new nations.

It is hoped that this book will also be read outside the West Indies, for both the past and the present of the West Indian people have much to offer those who wish to be informed about the twentieth-century world and, especially, about multi-racial and multi-cultural societies.

Readers may well have the more immediate aim of preparing for a public examination in West Indian history (of the Caribbean Examinations Council or of the London or Cambridge GCE Boards). This book is certainly intended to be a useful source of information for those in search of basic historical facts, but students need more than that. They must be able to think and be willing to question. There is much in West Indian history about which there is still fierce argument, and this book will have failed in one of its main aims if its contents are seen only as 'facts' to be memorized. Ideally, this book should lead to further inquiry, and to the challenging judgments implicit in much that is read and taught. And so the aim of this book is twofold; to furnish the reader with information, and to encourage him to further thoughtful inquiry into the West Indian past and present.

To help the student, there are extensive cross-references and a detailed index. There are also exercises at the end of each chapter, some of which provide suggestions for further study, while others may be used for practice in preparing for an examination.

One aspect of the study of history is the broadening of horizons, and no history is more appropriate for achieving this than the history of the West Indies. It is rich in events and covers a wide range of human experience and human emotions. But history is also a living process of which the student and his teacher are themselves a part. The West Indian can claim that this is indeed his heritage, and it is a heritage on which to build his own future and that of his children.

Contents

Maps and Diagrams

Tables

1 The European Discovery of the Caribbean

On 12 October, 1492, the Arawaks on the island of Guanahani welcomed the Spaniards to the Caribbean. It was the first meeting between the Amerindians of the West Indies and voyagers from Europe, and the Amerindians could have had no idea of the changes which would result in the islands from the coming of the Europeans. The meeting was recorded only by the Europeans, since the Amerindians were unable to write, but Christopher Columbus, who commanded the Spanish expedition, himself bore witness to the 'good will' of the Arawaks. He went on to write,

> 'They neither carry nor know anything of arms, for I showed them swords, and they took them by the blade and cut themselves through ignorance.'

Columbus's expedition had reached land ten weeks after sailing out of Palos. During those weeks, his sailors had been driven almost to mutiny as they faced the terrors of an unknown sea and feared that unfavourable winds might prevent them from ever seeing Spain again. They now claimed possession of Guanahani on behalf of the King and Queen of Spain, considering it of little importance that it was already the home of the Amerindians; and Columbus gave the island a European name, San Salvador, in honour of the Christian Saviour. The Spaniards' aims in coming to the Caribbean were to gain Gold and Glory and to serve God: they were looking for riches and for heathens whom they could convert to the Christian religion. But San Salvador* was a small island with an area of only sixty square miles, and it seemed to offer no riches. Its Arawak inhabitants were few, and so there were few heathens to convert. Yet Columbus's expedition did achieve a sort of Glory, since the Spaniards had discovered what, to Europeans, was a New World.

From 1492 until he died in 1506, Columbus busily visited and mapped many of the Caribbean islands and the mainland of central America (see Figure 1.2 and pages 3–7). At the same time, the Spaniards began to set up colonies in the New World. It fascinated them, and quickly became the scene of a frantic search for riches, of fierce competition between European nations and some of the worst crimes recorded in History of human beings against their fellow men.

The countries of the modern West Indies were born during the centuries which followed the first landing of the Spaniards on San Salvador. During these centuries, the countries acquired their racial and cultural mixtures and diversities, a rich heritage but one which was the product of many injustices and ferocious struggles. The injustices and the struggles began at almost the moment when the Spaniards first set foot on San Salvador. Before the end of 1492, Columbus had noted of the Arawaks 'a better race there cannot be' and he described the Indians as 'so simple'. But he also recorded that the Spaniards were 'so avaricious and grasping'. Being of Italian descent himself, Columbus could view the Spaniards with detachment, and he had thus already been able to identify the cause of the first Caribbean tragedy: the Europeans' desire for wealth, which was to go far towards destroying the Amerindians in the West Indies.

The Age of Exploration

Columbus believed that he had reached Asia. He called the Caribbean islands the 'Indies', and their inhabitants 'Indians'. Asia was a part of the world already known to Europeans for its riches and for its millions of people, who, it was thought, could be converted to the Christian faith. Marco Polo, a Venetian, had travelled extensively in

* Now known as Watling Island.

Cathay (modern China) in the thirteenth century, and had left records of his journeys which Columbus studied carefully. Marco Polo mentioned an island, Cipangu (probably modern Japan), which was believed to be about 9000 miles from central Europe. In 1492, the only known way of reaching Cathay and then Cipangu was by a long and dangerous journey overland to the east. Columbus, however, came to believe that the world was a sphere, so he argued that it would be possible to reach Cipangu and Cathay by travelling west. To the west of Europe lay the sea, and thus the journey could be made by ships—ships which could carry a much greater quantity of goods than could ever be carried by land. He also argued that the journey to the west would be shorter, only about a quarter of the distance which had to be travelled to the east. The prospect excited him but mathematicians doubted his arithmetic, and the sailors on his first voyage of 1492 doubted his belief that the world was round. As they sailed ever further into the unknown, the horizon seemed to them just as likely to mark the edge of the world, over which they could tumble in a gigantic waterfall—assuming they had not already been devoured by some previously undiscovered sea-monster.

In the fifteenth century, Europeans knew only the world of Europe, north Africa and, indistinctly, Asia. Viking voyages, which in earlier centuries had reached Greenland and north America, had been forgotten. Ships did not venture far out of sight of land, and journeys overland were often made difficult by hostile tribes and fierce conflicts about religion. Conflicts with the Moors of north Africa drew the attention of Prince Henry of Portugal (later known as Henry the Navigator) to the African land-mass, and his sailors began to explore that continent's west coast. When Henry died in 1460, the Portuguese had gone as far south as Guinea and had laid the foundations for a profitable trade between Portugal and the west African tribes. In 1481, the Portuguese reached the Congo, which added to Portugal's importance and prosperity; and the journey also advanced European skills in navigation. The full extent of the African continent was still unknown, though it was clearly vast. Hope was growing that, if the west African coast could be followed to its most southern point, ships could then turn eastwards and reach Asia. This would be a safer route to Cathay than the overland one, which was often blocked by Moslems who were hostile to Christian travellers.

Columbus at San Salvador, 1492. An early print shows the welcome extended by the Arawaks and the haste of the Spaniards to erect a Christian cross

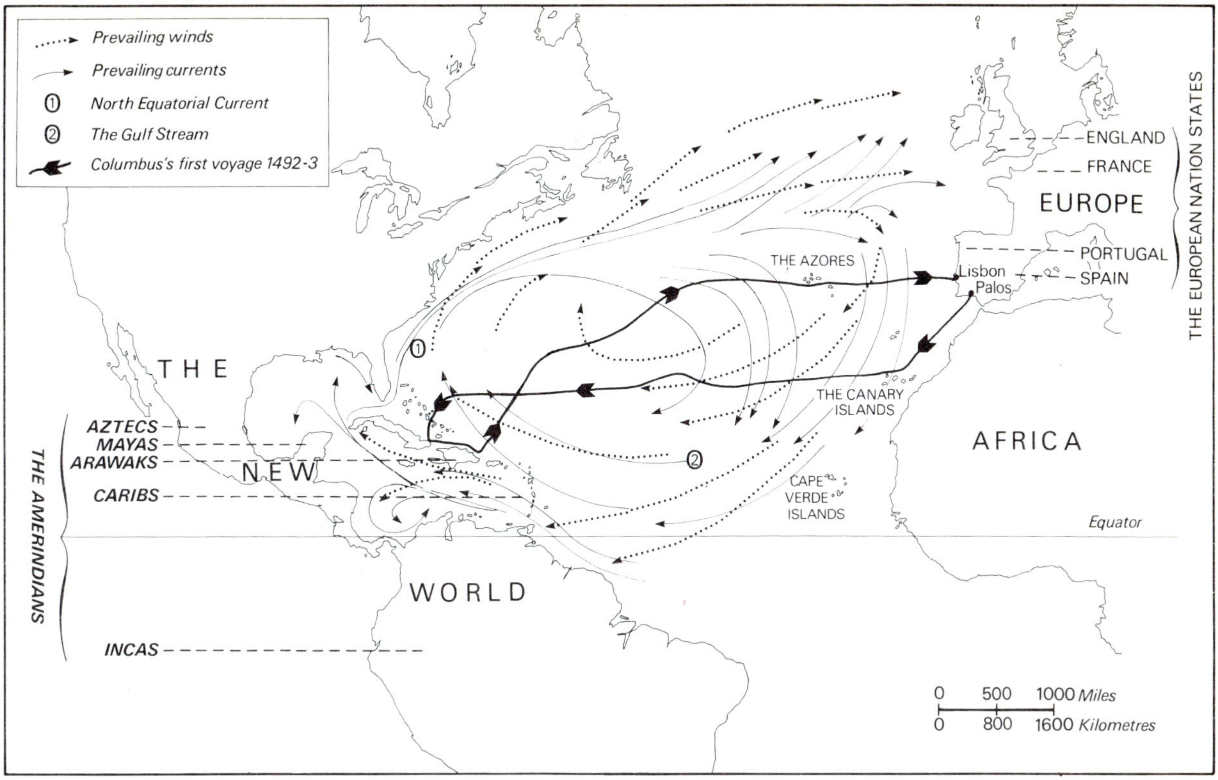

Figure 1.1 The Meeting of Two Worlds, 1492

The fifteenth century was a time when Europeans were growing increasingly curious about the world, and the development of the printing-press, the use of gunpowder and the improvement of navigational aids combined to make exploration and discovery more practicable. The prospect of a sea-route to Asia caught the imagination of growing numbers. For merchants, such a route held out the hope of great riches through trade. To the Catholic Church, it held out the hope of Christian converts. The rulers of Portugal, Spain, France and England, which were developing into nation states at this time, hoped for prestige and increased revenue. Each state was jealous of its neighbours, anxious to be stronger, richer and more important than they. So the Portuguese persevered in their exploration of the west coast of Africa until Bartholomew Diaz reached the Cape of Good Hope at its southern tip in 1488. Ten years later, Vasco da Gama carried the Portuguese flag round the Cape and across the Indian Ocean into the Indian spices-port of Calicut. The sea-route to Asia was open.

Columbus arrived in San Salvador during the years between the voyages of Diaz and da Gama. It suddenly seemed important to the rulers of Spain to obtain a sea-route to Asia as quickly as possible, if Portugal was about to reach Asia by a sea-route turning east round the southern tip of Africa.

The Voyages of Columbus

Christopher Columbus was the son of a weaver who, at one time, lived in the Italian city of Genoa. Columbus preferred to use the Spanish form of his name, Cristóbal Colón, but he was always handicapped by the fact that Spaniards regarded him as a foreigner. He became familiar with navigation in the Mediterranean Sea from an early age, and by the time he reached thirty he was beginning to look for a patron to support a voyage westwards, into the Atlantic Ocean.

The city of Genoa was not interested in such a venture. John II of Portugal also rejected Columbus's proposals for an Atlantic voyage, preferring more promising exploration along the African coast. Columbus then went to Spain where he secured the interest of a nobleman, the Count of Medinaceli, who recommended him to King Ferdinand and Queen Isabella. A commission of 'learned men and mariners' was appointed to study Columbus's proposals under the leadership of Hernando de Talavera.

Columbus did not argue his case well. In 1490, after four years of deliberation, Talavera advised Ferdinand and Isabella against supporting his venture. But curiosity about what lay to the west, together with the hope of riches and religious converts, proved stronger than the advice of learned men. Two years later, Columbus not only gained the support of the royal family but was allowed to name the terms on which he would agree to lead an expedition. Columbus's own investment in the voyage was supplemented by Queen Isabella, and Luis de Santagel was instructed to raise loans with which to equip the expedition under a guarantee that the Spanish government would repay them. To attract crews for the three ships which were to sail under Columbus's command, Ferdinand and Isabella held out the bait of pardons for past criminal actions. This *First Voyage* to the west set out from Palos in August, 1492, making for the Spanish-owned Canary Islands, where Columbus hoped to pick up favourable winds.

The flag-ship of the expedition was the *Santa Maria* which was barely thirty-five metres in length, and the *Nina* and the *Pinta*, the accompanying vessels commanded by the Pinzón brothers, were even smaller. In these tiny ships,

Columbus's flag-ship—probably a mere 100 tons (Anguilla, 1973)

the explorers left the Canaries early in September and headed out into the unknown. Reaching San Salvador on 12 October, Columbus knelt to kiss the earth and fervently thanked God for a successful landfall. The crews rejoiced with him, greatly relieved that they had survived in their cockleshells across the terrifying expanse of ocean. It was a gentle beginning to the European domination of the West Indies. San Salvador was Spain's first Caribbean conquest. 'Grand Admiral, Viceroy and Governor' of whatever he discovered (by decree of the Spanish royal family), Columbus took possession of the island without any resistance, encountering only astonishment and friendliness on the part of the Arawaks.

The Arawaks, indeed, offered to show the Spaniards the way to a more promising territory than San Salvador, the island of Cuba, over 200 miles away. Columbus's Journal reveals both his excitement and his confusion. His mathematical calculations suggested that this was Cipangu, and Cuba was certainly large enough to convince him that he had reached Asia. The Spaniards could not understand the language of the Arawaks nor identify the places by the names the natives gave to them. Travelling further and east from Cuba, Columbus was delighted to find an Amerindian girl with a gold nose-ornament in the land which the Arawaks called Haiti, and which Columbus named La Isla Española (Hispaniola). Here at last was the promise of riches. The explorer wrote down his hopes that great discoveries were imminent—'great riches', 'precious stones', 'pearls', 'spices' and, of course, 'gold'. He heard of Amerindian caciques with 'banners of beaten gold', but for the moment the great discoveries eluded him, and misfortune struck.

The *Santa Maria* ran aground on the north coast of Hispaniola. Columbus decided to leave the crew there, and they hastily built a fort (La Navidad) from the timbers of the wreck. It would be their job to search for the gold while he and the other adventurers hurried back to Spain with the news of the territories they had found. The small settlement at La Navidad was in the charge of Diego de Araña, and it was sufficiently well-armed to command the Arawaks 'with love and fear'. It was the first European colony in the West Indies, but it did not prove successful (see page 12). Meanwhile, in March, 1493, the *Nina* arrived back in Palos after a stormy passage, during which

Columbus had been almost convinced that they would drown and had considered committing the record of his exploration to a cask so that his successes should not be left unknown.

Honours and wealth were heaped on Columbus. Even so, he insisted on personally receiving the special reward which had been promised to the first of his crew to sight land, ignoring the humble sailor who had the more just claim. Preparation was quickly made for a *Second Voyage* so that Spain should not lose its advantage to any other European nation. This time, seventeen ships were fitted out, with a total complement of nearly 1500 persons. But personal rivalries and confusion as to the aims of the expedition delayed its sailing. Ferdinand and Isabella were anxious to give a high priority to Christianizing the inhabitants of the new lands, and they appointed a prominent churchman, Juan de Fonseca, to be in charge of 'Indian' affairs. It was also generally agreed that the lands should be settled and crops grown, but for many Spaniards the finding of gold had a higher priority. It was not until September, 1493, that the new expedition set out.

The Spaniards feared that the Portuguese would claim special rights in all discoveries on the route to Asia, so before Columbus's second voyage took place, the Spanish government was careful to get a legal title to whatever the explorer might find. They appealed to the Pope, the head of the Catholic Church, since in fifteenth-century Europe Christians believed that only the Pope possessed sufficient authority to grant a legal title in the New World. In May, 1493, the Pope granted Columbus's discoveries to Spain. The Pope's judgment and the Treaty of Tordesillas which followed it will be considered further on pages 11–12.

Armed with the Pope's authority, Columbus was ready to make more discoveries for Spain. The first West Indian island on which he now landed was Marie Galante and the list of Spanish possessions grew rapidly as he moved on, in succession, to Dominica, Guadeloupe, a host of smaller islands and Puerto Rico. Columbus himself still wanted to find the mainland of Asia. He did not have men to spare for settling these new islands, and, in any case, the islands seemed to offer little prospect of immediate finds of gold. Moreover, the aborigine people who inhabited many of these small islands were fiercer and more warlike than those the Spaniards had met on Columbus's first voyage. These were the Caribs, whom the Spaniards had already heard about from the Arawaks and whose name was to be given to the sea between the West Indian islands and American mainland, the Caribbean Sea. Columbus, therefore, continued westwards and returned to Hispaniola.

He found that the settlement at La Navidad had been wiped out by the Amerindians. This was the first of the many disappointments which Columbus was to meet in his efforts to plant colonies (see pages 12–13). A new settlement, east of La Navidad on the north coast of Hispaniola, led to the building of the first European township in the West Indies which Columbus called Isabella and entrusted to his brother, Diego; and a fort was built at Santo Tomás as a centre for mining operations and the search for gold. But Columbus himself was impatient to explore further. He went on to Cuba, still eager to establish whether it was the island of Cipangu or the mainland of Cathay; and in exploring the waters around Cuba he found the island of Jamaica.

Jamaica was the Admiral's last major discovery on his second voyage. Returning to Hispaniola in September, 1494, he became involved in the problems of administration. He appointed Bàrtholomew, another of his brothers, to take charge of the settlements, but it was evident that it was not easy to rule either the Europeans or the Amerindians. The search for gold poisoned all relationships. Columbus sent back to Spain some 500 Indians whom he offered as slaves to be employed in Europe, a substitute perhaps for the wealth not yet discovered. Queen Isabella disapproved, and sent the Indians back home. She also sent Juan de Aguado to find out precisely what was happening in the New World. Columbus saw Aguado's arrival as a threat to his own authority. And this, combined with his disappointment that only small amounts of gold had been found and that he had been unable to contact the Great Khan, the ruler of Cathay, persuaded the Admiral that he should now return in person to Spain. Bartholomew was left in charge of the settlements in Hispaniola with instructions to found a new colony on the south coast, at New Isabella (Santo Domingo). Columbus and Aguado sailed for Europe in the spring of 1496.

Columbus spent his time in Spain regaining the confidence of the Queen and preparing for his *Third Voyage*. Isabella had grave doubts about the

Admiral's apparent enthusiasm for enslaving the Amerindians. Referring to the traffic in Negro slaves from Guinea, Columbus boldly asserted that 'one Indian is worth three Negroes' and seemed to be mesmerized by the potential market for slaves from the New World. He persuaded himself that the man-eating Caribs, in particular, would be excellent slaves. The third expedition set out in May, 1498. Three ships sailed direct to Hispaniola. Three others, with Columbus himself, took a more southerly direction and reached Trinidad and the coast of the mainland. At this point, the Admiral made an error of judgment. He was still inclined to believe that Cuba was the mainland of Asia, so that he now thought the mainland of south America was yet another island. He turned north-westwards from Isla Margarita for Hispaniola.

Hispaniola again presented Columbus with problems. The settlement at New Isabella was more successful than that on the north coast, but there were still rivalries and indiscipline. Columbus resorted to executing disloyal settlers, and rewarded those who were loyal by allowing them, in effect, to enslave Indian labourers. Reports from the island again disturbed Ferdinand and Isabella, and early in 1499 they commissioned Francisco de Bobadilla to make ready to cross the Atlantic to investigate what was happening in Hispaniola. In fact, Bobadilla did not sail until the summer of 1500, and by that time he had been given authority to take over the island as Governor. Reluctantly, the rulers of Spain had been forced to the conclusion that Columbus was simply not competent to rule the settlements in the New World. Columbus himself vigorously protested that the problems of ruling in the Indies were underestimated in Spain. The Indies had 'neither a town nor any settled dwelling', and he claimed that he ought to be judged 'as a captain who went from Spain to the Indies to conquer a people, warlike and numerous' and who had brought under the authority of Spain 'another world'. When Bobadilla arrived at New Isabella

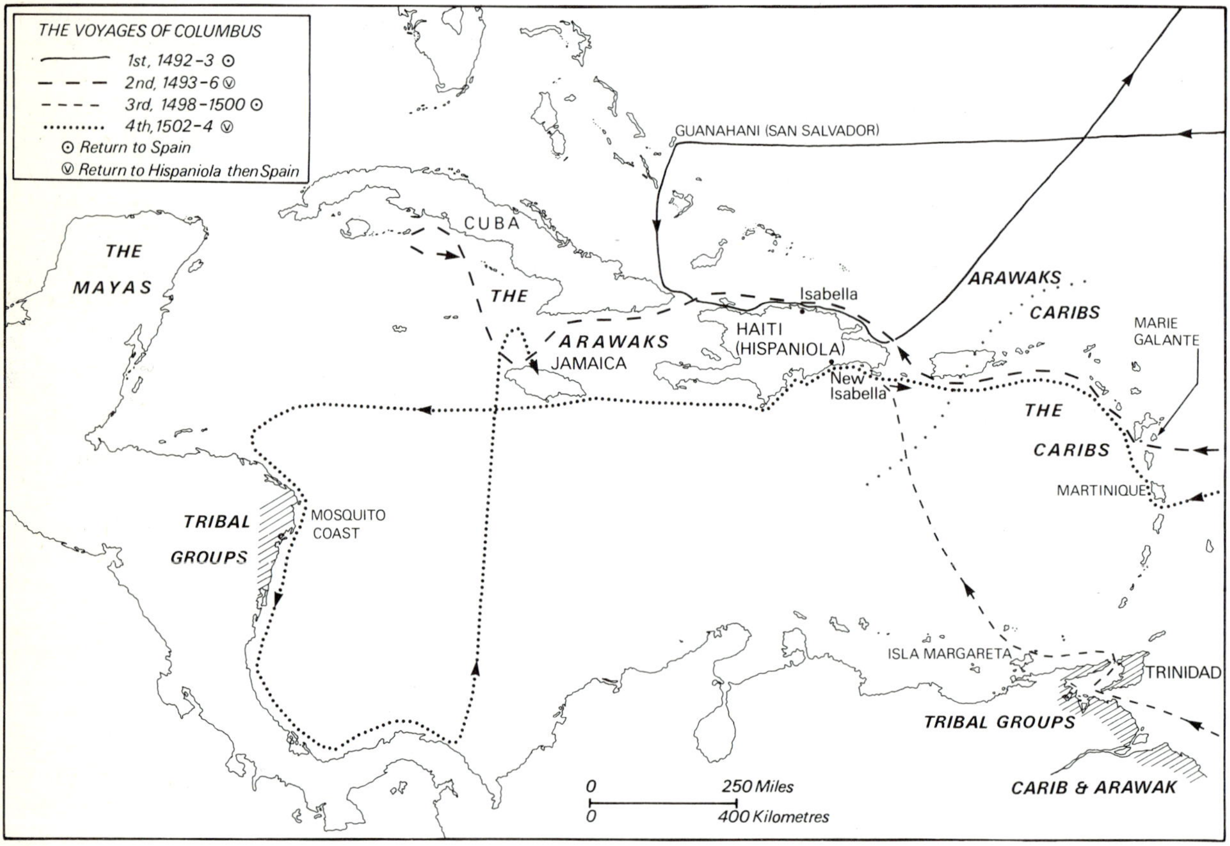

Figure 1.2 Columbus in the Caribbean

in August, 1500, Columbus and his brother Diego tried in vain to deny his right to take over control of the island. Bobadilla had both of them arrested and shipped back to Europe. They arrived in Spain in chains, but were then swiftly released.

Ferdinand and Isabella were willing to allow Columbus to make a *Fourth Voyage*, and even supplied him with four small ships. They were not, however, prepared to allow him to rule in the lands he discovered. He was no longer to be the Viceroy of the New World and was even forbidden to visit Hispaniola again. The fourth and final voyage began in May, 1502. In spite of the restrictions placed upon him, Columbus made for Hispaniola and was duly refused entry into New Isabella. He did, however, shelter from a storm further along the coast, the same storm in which Bobadilla, returning to Spain, lost his life. From this shelter, Columbus made his way to Jamaica and then, sailing first westwards and then south, his ships battered and wrecked by storms, he came to the coast of Honduras on the mainland. Still convinced that he was near Cathay, he planned to leave his brother Bartholomew and a small body of men in a new settlement, but they were driven away by the Indians. By June, 1503, what was left of the expedition had struggled back to Jamaica and there became stranded with the loss of its last seaworthy ship. Troubled by mutinous sailors and hostile Indians, it was the final humiliation for Columbus that he had to be rescued by a couple of ships sent from Hispaniola by Nicolás de Ovando, the Governor who had succeeded Bobadilla. Ovando had no wish to have Columbus lingering in Hispaniola and, within a few weeks of rescue, the Admiral was sent back to Spain where he arrived in November 1504.

Queen Isabella died in that same month. Columbus himself was a sick man, but he still petitioned King Ferdinand to restore him to his Viceroyalty in the Indies. That was out of the question. The Spanish empire in Hispaniola was taking shape under the able leadership of Ovando, and there was no place in it for an administrator who had failed as Columbus had. The Admiral died in May, 1506. His will, made on the eve of his death, showed that his heart was still in Hispaniola, 'which God gave me miraculously'. There he wished he could be buried, and his remains were eventually taken to the island in 1542.

Spain owed a great deal to Columbus. His voyages opened the way for the growth of an enormous Spanish empire in the New World. He had not, of course, reached Cathay or Cipangu. His Indies were not the East Indies but the West Indies. He had, in fact, opened the way to an unknown continent. By the time that he died, the Portuguese had also crossed the Atlantic, for Pedro Cabral reached the coast of Brazil in 1500. Amerigo Vespucci, another explorer, claimed to have reached the mainland of what is now Venezuela, and it was from him, not from Columbus, that America was to take its name. Nothing, however, can take away from Columbus the importance of his first Transatlantic voyage. Millions of Victorian school-children in Britain were later to learn the rhyme that,

> In fourteen-hundred-and-ninety-two,
> Columbus sailed the ocean blue.

What Did Columbus Discover?

This chapter and the map on page 6 have already shown that, from his arrival in San Salvador in 1492 to his exploration of the coast of Honduras ten years later, Columbus made known to Europeans the existence of a large number of territories in the Bahamas, the Greater Antilles and the Lesser Antilles. It was left for others to distinguish islands from mainland more effectively and to find out that, whereas the islands possessed only a little alluvial gold, the mainland would yield riches in plenty. It was also left to others to produce wealth from the islands by the cultivation of crops in the rich soil and under the hot sun. Chapter 2 will show that as a colonizer and administrator Columbus had little success but he paved the way for later generations to develop the Indies. His achievement was to prove that it was possible to sail westwards from Europe and to reach land.

Columbus himself was enchanted by the islands with 'such lovely vegetation' and 'the smell of the trees and flowers so delicious that it seemed the pleasantest thing in the world'. Many who travelled with him on his voyages were less sensitive. Their interest in the islands was in their profitability rather than in their vegetation, and they had little interest in tiny islands of volcanic origin which were merely the peaks of submerged mountains. Some of the larger islands were themselves mountainous, and almost everywhere there were dense forests which hard labour alone could clear. Other islands, particularly in the Bahamas, were of coral formation. In some cases, it was difficult to find a safe harbour, and some islands, like Barbados, were so far from their neighbours that not even Columbus found them. Europeans often found the climate harsh: it was difficult to endure the blistering sun even though the heat might be tempered by the north-east trade winds. Sickness and death lay in wait for many Europeans in the islands. Hurricanes too were likely to strike, as Bobadilla and Columbus himself found to their cost. Even so, from the time of the Admiral's second voyage in 1493, there was a steady stream of Europeans crossing the Atlantic to seek their fortunes in the New World.

They came for a variety of reasons. Some came only to plunder, to carry back to Europe whatever they could obtain with little effort. Some came in search of a new life, escaping from their debts, their disappointments and punishment for their crimes. Some came out of a search for adventure or through curiosity about the unknown. Some were sent by their governments to do a job of work, as administrators, justices and soldiers; and some, of course, came on behalf of their Church, to preach the word of God and to convert those who knew nothing of the Christian faith. The Catholics believed the Amerindians were urgently in need of Christianity.

For these aboriginal peoples, the World which Columbus discovered was Old, not New. What was new to them were the ways of the Europeans, their obsessive desire for gold, their dress, their weapons and ships, and their religious beliefs. The first and most important result of the Europeans' arrival in the West Indies was the cultural conflict which developed from the meeting of the Amerindians and the Spaniards.

The Amerindians

In the Greater Antilles in the fifteenth century, the Amerindians were mainly *Arawaks*. To them, Columbus paid tribute in 1493 when he wrote to Ferdinand and Isabella that,

> 'They exhibit great affection to all and always give much for little, content with very little or nothing in return.'

Arawak was the term used by the Spaniards to describe the Indians they found in San Salvador and other Indians who spoke a similar language. Arawakan-speaking Indians were also to be found on the mainland, but they lived mainly on the larger islands in the West Indies, having been driven, before 1492, from the smaller islands in the south by other Indians known as Caribs.

To the Europeans, the Arawaks seemed to be primitive people. They were illiterate, wore little in the way of clothing and their weapons were no match for those of the Spaniards. Columbus was impressed by their gentleness, but he also considered that they would be easy to conquer. Most of the Spaniards ignored the many virtues of Arawak society, eager only to 'civilize' them in the European fashion. In effect, the Europeans eventually destroyed the Arawaks, and their way of life can only be pieced together by archaeologists and historians. They lived in communities of perhaps fifty families or more, each community independent from its neighbours and ruled by a cacique (chief), whose office was often hereditary but whose power was small. They honoured their cacique by strangling him when he seemed to be dying, to speed him into the after-life. By studying their burial grounds archaeologists have been able to prove that the Arawaks believed in a heaven. Many bodies were buried with what they might need in the next world, such as decorated pottery and polished stone implements. It is difficult now to understand precisely what gods they believed in, but their religious ceremonies were often concerned with cures for diseases. The Arawaks may have believed that the first Spaniards they saw had come to them from heaven, for they had never seen European ships before and the horses the Spaniards rode astonished them. The Spaniards also carried weapons of iron and steel, which, it was sometimes suggested to the Arawaks, the

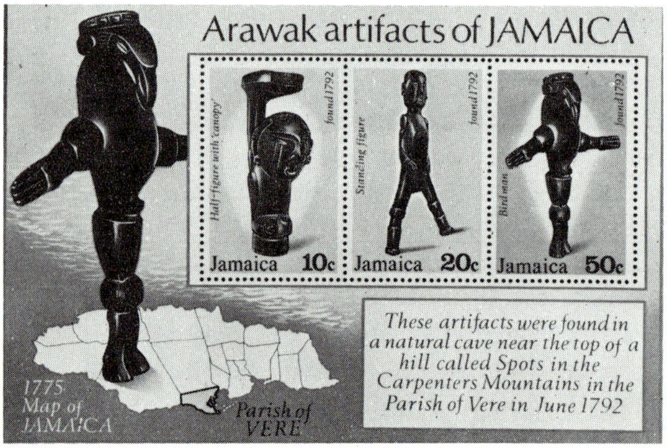

Arawak Artifacts, discovered in Jamaica (Jamaica, 1978)

Europeans would use to protect them from their enemies, the Caribs. So they welcomed the Spaniards, acted as guides, gave gifts such as parrots and willingly bartered their goods.

The Arawaks were by no means unskilled. They fashioned large dug-out canoes from the trunks of trees, and could confidently navigate across hundreds of miles. They grew crops, especially cassava, sweet potatoes, corn and yams. From stone, wood and bone they could make tools and weapons and, from shells, ornaments. From cotton, they could weave simple garments though they mainly went naked, occasionally painting themselves. They could also weave hammocks which were important in equipping their thatched houses, the houses being clustered in villages. They were, therefore, skilled in agriculture and in the making of simple articles, both useful and decorative, and they were, of course, expert fishermen and hunters. The Arawaks lived an orderly life, defending themselves when necessary, but in general respecting the rights of their neighbours and co-operating with members of their community. The search for wealth and the aggressive pursuit of power were not characteristics of the Arawak civilization.

But fifteenth-century Europeans thought of the Arawaks as uncivilized. The Indians had strange practices, such as flattening an infant's head between pieces of wood, either to have a fashionable appearance or to harden the skull. They were superstitious and appeared to be unambitious, even lazy, for, once the essential jobs had been done to provide food and shelter, they clearly preferred recreation to work.

A different race of Amerindians, the *Siboneys*, was almost extinct in 1492. The Siboneys were probably the first inhabitants of the West Indies, who had moved into the islands from the mainland more than 2000 years before the arrival of the Europeans. Nomadic and more primitive than the Arawaks, the Siboneys were driven northwards when the Arawaks entered the Lesser Antilles. By 1492, the Siboneys survived only in isolated groups, in western Cuba and south-west Hispaniola, for example. At this time, the Arawaks had been present in the West Indian islands for a thousand years or more, but within the last 400 years or so, they too had been driven northwards by the invasion of a third race of Indians, the *Caribs*.

Cariban-speaking tribes were still to be found

A descendant of the Caribs at work in Dominica today on a dug-out canoe

on the mainland of south America, especially in the Guianas, but the Caribs who, by the late fifteenth century, had taken over the Lesser Antilles from the Arawaks seemed to have developed a special ferocity. They were cannibals, who from time to time fed on the Arawaks; but then there were also Arawakan-speaking Indians on the mainland who included groups who were cannibals. What made the island Caribs especially fearsome was that their society was geared to warfare: the authority of a Carib chief (an obouto) rested on his strength and skill in fighting, and great emphasis was placed on toughness and courage in the bringing up of Carib boys. By 1492, the Caribs had reached as far north as Puerto Rico, forcing out the Arawaks from almost all the more southerly islands except Trinidad and making them retreat into the Greater Antilles and the Bahamas. Columbus saw nothing of the

Caribs until he made his second voyage. When he did meet them, he seemed to have two predominant thoughts: that the Caribs were 'very savage', and that they were 'suitable for the purpose' of being enslaved.

The Caribs were skilful and enthusiastic warriors (Antigua, 1970)

Like the Arawaks, the Caribs were skilled in the making and navigating of large dug-out canoes. They used these canoes to attack the Arawak communities and usually they out-fought them, burning their villages, eating their male victims and carrying off the women. Thus, Carib communities came to include considerable numbers of female Arawaks and became both Cariban-speaking and Arawakan-speaking. The Caribs also learned the skills of their captives. They learned quickly and Columbus considered them 'intelligent', but they were less interested than the Arawaks in the peaceful practice of agriculture. The Caribs preferred hunting and raiding though they were also capable fishermen. Like the Arawaks, they wore little clothing, but they painted and scarred their bodies, not merely for decoration as the Arawaks did, but also to give the appearance of ferocity.

The Arawaks' hopes that the Spaniards would rid them of the Caribs were to be disappointed. The readiness of the Caribs to fight was one reason why the Spaniards made little effort to settle on the smaller islands of the Lesser Antilles. The first European settlers concentrated on the larger islands, and there they became a greater menace to the unfortunate Arawaks than the Caribs had ever been, eventually working the Indians beyond the limits of endurance (see pages 22–6).

Amerindians on the mainland had developed more elaborate ways of life than those in the islands. The civilization of the *Mayas* centred on the Yucatán Peninsula, and was one of the most advanced civilizations in the Americas although by the end of the fifteenth century it was declining through civil wars and disease. The Mayas were capable of elaborate astronomical calculations, on which they based their calendar. They developed a form of hieroglyphic writing, and artifacts which have survived bear witness to the skills of Mayan craftsmen. Persons of rank wore rich garments, and Mayan architectural achievements included impressive temple-crowned pyramids. The Mayas also were eventually to be discovered, and in many cases destroyed, by the Spaniards. To the north, the *Aztecs*, who had developed an empire in Mexico, fell victim to the marauding conquistadors led by Hernán Cortés, and their fine stone temples were pillaged for their gold. The *Incas* of Peru suffered similarly at the hands of Francisco Pizarro (see page 16). Thus, the discoveries made by Columbus led to the disastrous impact of the Spanish civilization on the various civilizations of the American Indians. Neither the gentle Arawaks nor the comparatively advanced Aztecs were spared the Spaniards' greed for wealth. Eventually, the Spaniards and other Europeans were to build colonial empires in the New World, but the early years of Europe's contact with the Caribbean and central America were concerned more with demolishing the old than with building the new.

Exercises

1 'Fifteenth-century Europeans thought of the Arawaks as uncivilized' (page 9). Explain why the Europeans were likely to have held this opinion, and suggest ways in which the Europeans could have learned from the Arawaks.

2 Describe the ways in which the societies of the Arawaks differed from those of the Caribs. How did these island societies compare with the civilizations of the Mayas and the Aztecs on the mainland?

3 Why did Columbus come to the Americas? Which of his four voyages would he have been most likely to have considered the most successful?

4 Making reference to Figures 1.1 and 1.2, list the discoveries which were made by Christopher Columbus in the New World, and explain why, at the time of Columbus's death, Spanish colonizing activities were concentrated on Hispaniola.

2 The Development of the Spanish Empire

I THE FOUNDATIONS OF THE EMPIRE

Control and Demarcation

There was a short period in the 1490s when the islands which Columbus discovered seemed to be rather like his own personal empire. It ended in 1500 when Bobadilla arrived in Hispaniola (see page 6). From then onwards, the Spanish government made determined efforts to ensure that the islands not only belonged, on paper, to Spain, but that their inhabitants were obedient to Spain in practice. This was not easy to achieve. In the early years of the sixteenth century, many Spanish newcomers to the West Indies were interested only in gold and loot: they were greedy and undisciplined. Later, the Spanish government had to face the almost continuous efforts of other Europeans to break into the Spanish empire and steal from it. In 1523, a French privateer captured a couple of galleons which carried some of the Aztec treasures and saw for himself the wealth which Spain was obtaining from Mexico. When he took home his booty and the news, Spain's empire became an object of envy and a target for adventurers, and, before long, the Spaniards faced a lengthy and desperate struggle against the French, the English and the Dutch. The story of this struggle will be told in Chapter 3. At the same time, however, the Spaniards were trying to be constructive. They often worked with a strong moral purpose, since, in spite of the many crimes which were committed during the years in which the Spanish empire was built, their aim was to create orderly, prosperous and Christian societies throughout the Indies and on the mainland. The growth and development of the Spanish empire and its impact on the Amerindians will be the subject of this chapter.

Already, before 1500, the Spaniards had secured a legal title to their discoveries (see page 5). The problem of *Demarcation* had arisen when Columbus discovered San Salvador and claimed that he had arrived in Asia. Demarcation was clearly necessary to divide Spain's discoveries from those being made by the Portuguese. The Pope had earlier given permission to Portugal to take possession of Henry the Navigator's discoveries on the coast of west Africa. Spain had agreed to this by treaty, and the Pope had confirmed the treaty in 1481. But these Portuguese possessions were said to include the islands off the west African coast. Uncertain of the geography of Columbus's first voyage and eager to gain whatever profits might be forthcoming, the Portuguese claimed that Columbus's islands and discoveries must, by right, be theirs. They lay west of the African coast and were alleged to be on the route to Cathay, for which the Portuguese were still searching in 1492. Ferdinand and Isabella at once appealed to the Pope to settle the argument.

Pope Alexander VI issued the first Papal bull (decree) *Inter Caetera* before Columbus set out on his second voyage. He gave Spain the ownership of previously unclaimed lands which might be discovered in the search for the Indies. This was too vague for the liking of the Portuguese, and the Pope tried again in a second bull, similarly called *Inter Caetera*. This time, he drew a line from the North Pole to the South Pole, passing about 300 miles west of the Azores: discoveries west of this line would belong to Spain and those east of it, to Portugal. He went on,

> 'Let no person . . . presume to infringe this page . . . of our commendation. . . . For if any person does, he will incur the indignation of Almighty God, and the blessed apostles Peter and Paul.'

It was not known at the time, but this division would have given Spain the title to the whole of the Americas, including all of south America. The Pope also requested that all heathen peoples discovered by the Spaniards and Portuguese should be converted to Christianity.

Both John II of Portugal and Ferdinand and Isabella of Spain believed the Pope's line offered the basis of a settlement. In 1494, the two countries signed the Treaty of Tordesillas accepting such a line of demarcation, but they agreed to move it further west to give the Portuguese more space off the African coast. The line was now drawn about 1100 miles from the Azores, and the Pope confirmed this agreement in 1506. Thus, the islands of the West Indies were still allocated to Spain, but the new line had the effect of putting the east coast of Brazil into the Portuguese area of influence. When a Portuguese expedition under Cabral reached the Brazilian coast in 1500, the way was prepared for the later development of a Portuguese colony in south America.

The Treaty of Tordesillas provided a division between Portugal and Spain which lasted well. European Christians in 1494 were Catholics and they respected the bulls issued by the Pope, the head of their Church. In 1517, however, the Pope's authority was challenged by Martin Luther and other groups of Christians quickly developed who came to be known as Protestants. These Protestants did not regard the Pope as the head of their Church. Portugal and Spain remained firmly Roman Catholic, but the Reformation spread in the states which were further north in Europe and, during the sixteenth century, the English and the Dutch became Protestant. France remained Catholic, but French Catholics were inclined to pay less attention to the Pope when it was politically inconvenient to do so; France also came to include Protestant minorities known as Huguenots.

Even before the Reformation reached England, Henry VII sent the Cabots westwards to search for a route to Cathay, apparently assuming that the Pope's line of demarcation would not apply to the areas north of Columbus's discoveries. John Cabot discovered Newfoundland in 1497 and, although England did not take possession of it until 1583, Spain's rights had thus been infringed within a few years of the signing of the Treaty of Tordesillas. Henry VII had chosen to ignore the warning of the Spanish ambassador that he was likely to be trespassing on land 'already in the possession of' Ferdinand and Isabella. Therefore the Pope's ruling did not protect Spain from the states in northern Europe; and it was never, of course, regarded as legal by those who were not Christians, among them the Amerindians.

Columbus's Settlements in Hispaniola

The men left by Columbus at La Navidad in Hispaniola on his first voyage remained there mainly because the *Santa Maria* ran aground, and because they were willing to be the first to find the gold they believed existed there (see page 4). On his second voyage, Columbus came with the intention of founding a permanent colony. He brought settlers, farming tools and a dozen missionaries, to work amongst the Indians. The site was chosen, and the Spaniards began to build the new township of Isabella. But they saw no reason to plan carefully, and had learned little from the disaster which had occurred at La Navidad, where, in Columbus's absence, the Indians had been driven to fury by Spanish greed and arrogance and had wiped out the settlement. Columbus himself was anxious to leave Hispaniola, in order to continue his explorations. So the site of Isabella was chosen quickly, regardless of the fact that it was unsuitable for agriculture and that it even lacked a safe harbour. Columbus wished to put his brother Diego in charge of the settlement, regardless of Diego's lack of administrative ability, and it was not surprising that some of the settlers were soon plotting against the Columbus family. Disturbing stories of unrest and confusion in the colony reached Spain, and Queen Isabella rejected Columbus's proposal that he should send back Indian slaves in exchange for European cattle.

Without waiting to solve the many problems of the settlement, the Admiral sailed for Cuba and was away for more than five months. When he returned to Hispaniola, he transferred command of the settlement to his brother Bartholomew, went off on an expedition to capture Indians and sent 500 of them as slaves to Spain in spite of the Queen's disapproval. Columbus then angered the settlers by trying to tax them. It was at this point that Aguado arrived from Europe to remind Columbus of the authority of the Spanish rulers, and to try to improve the administration. Aguado and Columbus then returned to Spain and left Bartholomew in charge.

Before Columbus returned to Hispaniola on his third voyage to the islands, Bartholomew quarrelled with Francisco Roldán, one of the leading magistrates in Isabella. Once again, therefore, the settlement was in confusion and the arrival of Columbus himself did nothing to improve the situation. The Spaniards resented his rule as that of a foreigner. He continued to offend the Spanish royal family by trying to enslave the Indians, and he seemed unable to decide whether he should rule by seeking the goodwill of the settlers or by savagely punishing them. The most promising development in Hispaniola at the end of the 1490s was a new settlement which was made on the south coast on Columbus's instructions. It was a well-chosen site first known as New Isabella, and it was to grow into the important city and seaport of Santo Domingo where, as early as 1538, the Spaniards set up a university. It was clear, however, that neither Columbus nor his brothers had the administrative ability to make the settlement prosper. In 1500, Columbus's rule came to an end. He returned to Spain as a prisoner, leaving Bobadilla to sort out the unsolved problems of Hispaniola and to begin the business of establishing efficient government there. With some reluctance, Ferdinand and Isabella recognized that the proper role for Columbus was that of the sailor, not the ruler and Viceroy (see page 7).

The fourth centenary of the University of Santo Domingo was celebrated in 1938 (Dominican Republic, 1938)

Bobadilla and Ovando in Hispaniola

Bobadilla was himself replaced almost immediately. Queen Isabella was distressed that Columbus should be returned to Spain in chains and began to think that Bobadilla had perhaps exceeded his powers. In any case, it was now important that Hispaniola should have a new governor with proved ability and that a further batch of settlers should go to the island to work there and make the settlement successful. Nicolás de Ovando was chosen for this task. He was known to be an able organizer. So Bobadilla was recalled and Ovando sailed for Hispaniola in 1502 with 2500 persons, all that was thought necessary in seeds, livestock and tools, and the confidence of the King and Queen. When he arrived in Santo Domingo, he found that only 300 remained of Columbus's earlier settlers. The ill-fated Bobadilla took ship for Spain but drowned in a storm before he got clear of the islands.

Ovando was, officially, the first royal Governor of the Indies. He held office until 1508 and, though he was criticized for not rescuing Columbus more quickly when he was shipwrecked on his fourth voyage, and also for his treatment of the American Indians, it was Ovando who made the settlement of Hispaniola successful and made it a base for the expansion of the Spanish empire. His aim was efficiency and he showed ruthlessness in the pursuit of it. Troublesome settlers were weeded out and sent home, but it was the Indians who felt the full effects of Ovando's authority. Arawak caciques had already suffered at the hands of Columbus and Bobadilla, and it was Ovando who completed the 'conquest' of Hispaniola's Indians. Attending a feast given by the Arawaks to honour him, Ovando treacherously used the opportunity to seize Anacaona who had taken over the chieftancy from her dead husband. Anacaona was hanged as a demonstration, if it were needed, of Spanish power. Savage attacks were made on other Arawak communities, Ovando's example being followed by his lieutenants, amongst whom was Juan de Esquivel who was later to take control of Jamaica for Spain. The Arawak spirit was broken. They knew better now than to believe that the Spaniards had come as friends. Although Queen Isabella had instructed Ovando to treat the aborigines with justice, to see that they were taught Christianity and paid for their work, the Governor and the settlers saw the Indians as a pool of cheap labour to be used for the convenience of the Europeans. As early as 1503, Ovando was able to establish the principle that the Indians would be forced to work for their new masters (see page 22).

The labour of the Indians was of enormous benefit to the early settlers but Ovando intended that the Spaniards should also work to make Hispaniola prosperous. Spain expected to receive wealth from the New World, and, ideally, that wealth would be in the form of gold. Ovando organized mining and the panning for gold in the rivers and, for a time, before Hispaniola's small supplies ran out, the returns were satisfying, providing a substantial profit for the settlers and the Spanish government. But Ovando realized that Hispaniola must produce more than gold. The settlers needed food and it would be useful to offer something other than gold in payment for the supplies from Europe. It was, therefore, a time for experiment, to see what could be produced in Hispaniola and so, having established an orderly system of government, Ovando's next task was to organize the economy of the island.

The first year of Ovando's Governorship was not promising. Settlers died quickly, unaccustomed to the hardship and the tropical climate. A thousand died within a short time of arriving, but the service of the Indians made the settlement secure. To the crops of the Arawaks, the Spaniards added sugar-cane, rice and fruits such as dates and oranges. They quickly realized that these crops would grow more successfully than wheat and the plants which needed a cooler climate. They found it easy to rear livestock such as cattle, pigs and horses. They needed to operate on a scale sufficiently large to be able to send back produce to Spain in exchange for the European goods which would make life more comfortable. More settlers came from Europe. The population grew rapidly and, with the founding of new towns, the Spanish colony began to appear more permanent. It no longer clung precariously to just one site, and there was now a regular traffic to and fro across the Atlantic.

In 1508, Ovando expressed a desire to retire from the Governorship of Hispaniola and Diego Columbus, son of the Admiral, took over from him a well-established colony. It was one well-fitted to be the base for the further development of the Spanish empire.

The Extension of the Spanish Empire

The Spanish government sent out other adventurers to explore the New World even before the death of Christopher Columbus in 1506. Alonso de Ojeda, Vicente Pinzón (who had commanded the *Nina* in 1492) and others worked their way along what turned out to be the coasts of the mainland. Pearls were discovered, and Indian divers were used to collect them. Such profitable discoveries whetted the Spanish appetite for the founding of further colonies. The firm base in Hispaniola provided a foundation on which the empire could be built, and throughout the sixteenth century the empire grew steadily in size (see Figure 2.1).

This book is not primarily concerned with the mainland of the Americas, and it is enough to say that, by 1519, the Spaniards had mapped the coast of the mainland from Florida in the north to Brazil in the south. They had also made a settlement on the coast of Panama, and Vasco de Balboa, crossing the Isthmus of Panama in 1513, had discovered the Pacific Ocean. Soon, Spain's mainland empire stretched from Mexico to Chile, while the Portuguese developed an empire in Brazil. Moreover, in 1521, Ferdinand Magellan found a way round the southern shores of south America and opened the way into the Pacific.

During this time, the Spaniards also extended their empire in the islands of the West Indies. The extension began in 1508, when Juan Ponce de León settled in *Puerto Rico*. The island's Caribs put up a stout resistance and so did the Arawaks who had been conditioned to warfare by attacks from their fierce neighbours. But the Spaniards were now not only ruthless and well armed but also well organized, and the Indians could not hope to win in the end. Nevertheless, it took some years to complete the conquest of Puerto Rico for León went off on a fruitless expedition to Florida, prey to the restlessness which still hampered many of the efforts of the early Spanish colonizers. Compared with other Spanish islands Puerto Rico was slow to develop.

The Arawaks of *Jamaica* were able to offer little resistance. Diego Columbus sent Esquivel to occupy it in 1509 and Esquivel was already well-practised in the butchering of Indians. As Governor of the island, he followed the pattern of development which had been successful in Hispaniola under Ovando. The Indians were put to work. A search was made, in this case in vain, for gold which could be mined or washed from the rivers. Crops were planted and livestock reared. Towns were built and the population grew. In the course of time, Jamaica became important to the Spanish empire for its cattle ranches. It remained under Spanish control until seized by the English in 1655.

In 1511, Diego Velásquez began the conquest of *Cuba* and he, in turn, became Cuba's Ovando.

Arawak resistance took some three years to overcome since some of them had earlier fled from Hispaniola, bringing with them to Cuba a hatred of the Spaniards. All the Indians who survived this new encounter with the Europeans were enslaved. On account of its size and the able administration of Velásquez, Cuba soon became sufficiently prosperous to be almost independent of the parent-government of Diego Columbus in Hispaniola; and Velásquez began mounting his own expeditions to the mainland. But he did not neglect the island's development. Havana, which was founded in 1514, was among the towns he built, and by the second half of the sixteenth century it had become one of the most important Spanish ports-of-call, important particularly to the convoys which carried the wealth of the New World to Spain. Cuba yielded gold and had plenty of space for the prosperous development of agriculture and for the rearing of livestock.

In the early years of the sixteenth century, however, all of these islands were handicapped by the lure of the *mainland* and the restless searching of the Spaniards for easily acquired wealth. The quality of the administrators had improved since the 1490s and the settlements of Christopher Columbus, but comparatively few of the Spanish settlers were ready to commit themselves to a lifetime of hard work. The climate, moreover, continued to take its heavy toll through tropical diseases. The islands were like sieves: they needed constantly to be topped up with newcomers —Europeans, to replace the Europeans who moved on or died; and imported Indian labourers

Spanish brutality took a heavy toll. In Peru, the Conquistadors found both loot and Amerindians to carry it

to supply the work-force, as Arawaks fled or perished from their sufferings. Not until the first frantic period of conquest was over could the Spanish empire really settle down to a period of construction.

The Yucatán was explored by Francisco de Córdoba whom Velásquez had sent. The civilization of the Mayas was interesting, but it was the rumours of greater riches to the west which captivated the Spaniards, and in 1518 Cortés left Havana in search of them. His expedition owed much to the financial support of Velásquez and he set out with about 500 Europeans and a supporting force of Indians. But it was typical of the Spaniards to quarrel at this time, and Cortés had already clashed with Velásquez and renounced his overlordship. Cortés took some two years to locate and conquer the city of Tenochtitlán (Mexico City), the capital of the Aztec empire. When he did so, the Spaniards found astonishing wealth. Montezuma, Emperor of the Aztecs, was forced to accept the rule of Spain but lived only a brief time longer to endure his humiliation. News of the capture of Tenochtitlán and of its stone temples, ornamented in gold, inevitably drew other Spaniards to the mainland. A force, sent from Cuba to arrest Cortés and make him submit to the authority of Velásquez, simply joined him in the plundering. The riches of the Aztecs were what the Spaniards had dreamed of.

Their dreams of wealth were kept alive by the conquest of Peru by Pizarro. Pizarro's force of men was even smaller than that of Cortés when he reached Peru in 1532, but other conquistadors flocked to join him and to seize the riches of the Incas. The Inca ruler, Atahualpa, was put to death and his empire was subdued after two further years of fighting. Their conquerors carried off abundant supplies of silver and gold.

For some years, therefore, Mexico and Peru acted as magnets, draining the manpower from the Spanish islands in the West Indies. But Hispaniola, Puerto Rico, Jamaica and Cuba were never entirely abandoned and, by the middle of the sixteenth century, the Spaniards were ready to show more interest in agriculture and trade. European settlement on the islands increased, and this time the settlers stayed, populating the cities such as Havana and Santo Domingo, cultivating the land, and making themselves at home.

Spain's possessions on the mainland were so vast, however, that the islands of the West Indies were inevitably overshadowed in the Spanish mind. Almost all of the smaller islands were neglected. There was no evidence that they possessed much wealth and Spain had not the manpower to occupy them. But the Spaniards quoted the bulls *Inter Caetera* and the Treaty of Tordesillas as reasons why they should be considered Spanish property and why no other country should occupy them. Even the large island of *Trinidad,* which Columbus had discovered in 1498, was not occupied until 1532 when the Spaniards appointed its first governor. But the Spaniards showed little interest in the island itself and tended to regard it as little more than a base from which to search for riches on the mainland of south America. It was not until 1592 that permanent occupation began under the governorship of Antonio de Berrio.

By the end of the sixteenth century the Spaniards had established permanent settlements on all of the larger islands in the West Indies. Some of the islands were beginning to prosper in their own right, but in relation to the Spanish empire in the New World as a whole the West Indian islands were little more than outer defences. They formed a sort of barrier to keep away Spain's rivals from the settlements on the mainland, and served as staging-posts, useful harbours and bases, in the organization of Spain's busy Transatlantic shipping.

How the Spaniards Organized the Empire

It will be convenient to examine the organization of Spain's empire under three headings: political, economic and social.

Political

From the beginning, Spain faced the problem of making sure that the Spaniards in the New World remained loyal to their mother country. It was often suggested to Ferdinand and Isabella that Columbus was trying to build for himself a private empire, independent of their authority. Therefore, it seemed essential at an early stage to create a system of control which would both protect the rights of the Spanish government and allow some room for decisions to be taken on the spot in the West Indies and in America. Overall control of the empire was centred on the Supreme Council of the Indies, which sat in Spain and which the king

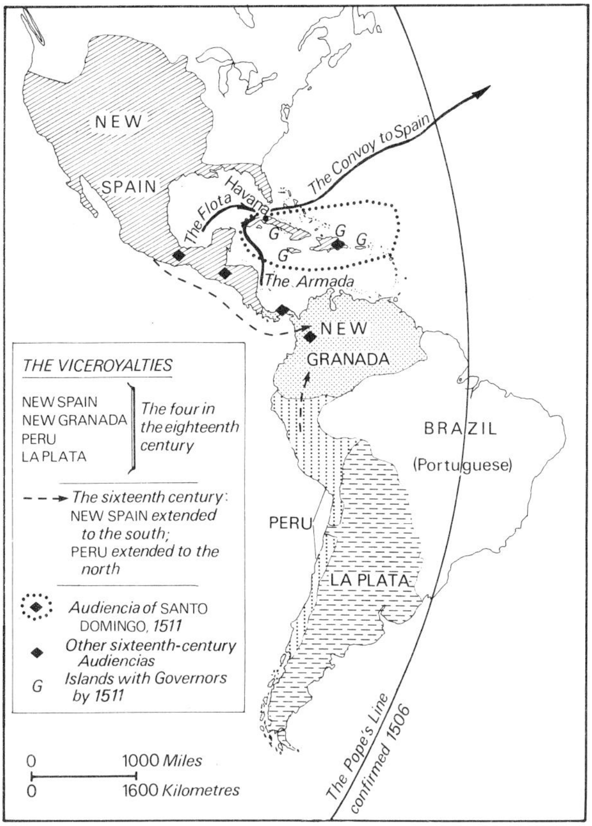

Figure 2.1 The Spanish Empire

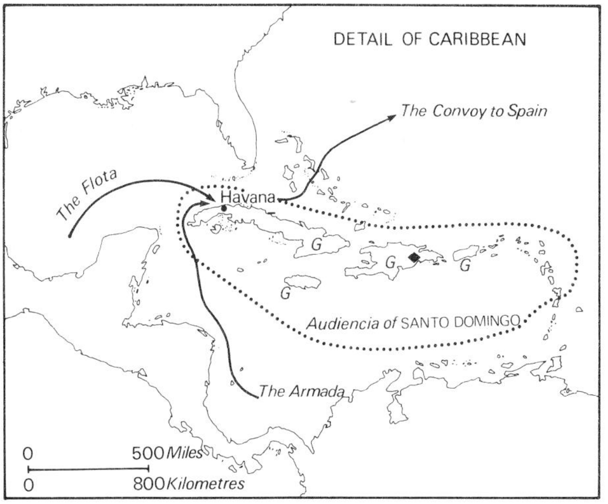

of Spain himself could attend since the colonies were thought of as being his personal possessions. The Council may be dated from 1511, but it originated in the staff of Bishop Fonseca who did much to prepare Columbus's second voyage. The duties of the Council, carefully defined by King Charles I of Spain after the death of Fonseca in 1524, were to decide policy, issue laws, make appointments, supervise the administration and, when necessary, act as a final court of appeal, in all matters which concerned the empire. The Council consisted of fewer than twenty members who were often chosen for their first-hand knowledge of the New World. The volume of their work was great and when, about 150 years after Columbus's voyages, the Council tried to codify (disentangle and summarize) the laws which had been issued for the Indies, they found that there were about 400000 of them. For the Council to operate successfully, it was necessary to create many other pieces of governmental machinery to whom administrative duties could be delegated, without, of course, surrendering the overall control which Spain was anxious to keep.

At first, Spain sent *adelantodos* to the New World as representatives of royal authority but they proved unreliable. There were also doubts about their powers and when Columbus took it upon himself to appoint his brother Bartholomew as an *adelantodo*, the office declined in importance. Ovando was sent to Hispaniola to be its Governor, and it became the regular thing in the sixteenth century for each island to be ruled by a governor. The governors were not always reliable either and, as Velásquez sometimes did, they were inclined to act as minor kings. They had important duties to perform in seeing that the islands were well-governed, that law and order were maintained, that taxes were collected and that the king of Spain received his share of the gold which was discovered. But it was thought that something was needed to keep an eye on them.

In 1511, the first *audiencia* was set up at Santo Domingo in Hispaniola. The islands needed courts of law and the *audiencia* was a committee of lawyers whose most important duty was to administer justice. It was soon realized, however, that these lawyers could perform other duties, among them that of assisting and reporting on the governor. The powers of the Audiencia of Santo Domingo grew quickly, taking in all of the islands and seeing that each was governed by a rather delicately balanced partnership of its governor and the lawyers. The Audiencia could deal directly with the Supreme Council in Spain and when *audiencias* were established also on the mainland they became the watchdogs of the Spanish government, supreme in judicial matters and possessed of the right to investigate the activities of all officials, no matter how important they were. The *audiencias* also took on other responsibilities; they not only safeguarded the interests of the Spanish king, but they were expected to protect the Indians. If the *audiencias* did their work properly, the empire would be governed efficiently, loyally and fairly.

But the very size of the empire seemed to call for the presence of a grand and regal figure, to represent the king of Spain himself and, in 1535, the Viceroyalty of New Spain was established, with the Viceroy having authority over the mainland as far south as Venezuela as well as over the West Indian islands. A few years later, a similar appointment was made in the Spanish empire further south when the Viceroyalty of Peru was set up. The conquest of the Incas had been followed by feuding among the Spaniards, and Blasco Vela's appointment as Viceroy of Peru ended with his murder in 1544. But the disorders were eventually curbed, and by the 1570s the Viceroyalty was functioning successfully. Mainland *audiencias* were created within these two viceroyalties. In the eighteenth century, the number of viceroyalties was increased to four by sub-dividing the earlier ones. At this time, the Viceroy of New Spain kept his authority over the islands but his mainland territories were now limited to Mexico and central America north of Panama.

The viceroys were magnificent and lordly rulers but they were allowed to keep office for only three years. The king of Spain had no wish to create overmighty subjects in the empire. He retained the power to dismiss a viceroy at any time and a viceroy was watched, and sometimes investigated, by the lawyers of the *audiencias*. In other respects, the *audiencias* assisted the viceroys in the administration of their territories. As these were so large, it was sometimes necessary to appoint further officials, especially to defend the outlying areas from Spain's enemies. In such areas, captains-general were appointed.

Day-to-day affairs were, of course, usually dealt with by local officials. In the West Indies, the Viceroy of New Spain tended to leave each island to the rule of its governor, and each governor worked in a sort of partnership with the Audiencia of Santo Domingo. This was a system of government which had emerged more by trial and error than as the result of some master-plan; and, because of the danger that the officials in the empire might be tempted to become disloyal and abuse their powers, they were frequently changed. Supreme power always rested with the Council of the Indies in Madrid, and for much of the time the officials in the New World were simply required to carry out orders and to enforce the laws sent from Spain. Moreover, the practice which had started when Aguado and Bobadilla were sent to the Indies to investigate the activities of Christopher Columbus, was continued. From time to time, Spain sent out a *visitador* to inquire into the government of the empire; and, as yet a further safeguard against incompetence, disloyalty and injustice, retiring officials could face a *residencia*, a judicial inquiry into their administration.

This system for the government of the Spanish West Indies had developed by the middle of the sixteenth century and it lasted, with only minor alterations, until the empire collapsed centuries later. It had become far more elaborate than that which existed when Diego Columbus took over Hispaniola from Ovando. Columbus ruled Hispaniola until 1523, struggling to assert his father's old powers as a Viceroy and to exercise authority over other governors, such as Velásquez in Cuba. He had several times to return to Spain, to press his claims and to defend himself against accusations of mishandling the Indians. When he died in 1526, the claims of the Columbuses to rule the lands the great explorer had discovered, died with him, and the way was clear for the development of an empire truly Spanish.

The empire was usually governed by officials who had been born in Spain, the result of a deliberate policy to try to make sure of their loyalty. The important officials of the empire, therefore, tended to regard the colonies as overseas territories, in which they would work but from which they would return to Europe. A similar attitude was later adopted by other European nations, such as the English and French, when they too gained West Indian colonies. This caused conflict between the officials and those Europeans who settled permanently in the islands. It was often a conflict of class, between the poorer settlers and the richer (sometimes high-born) officials. It also tended to become a conflict of race, between West Indians (sometimes of mixed blood) and

Europeans. In general, the Spaniards gave only a minor share in the administration of the empire to the *creoles* (Europeans born in the West Indies or those with only partly European parentage). The *creoles* were found mainly in the *cabildos* which were units of local government, rather like town councils, not elected but chosen from approved families. Certain *creole* families could attain a degree of importance and even local power, but they too had to obey the laws of the empire and could be dismissed if their work displeased those higher up the scale of authority. Once again, real power over the islands rested not in the West Indies but in Spain.

Economic

As early as 1503, part of the organization established by Fonseca, from which grew the Supreme Council of the Indies, began to specialize in matters concerning the economic organization of the empire. The Spaniards wanted to obtain wealth from the empire and they did not intend to share that wealth with other European countries. They first wished to make sure that the wealth came safely to Spain, but they also soon realized that the wealth would not consist of the silks and spices of the east nor even of cargoes of gold. Settlements in the New World began exporting the produce of tropical agriculture and the hides of the cattle. In return, the settlers wished to buy European goods. In supplying these goods and in selling the produce of the Americas, profits could be made; and the trade itself could yield taxes for the Spanish government. In 1503, the *Casa de Contratación* (the House of Trade) was set up. Its job was to organize and supervise the commercial and financial affairs of the empire. It made its headquarters in the Spanish city of Seville.

Working as a sort of department of the Council of the Indies, the House of Trade regulated Spanish shipping throughout what came to be known as the age of mercantilism. Mercantilist theories were not fully developed until the seventeenth century, when the English passed the Navigation Acts (see pages 59–61) and the French issued similar laws. But many of the ideas of the mercantilists were already popular in the House of Trade in the early sixteenth century. One of these ideas was that it was highly desirable for bullion (gold and silver) to flow into a country to make it richer and more powerful. The possession of gold was thought of as important in itself. Not only did gold possess purchasing-power but as the amount of gold in the world seemed to be very limited, it was necessary to obtain it so that other countries should not do so and become powerful. Thus the Spaniards became increasingly afraid that, unless they took precautions, other countries would penetrate into the New World and tap its wealth. It followed that if other countries began to trade with Spain's settlements they would obtain profits from that trade and again tap some of the wealth that belonged to Spain. The House of Trade insisted, therefore, that all traffic between the New World and Spain must be in the hands of Spaniards. In that way, Spain would gain all of the riches and all of the trading profits. Using the authority given by the Pope and quoting the Treaty of Tordesillas, the House of Trade forbade all foreign merchants to enter the empire. A system of licensing was also devised whereby traders could be registered and supervised and—a useful source of revenue—made to pay for the privilege of trading with the Indies. The Treaty of Tordesillas had recognized the rights of Portugal in Africa and in the sixteenth century the Portuguese began to settle in Brazil, and it was convenient sometimes to grant licences to Portuguese merchants. This was especially so when African slaves were later thought to be needed in the West Indies and when the *Asiento* was issued to allow the Portuguese to supply them. But, usually, licences were granted only to Spaniards.

The House of Trade became more than a licensing bureau and a tax-collecting body. It came to deal with navigation and maps, with harbours and the movement of migrants. Like the Council of the Indies itself, the House tended to have too many responsibilities for maximum efficiency, and one of its biggest problems was the protection of Spanish shipping. As early as 1523, it was unsafe for ships to sail alone since they ran increasing risks of being attacked by the privateers of other countries. At first, ships sailed in groups and with escorts as and when it was convenient; but as the empire and the traffic grew and as Spain quarrelled with the French, the Dutch and the English, something more orderly was needed. Admiral Pedro de Avilés devised a regular convoy system which began to operate in the 1560s.

Two fleets left Spain each year, carrying provisions to the empire. The *flota* sailed first, making for Cuba and then Mexico, supplying the northern part of the empire. The *armada* followed a few

The Spaniards were a devoutly Catholic people. Columbus had been quick to give thanks to God for his safe arrival in the West Indies

months later, supplying Panama and the southern settlements. Thus the empire received annual supplies, but although this traffic was seldom interrupted the settlers frequently complained that their needs were not adequately met. They felt a strong temptation to trade with interlopers such as John Hawkins from England whose goods would be welcome and could be cheaper—even though, of course, the House of Trade had forbidden such trade (see page 32). Both the *flota* and the *armada* wintered in the New World.

The return journey was made in one convoy. The two fleets assembled at Havana in Cuba, having collected the produce from all the settlements on the mainland, including the treasures of Peru which came along the west coast of south America and across the Isthmus of Panama by mule train. They then crossed the Atlantic to

Spain in a mighty and well-protected convoy. On the whole, Avilés's system was highly successful in protecting the wealth Spain obtained from the New World. Pirates were able to capture stragglers which became separated from the convoy and, occasionally, one or two ships on its fringes, but not until 1628 was a whole fleet lost—and that was when the Dutchman, Piet Hein, trapped the *flota* in a harbour near Havana.

Somewhat clumsily and inflexibly, the convoy system solved the problem of getting ships safely to and fro across the Atlantic. It was more difficult to protect the traffic around the West Indian islands and across the Caribbean Sea. Indeed, it was not only ships which were attacked: Spain's enemies would also attack ports in their search for booty. The Spaniards had to build fortifications and to equip fast-moving and well-armed squadrons. One squadron, towards the end of the sixteenth century, was based at Cartagena and another in the islands, at Santo Domingo, but they had to patrol an area too vast to make the defence really effective. This continuous struggle against other European countries began long before 1600, as Chapter 3 will explain.

Social

Administrators, lawyers, soldiers and sailors were vitally important to the working and protection of the Spanish empire, but it was unthinkable that the empire could exist without churchmen. They too arrived regularly in the New World from the time of Columbus's second voyage onwards, and they had, broadly speaking, two purposes. The Spaniards were a devoutly Catholic people and they needed priests to preach to them of their God, to hear the confession of their sins and to grant pardon to the dying; the Pope, Queen Isabella and Spaniards in general also thought it their duty to bring Christianity to the Amerindians. In addition, it has already been seen that Spain placed great importance on an empire which was loyal and orderly, in which everyone knew his place from the eminent viceroy to the most humble *creole*. Churchmen thus had an important role to play in helping to make society stable by providing moral leadership and persuading men to obey the law. Wherever there was a Spanish settlement there would almost certainly be found a Catholic priest. There were also friars, especially those of the Dominican order in white cloaks and black mantles, who were the first missionaries in the New World, and many of whom were deeply concerned about the welfare of the Indians. Not all churchmen followed their example. The worldly priest who sought his own comfort and looked for riches was not uncommon in Europe in the sixteenth century, and was savagely attacked by Luther and other reformers. Not surprisingly, there were among the priests who came to the Caribbean those who had little to offer in the way of moral leadership.

Churchmen were, however, often amongst the most educated people of the time, and governments found them of great value in matters of administration and in writing and keeping records. Bishop Fonseca, from 1493 to his death, had major responsibilities in helping the Spanish royal family to organize the affairs of the empire, and in all the Spanish settlements it was the custom to consult and use churchmen in government. They gave advice in a wide variety of matters and had a general duty to encourage good behaviour. But they had special responsibilities too. Churchmen supervised all matters to do with education. They often served as teachers and ran schools, collected and recorded knowledge about the New World and carefully considered what books should circulate in the empire. The time of the Reformation in Europe was a time when Humanists and Protestants were challenging many of the ideas of the Catholic Church and even the authority of the Pope. It was being suggested that Latin should no longer be the language of religion and that individuals should read the Bible for themselves, in German, English or their own language; and that they should decide for themselves what they should believe and not merely accept what the priests told them to believe. Most Roman Catholics thought that these were dangerous ideas and, in the Spanish West Indies, the Church did its best to keep them out. Books were checked, censored and sometimes burned, and among the books destroyed were those which threatened to undermine the authority of the Spanish government.

In Europe, it was also the custom for the Church to have its own courts which dealt with those matters thought to be 'spiritual'. These included matters to do with religious faith, lies and blasphemy, marriages and legacies, contracts and pledges. For a Catholic, the most terrible punishment that these courts could impose was that of excommunication which cut a man off from his Church and, they believed, from God. These courts came to the New World with the Catholic Church, but there was also a special court known as the *Inquisition* which had existed for several hundred years and which aimed to wipe out heresy. Those who deviated from the true beliefs of the Church were vigorously punished, and to be burned alive for witchcraft and Protestantism was not uncommon.

In the fifteenth century, the Inquisition had little influence in countries like France and England, but it was growing stronger in Spain where it often operated to protect not only the Church but also the monarchy. It became confused about its main aims but when it was introduced into the Spanish empire in 1569, it was a terrifying instrument, ruthless and savage. It dealt fiercely with Protestants, illegal traders, pirates and disloyal Spaniards, regarding them all as heretics. A special effort was made to keep Jews from entering the empire. It seems unlikely that many people were actually burned by the Inquisition in the New World, but it helped to maintain the authority of the government and continued in a shadowy existence into the eighteenth century.

Such intolerance must be set alongside the efforts of many churchmen to ensure that the early settlers were not only loyal and devout but were also humane and honest men. Their task was not easy in a society to which many had been drawn by greed, and in which one man was often contemptuous of another whose birth was more humble. As in Europe, some churchmen were content to use their influence for personal gain, or turned a blind eye in order not to offend a powerful neighbour. That some struggled to do their duty while others failed as Christian priests was apparent in the way that the Spaniards dealt with the Amerindians.

Queen Isabella is still remembered as Isabella the Catholic, 500 years after her birth (Dominican Republic, 1951)

II THE SPANIARDS AND THE AMERINDIANS

The Encomienda

It has been seen already that Queen Isabella disapproved of the persistent enthusiasm of Columbus for enslaving the Indians (see pages 5–6 and 12–13). At first, official policy was to Christianize them and to accept those who submitted to Spanish rule as subjects of the Crown, entitled to wages for their work. There were those, however, who resisted, especially the Caribs whom Columbus called 'a wild people' who needed to be conquered and cured of 'their cruel habits'. By 1503, Isabella's determination to make them Christian persuaded her that Columbus was right. Permission was given to capture them and bring them to the settlements or even to Spain,

> 'because if the Christians bring them to these lands and make use of their services, they will be more easily converted and attracted to our Holy Faith.'

So the first slaves to be sent across the Atlantic went from west to east, a strange mirror-image of the fact that millions of African slaves were later to be transported from east to west (see Chapter 6).

The basis of Spanish treatment of the Amerindians was the *encomienda* system, which was first introduced by Columbus following earlier Spanish practices in Europe. It bore some similarity to the serfdom of medieval Europe. Without scruple, the Spaniards took possession of the lands of the Indians which were then divided among the Europeans, and Indians were allocated to them to help with the work. Such Indians were said to be held 'in trust', and, in 1513, King Ferdinand issued a Code to define how they should be treated. It ended with the provision that no settler in Hispaniola should be allotted 'more than 150 or fewer than 40 Indians'. How the Indians were to be treated was the crucial question. There were several conflicting interests: humanitarians and religious men wanted them to be protected and Christianized; the settlers wanted them to work hard; and there was a general anxiety to make profits from the islands—an anxiety in which the Spanish monarchy shared. Queen Isabella had intended that the Amerindians would be free labourers who were treated well and paid. But she set a deplorable example by allowing forced labour to be used in the mines, which belonged to the royal family, merely limiting that labour to a period of less than a year. This was the thin end of the wedge, and, by 1503, Ovando could successfully claim that the *encomienda* system should be put into full operation with forced labour on the estates. Moreover, it seemed to be assumed very early that the Caribs would always be thought of as unfree—as Indians who had forfeited their freedom by resisting. In 1512, Ferdinand congratulated Ponce de León, Governor of Puerto Rico,

> 'You have done me a service by your efforts to pacify the island and by branding with the letter F on the brow the Indians captured in war, enslaving them, and selling them to the highest bidder, reserving a fifth part of the proceeds for me.'

Thus, from almost the very beginning of Spanish colonization, the Spanish attitude to the Indians was based on a confused mixture of greed and humanitarianism, combined with a measure of ruthlessness. Unable to refuse to work, the Indians were, in effect, slaves.

In 1492, there were probably about a quarter of a million Amerindians on the island of Hispaniola. When Ovando retired in 1508, death and flight had reduced them to about a quarter of that number. A royal decree of 1503 stressed the importance of humane treatment and of paying the Indians; of teaching them Christianity, allowing them private housing and of leaving them free to inter-marry with the Spaniards. But the settlers often ignored such humane intentions and too many churchmen failed to remind them of their duties. By 1512, the number of Indians in Hispaniola fell to about 20 000. The *encomienda* system took a heavy toll. Properly speaking, the *encomienda* was the pool of labour which the Spaniards could use. They were rapidly draining it dry.

The aborigines were not accustomed to the long hours of sustained hard labour which their Spanish masters demanded. Their treatment was often brutal, and their food and shelter inadequate. They fell victims to European-brought diseases, among which was venereal disease which was passed on to the Indian women by the Spaniards who raped them. Explaining to Philip II in 1582 why not a single Amerindian, of those originally resident in the island, remained in Puerto Rico, Governor Melgarejo mentioned particularly the toll taken by 'measles, colds and smallpox'. He also mentioned 'ill-treatment' which caused them to flee. But ill-treatment also killed them. The Spaniards 'beat them, struck them, kicked them and whipped them', according to Las Casas, who fought a lonely battle to restrain his fellow-countrymen. Owing to a strange lack of common sense as well as a lack of humanity, some Spanish settlers worked their Indians all the harder as the number of labourers dwindled. It was an age of cruel sports, and some Spaniards even took pleasure in hunting the Indians down like animals and seeing them die, for it was common to consider the Amerindians as little different from 'dogs'. Like the serfs in medieval Europe, the Indians also lacked protection for the crops they grew with which to feed themselves. The crops were trampled down by the Spaniards' livestock and by any Spaniard who chose to hunt in that direction. Las Casas struggled in vain to prevent such a callous destruction of the Indian people, and all he could do was to record it graphically.

The Struggle to Save the Indians

From distant Madrid, the Council of the Indies still issued decrees to try to save the aborigines. Towards the end of 1511, in Santo Domingo, a Dominican friar called Montesinos passionately reminded the settlers of their sins and begged them to treat the Indians humanely. The settlers reported him to Diego Columbus for interfering, but Montesinos returned to Spain and appealed to King Ferdinand. As a result, the Laws of Burgos were issued to emphasize, and perhaps clarify, royal policy. But the fundamental contradiction remained. The *encomienda* was confirmed, but Ferdinand hoped that the Indians would be better protected by a series of detailed regulations as to their working conditions, religious instruction, living quarters and legitimate punishments. Inspectors were to be appointed who would report to Fonseca on the treatment of the Indians by the Spaniards. Two years later, in 1514, only about 14 000 Indians survived in Hispaniola. There had been little change in the practices of the Spanish settlers, and a commission of 1516 justified the *encomienda* by arguing that 'if the Indians are given their freedom they will relapse into idolatry'. Religion and the need for labourers thus combined to make sure that the Indians remained slaves. The inspectors, appointed after the issuing of the Laws of Burgos, were themselves employers of Indian labour and, in general, the Laws were useless.

At this point, the Indians gained their most determined protector. Bartolomé de Las Casas committed himself, from 1514 onwards, to trying to save them. He began, as Montesinos did, by preaching to the deaf ears of the Spanish settlers about the injustices of the *encomienda*. Las Casas was an educated man, a graduate of Salamanca University who committed himself to the Church. He first came to the West Indies with Ovando, moved on to Cuba and was given lands where he himself employed Amerindian labourers. But his attention was caught by a passage in *Ecclesiastes* when he was preparing a sermon in 1514, and he became convinced that the *encomienda* was immoral. Neither Velásquez nor his fellow-settlers would accept this point of view and none followed Las Casas's example when he gave up his lands and set free his workers. Las Casas returned to Spain to seek support.

King Ferdinand was dying, but the Council was persuaded to appoint a commission of friars, men who were rightly considered to be more interested in the welfare of the Indians than were most of the priests of the Catholic Church. The commission was to explore the possibility of abandoning the *encomienda* system, and Las Casas himself was named 'Protector of the Indians'. It was little more than a gesture, for the Protector had little real authority. Spaniards were instructed to co-operate with him in all things concerning 'the liberty, humane treatment and salvation of the souls and bodies' of the Indians, but in the face of the hostility of the settlers it is said that the commission was able to set free only one Indian. The *encomienda* system remained.

King Ferdinand died in 1516 and Las Casas had fresh hope of the new and younger ruler, Charles I. He spoke passionately to the King of the 'gigantically tyrannical system' which existed in the empire, but the Spanish government did not share his sense of urgency, and the Indians continued to decline. Las Casas was granted land in Venezuela to experiment with the Indians working voluntarily. His settlement was raided by slave traders, and the Indians rebelled against the Europeans who remained amongst them while Las Casas was absent. Elsewhere, efforts to use the Indians as free labourers resulted in such a low level of production that the experiment was, financially, a failure—and that was intolerable to the Spaniards. In 1523, Las Casas joined the order of Dominican friars and spent the next twelve years in Santo Domingo, writing his *History of the Indies*.

In 1535, Las Casas was on his way to Peru.

Las Casas had great hopes of the Emperor Charles V, but neither could save the Amerindians (Cuba, 1944; Dominican Republic, 1959)

Contrary winds landed him in central America and he embarked on a new experiment with the Indians in Guatemala, remote from Spanish settlers and the *encomienda*. The Indians in this area were renowned for their ferocity and so far they had resisted Spanish attempts to subdue them. Las Casas aimed to teach them Christianity, offering them the Christian story in their own language. This, Las Casas considered *The Only Method of Attracting All People to the True Faith*, and he outlined his scheme in a booklet in 1537. He returned to Spain in 1540, at which time this most recent experiment seemed to be going well. With no pressures on them to work and to produce a quota of gold, the Indians showed interest in the Christian religion and became less aggressive.

In Spain, Las Casas helped to shape the New Laws which were issued in 1542. Most important among them was that Spaniards were forbidden to enslave any more Indians. When their masters died, existing slaves were to become the property of the Crown and might be expected to be given their freedom. For the West Indies, however, the New Laws came too late. Few Indians had survived, perhaps not more than a thousand in Hispaniola, and the Spanish settlers were determined to go on exploiting them for as long as they could. They therefore ignored the new provisions about the conditions in which the Indians should live and the loads which they should carry; they protested loudly, with the support of the Church; and in 1543 King Charles suspended the Laws. The destruction of the Indian peoples in the West Indian islands went on and today there survive only a few descendants of the Caribs who kept the Spaniards away from the smaller islands.

The 'gigantically tyrannical system' against which Las Casas protested: the Spaniards torture an Amerindian cacique

Las Casas recorded the sorry story in his *Very Brief Account of the Destruction of the Indies.* In 1544, he became the Bishop of Chiapas in Guatemala but left the New World for the last time in 1547, still unable to establish good relations with the Europeans of the Spanish empire. Even his final experiment in Guatemala ended in failure, for the Indians rebelled after Las Casas had gone, murdered some of his followers and were duly punished by the armed force sent against them by the Spanish government. Las Casas died in 1566. His writings have been of great help to historians and perhaps some of his readers were later influenced towards the more humane treatment of their fellow-men. But it was the tragedy of Las Casas that he could do little to alter the course of the history of his times. He could not save the aborigines of the West Indian islands from extermination by those whom the Arawaks had originally welcomed to San Salvador.

Searching desperately for a way in which to persuade the Spanish settlers to leave the Indians in peace, Las Casas was attracted to an idea earlier put forward by Dominicans. It was suggested that workers could be brought from Africa to the West Indies. The Portuguese were already collecting African slaves from the Guinea coast. They had indeed sold some to the Spaniards before the end of the fifteenth century, and from 1505 onwards the Spanish government began sending some of these to the New World. These early African arrivals died as readily as did the Indians and in 1511 King Ferdinand expressed his surprise. 'I cannot understand how so many Negroes have died. Take good care of them,' he wrote. The death of the Africans did nothing to discourage the Spaniards, and the trickle of slaves across the Atlantic grew steadily stronger. As early as 1517 a contract was signed for a regular supply, and merchants made arrangements with the Portuguese to meet the demand. Las Casas later maintained that he thought the Africans were legitimately captured in war and he came to regret the encouragement he had given to the traffic. He did not live to see the vast trade in human beings which was to develop in the seventeenth and eighteenth centuries (see Chapter 6), but he had already seen how Europeans callously ill-treated those weaker than themselves; and, ominously, by the middle of the sixteenth century, the settlers in Hispaniola were already busily replacing their dead Indians with imported Africans.

Las Casas could not save the Arawaks from extermination, but the more warlike Caribs survived in the smaller islands. Present-day descendants of the Caribs in Dominica

The New Society

That the Spaniards were white, the Indians and Africans brown and black came to have enormous significance. Throughout most of the history of the West Indies, white came to be associated with power, wealth and privilege. Not to be white became a ticket to servitude or, at best, second-class status. But it is perhaps worth remembering that European society in the sixteenth century was already class-ridden, and a considerable gap existed between the nobility and the peasantry. Many of those who ruled in the Spanish empire would have ruled in Spain itself. At the same time, many of those Spaniards who came to the West Indies were poor men, and some of the newcomers were even white slaves. Columbus carried criminals on his third voyage, and female white slaves were later sent to serve the needs of the settlers. To some extent, a new kind of society could be fashioned in the West Indies and many who had failed in Europe were hopeful that they could

Carib artifacts are a reminder of the Amerindian civilizations which the Europeans found in the West Indies (St Vincent, 1976)

succeed in the New World. From early days, therefore, the West Indian islands were a melting-pot.

Unfortunately, the first settlements were based on the pursuit of wealth and quick success. The society that was established was a competitive society which quickly got rid of the tolerant and gentle ways of the Arawaks. A new hierarchy developed which was a combination of much of the old system imported from Europe and a new system based on colour. The Spaniard often looked down on the creole, but a white man who was poor, even one whom his fellow-countrymen regarded as a criminal or an outcast, was still inclined to consider himself superior to an Amerindian or an African, a slave. The European settlers were better-armed, better-informed, more ruthless and no doubt more ambitious than the Indians. Thus, there developed the vicious legacy which was handed down to the twentieth century—the racialism which leads one people to consider themselves superior to another, measuring their superiority in any way that seems appropriate, in wealth, technological development, brute force or merely skin-colour. Tragically, therefore, the history of the West Indies began with the destruction of one people by another. The new society was full of divisions. Spanish officials, the representatives of authority, came and went. They had no great respect for the Europeans who stayed in the Americas, but the Europeans who stayed could at least achieve some sort of status by dominating their coloured workers. Only a handful of the settlers gave thought to serving their fellow-men. The majority looked for wealth and a social position, but it was difficult for West Indians of any colour to achieve the highest positions and real authority in the Spanish empire. This remained true even when the empire was coming to an end in the nineteenth century.

Exercises

1 Estimate the importance of the work of Christopher Columbus (a) as an explorer and (b) as a colonizer.

2 Compare the careers and exploits in the New World of Ovando and Cortés, and assess which of them gave the better service to the Spanish government.

3 Explain the methods by which the government of Spain attempted to control the political, economic and social life of its early West Indian settlements.

4 Describe the *encomienda* system, and explain why it was adopted by the Spanish settlers in the West Indies. How far did it fulfil the expectations that the Spaniards had of it?

5 What truth is there in the view that the Spanish colonists in the New World in the late fifteenth and early sixteenth centuries came to civilize the native peoples, but succeeded only in destroying them?

6 'It was the tragedy of Las Casas that he could do little to alter the course of the history of his times' (page 26). Explain the truth of this statement.

7 Imagine that you are an Arawak cacique on whose island the Spanish explorers have landed. Describe how you reacted to the coming of the strangers, and explain how and why your feelings towards them changed over the next few years.

3 The Challenge to the Spanish Empire

Europe in the Sixteenth Century

The Spanish discoveries in the New World were of particular interest to those nations in Europe which had coastlines facing west. Mention has already been made of the development of new nation states in Europe (see Figure 1.1) and of *Portugal*, whose sailors were exploring the coast of Africa long before Columbus sailed to the West Indies (see pages 2–3). After the Pope had confirmed the line of demarcation in 1506, Portugal seldom challenged Spain's possession of the American empire and was content to colonize Brazil. The Portuguese co-operated with the Spaniards, supplying them with slaves from Africa. From 1580 to 1668, Portugal was actually ruled by the king of Spain when the latter claimed to be the legal heir to the Portuguese throne. In any case, the two nations shared a common devotion to the Catholic Church.

The French, English and Dutch, however, were often in conflict with the Spaniards in Europe, and they soon showed themselves ready to invade the Spanish empire in search of whatever pickings they could acquire. *Spain* and *France* had only recently become nation states, creating, in each case, one country for the people of one nationality under a national monarchy, and driving away the foreigners who laid claim to parts of their territories. Now the rulers of Spain and France were deadly rivals. This rivalry was never more keen than in the 1520s when Charles I of Spain struggled with Francis I of France for the mastery of many areas of Europe. Charles of Spain also ruled large areas of Austria and Germany. He was the head of the powerful Habsburg family, and his importance in Europe was confirmed in 1519 when he defeated Francis in the election of a new Holy Roman Emperor. As Emperor, Charles became known as Charles V though, in Spain, he continued to rule as Charles I. So great was his power and wealth that the French sought almost constantly to challenge and weaken him and, when Charles was succeeded in Spain in 1556 by his son, Philip II, the Franco-Spanish struggle continued. Wars occurred frequently between the two countries in both the sixteenth and seventeenth centuries. And when a Bourbon became king in France in 1589, the struggle was sometimes referred to as 'Habsburg v. Bourbon'. The French regarded the Spanish empire as a legitimate and rich target at which to aim during the course of these wars. Although France was mainly Roman Catholic in religion, an influential minority of Frenchmen adopted the Protestant faith in the sixteenth century, and became known as *Huguenots*. The French, moreover, were less respectful of the Pope than the Spaniards and the Portuguese, and from the outset, therefore, they paid little attention to his ruling that the West Indies rightly belonged to Spain.

England became a Protestant country in the sixteenth century, and paid no heed at all to the Pope's ruling. From 1485 to 1603, the ruling family in England was the Tudors. The first Tudor was Henry VII who ruled from 1485 to 1509. Like all Christian rulers at the time, he was a Catholic, but even he sent the Cabots to the Americas to try to discover an English route to Cathay (see page 12). This was in spite of the fact that he considered himself an ally of the rulers of Spain and that he married his son to Catherine of Aragon, daughter of Ferdinand and Isabella. This son, Henry VIII (1509–47), came to quarrel violently with both the Spaniards and the Pope, partly because he wished, towards the end of the 1520s, to get rid of Catherine and re-marry. In this way, the English Reformation began and England eventually adopted many anti-Catholic ideas. Henry VIII's son, Edward VI (1547–53) was a keen Protestant and although he was for a short time succeeded by Catherine of Aragon's daughter Mary (1553–8) who restored the Catholic faith and even married Prince Philip of Spain (Philip II), England became a mainly Protestant country. The last Tudor ruler, Elizabeth I, came to the throne in 1558, and it was in her long reign that quarrels with Spain reached a climax. The English preyed on Spanish shipping and tried to break the Spanish monopoly of trade with the West Indies. In 1588, Philip II tried to invade England but the Spanish Armada was destroyed. Thus, well before the end of the sixteenth century, the English were a thorn in the flesh of the Spaniards and in the next century the English were to have even greater success in breaking into the Spanish empire.

The Dutch of *Holland* also caused considerable trouble for the Spaniards. Holland in the sixteenth century was part of the Spanish Netherlands and was ruled, therefore, by Charles of Spain and then by Philip II. But the Dutch were frequently in revolt. They adopted rather extreme Protestant ideas (Calvinist ideas from the teachings of John Calvin) and hated the Catholics. They resented the taxes imposed on them by the Spaniards, and they wanted to be a free nation. Particularly after the middle of the sixteenth century, and sometimes in league with the English, the Dutch fought stubbornly against Spanish rule. They were adventurous seamen and successful traders, and they carried their struggle to the New World. Unable to find a way of defeating the Dutch, Spain had to seek a truce and, although the war was later renewed, Holland had in effect already won its independence. In 1648, the Spaniards finally accepted this. By that time, the Dutch had become the most important merchants in the West Indies.

In the sixteenth century, therefore, the Spanish empire was troubled by the French, English and Dutch. The seamen of these three nationalities were drawn to the New World mainly by the hope of gain and the desire to grab a share of the Spanish wealth, but they had other reasons too for their activities. They thought of themselves as patriots, helping the development of their own countries, weakening Spain, the enemy. Those who were devout Protestants considered the Spanish Catholics backward and, with their Inquisition, cruel. They were inspired also by a love of adventure and by a curiosity about the unknown—qualities characteristic of the European Renaissance. The Spanish empire also offered a challenge. The Spanish government regarded every activity by foreigners west of the Pope's line as illegal. To sail in these waters was an act of defiance and something of an achievement in itself. To steal Spanish gold or to make a profit from illegal trading would be even more of an achievement.

The Adventurers

None of Spain's rivals was rich and strong enough in the sixteenth century to make a full-scale attack upon the Spanish empire. They could only afford comparatively small armies which were needed in Europe, and navies, like the English navy, were needed to protect the home countries. All that governments could do, therefore, was to encourage adventurous subjects to undertake what were almost private voyages. Sometimes they received financial help for their voyages and sometimes the ruler took a share of the profits, as Elizabeth I of England did. But the adventurers were essentially *privateers* who mixed patriotism with their quest for private gain.

Privateers claimed to be different from pirates because they carried permits from their governments giving them a sort of right to prey upon the enemy. Their countrymen regarded them as heroes, but their victims were not persuaded by legal niceties to think of them as anything but robbers. The privateers received from their governments *letters of marque* or *letters of marque and reprisal*, giving a right to sail in foreign waters and to seize enemy property. If captured, the privateer could claim to be treated as a prisoner-of-war and not as a pirate. Perhaps there was some force in this claim if countries were actually at war. Letters of marque had first been issued by the English during the middle ages for use in wars against the French and the practice was not finally outlawed until 1856. In the sixteenth century, however, the letters were issued by the English, French, Dutch and even the Spaniards, and governments became less concerned about whether a state of war existed officially or not. As the distinction between privateers and pirates became hopelessly blurred, the Spaniards insisted that all foreign privateers were really pirates and, for good measure, often assumed that they were Protestants too and therefore heretics.

It was often similarly difficult to distinguish pirates from illegal traders. In Elizabeth's reign, the ships of English merchants were frequently used almost indiscriminately for trading, raiding and defending the home country. The Queen's ships could be used in the same way so that it was not even easy to tell the difference between the navy and the merchant marine. Ships' captains had to be prepared not only for sailing and trading but also for fighting. John Hawkins sailed to the Spanish empire mainly to trade, in spite of the Spanish veto, but in 1568 he was quite ready to use violence at Rio de la Hacha to storm the town and force the Spaniards there to purchase 200 slaves.

The ships of Spain's rivals sailed for the New World in increasing numbers, especially in the second half of the sixteenth century. Although each voyage usually had a main purpose, to trade or to pillage or, in some cases, to explore, the sailors were versatile. Many of the voyages ended in violence, though few set out with the single-mindedness shown by Francis Drake after 1568 when his intention was to load his ships with plunder and take revenge on the Spaniards for what he regarded as their treachery (see page 34). By means of the convoy system, already described in Chapter 2, the Spaniards were able to protect the bulk of their wealth, and by 1600 the convoy which left Havana consisted of about ninety cargo ships escorted by about a dozen warships. This force was too formidable for a serious attack to be made on it, but local shipping around the West Indies and the settlements themselves were far more difficult to protect.

The French

The wars between Charles I and Francis I in the 1520s gave the French an excellent opportunity to test the strength of the Spanish empire. French pirates had troubled the Spaniards as early as the 1490s but they had so far seen little of the wealth of the Americas. That was changed with the capture of three ships which were carrying the gold and jewels of the Aztecs from Mexico. The ships were intercepted near the Azores in 1523 by Giovanni da Verrazano, an Italian in the service of France, and some of the booty reached Francis I himself. The treasures surprised and delighted the French, but they also alarmed them. If Spain were receiving such cargoes, Spain would be richer and better able to sustain a war than the French. Francis I immediately questioned by what authority he had been denied his share when the world had been divided, and letters of marque were quickly put into circulation in an attempt to cripple the Spaniards.

The French preyed on Spanish shipping and they also raided the harbours of the Spanish empire. An expedition attacked Honduras in 1537 and seized nine ships of the treasure fleet. Mainland towns along the Venezuelan coast were burned in 1543. French privateers infested Caribbean waters and it became difficult for the Spaniards to conduct their normal business about the empire. There was relief for the Spaniards in the New World only when periods of peace interrupted the Franco-Spanish wars in Europe. But they were at war again in the 1550s and this time Cuba and its neighbouring islands bore the brunt of French pillaging. François le Clerc savaged Santiago de Cuba in 1554 with a force of ships which bore some resemblance to an official naval squadron. A year later, Jacques Sores raided Havana itself, the most important harbour in the islands. There was butchery as well as pillaging and, though the Spaniards struggled to repair their defences, it was obvious that they could not adequately defend the empire as a whole. The Spaniards had to learn to live with the fact that the waters of the Caribbean would never be entirely safe in the sixteenth and seventeenth centuries.

The agreement that there would be 'no peace beyond the line', as part of the Treaty of Cateau-Cambrésis in 1559, marked Spanish recognition of this fact. 'The line' was actually two lines—the prime meridian (Longitude 0°) and the Tropic of Cancer. Although there was to be peace in Europe, Spain and France agreed that 'West of the prime meridian and south of the Tropic of Cancer ... violence done by either party to the other shall not be regarded as a contravention of the treaty.' It seemed inevitable that adventurers would be lured to the West Indies and the Atlantic sea-routes by the hope of booty: they would grab what they could, and the Spaniards would fight back to the best of their ability. Otherwise, France made a hollow acceptance of Spain's right to its empire but only as far north as the Tropic of Cancer. Beyond that, there would be room for other empires and French Huguenots made an unsuccessful attempt to settle in Florida. In the remaining years of the sixteenth century, however, the English and the Dutch caused greater problems for Spain than did the French.

The English

After brief clashes in the first half of the sixteenth century, England did not officially go to war with

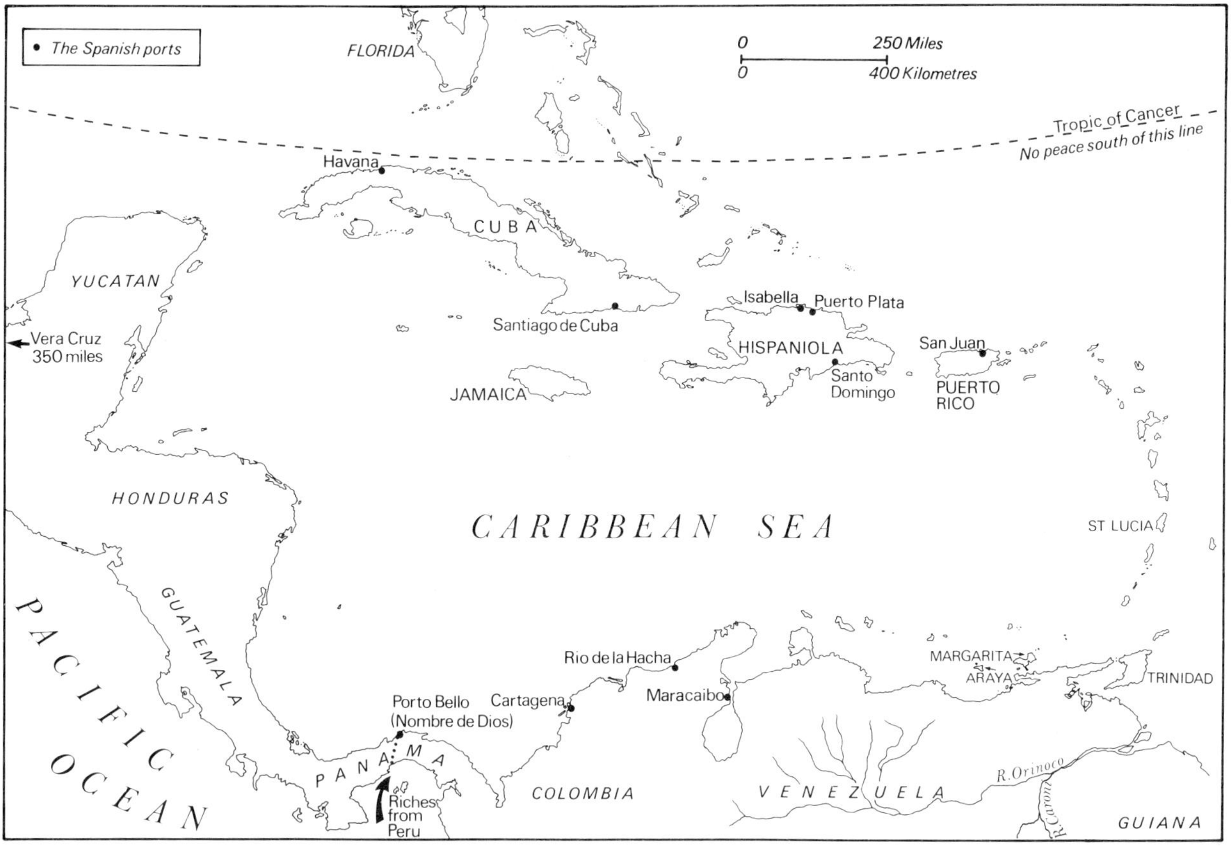

Figure 3.1 No Peace Beyond the Line in the Sixteenth Century.

Spain until 1585. The war then lasted until 1604. Long before 1585, however, Anglo-Spanish relations were badly strained. Elizabeth I consolidated the Protestant religion in England. She was excommunicated by the Pope in 1570, and those Catholics who argued that she had no right to be Queen and that the throne should have passed to Mary Stuart, the Catholic Queen of Scots, looked to Philip II of Spain to overthrow her. For her part, Elizabeth cautiously helped the Dutch to resist Spanish rule in the Netherlands and to keep Philip occupied. In 1568, Spanish ships, which were carrying silver coins to Spain's army in the Netherlands, took shelter in English ports and Elizabeth seized the money for herself. Against this background, it was not surprising that English sailors cast envious eyes on the Spanish empire and that the English government encouraged them to go privateering.

The English were also interested in finding their own route to Cathay in the sixteenth century, either by going round the north of the Americas or by going round the north of Europe and Asia. The problem was to find a passage through the ice. Such explorations were not successful but they encouraged English seamen to a spirit of adventure, and for many English sailors the known Spanish empire in the New World began to seem more attractive than the mere hope of a route to Cathay through the frozen northern seas. After the Cabots, John Rut explored the Atlantic in 1527. Block by ice to the north, he turned towards the West Indies and seems to have been the first Englishman to visit Hispaniola. It may be that he attempted to trade in Santo Domingo but that the Spaniards drove him away. In 1528, however, Charles I wrote to accuse the judges of the Audiencia of Santo Domingo of 'great carelessness and negligence', for he had heard that an English ship entered Santo Domingo harbour and had been allowed to sail away unmolested.

About the same time, Robert Thorne suggested a South Sea Project to Henry VIII. Thorne was a merchant of Bristol who lived in Seville in Spain and who knew of Magellan's voyage into the Pacific Ocean. It was his plan to follow this up with an English expedition, somehow reaching the Pacific by way of the Arctic and then claiming for England the islands which Magellan had discovered. The Project left many questions unanswered, not least that of how the English were to reach the islands; and Thorne died before he could persuade the King to take it seriously. But the King or his Secretary, Thomas Cromwell, gave encouragement to William Hawkins, and Hawkins became the first Englishman to trade successfully with the Portuguese in Brazil, thus establishing an English link with the New World. During the 1530s, Hawkins went regularly to the Guinea coast of Africa for ivory and to Brazil for dyewood, and by 1542 the English had a fortified base on the Brazilian coast at Bahia. One voyage brought back goods twenty times the value of those taken out of England.

In the middle years of the sixteenth century this trade may have lapsed for the records are silent. Thomas Wyndham, however, sailed to the African coast in 1553 and brought back gold, enough to lead to a further expedition the following year which brought back more gold. This invasion of the Portuguese monopoly was obviously profitable. In reply to Portuguese protests, the English merchants claimed,

> 'We be merchants who, by common usage of the world, do use traffique in all places of the world, as well Asia and Africa and Europa.'

The traffic continued, disregarding the Pope's line of demarcation, and in the reign of Elizabeth the English began collecting not only Africa's ivory and gold but also African slaves. Elizabeth herself told the Portuguese that she would instruct the merchants not to trade with Portugal's African territories. She did not say, however, that she did not regard African territories as Portuguese unless they actually had a Portuguese settlement!

The same recipe could be applied to the Spanish empire which was a suitable market in which to sell the slaves collected from Africa. The Spanish monopoly, it was hoped, would be no more effective than the Portuguese monopoly. So there came to the Spanish empire a plague of Englishmen, some to trade illegally, some to rob and some to do both. The records of the exploits of most of these adventurers are far from complete. The papers of the Admiralty Court in London show that a tiny eighteen-ton ship with only three small guns raided the coast of Colombia and came away with several thousand pounds worth of booty, at that time a rich haul. Exploits such as this were no doubt commonplace. It was referred to as 'adventuring on thirds', in other words on third-shares: the ship's owners, the crew and the financiers of the voyage each took a third of the profit.

But three Elizabethan adventurers stood out from the rest, and their histories will illustrate how Englishmen penetrated the Spanish empire. The first was John Hawkins, son of the William Hawkins who traded in Africa and Brazil. The second was Francis Drake, the third Walter Ralegh.

John Hawkins arrived in Hispaniola in 1563, making great play of the fact that he had applied to the House of Trade for a legal permit to trade but less of the fact that the permit had not been granted. In three small ships, of which the *Salomon* was the largest, he brought to the Spaniards 300 African slaves from Guinea. At Isabella and Puerto Plata, according to Hakluyt (*The Principal Navigations and Voyages of the English Nation*), he then 'made sales, standing always upon his guard'. Having got rid of the slaves and taken on board 'hides, ginger, sugars and some quantities of pearls' to be sold in Europe, he then arrived home in September, 1563, with a handsome profit from a year-long voyage. Back in Hispaniola, the Spaniards reported to their government that Hawkins had come 'well supplied with artillery'. A lawyer of the Audiencia of Santo Domingo described how a force of seventy horsemen had tried in vain to capture the Englishmen. He went on to explain that the Spaniards had then bought slaves, apparently because they needed them, and ended with a complaint that 'people oppose justice here' and would not co-operate with those who tried to enforce the law. He himself, therefore, would like to be transferred to another appointment.

This letter clearly revealed the problems of Spanish officials in the New World. The House of Trade forbade trade with foreigners, but supplies from Spain were often insufficient and expensive. Officials, therefore, found it difficult to prevent the settlers from trading with those who, whether legally or not, had goods to offer, especially slaves.

Now that Hawkins had made one profitable voyage, he hastily got ready to make another, and this time Elizabeth I and her ministers were eager to help to finance him and to gain a share in the profits. The voyagers of 1564–5 visited the American mainland and sold slaves at Rio de la Hacha. Hawkins paid harbour dues and even got a permit to trade which the harbour authorities had no power to give him and which was, legally, useless.

Once more, however, the House of Trade only heard about Hawkins's voyage when it was too late to stop him. But feverish instructions were sent to try to prevent future trading and a voyage of 1566, without Hawkins himself in this case, found the mainland ports less welcoming and some Africans had to be released, unsold.

Hawkins took an expedition of nine ships in 1567, led by the large and well-armed *Jesus of Lübeck*, loaned to him by Queen Elizabeth. It was on this voyage that the citizens of Rio de la Hacha were persuaded by violence to buy (see page 30). Hawkins's ships were then caught in storms. During a lull, he turned to privateering and captured three small Spanish vessels, but the English needed the shelter of a harbour to repair their storm damage and they put into Vera Cruz.* A welcoming party mistook them for a Spanish fleet and they were duly made prisoners of the English for their short-sightedness. The English were in control of Vera Cruz for a night, but the following dawn showed a fleet of a dozen Spanish ships outside the harbour. Hawkins was able to make a brief truce that neither would attack the other, but the Spanish fleet had aboard the new Viceroy of New Spain who was eager to take up his command with a resounding success. The truce was broken and the English ships smashed. Only two English ships escaped, so over-loaded with the sailors from the other vessels that Hawkins, now on the *Minion*, had to put half his men ashore where they were hunted down by the Spaniards. The other ship to escape was the *Judith*, commanded by a cousin of Hawkins, Francis Drake. Reduced by disease and hunger on the voyage home, Hawkins landed only fifteen men in England at the beginning of 1569 and Drake's ship fared little better. All the money invested in the voyage was lost along with seven ships and almost all their crews.

* The sixteenth-century port was nearby, at San Juan de Ulloa, founded in 1519.

The Spaniards routed Hawkins and the English at Vera Cruz. Only two English ships escaped

Elizabeth I, Hawkins and Drake—English thorns in the flesh of the Spaniards (Barbuda, 1971; St Christopher-Nevis-Anguilla, 1970)

Hawkins had been the first Englishman to sail on the triangular route, from England to the coast of Africa, with slaves from Africa to the New World, and from the New World home to England. This triangular route was later to yield enormous profits to those who sailed it and to bring unimaginable misery to millions of African slaves. But Hawkins himself had little further contact with the Caribbean. He became Treasurer of the English navy and a member of parliament, and did not return to the Spanish empire until the Spanish attempt to invade England in 1588 had been beaten off. Along with Martin Frobisher, he made an unsuccessful attempt to seize the Spanish convoy near the Azores in 1590 and five years later, now aged more than sixty, he sailed with Drake to raid the islands of the West Indies. He died off Puerto Rico, during the night before a fruitless assault on the island. By that time the English infested the Caribbean and constantly added to the troubles of the Spanish officials who tried to rule the empire. De Berrio wrote from Trinidad to Philip II in 1593 to complain particularly of the English and the Caribs,

> 'Besides these Englishmen whom I loathe and always injure, I am surrounded by Caribs who have tried to destroy this Island and have eaten a great number of Indians. . . .'

Meanwhile, the disaster at Vera Cruz poisoned Anglo-Spanish relations and began a new chapter in England's dealings with the Spanish empire in which the principal figure was *Francis Drake*. No single Englishman was more loathed by the Spaniards—they called him *El Draco*, the dragon. Returning from Vera Cruz in 1569, Drake had vowed to take revenge on the Spaniards and punish them for their treachery, conveniently disregarding the illegalities and occasional violence of the English themselves in the New World.

Drake made some pretence of returning to the Spanish empire as a trader, and made regular voyages in the years 1570 to 1573. One of his companions recorded that when the Spaniards asked him his business, Drake replied that he 'meant to traffic with them, for he had tin, pewter, cloth and other merchandise that they needed'. When the Spaniards reminded him of the ban on trade with foreigners, Drake answered that he 'was come from his country to exchange his commodities for gold and silver' and did not intend to return 'without'. These early voyages were mainly expeditions for plunder.

The Isthmus of Panama and the city of Nombre de Dios (Porto Bello) particularly attracted Drake. The treasures from Peru came through Nombre de Dios, reaching the city by mule-train across the Isthmus. In 1572, Drake achieved a spectacular success. Two small ships sailed from England with a force of fewer than a hundred men. They made an unsuccessful attack on Nombre de Dios and Drake was wounded for his recklessness. But the so-far modest booty was vastly increased by the great haul won by ambushing the mule-trains in the Darien Hills. So much silver was taken that the ships could not carry the whole load. It was at this time that, like Balboa before him, Drake saw the Pacific Ocean, a feat he is alleged to have accomplished by climbing a tree. The Englishmen then headed for home with their plunder, and Drake himself began to plan the future voyages which would carry him into the Pacific.

In fact, Drake was not the first Englishman to sail on the Pacific Ocean. John Oxenham made some profitable voyages to the Spanish empire. He crossed the Isthmus on foot, built himself a small ship, and attacked the Spanish vessels which carried treasures northwards from Peru. But Oxenham's good fortune did not last. He was captured by the Spaniards and hanged.

Drake's assault on the Pacific was not such a casual affair. An expedition of five ships sailed from England in 1577. The flag-ship of the fleet was the *Pelican* (re-named the *Golden Hind* during the voyage), and the intention was to follow Magellan's route south of south America. This route brought Drake into the Pacific and to the western shores of Peru where towns were looted and vessels plundered. After exploring America's west coast almost as far north as present-day Canada, the *Golden Hind* headed westwards and round the world for England. The world voyage lasted three years and thus kept Drake away from the West Indies for a time. But the Spaniards realized that even the west coast of the Americas was now not safe from marauding foreigners. Those who had invested in this voyage got a return of 4700 per cent.

In 1585, the year in which Spain and England officially went to war, Drake led an expedition of thirty ships, two of them the Queen's. They attacked the Cape Verde Islands, and headed for the West Indies where they bombarded Santo Domingo. From there, they made for the mainland and sacked Cartagena, extracting an enormous ransom to leave the city. This was even more profitable than trading with the Spaniards: the

The Spanish galleon *Cacafuego* provided booty for Drake and the crew of the *Golden Hind*—an encounter in the Pacific from Bry's *Americae*

Spaniards could be persuaded to pay the privateers to go away. However the English paid a high price for their plunder. Disease almost invariably ravaged the crews of their ships and, without a base in the New World in which to shelter and re-fit, the homeward voyages were always an ordeal. Many adventurers died so that the investors and the survivors might obtain their profits. Drake limped home with his loot in 1586 and remained in European waters during the next few years, savaging the Spanish port of Cadiz and defending England against the Armada.

Drake's voyage of 1595 to the West Indies was a failure. Neither he nor Hawkins survived the expedition, and the attempts to invade Puerto Rico and to pillage Panama were unsuccessful. Drake himself fell victim to the disease which had so often killed off his sailors, and he died off Porto Bello at the beginning of 1596. The death of *El Draco* caused great rejoicing throughout the Spanish empire. But others followed in the footsteps of Drake. Some still dreamed of capturing the Spanish convoy, the richest prize of all. An English fleet had lurked in waiting for the convoy in 1591, near the Azores, but the Spaniards sent out warships and all the English ships were driven away, except the *Revenge*, commanded by Richard Grenville. Grenville did not gain Spanish treasure but he achieved immortality in the history books. Single-handed, the *Revenge* fought the whole Spanish fleet in a battle so absurdly one-sided that Grenville could not help dying as a hero. Less quixotic, and with more profit, William Parker sacked Nombre de Dios in 1601, reminding the Spaniards that the pillaging of the sixteenth century would continue in the seventeenth.

Grenville assured himself of immortality (Turks and Caicos Islands, 1972)

Walter Ralegh first made his mark in the New World when he attempted to found a colony in north America. The idea seems to have originated with Humphrey Gilbert, who had followed the Cabots in exploring Newfoundland and lost his life at sea. The basis of the idea was that a settlement in the Americas would be convenient for dumping English subjects who were 'mutinous' or 'burdensome' and who fell into 'pilfering and thieving and other lewdness'. The Portuguese allege that, in 1579, an English expedition tried to get a foothold in Brazil, but English records of this seem not to exist. Some of Elizabeth I's ministers liked the idea of depositing stubborn English Catholics in the New World, but it is likely that they thought of north America rather than south America. Ralegh certainly got permission in 1584 to found a colony, and he chose a site on the east coast of north America which he called Virginia in honour of England's unmarried Queen. Grenville was given the task of taking out the first settlers, and they went by way of Hispaniola, drawn there perhaps by the magnetic appeal of Spanish treasures. But they sailed on, and if Grenville thought of a West Indian colony instead of one in Virginia it came to nothing. Even in Virginia, however, the settlement was a failure. Drake called there on his way home from the voyage of 1585–6 and the settlers insisted on returning to England with him. A permanent settlement in Virginia was not made until 1607.

Meanwhile, Ralegh turned his attention to the northern coast of south America. Ralegh was a scholar and he eagerly read Spanish accounts of their activities in the New World. He became fascinated by rumours of *El Dorado*, an Indian ruler believed to command a city of astonishing wealth somewhere along the River Orinoco in the uplands of Guiana. Such a city offered a more tempting prize than did Virginia and, in 1594, Ralegh sent a small expedition to investigate. The expedition reached Trinidad, near the mouth of the Orinoco (see Figure 3.1), where the Spaniards had made de Berrio the Governor and were themselves planning exploration. The next year, Ralegh went in person, sacked Spanish settlements on the islands and added to de Berrio's troubles by taking him prisoner. Ralegh then began to follow the course of the Orinoco. The local Indians seemed friendly. They confirmed the stories of a golden city and took the Englishmen to the River Caroni, a tributary of the Orinoco,

An artist's impression of Walter Ralegh and his followers in Trinidad which, they indicated, would lead to the riches. Flood-waters prevented an immediate investigation, so Ralegh optimistically declared the area English property and hastened home to seek further support. He wrote up his story in *The Discovery of Guiana*, and his enthusiasm overflowed. He did not doubt that untold riches existed,

> 'The graves have not been opened for gold, the mines not broken with sledges, nor their images pulled down out of their temples. ... Whatsoever prince shall possess it (Guiana), shall be greatest.'

Queen Elizabeth and her government were, apparently, not impressed. Ralegh was personally out of favour and he could get no support for a new expedition. For some years, he sailed only in European waters with nothing much to show for it except a successful raid on Fayal in the Azores. Worse followed. When James I came to the throne in 1603, Ralegh was accused of treason and lodged in the Tower of London under sentence of death.

James spared his life but it was not until 1616 that Ralegh was able to bribe the King's chief minister and obtain his release. He also got permission to revisit Guiana. James, who liked to be thought of as a peace-maker, insisted that on no account should Ralegh fight with the Spaniards. The Anglo-Spanish War had ended in 1604 and, for the time being, the English had promised not to trespass on the Spanish empire. Ralegh claimed to know of a mine which would yield gold, so that it would not be necessary to search for El Dorado, but there was little hope that he could avoid conflict with the Spaniards. He sailed in 1617 but, when he reached Guiana, he was obstructed by a Spanish fort which he despairingly attacked. He found no gold, and returned to England with the crews wasted by disease. His life was forfeit and he was executed.

But Ralegh's efforts had not been entirely in vain. Others took up the idea of establishing an English colony south of the Tropic of Cancer. An attempt was made to land on St Lucia in 1605, but the Englishmen were routed by the Caribs. Attention therefore turned again to the mainland and the 'Wild Coast' which was south of the mouth of the Orinoco and the home of the primitive Warrau Indians. Roger North managed to gain a foothold for a short time, but the English were generally less successful than the Dutch on the mainland. It was an expedition travelling home from a visit to the mainland which first established a lasting English colony in the West Indies, on the island of St Christopher (see Chapter 4).

The Dutch

The Spaniards discovered the strength of the Dutch as seamen when Dutch privateers, whom the Spaniards contemptuously called Sea Beggars, harassed Spanish supply-lines to the Netherlands. Dutchmen soon realized that it would help their struggle for freedom from Spain if they were to attack their enemies in the New World. Thus, during the last thirty years or so of the sixteenth century, Dutch privateers joined the French and English in the West Indies. At first, they produced no national hero of the reputation of Drake to cause panic in the Spanish empire. The main aim of the Dutch remained that of winning their independence in Europe.

A letter of 1604 to Philip III of Spain from Don Juan Barnuevo described the Dutch as being chiefly traders in salt. They took it from 'Point Araya where there is an immense quantity of it', to use in the Netherlands and to sell at a profit in Germany. Barnuevo reckoned that Holland had as many as 2000 ships, many of them trading far away from Europe. The Dutch East India Company was founded in 1602, to challenge Portugal for the trade of Asia. The Dutch West India Company, to make a similar challenge to Spain in the west, was not founded until 1621, but before that there were already enough Dutch traders in the Americas for the Spaniards to consider poisoning the salt deposits in order to discourage them. The Spanish Governor of Margarita was so angry at Dutch and English raids on his pearl fisheries that, in 1612, he suggested that less tobacco should be grown in Trinidad: he was convinced that it was tobacco which attracted illegal traders to the area. But there was no way in which the Spaniards could stop the Dutch, and in the early seventeenth century Dutch merchants were a powerful force in the West Indies (see pages 45–6).

The Sixteenth Century in Retrospect

It may well be asked, who gained from the turbulent marauding of the sixteenth century? What had the Europeans achieved for themselves and for others in the New World when Philip II of Spain died in 1598 and Elizabeth of England died in 1603?

In spite of the plunder and produce which flowed from the empire into Spain, Philip II was often bankrupt. Time and again, he was forced to borrow in advance of the arrival of the convoy, and Spain faced a constant struggle to pay its way and finance its wars. The gold and silver from the New World had the effect of causing prices in Europe to rise rapidly, for there was now more money with which to purchase goods but little increase in the quantity of goods to be purchased. Thus inflation seriously hurt Spain and Portugal and then spread rapidly to other parts of Europe. In exchange for the prestige and the produce of the empire, Spain incurred financial problems and, during succeeding centuries, the Spanish economy may be said to have stagnated or developed only slowly. This was partly because the Spaniards relied too much on easy wealth from the empire and too little on the development of Spanish agriculture and industry.

It is also unlikely that privateering brought any real profit to Spain's enemies. Many voyages ended in disaster and loss. The toll in human life was high and the financial profits small. But the voyages did play a part in the accumulation of capital by the more fortunate backers and they did encourage ship-building and trading in distant parts. The comparatively small-scale activities of the sixteenth century provided a foundation on which the English and Dutch, especially, built considerable commercial successes in the seventeenth century. In the sixteenth century itself, however, the main importance of the voyages was probably political: they weakened Spain and they boosted the reputations of Spain's rivals, helping the Dutch to gain freedom and the English to survive a Spanish-Catholic assault. By the beginning of the seventeenth century, however, many countries were becoming convinced that permanent settlements in the New World were desirable. The next task was to establish them.

Europeans liked to think that the New World itself benefited from their settlement. In the sixteenth century, there was little evidence to support this conceit. Chapter 2 has shown how the Europeans all but destroyed the aborigine population of the West Indies and tore down the civilizations of the Aztecs and Incas. It has also been seen that by the middle of the sixteenth century there was already a small but steady trade in Africans, the beginnings of an enterprise as inhuman as any in history. Indians who survived in the Americas were often enslaved and almost always degraded. In exchange, it was argued, they were introduced to Christianity and to the white man's civilization which was usually said to be more 'advanced'. The Europeans built towns, established plantations, opened mines and made trade links—even though other Europeans spent much of the sixteenth century trying to destroy these. The Europeans brought knowledge and sometimes set up schools not only for the immigrants but also for the Indians, so that, if they survived, Indians might learn to read and write. There is very little evidence that, by 1600, the Indians had gained from this. In the West Indies, almost all the Arawaks were then dead; and the Caribs survived, in the main, by resolutely keeping the Europeans out of the Lesser Antilles. So far, the Spanish empire had added to the property and prestige of the Spanish monarchy. It had added to the Europeans' knowledge of the world. It had caused great excitement in Europe and provided a theatre for many deeds of bravery—and many more of foolishness, cruelty and downright barbarism. Las Casas had found little to praise in Spanish colonization, and much to condemn. He died in 1566, sad and frustrated. Forty years later, beset with privateers, the empire would have given him no better cause for rejoicing.

Exercises

1 'The Spanish discoveries in the New World were of particular interest to those nations in Europe which had coastlines facing west' (page 28). Explain the reasons for this interest, and show how this interest affected the development of the West Indies in the years before 1600.

2 What can you learn of the development of the Spanish empire in the sixteenth century from a study of Figures 2.1 and 3.1?

3 Describe the activities in the Caribbean of (a) Hawkins and (b) Drake. How far would you agree that these activities of Hawkins and Drake were rewarding for the English, damaging to the Spaniards and unhelpful to the West Indies?

4 What do you understand by *privateering* in the sixteenth century? Argue for and against the claim that privateers were 'different from pirates' (page 29).

5 Imagine yourself to be a member of the Audiencia of Santo Domingo in 1596. Write a letter to Philip II of Spain to report that you have just heard of the death of Drake and expressing your feelings at this news in the light of Drake's past activities.

4 Settlement and Fragmentation in the Seventeenth Century

The Newcomers

The enemies of Spain came to the West Indies in the sixteenth century to pillage, and to profit from whatever illegal trading they could persuade the Spanish settlers to do. They continued to pillage and to trade in the seventeenth century, but they were now also looking for places in which to establish permanent footholds. The area which Spain had claimed in the Treaty of Tordesillas was so vast that it was impossible for the Spaniards to keep out the English, French and Dutch for ever. The English and French showed the greater enthusiasm for settlement, for farming the land and building colonies. The Dutch preferred to concentrate on trading with whichever settlements welcomed them, and they looked on their own territories as trading posts rather than as agricultural colonies. They chose their territories for their safe harbours, and they were more eager to build warehouses than to create plantations from the wilderness. For much of the first half of the seventeenth century, the Dutch became the principal traders of the West Indies and soon proved themselves essential in supplying the needs of the early English and French settlers.

Two major struggles dominated the second half of the seventeenth century. This chapter will deal with the first one, in which the French and the English forced the Spaniards to recognize the legality of their settlements. The buccaneers were a powerful aid to the French and the English in this struggle, of which the outcome was the fragmentation of the West Indies, split up among various European nations. The second struggle, in which the English and French took control of the profitable trade with their own colonies and squeezed out the Dutch, will be considered in Chapter 5.

English Settlement

Repeated failures to gain a successful foothold on the coast of the south American mainland led the English to turn their attention to the Lesser Antilles. In 1622, members of the Amazon Company, among whom was Thomas Warner, landed on the island of *St Christopher* as they were returning, disappointed, from the mainland. The Carib obouto, Tegreman, did not resist the newcomers. There were no hostile Spaniards, and the island seemed to be very suitable for the planting of tobacco for which there was a lively demand in Europe. Warner returned to England and interested the merchant, Ralph Merrifield, in the island. Merrifield gave financial support to Warner who came back to St Christopher (St Kitts) with a tiny group of settlers at the beginning of 1624. Their intention was to create a settlement and grow tobacco which Merrifield could sell in

The beginning of the first English settlement in the West Indies (St Christopher-Nevis-Anguilla, 1973)

England. It was a peaceful and constructive intention, not a destructive attempt to plunder. But the Englishmen were settling on a Carib island, and ill-feeling grew between the newcomers and the Amerindians. Caribs were killed in the skirmishing and Warner's settlement survived only because more Europeans arrived, albeit Frenchmen. These Frenchmen were led by Pierre d'Esnambuc and du Rossey, and they were all that remained of a privateering expedition which had been mauled by the Spaniards. Combining together to fight off a Carib attack, the English and French then chased the Indians away from their island.

D'Esnambuc went home to France and promptly enlisted the backing of the king's chief minister, Cardinal Richelieu. In 1627, Warner agreed to partition St Kitts with the French: the English took the centre and d'Esnambuc's settlers took the northern and southern ends. Thus began an uneasy partnership which lasted until the French gave up their interest in the island in 1713. It was significant of Anglo-French rivalry to come, however, that Richelieu included in his grant to d'Esnambuc in 1626 'exclusive rights to settle the islands of St Christopher and Barbados and the surrounding islands', assuming, as the Spaniards had previously done, that a European nation could monopolize what it chose. Richelieu also echoed Spanish ambitions by referring to the Christianizing of the Indians and the working of 'mines and metals'.

About the same time that Richelieu was granting islands to d'Esnambuc, the King of England made a similar grant to Warner and appointed him the Governor of St Christopher, Nevis, Barbados and Montserrat. The English were quicker off the mark than the French. In fact, John Powell had already claimed Barbados for England in 1624; and the English settled on Nevis in 1628 and on Antigua and Montserrat four years later. The French had therefore to look elsewhere and they took possession of Guadeloupe and Martinique.

John Powell had been trading with Brazil and he came to *Barbados* by chance. It lay to the east of the Windward Islands and at that time few ships passed near it. It seemed a suitable island to claim for King James, and Powell nailed to a tree a notice to stake the English claim. He was able to return there in 1627 with his brother Henry and a substantial number of settlers. Like Warner, he had obtained financial support from merchants,

Barbados never lost the Assembly which Charles I granted to the settlers in 1639 (Barbados, 1939)

the Courteens, and Dutch connections on the mainland in Guiana persuaded Indian labourers to come voluntarily to Barbados to assist with cultivation. Barbados too concentrated on producing tobacco for export to England and Europe.

These first English settlements were not established without difficulties. There were massive trees to be felled and the land had to be cleared for cultivation. The Caribs continued, spasmodically, to raid St Kitts and its first tobacco crop was destroyed by a hurricane. Then there was fighting between the English and the French which gave Spain the opportunity to destroy both their settlements. Except for Barbados, remote from these clashes, the English and French footholds in the islands seemed on the point of extinction. But the Spaniards had not the manpower to garrison the Lesser Antilles. When the Spanish fleet disappeared, English and French survivors came out of hiding, rebuilt what had been destroyed and by the middle of the 1630s were firmly in possession. They relied heavily on Dutch traders to bring food and equipment, but stocks were sometimes perilously low.

Like the Spaniards at the end of the fifteenth century, the English faced the problem of how the islands were to be governed. There seemed, perhaps not surprisingly, to be some confusion in England as to precisely what the English properties were, and where they were. Warner's first royal grant included Barbados though it was nearly 400 miles from St Kitts and was settled by Powell. In 1627, Charles I granted to the Earl of Carlisle the right to be the Proprietor of England's

West Indian islands. *The Proprietor* was a sort of overlord, and the English sometimes used this system in the colonies they established on the mainland of north America. The Proprietor appointed governors to the colonies, supervised their administration (from England), taxed the settlements and punished the settlers for misdeeds; and he issued laws, although the settlers were supposed to be consulted in the law-making. It was easy, of course, for a Proprietor to be most interested in his power to collect taxes.

Confusion followed when, in 1628, Charles I granted to the Earl of Pembroke the right to be the Proprietor of Trinidad and Tobago (which England did not possess) and of Barbados (which Carlisle already held), throwing in for good measure the perhaps non-existent island of Fonseca. A bitter conflict about Barbados now developed between Carlisle and Pembroke and their respective supporters. It ended in the triumph of Carlisle and, when he died in 1636, his rights passed to his son. Pembroke's supporters, who included the Courteens, lost their influence and investments in Barbados, while Carlisle began to exploit the island and to squeeze the settlers for taxes. In its first years, Barbados had been more stable than St Kitts, but St Kitts now began to forge ahead under Warner's able Governorship, which lasted until his death in 1648.

Meanwhile, the Civil War broke out in England in 1642, between the Royalists, who supported Charles I, and the Parliamentarians who wanted to limit the powers of the King. Charles I was eventually defeated. He was executed in 1649 and England became a republic under the leadership of Oliver Cromwell. The English West Indian settlements were left very much to themselves during the 1640s, in spite of the fact that the Parliamentarians nominated the Earl of Warwick to supervise them. Barbados considered itself almost independent. Its settlers traded with the Dutch and, initially, took little interest in the quarrels at home, seizing the opportunity to avoid paying taxes to the Proprietor. But whereas St Kitts and the other islands wisely remained neutral in the quarrels at home, Barbados was eventually caught up in them. In 1647, Carlisle had named Francis Willoughby to rule Barbados and to share its profits with him, and Willoughby arrived in the island in 1650, now a Royalist refugee. He promptly proclaimed Barbados a stronghold of the monarchy, loyal to Charles II, the son of Charles I. His action divided the settlers but the majority rallied to him when he went on to issue a Declaration of Independence, the first English colony ever to take such a step. But it could be no more than a gesture. Cromwell sent George Ayscue with a powerful republican force to subdue the rebellious island and, in 1651, Barbados had to surrender. Daniel Searle was appointed its new Governor.

Cromwell's policy was to make the English islands in the West Indies the property of the government and to end the system of farming them out to proprietors. But the monarchy was restored in England in 1660 and Charles II then briefly revived the Carlisle proprietorship: Willoughby was restored as the Governor of Barbados. Almost at once there was an outcry in Barbados at the taxes Willoughby imposed and, having second thoughts, Charles II abolished the proprietary system in 1663. From this year forward, the English islands were *crown colonies*, in that they were the property of the English monarchy as the Spanish empire was the property of the Spanish monarchy. The crown colonies would be ruled by officially appointed governors, which was what Cromwell had planned at the time of the Barbadian surrender in 1651. At the same time, however, each governor would be assisted by a council, and each colony would have an assembly made up largely of the settlers themselves (the more prosperous and important of them), to help in making laws and to give consent to taxation. On these principles, the English islands were ruled for centuries. It was a system which, at least on the surface, was less rigidly directed from Europe than that of the Spanish empire. But the islands were left with one deep grievance. To compensate Carlisle for the loss of his proprietorship, Charles II insisted that the colonies should pay a 4½ per cent tax on exports, a grievance which remained into the nineteenth century.

Meanwhile, the English at last gained a territory on the mainland in Surinam; and Cromwell, pursuing his Western Design, added to the English possessions the island of Jamaica. *Surinam*, part of the Wild Coast of Guiana, was occupied by Willoughby and a party of settlers most of whom had left Barbados when that island's brief independence had been snuffed out in 1651. Surinam had good agricultural prospects but, having gained it, the English did not apparently want it. They gave it to the Dutch in 1667 in exchange for what was to become New York on the coast of north America.

Efforts to gain further West Indian islands came to nothing for the time being. The Caribs beat off an attempt to seize St Lucia in 1638, as they had beaten off the attempt made in 1605. It was the French who eventually overcame the Caribs on the island, and thereafter the English, from time to time, challenged the French for its possession. The Caribs defended Dominica and St Vincent even more stubbornly and, in 1660, the English and French agreed to leave them alone for the present.

Cromwell's Western Design and the Conquest of Jamaica

> 'The design in general is to gain an interest in that part of the West Indies in the possession of the Spaniards.'

With these words, Cromwell began his instructions to Robert Venables at the end of 1654. He went on to suggest that Venables should take Hispaniola and Puerto Rico, and then go on to capture Havana in Cuba. Or perhaps, Cromwell continued, start with Cuba. Becoming even more flexible, he went on to suggest another possibility: to by-pass the islands and attack the mainland. But the main aim was clear: to become 'master of the Spaniards' Treasure'. In fact, Venables and William Penn who commanded his fleet captured Jamaica! And they did little to 'pursue, kill and destroy', as Cromwell advised, because the Spaniards put up little resistance in defence of an island whose development had been slow and whose geographical position was rather inconvenient to their main trade routes. Venables and Penn hurried back to England to inform Cromwell that Hispaniola was better defended than they had expected and had twice beaten off their attacks. Perhaps they felt it necessary to justify their conquest not of a treasure-house but of a rather sleepy cattle-country. Cromwell put them in the Tower of London for a month, more for deserting the island when he had expected them to stay to consolidate an English settlement than for handing him a useless conquest.

In fact, Jamaica was far from useless and England was fortunate to secure it with an expedition as badly prepared and incompetently led as that of Venables and Penn. They had left England with 2500 men, most of them ill-trained, and collected a rabble of 4000 more from English settlements in the West Indies. The force was weakened by disease and the adventurers were generally more remarkable for their fright and cowardice than for their desire to make a spectacular conquest. The panic of the Spaniards at Santo Domingo was exceeded only by the terror of many of those attacking the city. It was a great relief for the Englishmen to turn away from the barking dog of Hispaniola to pounce on the rabbit of Jamaica. What they captured, however, was a first-class base from which to launch the attacks of the buccaneers against the Spaniards in succeeding years, and it was the largest West Indian island that the English were ever able to seize.

The English settlement of Jamaica took some time before it began to prosper. To begin with, it took time to clear the island of Spaniards and African slaves who remained loyal to them. Rather more serious was the sickness to which many of the settlers fell victim, weakened as they were by hunger. The writer of a letter in November, 1655, said he had never seen so many funerals, that the settlers were eating dogs (and the dogs digging up and eating the dead). He himself, he said, suffered from 'bloody flux, rheum, ague and fever' and had 'fallen away five inches'. The brother of the person to whom he wrote had died of 'dropsy, consumption and other complicated diseases'. The Spaniards were overcome by the end of the 1660s and more hardy English settlers soon arrived to build up the colony, but for many years they were harassed by the maroons, the name given to the runaway slaves.

A succession of able governors helped the colony to succeed. General D'Oyley arrived in 1657, Lord Windsor in 1661. Thomas Modyford ruled the island when buccaneering was at its height (see pages 46–9), and then the most outstanding of the buccaneers, Henry Morgan, himself succeeded to office. Jamaica was large enough to permit the development of extensive sugar plantations (see Figure 7.1) and, once the early difficulties were overcome, the main problem was to build up a population large enough to develop the potential of the island.

French Settlement

The French clung to the two ends of St Kitts—won for them by d'Esnambuc—

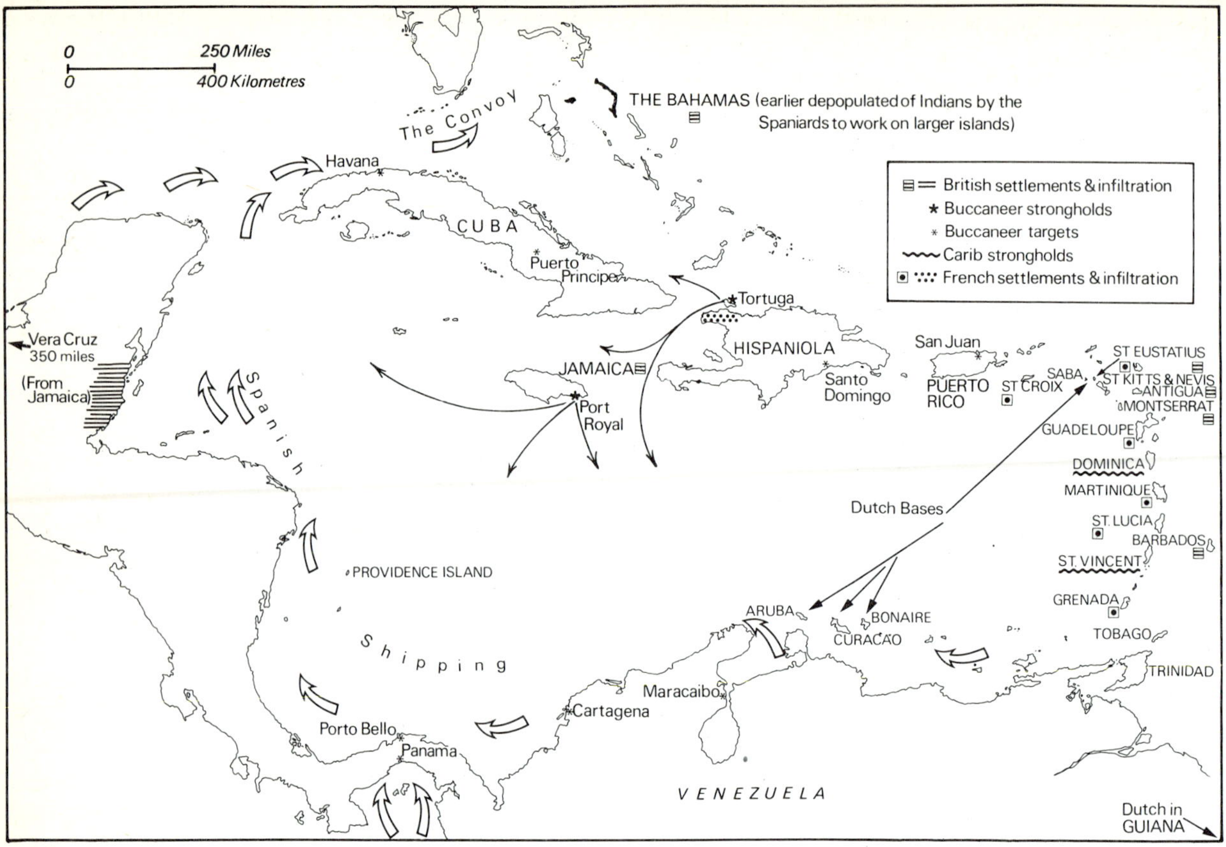

Figure 4.1 Seventeenth-Century Fragmentation

throughout the seventeenth century, but it did not satisfy their national pride merely to share a small West Indian island with the English. In 1635, Richelieu organized the *Compagnie des Isles d'Amérique** for the purpose of extending the French possessions and, from this early date, to impose a more tidy governmental control over the French territories than the English had so far managed. D'Esnambuc was appointed Governor-General and, before the end of 1635, Guadeloupe and Martinique were claimed for France. These became the principal French islands in the West Indies. European settlement was now extending steadily through the Lesser Antilles. The French probed northwards from their settlements on St Kitts and occupied St Bartholomew, St Croix and St Martin, the last of which they agreed to share with the Dutch in 1648. Further south, among the Windward Islands, they occupied St Lucia and Grenada in the middle of the seventeenth century. But, for the time being, the Caribs kept the Europeans out of Dominica and St Vincent.

The seventeenth century, like the sixteenth, was a century of wars in Europe. The struggle between Bourbon and Habsburg continued, and so the French still regarded the Spaniards as a legitimate enemy. The French also began to clash with the Dutch who were now independent of Spain. From 1643 to 1715, France was ruled by the aggressive Louis XIV and in the course of the many wars which the French fought during his reign, Tobago was taken from the Dutch in 1678. About this time, the French also gained territory on the mainland, establishing themselves at Cayenne in Guiana in 1674.

While the English were moving from the proprietary system to the more tidy one of the crown colonies, the French moved in the opposite direction. The *Compagnie des Isles d'Amérique* went

* Company of the Isles of America.

bankrupt and the French islands were sold to men who were, in effect, proprietors. In 1649, a group of islands centred on Guadeloupe and Marie Galante made up the first sale. Others quickly followed, Martinique with French islands to the south in one package, the French share of St Kitts and the small islands to the north in another. The French islands were thus farmed out amongst three proprietors; however, they tried to avoid the problems which the English encountered in the days of the Earls of Carlisle, by requiring the three proprietors to live in the West Indies rather than in Europe.

The proprietary system was as unsatisfactory as the Spaniards had found the personal rule of Columbus to be. Too often the colonies were held back in their development by private feuds and personal self-interest. Proprietors seldom took a long-term view: their main interest was in short-term profit. In the 1660s, Louis XIV was served by probably the most able minister that his reign produced, Jean Colbert, and Colbert organized the founding of a new French West India Company. This Company represented the French government and was expected to apply government policy. From its foundation, in 1664, it took over the French islands of the West Indies so that France was able to establish an official and united policy in the islands in all matters to do with government, the society and the economy. The English had just arrived at almost the same point, Charles II having abolished the proprietary system in 1663.

Dutch Settlement

Dutchmen settled in three main areas—on the mainland in Guiana; on a batch of islands off the coast of Venezuela of which the largest was Curaçao; and on other tiny islands north of St Kitts which included St Eustatius. The fact that many of these islands were mere pin-points of land was of no great importance to the Dutch, for, except on the mainland, their main business was to trade and they needed space only for the purpose of setting up depots.

Dutch settlements in Guiana were usually to be found a few miles inland, on the larger rivers. By 1616, such settlements existed on the Courantyne, the Essequibo and the Cayenne. About ten years later, a settlement was founded on the Berbice, and by that time the Dutch were working their way further inland.

The foundation of the Dutch West India Company in 1621 was an important landmark in the history of Dutch activity in the West Indies. 1621 was also the year in which the truce of 1609 with Spain expired. When the Spaniards then resumed their efforts to force the Dutch to abide by Spanish rule in the Netherlands, the West India Company took as one of its main aims the 'humbling' of 'the pride and might of Spain'. The struggle for Dutch independence became part of the Thirty Years War in Europe, and when the War ended in 1648 Spain had finally to renounce its claim to rule Holland. By that time the Dutch had become the most successful traders in the West Indies. They had added to their possessions from 1634, the islands of Curaçao, Aruba and Bonaire, ideal bases for trading with the mainland; and by 1640 they had claimed St Eustatius, St Martin and Saba, which were ideally placed to trade with the English and French settlements in the Leeward Islands.

Curaçao and its sister islands had deposits of salt which was much used at this time for preserving foodstuffs, and the Dutch were able to grow crops in Guiana and on most of the islands. But, above all, the islands were well-placed for the smuggling of goods into the Spanish empire and for preying on Spanish shipping. For a time, the Dutch were able to hold Tobago but they directed their energies towards dominating the trade routes rather than towards capturing islands and founding colonies. They were forbidden to trade in the Spanish empire and in the French colonies, and the English government strongly preferred the English colonies to trade with Englishmen, but it was not possible for other Europeans to keep the Dutch out in the early seventeenth century. Dutch traders were indispensable, and it is unlikely that the early French and English settlements could have survived without them. The Dutch West India Company prospered. Tobacco was collected regularly from the Spaniards in Venezuela and hides were collected from the Spaniards in Hispaniola. It was a measure of the weakness of the Spanish government that it could think of no other ways to stop the Dutch, than to forbid its Venezuelan subjects to grow tobacco and to expel from Hispaniola those subjects found trading with the enemy.

The Charter which the Dutch had given to the West India Company had made it all-powerful, granting sole rights for twenty-four years to sail, trade, make contracts and appoint governors (subject to government approval) in the western hemisphere. Piet Hein sailed under the authority of the Company when, in 1628, he scored one of the most spectacular successes against a Spanish convoy, driving the treasure ships ashore near Havana and weighting down his own fleet with the plunder. The shareholders of the Company rubbed their hands with glee at the dividends of that year's operations. But Hein was only one of scores of privateers who took a steady toll of Spanish wealth. As they weakened Spain, they enriched Holland and showed well the truth of the claim in the Company's Charter that,

> 'the prosperity of this country and the welfare of its inhabitants principally consist in the navigation and commerce ... carried on ... with all countries and kingdoms'.

Other Settlements

Three other European countries also looked for pickings in the West Indies. Denmark looked for a base to the east of Puerto Rico and found one on St Thomas, which the Dutch had held but abandoned. A Danish West India Company secured regular possession in 1672 and the Danes eventually sold the island to the USA in 1917.

Brandenburg gained an even smaller prize, the rock of St Peter in the Virgin Islands. This was in 1689, after the Brandenburgers had made a variety of bids to purchase something more promising, at one time setting their sights even on Tobago. Brandenburg too set up a West India Company in pursuit of profits like those of the Dutch.

Sweden had two companies, one for operations in the Americas and the other, the Swedish African Company; but not until the eighteenth century did the Swedes persuade the French to give them a West Indian base on the little island of St Bartholomew.

Denmark, Brandenburg and Sweden had, in effect, missed the boat. Even the tiniest islands had by now been claimed, except where resolute Caribs still kept away the Europeans. Privateers could still seize an occasional juicy cargo and engage in a profitable trading deal but there was little room for more newcomers. Instead, attention began to centre increasingly on Africa and the lucrative business of transporting slaves. So vast did that trade become in the eighteenth century that, in spite of claims to monopolies, it was difficult to keep anyone out of it (see pages 71–4).

The Buccaneers

> 'Here are a sort of vagabonds that are saved from the gallows in Spain.... These go by the name of cow killers, and indeed it is their trade.... These are those that doth all the mischief, and here are Negroes and Mulattoes which are their slaves.... If it were not for these cow killers and the Negroes, the Spaniards were not able to hold up his hand against any enemy, for the Spaniards are so rotten with the pox and so lethargic.'

In these words, Henry Whistler recorded some of his impressions of Jamaica in 1655. He was referring to those who gave most trouble to the English and who, at that time, defended the Spaniards. Within a few years, however, the cow killers became the deadly enemies of Spain and perhaps the most effective fighting-force that England and France had yet found on which to rely. These *buccaneers* were seventeenth-century pirates who took their name from the word *boucan* which was a sort of grid-iron used as a cooking device by the cow killers. They consisted of a miscellaneous collection of vagabonds, cow killers, runaways and outcasts who matched greed only with ruthlessness. Encouraged by the English and the French, they brought down fire and destruction upon the Spaniards.

It is impossible to draw a precise line to divide the buccaneers from earlier privateers and pirates, and it is easy to exaggerate the extent to which the buccaneers deliberately served the interests of the French and English governments. They were certainly useful to those governments in so weakening the Spaniards that the latter were forced to end the nonsense of maintaining that the whole of the West Indies were part of the Spanish empire, and that the other countries' settlements were illegal. The buccaneers are said, therefore, to have forced Spain to recognize the settlements of England and France, and it is certain that some, particularly Henry Morgan, were honoured by their governments. But the buccaneers served, above all, themselves.

By the middle of the seventeenth century, the privateers were so numerous and had existed so long that they had begun to develop their own pirate code. They elected their leaders, shared out the booty on the basis of a sort of contract, and compensated the casualties in pieces of eight for lost limbs, eyes and fingers. They also compensated widows for lost pirate-husbands.

Perhaps the first of these well-organized privateers to be identified as buccaneers were the inhabitants of the island of Tortuga off the north-west coast of Hispaniola, a motley collection who had already murdered their governor. They were of mixed nationality but they claimed protection from the French. Many of them had arrived in Tortuga as refugees from the Spaniards who had uprooted them from Hispaniola on the eve of the attack by Venables and Penn in 1655. They named themselves the Brethren of the Coast and took to the seas. For some ten years, they attacked the Spaniards with a brutal savagery outstanding even in the blood-soaked history of the West Indies, and attracted to their crews cow killers and outcasts from the entire area.

In 1665, Bertrand d'Ogéron restored Tortuga to something like normal French rule and even imported 150 hardy French women to try to tame some of the ruffians by marriage. But at the same time, d'Ogéron issued letters of marque in a bid to organize the buccaneers for the defence of the island and the weakening of the Spaniards. Meanwhile, the English had taken Jamaica where buccaneers gathered at Port Royal and did their best to make it 'the wickedest town in the Americas'. Plenty of rootless drifters remained from the Venables–Penn expedition and, like d'Ogéron, Governor Modyford saw the advantage of tolerating the buccaneers in exchange for a sort of loyalty, especially as he had no great force with which to control them. It would take many decades of hard work to establish Jamaica as a prosperous English colony and plunder was, for a time, its main source of income.

Buccaneers in Port Royal, therefore, provided a sort of protection for the English. Buccaneers in Tortuga provided a sort of protection for the French. All the buccaneers provided a destructive enemy for the Spaniards. Some of the buccaneers were Dutchmen but it would be wrong to assume that English, French and Dutch were united against Spain. There were many wars in Europe in the second half of the seventeenth century and England, France and Holland often fought against one another. These wars affected the West Indies so that, for example, in the 1660s the Dutch bombarded the English island of Barbados and the French fought the English in St Kitts.

The 1660s was also the decade in which *Henry Morgan* emerged as the leader of the buccaneers. Born in Wales, it remains something of a mystery how and when Morgan arrived in the West Indies but he may have been on the Venables–Penn expedition. He became known to Governor Modyford when, already a member of the Brethren at Port Royal, he was sent with Edward Mansfield to raid Curaçao in 1665, England being at that time officially at war with the Dutch. Curaçao's salt and even its warehouses were of little interest to buccaneers and, with a disregard for instructions that was often typical of privateers, Mansfield and Morgan attacked Cuba and then the mainland instead. These Spanish possessions were likely to offer richer booty. They came back to Jamaica claiming to have secured Providence Island for the English, in the south-west of the Caribbean Sea. Englishmen had been there before, when the Providence Island Company, founded in 1630, had for eleven years turned the island into a pirates' lair to prey on Spanish shipping travelling from Cartagena to Havana. The Spaniards rooted them out in 1641. Now, English interest revived. Modyford accepted the buccaneers' gift but by the time his brother, James Modyford, was ready to take charge of the island the Spaniards were back in control of it.

With the death of Mansfield, Morgan took command of the Brethren, and from 1666 onwards Modyford issued letters of marque against Spain. Morgan sacked Puerto Principe in Cuba and then raided Porto Bello on the Isthmus of Panama in search of richer booty, an attack made with far more savagery than that of Drake nearly a century earlier. Buccaneers from Tortuga meanwhile ravaged Maracaibo and seized such plunder that Morgan made Maracaibo the target for his next expedition. But he did not find riches for the taking such as there had been at Porto Bello. Instead of a riotous month in which to loot and rape, the buccaneers had to scour the countryside for any plunder at all, get themselves out of a Spanish trap, and return to Port Royal with their appetites unsatisfied. After a brief lull, Morgan prepared for a new expedition in 1670 with Modyford's support. Thirty-six ships and nearly 2000 men, a quarter of them French, were painstakingly assembled.

They sailed in December, 1670, their destination Panama. By that time, Spain had signed the Treaty of Madrid. Officially, England no

Maracaibo, 1669. Morgan and the buccaneers battered the Spanish warships but could find little booty on the mainland—an illustration from Esquemeling's *Buccaneers of America*. With Morgan and his Port Royal base (Jamaica, 1971)

longer had a reason for quarrelling with the Spaniards, but Modyford had no real control over the buccaneers: nothing could stop them now. The city of Panama was reduced to smoking ruins in a month of pillage, but the Spaniards had wisely removed many of its treasures before the buccaneers arrived and devastation rather than profit was the chief result of the attack. Morgan returned to Jamaica in April, 1671, with only modest booty.

Recognition

Modyford had accepted and even supported the buccaneers of Port Royal chiefly as a way of protecting Jamaica. Cautiously, the English government in London had made use of them, as a way to put pressure on Spain to agree to the legality of English settlement in the West Indies and to acknowledge the English conquest of Jamaica. In the Treaty of Madrid of 1670, the Spaniards recognized the English claims, insisting in return that the English should cease to attack Spanish property. Spain was outraged that almost as soon as the Treaty had been signed, Morgan destroyed Panama. Charles II, the King of England, dismissed Modyford from his Governorship and had him brought home to be imprisoned in the Tower of London. Thomas Lynch became Governor of Jamaica in his place and was strong enough in 1672 to send Morgan back to England too.

Charles II was not a king who acted in haste. With Modyford and Morgan now in England, the Spaniards protested less loudly, and within a few years Charles was able to make Modyford chief justice, in reward for past services, and to grant Morgan a knighthood. The buccaneers were now a nuisance. They plundered Trinidad in 1673 and Vera Cruz ten years later. Spain had not yet recognized French settlements in the West Indies and so the French were still inclined to condone buccaneering. But the English now wanted peace, so that their settlements could grow into orderly and prosperous colonies. Charles apparently believed that the best way to catch a thief was to use another thief to do it. He appointed Morgan to be Deputy-Governor of Jamaica, the man who seemed most fitted to suppress the buccaneers, now that he had apparently accepted respectability.

Spain and France signed the Truce of Ratisbon in 1684, agreeing to peace both in Europe and in the Americas. This was not quite the end of their enmity and the Spaniards did not fully accept the French right to settlements in the West Indies until the Treaty of Ryswick in 1697. By that time, the buccaneers had also become respectable. Those who had not already been persuaded to turn to the more peaceful work of growing tobacco or other small-scale crops, were enlisted in the 1690s to serve their countries in the War of the Grand Alliance. When the Treaty of Ryswick was signed, their numbers were comparatively small. Disciplined naval squadrons were now a match for them. Conveniently, Port Royal was destroyed by an earthquake in 1692. Morgan had died in 1688, having become something of a model citizen.

After 1697, the European governments still used privateers in wartime. Some of them were ex-buccaneers like Laurent de Graff, who had helped the French in the 1690s with an old-fashioned type of attack on Cartagena. But the pirates of the eighteenth century were rather lonely figures, no longer hunting in packs as the buccaneers had done and no longer half-accepted by the governors of the islands. There was a place for them in wartime as long as they were reasonably well-disciplined, but in peacetime most men were now united against them. Some buccaneers found an outlet for their adventurousness in exploration, especially in the Pacific. A few even turned to writing, as William Dampier did in his *New Voyage Round the World* (1697). They showed great interest in the Isthmus of Panama, no doubt fascinated partly because of its old connection with Spanish treasures. The stories of their explorations and adventures did much to spread through Europe an interest in the Americas and the West Indies, as well as in the South Seas of the Pacific. The West Indies, however, were glad at last to be rid of them.

Port Royal in the days of Henry Morgan—a reconstruction with the governor's house in the centre. Morgan lived there as the Deputy-Governor of Jamaica

The Spanish Empire in the Seventeenth Century

Morgan's vicious destruction of the city of Panama was an example of the danger in which many Spanish settlements stood. But although frequently damaged, the Spanish empire remained generally intact. The islands on which other nations settled had almost all been ignored by the Spaniards, and Jamaica was Spain's only significant loss. D'Ogéron, however, had established the French in a corner of Hispaniola and defended them by using the buccaneers on the off-shore island of Tortuga. From this settlement was later to develop France's most prosperous colony of St Domingue. The mainland of the Spanish empire remained similarly intact except for the foreign settlements in Guiana and Honduras, areas which, again, the Spaniards had neglected. It had not been possible to keep foreign

A Spanish settlement in Hispaniola in the seventeenth century. Such settlements tempted the buccaneers, but there was richer booty on the mainland

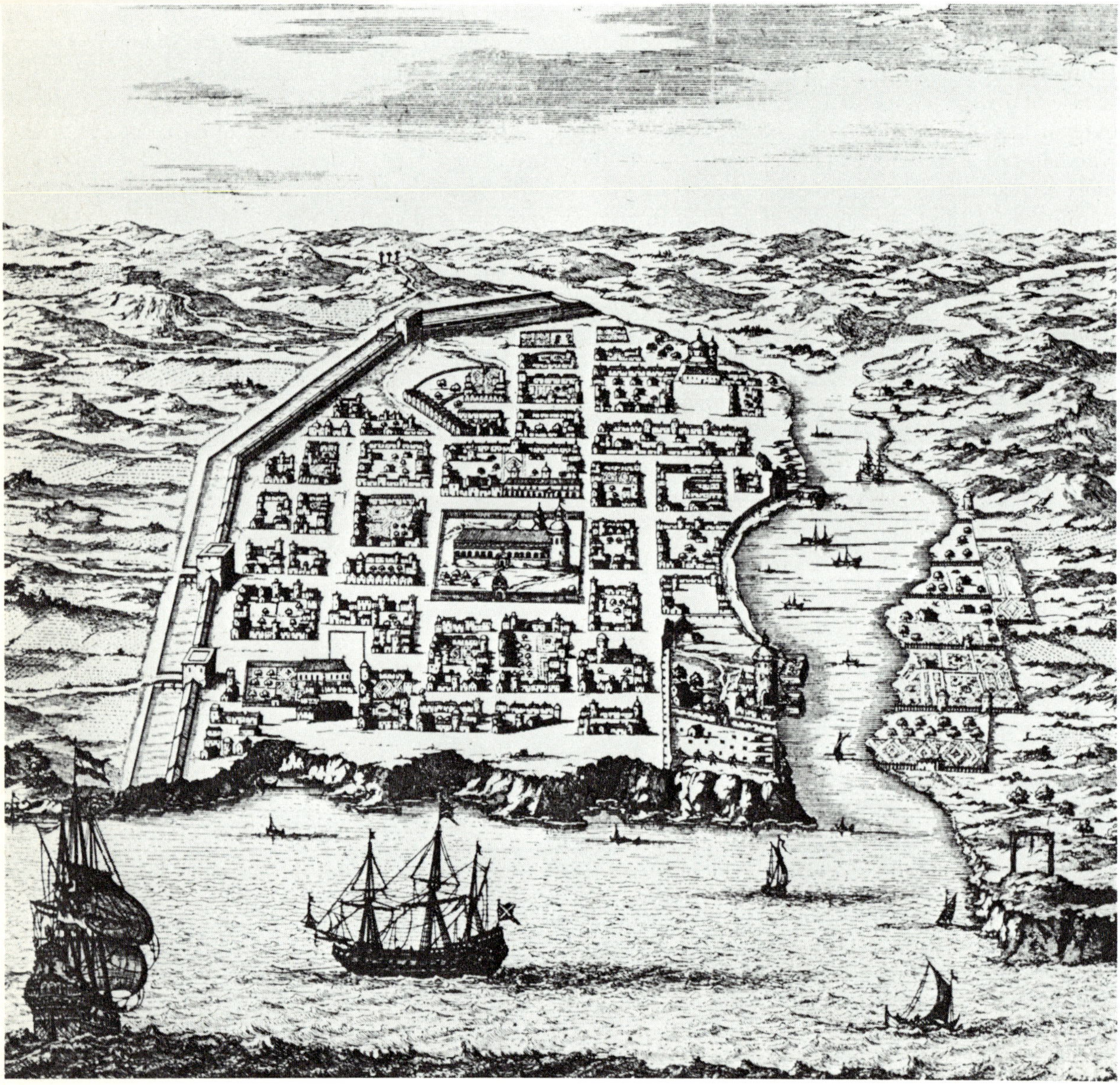

traders out of the empire and it was certainly not possible to protect every Spanish ship around its shores. But the convoy system provided a usually effective protection for Spanish fleets across the Atlantic throughout the seventeenth century. So that century was by no means an unsuccessful one for Spain.

The extent of the Spanish empire, and the basic system of its government had been largely determined before the end of the sixteenth century. The seventeenth century was one of consolidation and some limited improvement. In 1681, for example, the Council of the Indies completed its work in revising the code of laws by which the empire was ruled, and issued the *Compilation of the Laws of the Indies*. But the most important developments were those which concerned the societies and the economies of the Spanish colonies.

Social divisions in the Spanish empire were still extensive. Power almost always rested with the *peninsulares*, the true-born Spaniards. Those of high birth, the *hidalgos*, held high positions in the administration, in the military and in the Church. Those of more humble birth still considered themselves superior to the creoles. After the creoles came those of mixed blood, the mulattoes; and lower still were the Amerindians and, bottom of the social scale, the Africans. By the seventeenth century, the vast majority of the Africans in the empire were slaves. Much jealousy existed between poor whites, creoles and mulattoes; and poor whites and creoles tried desperately to maintain an imagined superiority against fellow-artisans and fellow-clerks. If occupation and wealth (or lack of it) seemed to deny such a superiority, it became essential to boast of one's birthplace or parentage. Each social group tended to look down on those 'below' it, and everywhere there was a fear of change. The king, the hidalgos and the Council of the Indies feared disloyalty, which would weaken the empire from within, and expose it to the onslaughts of the English, French and Dutch. Other classes feared those below them—ambitious mulattoes, sullen Amerindians and rebellious Africans. It was therefore a conservative society, anxious to preserve that which existed.

Such a society tends not to be enterprising. When one adds to this the almost fanatical obsession of the authorities with economic monopoly, to shut out other Europeans from the economic life and trade of the empire, it was inevitable that development would be slow. It has been seen that the authorities preferred to abandon tobacco-growing in Venezuela rather than sell the crop to the Dutch. The empire, therefore, became distorted because of the need to ship its produce to Spain and to send it along a limited number of fairly safe routes. Havana became the centre of the Spanish empire in the West Indies because of its key position. In consequence, Hispaniola tended to be neglected, and the French seized their opportunity to take possession of a corner of it. Jamaica too had been neglected, letting in the English. On the mainland also, outlying parts of the empire remained poorly developed because of the tendency for wealth to be sucked towards the Isthmus and Porto Bello and the route to Spain. Thus, prosperity was unevenly spread in the Spanish empire, a fact from which the buccaneers were able to profit, for they needed only to identify a limited number of rich targets, such as Porto Bello and Panama.

Economic activity was also thought of as being mainly to serve the interests of Spain. Mining was extensive but chiefly on the mainland. From the mines, minerals would flow to Spain. Where there was comparatively little to mine, for example in the islands of the West Indies, agriculture became the most important activity. Crops such as tobacco and sugar would be sent to Spain. But what was lacking was a major effort to develop all the islands. Development was spasmodic and patchy, and areas of the empire such as western Hispaniola remained untouched by prosperity. On the other hand, manufacturing was not generally forbidden as it sometimes was in the colonies of other European countries. Spain was not a manufacturing country, and the Spaniards found it difficult to supply the needs of the empire without making manufactured goods at home scarce, and therefore expensive. Many daily needs thus came to be supplied by artisans working within the empire itself.

The Spanish West Indian islands, however, had to face the fact that they were simply a small part of a large empire much of which was more profitable than they were. It was natural for Spain to tend to neglect them, except in so far as they could produce a ready profit, or could be used to protect the trade routes for the produce of the mainland from other Europeans. Of the two, the latter was perhaps the more important. Spain was anxious that the island societies should be stable and that each man should know his place. In this work, the Catholic Church proved important. Churchmen held extensive grants of land which few of them showed much enterprise in developing, but they used their influence to make the settlers loyal to Spain, loyal to authority, including that of the Church, and—sometimes at least—loyal to the teachings of the Christian religion. Only a minority of churchmen like Las Casas found slavery to be against the Christian religion, but churchmen often used their influence to make the slave's lot less harsh. In teaching the slaves Christianity, churchmen sometimes taught them other things such as reading. Among the Catholic churchmen were the Jesuits, members of the Society of Jesus, which had been founded in 1540 mainly to fight against the spread of Protestantism. The Jesuits had a special interest in teaching and they were often associated with the schools of the Spanish empire and with the missions to the fringes of the empire, where they worked amongst the Indians. But even the Jesuits saw nothing fundamentally wrong with the system of slavery. In the seventeenth and eighteenth centuries many Jesuits became rich slave owners, and they were so arrogant and powerful that they were expelled from the Spanish empire in 1767. But though churchmen, almost alone, had sought to curb the cruelty of white men to Amerindians and Africans, the influence of the Catholic Church was mainly used to preserve the system; and its schools, together with the universities of the empire, benefited most of all the most privileged whites. The school of the Dominican order of friars at Santo Domingo was called a university in 1538, but the first real university in the West Indies was probably that of Havana, founded in 1728. The main function of the first schools and universities was to train new churchmen. Secondly, they taught the children of the government officials and the rich whites. In general, the early settlers of the empire were poorly educated and often illiterate. Lucky indeed, therefore, was the Indian or African who gained any education at all, for that might make him better than his master; and the society of the Spanish empire did not encourage any man to rise above his station.

Exercises

1 Where, and in what circumstances, were settlements founded in the Caribbean before 1651 by (a) the English, (b) the French and (c) the Dutch? (Refer to Appendix III as well as to this chapter.)

2 Why did the European governments decide that the proprietary system was not a satisfactory one for the administration of their West Indian colonies?

3 Write an article for publication in a Jamaican newspaper in 1688 on the occasion of the death of Henry Morgan, expressing your views, as a seventeenth-century West Indian, on the past activities of Morgan and other buccaneers.

4 'The Spanish West Indian islands had to face the fact that they were simply a small part of a large empire much of which was more profitable than they were' (page 51). In what ways were the West Indian islands handicapped by this fact?

5 Explain why the title 'Seventeenth-Century Fragmentation' has been given to Figure 4.1. Explain what further information about the West Indies in the seventeenth century can be obtained from this map.

6 Find out more about the appearance and construction of the shipping which was employed in the West Indies in the sixteenth and seventeenth centuries. In what ways were these ships designed to serve the purposes for which they were used at this time?

5 Production and Trade in the Seventeenth Century

I PRODUCTION

Self-Sufficiency

'Here is their lord whom they serve and adore.' These words, according to Las Casas, were once used by an Arawak cacique to warn his people against the Spaniards' lust for gold. Even if the Amerindians were to swallow their gold, he warned, the Spaniards would get it out of them. But the West Indian islands had only very limited amounts of gold. The quantity was far from sufficient to enable the island settlements to survive for long simply on the basis of exporting gold.

In any case, the settlers had to eat. It was impossible in the sixteenth and seventeenth centuries for all their foodstuffs to be obtained from Europe; and any European food which was obtained would have to be paid for. So crops had to be planted in the West Indies for the settlers to feed themselves. It was good sense for the newcomers to give a high priority to agriculture and to aim to supply as many of their own needs as possible: that is, to become self-sufficient.

Some of their needs the early settlers could not hope to supply. To begin with, very little could be manufactured in the Spanish empire. Finished goods had to be brought from Europe—such things as tools, clothes, books and household utensils. To pay for these, it was necessary to export. There was a demand in Europe for gold and other precious metals, but if these could not be found in sufficient quantities something else must be produced. Unless that 'something else' were found, the settlers would not be able to buy: they would have no purchasing-power. Food crops were grown to be eaten in the islands, but other crops had to be grown too, for export. It was essential, therefore, to find out what would grow well in the West Indies and what, at the same time, could be sold in Europe. The mining of minerals would simply not produce enough exports. In any case, from the time of the earliest settlements, the Spanish royal family expected to receive a large share of any gold which was discovered. Ferdinand and Isabella firmly laid it down in 1501 that 'mines of metal ... belong to us'. With the royal fingers in the pie, it would be difficult for the early settlers to pay their way with gold.

Crops

The Amerindians were, of course, self-sufficient before the coming of the Europeans. Agriculture, hunting, fishing and a little bartering provided all that these simple people needed or wanted. But Europeans would not be satisfied to live so simply. They could, however, learn from the Arawaks about the crops which traditionally grew in the West Indies. On his first voyage, Columbus noted that the Indians grew corn and yams and that they made a sort of bread from the roots of the yams. He was also impressed by the Indian cultivation of cotton, and of a herb which they smoked. The 'sweet waters' and open spaces convinced him that the islands would be excellent for agriculture and cattle-raising although, as he found no large quadrupeds, it would be necessary to import cattle, pigs and goats from Europe.

The very first settlers could exist on the same food crops that the Indians grew, not only corn and yams but sweet potatoes, pumpkins and cassava. Like the Indians, they could hunt and fish though the game was small, principally the agouti. From their crops, the Indians were able to make intoxicating drink, but the Spaniards wanted wine such as they were accustomed to in Europe. They also wanted more variety in their foods. They, therefore, experimented to see what could be grown in the West Indian climate.

As early as 1495, Columbus was urging that wheat, barley and grapes should be planted. He expected wheat to grow quickly in the fertile soil but that it would take longer to establish fruit trees. In fact, wheat and barley did not grow well in the hot sun but when Ovando came to Hispaniola he brought a wide variety of plants, and could not, therefore, be sent to Europe. Timber was useful but too bulky, so that it was more profitable for Europeans to seek supplies nearer home. Cotton was in some ways an ideal crop, but Europe had sufficient supplies from elsewhere; also, it was an age when wool was more popular for the manufacturing of cloth and clothing and, until the late eighteenth century, the demand for

Tobacco was the first export crop of the English settlers, but supply soon outran demand (St Christopher-Nevis-Anguilla, 1973)

those from the warmer areas of Europe and the Mediterranean, including sugar-cane and citrus fruits, did well. Livestock prospered too, cattle, pigs and goats, although Europeans soon realized that the West Indies were unsuitable for rearing sheep. There was no reason why the Spaniards should starve if they were prepared to work at the production of food, or if they could force others to work for them.

The problem of a crop for export was rather more difficult. What was needed was a crop which was needed in Europe over and above what Europe itself produced. It would have to be light and compact because sixteenth-century ships were very small, most of them hardly more than twenty metres in length; and also non-perishable because the ships sailed slowly, dependent on the winds. Even on a fast passage, fruits and vegetables would be likely to be rotten by the time the ship docked.

Much that was produced in the New World cotton in Europe was comparatively small. There was a small market for such produce as coffee, tea, spices and dyewood, but in view of competition from other parts of the world, especially the east which now supplied Europe along the trade routes discovered by the Portuguese, the demand was not large enough to support extensive cultivation and production in the West Indies.

More promising were tobacco and sugar, and these, with dyewoods, and hides from cattle, became the important exports of the Spanish West Indies. Tobacco was sold by the Spaniards to other European countries and in the early seventeenth century the high price of this tobacco was one of the reasons why others, such as the English, wanted West Indian islands of their own. They could then grow tobacco for themselves and cut out the Spaniards' profit on it. In the long run, however, sugar was to be of much greater importance than tobacco in the development of the West Indies.

Tobacco v. Sugar

Apart from small bulk and the ability to survive a voyage across the Atlantic to markets where demand existed, tobacco had other advantages to recommend it. Cultivation could be undertaken on a small scale and it did not need the outlay of much capital. The settlers could grow their crops on a comparatively small area of land and with only a few helpers, perhaps the members of a family. The tobacco could then be sold to merchants for ready money and further crops cultivated. In many ways, this was an ideal small enterprise for the newcomers to the West Indies. But, perhaps more so than other plants, the tobacco plant had to be nurtured carefully and protected from disease and from storms which might easily destroy it.

About the end of the 1630s, however, a more serious problem arose. The new English and French settlements in the West Indies embarked on the growing of tobacco with great enthusiasm, only to discover that supply began to outrun demand. By this time, there were many settlements on the mainland of the Americas, including the English colony of Virginia, where the soil and climate were rather more suitable for tobacco-growing than those of the West Indies. West Indian tobacco, it was alleged, was less mild and less palatable than that of Virginia. Moreover, Virginia had the advantage of being able to produce tobacco in great bulk from a large area of land. Merchants found it less convenient to trade with the scattered islands of the West Indies than with Virginia whose supplies, particularly for the English market, came near to meeting the demand.

Throughout the West Indies, those who relied

This 1628 Dutch cartoon was a comment on the popularity of smoking (and on some of its after-effects). The West Indies competed with Virginia to supply the tobacco

on tobacco-growing found their profits falling. By 1639, prices had dropped alarmingly. The Virginians, moreover, were protesting loudly to the English government that settlers in the West Indies had been allowed to grow tobacco and thus compete with them. In Barbados and the other British islands there seemed to be no alternative but to find a different export-crop. The first choice was cotton, but neither the demand nor the amount of land available in the small English islands favoured this crop. The result was a rapid and dramatic changeover to the production of sugar. A similar changeover took place in the French islands, for similar reasons. In the case of the French, however, the settlers were commanded by Philippe de Poincy, Governor-General of the West Indian islands, to halt the production of tobacco under the threat of the confiscation of their plantations and a year in prison.

The production of sugar was a less simple operation than the growing of tobacco. In the English and French islands, the changeover needed expert advice and assistance, both of which were supplied by the Dutch. Sugar production required a knowledge of technology, a considerable amount of capital and a large supply of labourers. There were, therefore, many problems to be overcome before sugar production could become established.

The Dutch were not the only ones who had experience, however, for sugar was established in the Spanish islands early in the sixteenth century. It was obvious from the beginning of Spanish colonization that sugar-cane would grow well in the West Indies, but it was also recognized that the industry was expensive to set up. In 1518, King Charles I of Spain offered loans to settlers who wished to build sugar mills. A year later, he exempted the building materials and machinery for the mills from customs duties and, about the same time, encouraged those experienced in sugar production, for example in the Canary Islands, to bring their skills to the New World.

By bringing the first sugar mill to Hispaniola in 1516, Gonzalo de Vedosa began the process which was to make sugar cane the king of West Indian crops and establish sugar production as the leading industry. The first mills were turned by animals or slaves, but these were quickly replaced by water power wherever it was available. The water-powered mill, known as an *ingenio*, could grind the cane more efficiently to extract the juice, which was then turned into sugar by boiling. Each *ingenio* employed about a hundred workers; and each mill could grind such vast quantities of cane that enormous amounts of it had to be grown. Such an operation required heavy capital investment but it could also produce substantial profits. By 1541, Hispaniola already had forty mills, the majority of them *ingenios*, and the industry had already spread to Puerto Rico and Jamaica. The enthusiasm for gold had given way to a new enthusiasm, for sugar.

But if the rise of sugar production in the Spanish empire was rapid, so too was its decline. In 1582, the Governor of Puerto Rico reported twelve mills in the island but complained that production was handicapped by a shortage of African slaves. In 1602, another Governor reported that the *ingenios* had been abandoned. Sugar production also declined in Hispaniola and, in the second half of the sixteenth century, it was Cuba rather than Hispaniola which dominated the industry. Sugar production in Cuba probably dated from about the 1530s, but it was expanded more cautiously than had been the case in Hispaniola. Production in Spanish Jamaica seems always to have been on only a small scale. Apart from producing sugar in the West Indian islands, however, the Spaniards were also producing it elsewhere in their empire, and in the sixteenth and early seventeenth centuries the supply of sugar was adequate for the demand. The sugar industry was known to the Spaniards, therefore, and it was not unimportant in their Caribbean islands, but, except for the boom years in the middle of the sixteenth century, it did not achieve the towering eminence which was to come later in the English and French islands.

The Sugar Revolution

About the middle of the sixteenth century, Las Casas was worried that the emphasis on sugar led to the neglect of other crops. When the craze for sugar was at its height in Hispaniola, the island had to import food. But when the Spanish islands ceased to concentrate heavily on sugar they could give more attention to a balanced agricultural programme, and to supplying their own food. In later centuries, many West Indian islands were to realize the disadvantages of being over-dependent on sugar, at the mercy of the varying prices it could command. Moreover, sugar tended to make profits for a comparatively small number of large plantation owners. There was little room in the industry for the small producer.

Sugar production was important not only to the economies of the West Indian islands but also to their societies. Sugar needed extensive lands for enough cane to be grown to feed the mills. Small landowners were, therefore, often bought out by their richer neighbours. In 1645, Barbados had over 11 000 smallholders holding about ten acres each. In 1667, the land was concentrated in the hands of about 700 great estate owners, the average plantation being of some 300 acres. This led to a major change in the structure of society, a change which was to be repeated throughout the West Indies. There were fewer small landowners; in their place had emerged a powerful group of capitalist planters, businessmen who sought profit from their large estates and vast labour force.

An early sugar mill in Barbados. Sugar quickly dethroned tobacco (Barbados, 1970)

The labour force will be considered further in Chapter 6. It has already been mentioned that the sugar mills of Puerto Rico declined because of a lack of African slaves. Nothing was more important to the sugar plantations than a labour force of slaves. In 1645, Barbados had about 5500 African slaves. In 1667, it has been estimated that there were over 80 000; and this again was a pattern commonly repeated elsewhere. Sugar in the West Indies produced a society predominantly African in terms of numbers. But the Africans were denied even the most basic human rights.

On the backs of the Africans there developed a pyramid of social groups. At the top were the plantation owners, some of them absentee, content to appoint agents in the islands and to run their estates from Europe. It was generally the intention of these estate owners to retire to Europe when they had made sufficient profit. Thus, the richest and often most powerful men of the West Indies were those who had the least interest in the future of the islands. Next in the social scale came the agents and attorneys, a class of professional whites, many of them also looking for an opportunity to retire to Europe rather than to make a permanent home in the West Indies. For the rest—overseers and foremen, craftsmen and artisans, shopkeepers and clerks—there might be little to divide them in wealth, but they were divided by colour: whites, mulattoes and occasionally freed blacks. Those with white blood struggled to insist on a superiority over those with less white blood or none at all. By universal agreement, the African slave was at the bottom of the scale.

It is unlikely that the sugar revolution brought much benefit to the West Indies in the seventeenth and eighteenth centuries. The concentration on sugar postponed the day when a serious effort would be made to develop the full potential of the islands and their people. All that mattered at this time in many islands was to produce sugar. The wealth the sugar produced went mainly to Europe in the form of merchants' profits, the profits of the slave traders, the profits of returned emigrants and, to a lesser extent, the taxes imposed by European governments. During these two centuries, the English and French governments were less concerned than the Spaniards had been to build something of permanence in the West Indies. English and French settlers, expecting to retire to Europe, had less need of schools, libraries and fine public buildings. Like the conquistadors who searched for gold, many of them were also searching for wealth in the shape of profits from the sugar industry. So the West Indies had to endure another age in which the emphasis was on extraction rather than on construction. Symbolic of the concern of the English and French with their profits was their determination to deny any of those profits to the Dutch.

The seventeenth century, therefore, witnessed the beginning of a new age of greed, which was to reach its peak in the next century (see Chapter 7). In the West Indies, greed led to the production of as much sugar as possible at the least cost. In Africa and on the Atlantic, it led to fierce competition to extract profits from the slave trade without which sugar would not prosper (see Chapter 6). In Europe, it led to a struggle to dominate the sugar markets and a struggle between England and France which also extended to the Americas and to India. An earlier battle, however, waged and won before the end of the seventeenth century, was to destroy the commercial supremacy of the Dutch West India Company in the Caribbean.

II TRADE

The Dutch Foster-Fathers

Chapter 4 showed how the first English and French settlements depended on the Dutch whose ships called more regularly with supplies and came more regularly to buy produce than the ships of other nations. Like the earlier Spanish settlers, the English and French tended to ignore the instructions of their governments that they should trade only with their fellow-countrymen. Nevertheless, the instructions were endlessly repeated; for example, in a charter for the establishment of sugar production in Martinique and Guadeloupe in 1638, the *Compagnie des Isles d'Amérique* laid it down that 'the sugar ... be transported only to France and its sale to foreigners ... be strictly forbidden'.

Hugo Grotius put the Dutch point of view in 1609 in his *Mare Liberum*. He denied the right of the Pope, the Spaniards, the Portuguese or anyone else to close the seas to the merchants of other nations. He asserted that trade should be free to all nations. Adopting this principle, Dutch merchants sailed to any harbour where there was trade to be done, and their depots in the New World and the large number of ships which the Dutch West India Company could command, gave them a flying start when the first English and French settlements were founded. At first, their trade was mainly in tobacco. When tobacco glutted the markets, they turned to sugar.

Unlike the Spaniards, the Dutch were very ready to teach the newcomers the skills of sugar production. They had themselves gained experience in Brazil and Guiana and, scenting future advantage for themselves, they brought equipment and expertise to the English and French islands. Barbadians were taken to see how sugar was produced in the Dutch settlements. Whatever the problem, the Dutch had a solution for it. If capital was lacking, a Dutch loan could be arranged against the security of the crop. If labour was lacking, the Dutch would bring African slaves. If the sugar was of poor quality, the Dutch would offer advice and bring more technical knowledge. Because of their skills, their loans and their ever-present shipping, the Dutch inevitably secured a large share of the profits of early sugar production in the English and French islands. In 1662, over 70 per cent of the shipping which visited the French islands was Dutch. By that time, however, there was considerable anxiety, both in London and Paris, that the profits which might have come to them from the West Indies were accumulating in the pockets of the Dutch.

Mercantilism

Most of the economic theorists of the seventeenth century were mercantilists (see page 19), save for Dutchmen who were in favour of free trade. The essence of mercantilism was that trade should not be free. Many mercantilists believed that the actual fund of trade was fixed and that the overall profits from trade could not be increased, so each nation must strive to get the largest share of them for itself. An English mercantilist, for example, would argue that trade should be controlled by the English government in order to produce the most favourable balance of trade possible: England should export more than it imported and achieve a surplus. The mercantilists who were also bullionists believed that the surplus should be in the form of gold and silver, and thus add to the nation's stock of precious metals. Edward

Misselden summarized the argument in 1623 in his *Circle of Commerce*,

> 'If the native commodities exported do weight down and exceed in value the foreign commodities imported, it is a rule that never fails that then the kingdom grows rich and prospers in estate and stock: because the overplus thereof must needs come in in treasure.'

These beliefs were in many ways similar to the beliefs of those who had founded the Spanish House of Trade.

But the theories could be developed further. As far as possible, a country should be self-sufficient so as not to need to buy from foreigners. If a country had colonies, these colonies should supply the mother country with things that were needed and things which could be sold abroad so as to create Misselden's 'overplus'. Those who lived in the colonies should buy only from the mother country, and thus stimulate production within the mother country. Trade itself should also be carried on, as far as possible, in the ships of the mother country and by the nation's own merchants. In this way, ship-building would be encouraged, builders and sailors employed, and the profits of the carrying trade would similarly be kept out of the hands of foreigners.

In short, foreigners should be allowed to earn only the minimum amount of wealth—by buying from them as little as possible, and using their services, such as their shipping, as little as possible. At the same time, foreigners should be persuaded to buy as much as possible so as to extract payment and wealth from them. To the mercantilists, this seemed to be an excellent recipe for increasing their own country's prosperity and power. But it was also a narrow-minded recipe for a strange blend of national competition and restrictions, from which colonies could be expected to benefit very little. Nevertheless, such theories remained popular until challenged by a new school of economists at the end of the eighteenth century. In Britain, one of the most eminent of these was Adam Smith. Earlier, the theories had been so popular in England that even Scotland, which from 1603 shared the same monarchy with England, was excluded from English colonial trade until the Act of Union of 1707 created the United Kingdom.

It was the Dutch, however, who were the main enemy to the mercantilists of England and France in the seventeenth century. They constantly drained away wealth, so it seemed, by their carrying trade and the profits which Dutch merchants and financiers made. Parliamentarians in England and Jean Colbert in France, set out to destroy the Dutch commercial supremacy.

The English Navigation Acts

With the execution of Charles I at the end of the English Civil War in 1649, members of the Rump Parliament became the most powerful men in England. It was they who determined to make the Navigation Acts effective and who went to war with the Dutch in the first of a series of Anglo-Dutch Wars.

The Navigation Acts were not new. Several such acts had been issued, in 1382, 1485 and 1540, and they had been quoted and repeated many times including, in recent years, in ordinances issued by James I and Charles I. As has been seen, however, settlers in St Kitts, Barbados and other West Indian islands tended to ignore them. In 1650, the English Parliament took advantage of Barbadian support for the Royalists to issue a new Navigation Act to reinforce the old ones, and to ensure that the old acts applied to England's new colonies. Foreign ships were forbidden to trade with English colonies except when given a licence to do so by the English government. In 1651, a further Navigation Act was passed, spelling out in detail the regulations for trade. Trade with England's colonies must be carried out in English or colonial ships with predominantly English crews. And English trade with foreign countries must be carried out in English ships or the ships of the foreign country in question. If this Act could be enforced, the Dutch, who depended on carrying the goods of other countries, would have no part left to play.

The Navigation Acts of 1650 and 1651 were partly the reason why England and Holland went to war in 1652. Two years later, the Dutch accepted defeat, having been out-gunned in European waters by the English navy. In Europe at least, the Navigation Acts were now generally enforced.

It was less easy to enforce them in the West Indies and Barbados in particular kept up a constant protest about the ban on Dutch merchants. English merchants, however, had more influence on the English government than had Barbadian

An artist's impression of the surrender of New Amsterdam to the English by the one-legged Peter Stuyvesant. The English thought New Amsterdam a better prize than Surinam

settlers. Oliver Cromwell died in 1658 and two years later the monarchy was restored in England. Charles II promptly confirmed the trade laws with another Navigation Act (1660). This Act also added a list of items which were produced in the colonies and which could now be sent only to England or to another English colony. This list of enumerated articles could be altered from time to time to make certain that England controlled the destination of all produce considered important. Yet another Act was passed in 1663, the Staple Act, which prevented the delivery to the colonies of any foreign goods except by way of England. Therefore, foreigners could only bring their goods to England, and from England the goods would have to travel on to the West Indies in English ships. In 1673, the Plantation Duties Act was added, imposing a tax on goods sent from one English colony to another. The Act added to the revenue of the mother country and had the effect of doing even more to channel the trade of the colonies through England. A further Act of 1696 completed the web in which the trade of the English West Indies was trapped.

In the reign of Charles II, two further Anglo-Dutch Wars were fought, not entirely about the Navigation Acts but to a large extent because of commercial rivalry. The Second Dutch War lasted from 1665 to 1667 and ended with the humiliation for England of a Dutch raid into the estuary of the River Thames. There had been fighting in Guiana and skirmishes in the slave-trading areas of the African coast. The English captured New Amsterdam (New York) from the Dutch and kept it at the Treaty of Breda, giving Surinam to the Dutch in exchange. But England had been unable to win a decisive victory which would totally destroy Dutch seapower.

The Third Anglo-Dutch War broke out in 1672 and again the Dutch held their own at sea. The war ended in 1674, with both countries now more alarmed about the growth of French power than about the Navigation Acts. England's real victory in the struggle for the trade of the West Indies came not with wars but with the growth of a large English merchant marine, a fleet sufficient to handle the trade of the English islands. In any case, in 1688, William of Orange, a Dutchman, became King of England. In the years which followed, England and Holland, both fearful of the might and aggressiveness of Louis XIV, were often united in wars against the French.

The Navigation Acts were primarily designed to benefit England, and they made the West Indian islands of the British empire utterly dependent on England for their markets and their supplies. A major disadvantage of this was that the prices, both for West Indian produce and the supplies, were usually fixed in England. Moreover, the English government insisted on collecting duties on the trade. It was often necessary for West Indian planters to employ agents in England to represent them. On the other hand, they were usually guaranteed a market in England and their goods were unlikely to remain unsold. In time, English ships became as numerous in the Caribbean as Dutch ships had been, and Britain was also developing a large empire on the continent of north America. This was a great advantage enabling a useful two-way trade to grow between the English West Indies and north America (see pages 97–8). But the mercantilist system, enshrined in the Navigation Acts, was always a European imposition. Although it provided the West Indies with a measure of protection, military and naval as well as economic, the West Indian islands were made subservient to the interests of England. They were also exposed in the years to come to a new peril. Since they were, in effect, outposts of England, they inevitably became the targets of England's enemies, liable to be attacked in times of war.

The French Commercial Regulations

Colbert became Controller-General in France in 1665. From that date to his death in 1683 he was the most powerful of the ministers of Louis XIV. His influence extended into all the branches of the French government but he showed a particular interest in the French economy and the colonies. His aims included the creation of a thriving economy and of a comprehensive system of state regulations. He wanted to develop industry and agriculture, to make trade prosper, to develop a strong French merchant marine and to ensure the stability of the colonies, which would be subject to strong central control from Paris. The keynote of Colbert's policy was regulation by the state. Some of the regulations were inevitably aimed at the Dutch who monopolized much of the trade with the French West Indies. But Colbert was also willing to learn from the Dutch, and he followed their example by establishing new French trading

Paramaribo, Zeelandia Fort: *c.* 1670. By the Treaty of Breda, the English gave Surinam to the Dutch (Surinam, 1967)

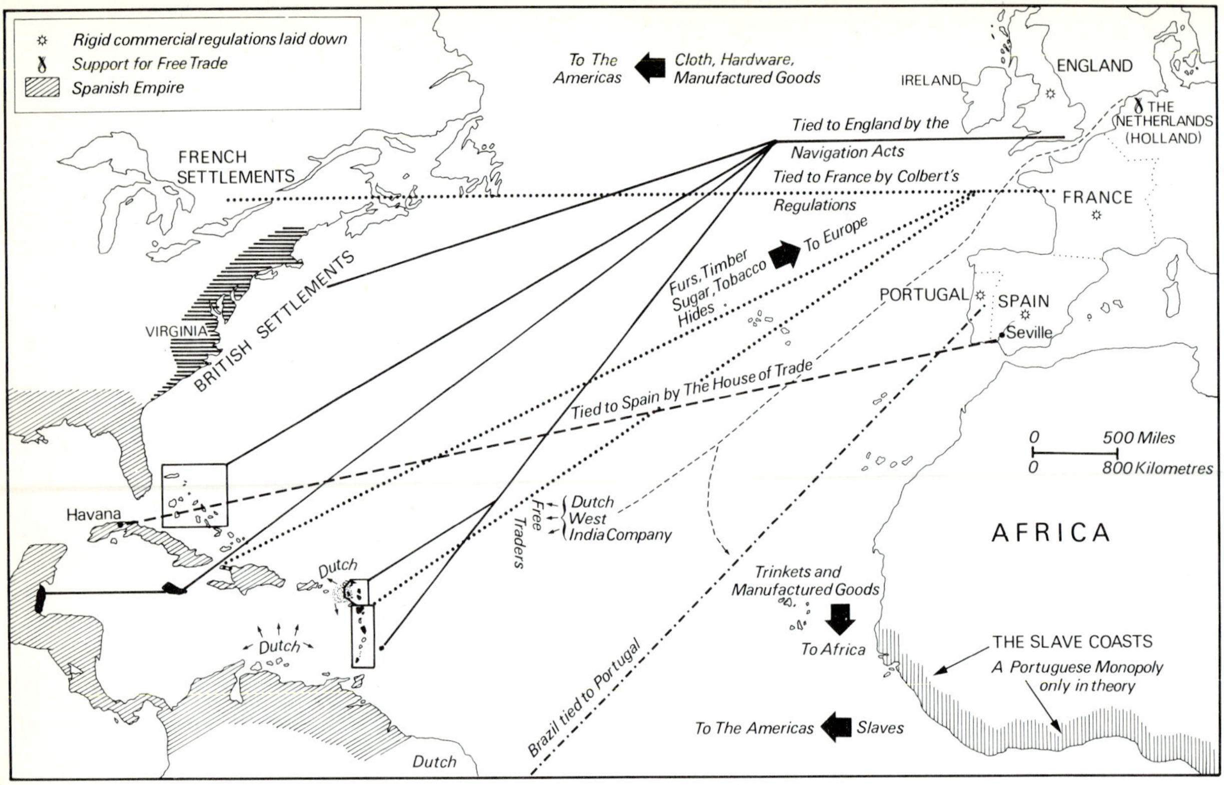

Figure 5.1 Trade Patterns in the late Seventeenth Century

companies, an East India Company and a West India Company.

The basic ideas behind Colbert's policies were essentially those of mercantilism. The islands of the French West Indies were seen mainly as territories which would supply goods needed in France or which the French could sell at a profit, and which would buy French goods and thus stimulate French production. They would use French ships and stimulate French shipping; and they would be loyal to France in every way. In this connection, Colbert thought it necessary to attempt to regulate French West Indian society and to draw up a code of regulations for the treatment of African slaves, the *Code Noir* (see pages 84–5).

The French West India Company was not an unqualified success. In 1674, its privileges were cancelled. Colbert had realized that there was value in encouraging private traders, although he insisted that they should be Frenchmen. A monopoly was always likely to be challenged by interlopers. Colbert was less concerned about preserving the monopoly of the Company as long as he could preserve the monopoly of the nation, and by 1674 French traders, Company and private, were steadily taking trade out of the hands of the Dutch. From a mere handful only ten years before, the French now had a hundred ships trading with the West Indies. In 1678, at the Treaty of Nijmegen, which closed one of the many wars fought between the French and Dutch in the late seventeenth century, the Dutch were forced to recognize the French trading monopoly. Colbert was critical of his King's frequent resort to war since that handicapped France's economic development, but the French–Dutch Wars also did much to sap the strength of the Netherlands. Five years after the Treaty of Nijmegen, the French had 200 ships trading in the West Indies.

There were protests, of course, from the French islands, just as the English had had protests from

Barbados. Goods from France were often expensive. In some cases, supplies were not adequate. To feed the African slaves, it was necessary to have a steady supply of salted beef which the Dutch were able to provide, often collecting it from Ireland. In 1680, Colbert had to give way on this issue since French beef was insufficient and the French islands too small for cattle-rearing. But a strict control was generally maintained over the islands and, though he sometimes gave way in matters of detail, Colbert was satisfied that, overall, his policy was effective. Most of the trade was monopolized by the French themselves; shipping developed rapidly and the islands produced what the French wanted them to produce.

What Colbert especially wanted was sugar. Sugar from the West Indies became the basis for the sugar-refining industry in France. At first, Colbert seems to have thought that it would be useful to the West Indian islands to refine their own sugar. But European interests triumphed as they did in most matters at this time. It suited French sugar-refiners to receive raw Caribbean sugar which they could process and then sell at a profit. By varying the duties, therefore, Colbert and his successors strangled at birth the sugar-refining industry in the West Indies, encouraging the French colonies to export raw sugar which was subject to only a low tax, and discouraging them from the refining process by taxing heavily their refined sugar.

At the beginning of the eighteenth century, therefore, the newcomers had established themselves in the West Indies, alongside the Spaniards. Spain had been forced to recognize the Dutch islands (1648), the English islands (1670) and the French islands (1697). If not entirely excluded from the trade of the English and French islands, the Dutch had lost their commercial supremacy. In the eighteenth century, they would be outclassed totally by the growing maritime importance of England and France. After a brief concentration on tobacco-growing, sugar had become the king of crops in the new settlements, and with sugar the massive enterprise of importing African slaves had begun to flourish. At the same time, the West Indian islands had fallen victim to the full force of European mercantilist ideas. They existed not so much in their own right but as appendages to their mother countries. They too were in a kind of slavery, or at least bondage, being denied any effective right to produce what they wished; sell where they liked; buy in any market; or in any way that mattered, control their own destinies.

The Decline of the Dutch

By the beginning of the eighteenth century, the great days of the Dutch were passing. The Dutch West India Company was dissolved in 1674 and a new Company, founded in 1675, never achieved the successes of the old. The Dutch retained their settlements in the West Indies, but the prosperity which had come to them from trade in the early seventeenth century could not be recovered. The government of the Netherlands lost interest in them, except to provide any defence that was necessary and to appoint a succession of governors to go through the motions of carrying on the administration. In Guiana, in fact, the Dutch reverted for a time to the discredited practice of appointing proprietors to run the settlements almost as private estates.

Admiral de Ruyter visited St Eustatius in 1666 but he could not preserve the supremacy of the Dutch West India Company (Netherlands Antilles, 1966)

Dutch experience in the western hemisphere had been generally disappointing. Although they made considerable profit from the trade in African slaves, they could not monopolize it. Their commercial supremacy in the West Indies had been short-lived, and they had now missed the opportunity to settle on any of the larger islands. Apart from Guiana, they had almost nothing to show for their efforts on the American mainland, having been expelled from Brazil by the Portuguese in 1654 and from New Amsterdam by the English in the 1660s.

Their tiny West Indian islands remained, however, and except for a brief period during the Napoleonic Wars when the British occupied Curaçao and its sister islands, Dutch possession was undisturbed. These West Indian islands could not rival the importance of the larger Dutch East Indies. In 1949, the latter successfully demanded their independence and went their own way under the name of Indonesia, but Holland still retained the West Indian islands. As the Netherlands Antilles, they became an integral part of the Kingdom of the Netherlands in 1922 and achieved self-government in 1954, remaining in the late 1970s among the comparatively few Caribbean islands which still belong to European governments. Their combined population was, even then, less than a quarter of a million, the majority of whom lived in Curaçao.

Exercises

1 Show how, in the second half of the seventeenth century, French and English influence in the Caribbean grew, while that of the Spaniards and Dutch declined. (Refer to both Chapter 4 and Chapter 5.)

2 'Foster-Fathers' (page 58). Explain and illustrate this description of the Dutch in the West Indies in the seventeenth century. What factors combined to weaken Dutch influence in the area?

3 What do you understand by *each* of the following terms: self-sufficiency; mercantilism; free trade? What were the effects on the islands of the West Indies of the mercantilist laws which were enacted in Europe in the second half of the seventeenth century?

4 Make a list of the crops which a settler in Barbados might have considered planting in the late 1640s. *In each case,* add notes of the arguments in favour of planting the crop and the arguments against planting it. What overall conclusions would the settler have been most likely to reach?

5 Divide a large sheet of paper into the sections shown below, and (making use of Chapters 2 and 5 and Figure 5.1) insert the appropriate information into each of the twelve boxes.

How the Europeans Controlled the Trade of their Empires			
	Spaniards 16/17th c.	English 17th c.	French 17th c.
Trade routes	From mainland and islands to Havana. From Havana to Spain, especially Seville. Making use of winds and currents.		
Trade commodities			
Ships used (nationality)			
Licensing and duties			

6 The Labour Supply

I WHITE LABOUR

The Problem

From the moment the Spaniards first arrived in the West Indies, it was obvious that labour was needed in order to extract wealth from the islands. It has been seen in Chapter 2, that the *encomienda* system provided the labour of the aborigines for use by the Spaniards, but the Amerindians were comparatively few in number and they quickly fell victims to overwork. Where then, if it could not be found in the islands, was a labour force to come from? Most of the early economic activities in the West Indies were labour-intensive. Without machinery and with only simple tools, there was no alternative but to make use of intensive human effort in land-clearance, mining and building, and this called for much back-breaking work in the hot sunshine. Such work was traditionally the lot of the poor; and there were plenty of poor in Europe. One solution, therefore, was to transfer poor labourers from Europe to the West Indies, by encouragement and the hope of reward or by compulsion and threats of a worse fate. But there were two major obstacles: the first was that Europeans were unused to the fierce heat of the West Indies and, since hygiene was little regarded in the early settlements, they were often ravaged by diseases; the second was that Europe itself needed labour and so the white labour which was spared for the West Indies was commonly of low quality.

The Spaniards faced the additional problem that labour exported to the West Indies often moved on, lured by gold to the mainland. At no time, therefore, was white labour ever adequate in itself. A small group of whites could well grow tobacco, with or without a little Indian help, but when sugar-planting became common there was no hope that a white labour force could adequately cope with it.

Columbus carried a few convicted criminals to the West Indies, on his third voyage. The Spaniards also made some use of white slavery, mainly female, and the authorities issued decrees from time to time to encourage settlers to marry and breed. Sometimes, the Spaniards admitted non-Spanish settlers—the subjects of the Habsburg Empire, because they were the subjects of Charles I (Emperor Charles V), and Portuguese, because they were at least Roman Catholic. But, in general, the Spaniards relied on the emigration of their own people to the American empire. A decree, issued by King Charles in 1529, shows the kind of encouragement which was given,

> 'Two or three square leagues of land (depending on the location) would be granted, with the right of ownership and succession. The founders were to be knighted. To begin with, they would be excused duties on what they imported. They were entitled to any profits from mines and pearl-fisheries subject to a royal levy, and to the fruits of patronage, for example from the appointment of a notary.'

For their part, the founders were to take to the settlement at least fifty married couples, a priest and fifty Africans; and they were to build a church and take enough supplies to build stone houses and set up a flourishing community, complete with livestock.

Charles was thus relying on his richer subjects to pay for and create West Indian settlements, in return for the granting of land (taken, of course, from the Indians) and certain legal and financial concessions. At other times, settlers were tempted with free transport, land and the basic equipment to start farming. But it was still not possible to populate the West Indies with an adequate number of whites. From as early as 1505 (see page 26), Africans were imported, and within a short time it was they who became the backbone of the labour force. By 1514, Ferdinand I was warning that there would be the danger of trouble if there were too many Africans, especially young ones. In 1518, a member of the Audiencia of Santo Domingo reported that some Africans in Hispaniola had fled to the hills; but he seemed to have dealt with the problem to his own satisfaction, for he added, 'I whipped some, cut the ears off others and there were no further complaints.' Thus the Spaniards adjusted to a West Indian population in which Africans were growing in number. The Africans provided the labour force, and the Spaniards gave their attention to controlling them. To the Spaniards, this seemed to be the best formula which could be devised to ensure that the islands were populated and worked. Other Europeans, who came later to the West Indies, settled for the same formula but, to begin with, the English and French experimented with a different system, that of indentured white labour.

Indentured Servants

The English and French, unlike the Spaniards, found very little Amerindian labour available when they made their first settlements. The Caribs could be killed but few of them could be forced to work, and more peaceful Indians were now so difficult to find that it seemed more sensible to concentrate on a European labour force. In 1647, the English parliament noted the 'great want of servants' in the West Indies and made it legal for 'any person or persons' to transport to the settlements any persons who 'be willing to serve or be employed', providing only that there should be an official register of these servants. This was almost a licence for seizing and transporting unfortunates who could easily be misrepresented as 'willing', particularly because the authorities in England generally seemed to regard the colonies as ideal for dumping criminals and other undesirables. In 1646, the Keeper of Winchester House Prison had suggested that it would be a convenient way of clearing his jail to send the petty criminals to Barbados. This scheme appealed to him all the more because he was not being adequately paid for the upkeep of the criminals. Barbados was also thought to be a suitable destination for the Irish rebels whom Cromwell wished to punish for supporting the Royalists. Moreover, Europeans were preying on each other, capturing foreigners to sell as servants: the Dutch offered to Barbados fifty Portuguese whom they had taken prisoner in Brazil.

The theory behind the law of 1647 in the English parliament was that the 'willing' servants would undertake to work in the colonies for a period of years, usually three or five, under a sort of contract, an indenture. Their passage to the West Indies was paid for by the contractor. When their term was up, they became free, perhaps to return home or perhaps to receive a small parcel of West Indian land. But many indentured servants failed to survive their term of bondage; and many others were simply left to fend for themselves when their terms expired, without the money either to return home or to set themselves up as free men. A similar system was operated by the French, the French indentured servant being known as an *engagé*.

The employers of the indentured servants in the colonies almost always worked them to their limits. Since almost no one who was secure and respectable would choose to put himself in this kind of bondage, many of the 'servants' were riff-raff and many others were too young or too feeble-minded to escape it. Unscrupulous contractors trapped them with romantic tales about the opportunities which awaited them in the colonies or, not infrequently, simply kidnapped the unsuspecting. Kidnapping became commonplace in Bristol. The owners of Caribbean plantations saw nothing wrong in extracting the maximum work possible: they merely regretted that so many of the indentured servants died—from malnutrition, tropical diseases and labour in the heat of the islands. The servants who survived were quite likely to be cheated out of their due rewards after their years of unpaid toil. Sugar plantations gobbled up the available land so rapidly that, in places such as Barbados, little was left for the indentured servants who completed their terms. The Barbadian planters began to pay off their time-expired labourers with two or three hundredweights of sugar instead of land, no doubt considering this shrewd business practice; but the sugar was too little even to pay for a passage back to Europe. In view of the conditions, it is not surprising that white indentured labour failed completely to provide an adequate labour force.

While it lasted, however, the indenture system brought a steady stream of whites to the English and French islands. Some were quick to run away, perhaps to join the buccaneers. Many died. Some survived to return to Europe or to make good in the West Indies; but most of those who survived swelled the ranks of the poor whites. These were often 'poor miserable creatures' who made a living as best they could in a society which was increasingly dominated by wealthy estate owners, served by a huge African labour force. The hey-day of the indenture system was from about the 1640s to the 1680s. The system came in at about the time when the white population of Barbados had already reached a peak of over 30 000 and was beginning to decline. But the influx of indentured servants could not even keep up the numbers of the white population in the West Indies. From 1654 to 1660, Barbados received over 2300 servants; and from 1654 to 1685, some 10 000 were shipped out of Bristol alone, bound for the West Indies and north America. Even so, and even though the indenture system persisted into the eighteenth century, it could hardly maintain what the authorities considered to be an adequate white presence in the face of the great increase in the number of African slaves. Further inducements had to be looked for, and in 1749 Jamaican planters were offered twenty acres, a house, money and an African for each white family they imported. In five years, the planters collected about 350 whites, but they attracted them from the smaller islands rather than from Europe. More constructively, Barbados began to make hesitant steps towards establishing a textile industry in 1781, offering the prospect of regular work to white immigrants.

There were several weaknesses in the indenture system. The first was that, from the beginning, it was too heavily associated with society's cast-offs and too much like slavery. It offered little inducement to the more stable and successful elements in European society. It was also a short-sighted system which made a totally inadequate provision for giving a permanent and secure place in West Indian society to those who completed their terms. The main reason for this was that, except perhaps in Jamaica, sugar estates left little land to spare for other landowners. Similarly, there was little opportunity for employment. Planters could not see the sense of employing a white man at a living wage when African slaves could be employed unpaid. Sugar had tended to squeeze out the smallholders, and now, in effect, it rejected a European labour force. Unable, or unwilling, to tackle the problem at its roots, English colonial governments took refuge in useless laws which were known as Deficiency Laws.

Sugar, which was established in Cuba as early as 1535, created an insatiable demand for labourers wherever it was produced (Cuba, 1937)

Deficiency Laws

At the beginning of the eighteenth century, blacks outnumbered whites almost everywhere in the West Indies. Whites arrived in no more than a trickle, but the slave ships brought Africans in a flood. In 1700, in spite of the indenture system, the ratio of white males in Barbados to the African population was only 1:18. Many indentured servants who came to Barbados were Irishmen who made haste to leave the island as soon as their terms expired. In the Leeward Islands, there was a similar emigration from the English colonies, so that the ratio of whites to Africans was seldom more than 1:2 and was sometimes as low as 1:4. In Jamaica, the ratio was 1:6. In all the British islands at that time, there were about 25 000 whites and about 125 000 Africans.

In the French islands, the importing of Africans had proceeded less rapidly but some 7000 whites were outnumbered by over 3:1 in Martinique and almost 2:1 in Guadeloupe. In St Domingue, the area of Hispaniola successfully claimed by the French, there were 30 000 whites by 1726 but again they were outnumbered 3:1 by African slaves.

In all the settlements, as the eighteenth century went on, white numbers grew with painful slowness or even fell, while those of the Africans raced ahead. In the 1770s, Jamaica had over 200 000 Africans, St Domingue 250 000. Martinique had at least 70 000 slaves, Guadeloupe even more.

Barbados had some 65 000 Africans. The pattern was similar in the smaller islands and English and French whites were now outnumbered in the West Indies as a whole by about 10:1. But the Spanish islands were less committed to the sugar revolution at this stage and it was only there that the whites were more than a small minority. Cuba, for example, was still geared largely to the production of tobacco and in the 1770s the island had over 100 000 whites compared with a slightly smaller number of Africans, of whom more than 20 000 were freemen. Spanish Hispaniola had only 15 000 slaves in a population of 125 000, and Puerto Rico, preferring the cultivation of coffee to that of sugar, had a population in which white and non-white were in roughly equal proportions, the majority of non-whites being mulattoes.

The difference between the Spanish islands and those of later European settlement lay essentially in the main crop. The logic of the emphasis on sugar production in the English and French islands in the late seventeenth and eighteenth centuries was to have a vast, cheap labour force. Every plantation owner knew that it was cheaper to buy an African slave than to employ a white man. The Deficiency Laws were, therefore, little more than pieces of paper. The aim of the Laws was simple, but unrealistic. Planters should employ white workers in a fixed ratio to Africans so that the white minority would not be overwhelmed utterly.

Jamaican laws provide an example of this legislation. In 1703, planters were required to employ white workers in a ratio of 1:10 of the slave labour force. Those who failed to do so were to be fined. In 1730, a new Deficiency Law fixed the ratio at 1:30 and made the fine smaller, clear evidence that the earlier law had failed. It was much cheaper to pay the fine than to employ white labour, and paying the fine seems to have suited both the planters and the colonial government, which thus gained useful revenue. Deficiency Laws were probably slightly more successful in Barbados, where unemployed whites were still to be found who would work for low wages, but as a solution to the problem of the imbalance in the population the Laws achieved virtually nothing. At the same time, however, the Laws tended to emphasize differences in colour and to divide society by colour rather than by class. Their basic aim was to preserve white supremacy and they reinforced in whites, even in the poor whites, the idea that whiteness was linked with superiority. But they were irrelevant to the real problem of curbing the greedy obsession for sugar, and of seeking far-reaching constructive measures which would bring to the islands more balanced economies and more just societies. In the eighteenth century, only the Spaniards were proceeding in that direction, albeit slowly. England and France demanded sugar and more sugar. Sugar demanded slaves and more slaves.

II AFRICAN SLAVES

Africa

The first African to be captured on the Guinea Coast and taken to Europe was a prisoner of the Portuguese. The year was probably 1441, or at least early in the 1440s. About that time, the Portuguese found a young African boy, fishing along with his younger sister. The children were seized, and taken to Portugal where they were made Christians and educated. During the next 300 years, slave-trading stations mushroomed along 4000 miles of the west African coastline from the Gambia to Angola, south of the Congo. During the years before 1815, when the Congress of Vienna condemned the slave trade, few of the millions of Africans who were to be seized and transported received the comparatively gentle treatment accorded to the fisher-boy and his sister.

The Africans lived in tribes. Slave traders and West Indian plantation owners soon came to recognize that not all Africans were alike. Ibos, from what is now eastern Nigeria, had a reputation for pining and ending their sufferings with suicide. The Ashanti, from present-day Ghana (usually called Coromantees in the West Indies since they were shipped from the trading station at Cormantine) were strong and efficient but not easy to subdue. One West Indian planter observed that they were 'habituated from infancy to war'. Tacky, who led a slave rebellion in Jamaica in 1760, was of the Ashanti. The Mundingoes, who lived near the mouth of the River Gambia, and their neighbouring tribes of Senegambia were less troublesome, but they were considered to be poor field workers and more suited to domestic service. Plantation owners tended to judge their African slaves on only two criteria: their capacity for work and their inclination to cause trouble. But each

An Obeah man in Jamaica, sketched in the late nineteenth century

African tribe also had its own crafts, religious practices and other social customs, some of which were to survive and enrich West Indian society in later years. In general, however, the planters were little interested in these, except those practices and customs which they regarded as a nuisance or even dangerous. Many Africans were expert in poisons, which they obtained from vegetation, and which made a formidable weapon to use against their white masters. The latter took what precautions they could. Africans had no common language, and so it was convenient for the whites to build up a labour force from a variety of tribes, so that slaves could not easily communicate with one another. This did not always overcome the problem of *Obeah,* however.

The cult of *Obeah* was particularly widespread in Jamaica. It was based on a belief in incantations which could maim and destroy, or fortify and protect. Tacky's supporters believed they had been made invincible by an Obeah-man on the eve of their rebellion. When Tacky and his followers had been killed after rampaging violently through the plantations leaving a bloody trail of destruction, the Jamaican authorities tried hard to suppress *Obeah* but without complete success. Before the end of the eighteenth century, an even more violent outbreak occurred, this time in St Domingue, the French part of Hispaniola, where African beliefs had taken firm root in the practice of Vodun (often referred to in England as *Voodoo*). Vodun developed out of what seemed to the Europeans to be a mixture of superstitions and harmless recreations such as dancing. But in the 1790s it provided a powerful unifying force for a mass-rising of the slaves which was to result in Haiti (St Domingue) becoming the first independent West Indian state (see pages 102–4). Vodun has remained a powerful force in Haiti down to the present day.

Just as the earlier settlers in the West Indies had dismissed the customs of the Indians as primitive and unimportant, so Europeans dismissed African customs as similarly uncivilized. Only in recent years have Europeans begun to recognize that, before their own arrival there, much existed in Africa which was by no means barbarous. Apart from African arts and crafts, many tribes lived in orderly societies which carefully safeguarded human rights, respected human dignity and promoted co-operative living. Uninterested in these values, however, the slave traders noted only African superstitions, an apparent economic backwardness, a primitive near-defencelessness against European weapons, and the practices of some African tribes of keeping slaves themselves and of indulging in wars against their neighbours. Thus there developed the argument, sometimes put forward to justify European slave trading, that many Africans were slaves in Africa. While undoubtedly true, this argument is somewhat misleading. Not only did practices differ widely from tribe to tribe, but many slaves were very well treated, by the Mundingoes for example, and they were not without certain much-respected rights. They were, nevertheless, slaves. Some had become slaves as payment of a debt, others as punishment for a crime. Some were the prisoners who had been taken in tribal wars. They therefore lived in a sort of bondage which had some similarities to the serfdom of medieval Europe. This bondage was usually very different from the naked exploitation of African slaves by the European slave traders and West Indian plantation owners, both of whom were motivated mainly by the desire to make a financial profit.

Africans cannot, however, escape all blame for the fact that the slave traders on the African coast were often well supplied with human cargoes. There were Africans, chiefs among them, who were willing to sell their fellow-men. The kings of Dahomey were willing to provide slaves, although in the 1720s, Agaja Trudo, the then King of Dahomey, recognized the damage the trade did to Africa and for a time sought to stop it by burning and looting the trading stations. In 1730, however, Dahomian slaving was resumed, with some restrictions and under royal control. Further west, the king of Sherbro also found profit in supplying slaves to the Europeans, for the goods which could be obtained in exchange were hard to resist. African rulers were eager to acquire 'firearms and cowries'.

Other African chiefs made the mistake of seeking European help in their tribal wars, and thus gave the slave traders a chance to meddle in local affairs and collect up the prisoners. Freelance African slave merchants also set themselves up in the business of supplying slaves. In the eighteenth century, it was necessary to go far inland to secure a sufficient number of slaves and, since Europeans seldom moved far from the coast at this time, such raids were usually undertaken by African middlemen. The slaves thus acquired, sometimes by purchase and sometimes by violence, were brought to the Europeans in a *coffle,* a sort of human convoy. The slaves were yoked together with leg-irons and a Y-shaped branch, the latter being fastened round the neck of one slave at the fork, the stem resting on the shoulder of the following slave. The captives were escorted and guarded by their armed captors. Often for months, sometimes for years, such coffles shuffled their way to the coast. Tribes along the route would sometimes exact a tax in exchange for permission to pass. Eventually, those captives who survived would be delivered to one of the many trading stations, for example at Whydah or Elmina, where Europeans were usually eager to buy (see Figure 6.1).

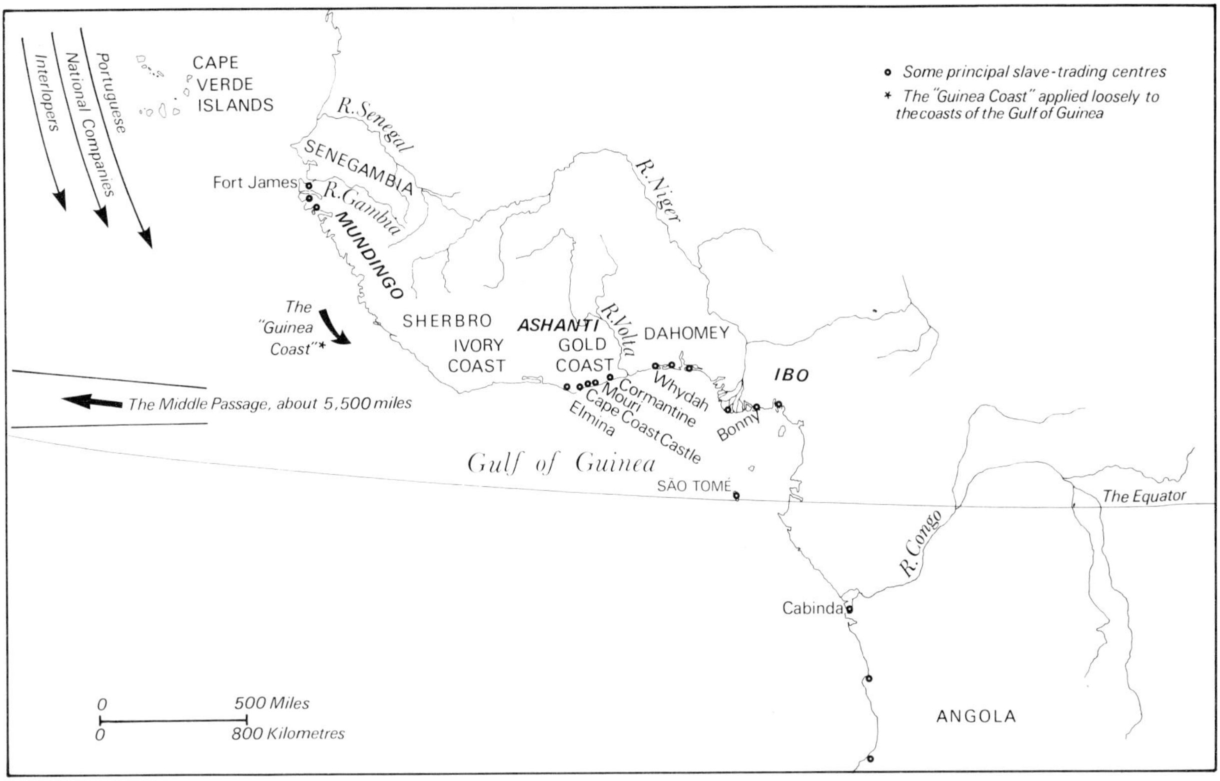

Figure 6.1 The Supply of African Slaves: West Africa in the Eighteenth Century

The Transatlantic slave trade continued and developed over some three centuries, the sixteenth, seventeenth and eighteenth. At first, the Portuguese had exchanged horses for slaves. Then there was a period when Europeans bought with cowrie shells, which African tribes often used as currency. For a time, African chiefs could be won over with beer and brandy, silks and cloth. But by the eighteenth century, Africa wanted firearms and European hardware, and West Indian rum was also finding its way to Africa. By this time, the triangular trade was firmly established: Europeans carried the products of European industry to west Africa to be exchanged for slaves; the slaves were then carried to the West Indies to be sold or exchanged for West Indian produce; that in turn was then taken to Europe to realize a final profit. The two vital elements in this triangular trade were slaves and sugar.

The European Slave Traders

As early as the middle of the sixteenth century, the Portuguese had organized slave-trading centres on the island of São Tomé and on the coasts of Senegambia, the Gold Coast and Angola. Trading-stations were set up within protective forts to act as collecting points for slaves and centres for bargaining. Such forts came to have compounds known as barracoons in which slaves could be kept until ships arrived to carry them across the Atlantic. The coastline of Africa was so vast, however, that there was no way in which the Portuguese could keep out other European nations, although in the sixteenth century non-Portuguese visitors were comparatively rare and their first visits were made more from curiosity than from a desire to capture slaves. Nevertheless, by the end of the sixteenth century, French, English and Dutch privateers had become acquainted with the African coast and aware of the profits which could be made out of cargoes of African slaves. In 1588, Elizabeth I had given permission for an English company to trade in Senegambia but the trade was in goods, not in human beings, and for the moment the English seemed to have abandoned the slave trading which Hawkins had pioneered (see pages 32–4).

The Dutch knew the value of African slaves as a commodity for trade, but they could be as ruthless as other Europeans towards Africans who rebelled: an African executed by the Dutch in Surinam in 1730

Portugal thus continued to be the main supplier of slaves to the New World throughout the sixteenth century.

The first major intervention in the slave trade was made by the Dutch. The Charter of the Dutch West India Company (1621) specifically mentioned 'the coasts and lands of Africa', since the Dutch refused to recognize either the Spanish monopoly of the West Indies or the Portuguese monopoly of Africa and the East (see page 45). The Netherlands struggle for independence during the Thirty Years War (1618–48) gave the Dutch the opportunity to seize many of the west African forts of the Portuguese. There was a

Dutch fort at Mouri, near Elmina, as early as 1612, but in 1637 the Dutch took Elmina itself and soon afterwards had effective control of the whole of the Gold Coast. They aimed to become the suppliers-in-chief of African slaves, exporting them to their own settlements in Brazil and north America, selling them to the new English and French West Indian settlements, and smuggling them into the Spanish and Portuguese empires. Their ruthless business methods soon earned them a reputation for harshness on the African coast.

But Dutch supremacy in the slave trade was short-lived. The loss of their foothold in Brazil and the surrender of New Amsterdam to the English restricted their own market, and Portugal kept a sufficient presence in parts of Africa, other than the Gold Coast, to meet most of the demands for Africans in the Portuguese and Spanish empires. It was, therefore, greatly damaging to the Dutch when the English and French set up their own national companies as part of their campaigns to destroy the Netherlands carrying-trade. But that destruction was not accomplished overnight and the Dutch continued to share in the slave trade throughout the eighteenth century. Not until slave trading had become illegal did the Netherlands abandon the Gold Coast completely, selling Elmina and other forts to the British in 1872.

Meanwhile, in 1663, there was formed the Company of Royal Adventurers of England Trading in Africa, a short-lived English company which in the Anglo-Dutch Wars got the worst of it on the African coast. In 1672, the more famous Royal African Company was founded which was to last until 1750. The Company took over the English fort on the Gold Coast at Cape Coast Castle and by 1690 controlled a string of eight forts. But the Royal African Company also found it impossible to control the slave trade from a handful of scattered forts. The expense of the forts was considerable. Although the Company had government support, sometimes as much as £10 000 a year, it was claimed that it cost twice that sum simply to maintain the forts. The Company was, therefore, forced to charge high prices for slaves in order that those who had subscribed to its stock could make a profit. It was soon obvious that freelance traders, who were prepared to ignore the monopoly which had been granted to the Company by Charles II, could supply Africans more cheaply; and it was obvious to financiers that they would gain more by backing the interlopers than by buying the stock of the Company. Thus the Royal African Company was engaged in a continuous struggle to preserve its monopoly not only against foreigners but also against English interlopers. After 1750, English merchants traded in a much looser association which anyone was free to join, the Company of Merchants Trading to Africa. But by that time, it was generally recognized that the slave trade could not be monopolized, neither by one company nor even by one nation.

The monopolistic companies could, at best, control only short sections of the African coastline. Interlopers simply went elsewhere, extending the blight of the slave trade to yet more sections of the coast. In 1673, the monopoly of the French West India Company was transferred to the *Compagnie du Sénégal*. Another French company was founded to trade in Guinea. But these companies too found their monopolies infringed. European countries with very few West Indian possessions, or even none at all, could not be kept out of the African trade. Sweden set up a Guinea Company as early as 1647. Denmark joined the scramble for Africans in the 1670s, Brandenburg in the 1680s, each with a national company from which their rulers hoped personally to profit and which they trusted would develop the country's shipping in the Transatlantic trade. When national companies faltered, private traders carried on, and although Sweden and Brandenburg dropped out of the business in the eighteenth century, the other countries made sure that the trade continued unabated.

Certain European ports became particularly closely associated with the slave trade. In France, the centre was Nantes although most of the ports on the Atlantic coastline shared in the trade. English slave-trading ports included London, Plymouth, Bristol, Liverpool and Lancaster; in Scotland, Glasgow became involved. But London, Bristol and Liverpool outshone their rivals, with Liverpool gaining a special ascendancy. From 1783 to 1793, Liverpool merchants sold over 300 000 slaves with a net profit to the town of about £10 on each one. Not all the voyages returned a uniform profit, however. The merchants had to face risks. On the African coast there could be delays in filling the slave ship with its cargo, and the expense of obtaining the Africans varied according to the readiness of the supply. The African coast was also notoriously unhealthy for Europeans and the crews of the slave ships were always likely to be decimated by disease. The voyage across the Atlantic was also hazardous with dangers to be faced from storms, pirates, epidemics and slave rebellion. The slaves who survived then had to be sold in the West Indies, where prices again varied according to the current supply as well as to the condition in which the slaves arrived. Even so, Liverpool and its merchants prospered on the profits of the traffic in human beings. This prosperity spread also to the suppliers of goods to be traded with the Africans and to the manufacturers of the varied equipment which was essential to shackle and subdue the slaves. Shackles and thumb-screws were marketed at about 14 shillings a hundredweight. In the West Indies, a slave might bring about £50 if fit and strong and if supply was not plentiful. At other times, a price of £37 was not unusual. And slave ships were almost always packed to their limits with their human cargo.

It has been estimated—and there can be no way of knowing the exact number—that about 20 million Africans were taken from their continent during the years of the Transatlantic slave trade.* Perhaps 5 million went to the West Indies, the rest to the American mainland. Many who left Africa, however, did not survive the voyage, just as many who were captured did not even reach the African coast. It is likely that between 10 and 15 per cent of the slaves who set out across the Atlantic did not live through the voyage. But of those who landed in the West Indies, the largest numbers were carried by the English, whose Caribbean settlements were to a considerable extent responsible for developing the slave trade with the Gambia. The French were the closest rivals to the English in the numbers of slaves transported, the Dutch coming third. This Anglo-French dominance reflects the importance of the sugar plantations in the English and French islands. The third place of the Dutch was the result of the comparatively short-lived ascendancy of the Dutch West India Company. It was scarcely due to any lack of Dutch enthusiasm, for the capture of Pernambuco in 1634 had immediately prompted the Company to seek slaves east of the Volta with all speed, and to ship them across the Atlantic.

Monument to the Unknown Slave. Millions of his brothers were shipped from Africa to the Americas (Haiti, 1968)

The Middle Passage

The triangular trade (from Europe to Africa; from Africa to the West Indies; from the West Indies to Europe) had, as its Middle Passage, the voyage of the slave ships across the Atlantic. Once the slaves had been collected from the barracoons and the ship filled to capacity, they faced an ocean journey of something like six weeks, perhaps longer. But few masters were lucky enough to fill their ships at one fort. Weeks were likely to be spent working along the African coast in search of a full cargo, sometimes two or three months. The slave's ordeal could, therefore, last for as long as four or five months on top of the time which he might already have spent in a coffle and a barracoon. It is difficult to imagine the physical and mental torture the slave had to endure. His captors had a vested interest in trying to preserve his health but, often packed like a parcel on a shelf, deprived of liberty and even of fresh air, always regarded as a commodity and not as a human being, the slave

* Other estimates have varied from 'a few millions' to 'a hundred million'.

had to endure surroundings which were cramped, hot, insanitary and indescribably uncomfortable. His captors could well be vicious and cruel; almost always they were callous. To acute physical discomfort and sometimes brutality, must be added the mental anguish of the African, leaving his homeland for ever and going to an unknown land about which he could only speculate, quite likely leaving family and friends, and perhaps unable to understand the speech of either his masters or his fellow-prisoners. It would not be surprising if he were terrified, especially when he imagined what might await him across the sea. For many slaves, death was preferable to further torment. Some were able to jump from the small boats which took them from the shore to the slave ships lying in deeper waters. Some managed to plunge into the sea from the ships themselves. Others found different ways of ending their lives, perhaps in a hopeless rebellion against their captors for which death would be a likely punishment. Thousands, perhaps millions, of others died from dysentery, 'fluxes and fevers' and sometimes simply suffocation. Captain Thomas Phillips, master of the *Hannibal,* took over two months to reach Barbados from Africa in 1694. Of his cargo of 700 Africans, over 300 died on the voyage, twelve of them from smallpox. Another twelve had managed to drown themselves before the *Hannibal* left the African coast. Disease also killed fourteen of the crew. In his Journal, Phillips noted sadly that the slave-deaths had lost him £6560.

Female slaves were commonly raped on the voyage by the members of the ship's crew. Slaves of both sexes were likely to be flogged for misdemeanours. Food was no more than the minimum and the cheapest which, it was hoped, would keep the slaves alive. The best the African could hope for was a quick voyage, calm weather and a ship's master who, if not sensitive to the slave's sufferings, was at least a good enough businessman to realize the advantages of humane treatment and of delivering his catch in good condition. The worst would be a slow and prolonged passage, a brutal master and bestial crew, and storms, which added sea-sickness to the torments and vomit to the urine and excrement in which the slaves had to travel. So foul and rotten did most of

A French print of slaves being forced to exercise during the Middle Passage

the slave ships become that, in Liverpool, it was reckoned that they were fit for only eight voyages on the Middle Passage. Each of the eight voyages was one of unmitigated misery for hundreds of Africans and an ordeal hardly less grim for the members of the crew. To the stink, the risk of disease and death, and the usual primitive conditions of the seaman in the seventeenth and eighteenth centuries was added the fear of slave revolt. But only a careless captain and crew allowed the slaves to get out of control. The greatest threat lay probably in the danger that a crew might be weakened by disease and death and no longer able to dominate the slaves. Such was the case when the slaves rose on the *Don Carlos* in 1701—an English ship in spite of its name. The revolt was suppressed, as was usually the case, and its leaders were savagely flogged. Thirty Africans had died in the struggle, but they had cut the cook's throat, killed another seaman and wounded several more of their tormentors.

The number of slaves lost on the voyage of the *Hannibal* was abnormally high, but losses of 20 or 30 per cent of the cargo were not uncommon during the Middle Passage. When the slave ships reached the West Indies, the aim was to sell the surviving Africans at the best price possible. An attempt was made to cleanse them of the filth of the voyage, then to oil them so that a shiny skin might attract a buyer. Like a shopkeeper polishing his wares, the ship's master prepared his slaves for market. Some were even fattened on improved foodstuffs during the last days of the Passage. The first task was to get the slaves ashore, which was not usually a problem as the Africans were only too eager to leave their floating prison. But a hundred slaves leapt into the sea from the *Prince of Orange* when it reached St Kitts in 1737, and thirty-three succeeded in drowning themselves, leaving the captain to lament the loss of thirty-three prices. The others were pulled from the water and sold as quickly as possible, before the buyers could realize that some of the slaves they bought had been half-drowned and would suffer the after-effects of their immersion.

Weak and dying slaves, referred to as 'refuse slaves', were often auctioned first. Bidding could then begin for the fitter Africans, the estate owners assessing them as shrewdly as they could for the labour which could be extracted from them. Many regulations were issued to forbid the splitting up of African families in the sales, but the regulations were commonly disregarded. Once again, therefore, the slave's destiny was a matter of chance. The buyers looked on the transaction as a farmer might look on a cattle-auction: they wanted value for money and very few were motivated by feelings of compassion. Some of the buyers, indeed, could well be dealers, investing in slaves to dispose of them later at a profit. Even worse for the slave than the auction was the 'sale by scramble' which sometimes took place. Herded on the deck of the ship or into a compound on land, the slaves were sold at a fixed price. At a given signal, buyers were admitted, often in a headlong rush, to claim their bargains, jostling and squabbling over the Africans who could have had little understanding of this new ordeal in their lives. Once bought, however, the African was about to come face to face with the main reason for all his sufferings. Unless he had had the rare good fortune to be bought by a slave owner who preferred some different crop, he was about to be introduced to a West Indian sugar estate (see Chapter 7).

The African Population of the West Indies

It has been seen that whites were soon heavily outnumbered by African slaves in the sugar islands (see pages 67–8). The transporting of Africans into the Americas was one of the largest migrations in history. In spite of an appallingly high death rate on the plantations, the African population of the West Indies grew enormously from about the middle of the seventeenth century to about the end of the eighteenth century. The high death rate of the slaves was often the result of deliberate policy on the part of their masters. In Antigua, for example, in the middle of the eighteenth century, some planters argued that it was more profitable to work Africans fiercely, even to death, and then to buy new slaves, than to impose a lighter load and spend more on food and decent living conditions so that slaves would live longer. Throughout the West Indies there were slave owners whose calculations led them to the same conclusions. Some owners also experimented in the breeding of slaves. Antigua and Barbuda had stud farms for the producing of African children. Since the children of slaves automatically became the property of the slaves' master, this might be cheaper than purchasing the cargo of the slave ships, though it needed fine calculation to weigh the cost of rearing the babies against the current market prices. Of course, it might be possible to breed super-slaves if one carefully controlled the parentage. Such an experiment was tried in Barbuda where a collection was made of slaves of massive physique in an effort to produce even bigger Africans, some of whose descendants retain their imposing stature to the present day. The letters and diaries of the eighteenth-century plantation owners show a considerable concern with the most economic ways of increasing the African labour force. Equally, the owners often squandered their slaves as the Spaniards had earlier squandered the Indians, killing them off almost casually with overwork, ill-treatment and too little nourishment. Eric Williams* has calculated that, on the basis of the African population of Barbados in 1764 and subsequent importations, the island should have had over 112 000 Africans in 1783. In fact, it had only 62 000, actually fewer than in 1764. Barbados was not unique. For much of the eighteenth century, Jamaica imported, on average, about 7000 Africans a year and St Domingue over 8000. But, although the slave population increased substantially in each case, the increase bore little relation to the total importations. The explanation lies in the heavy toll of African lives which was taken by the sugar estates. The malnutrition from which many slaves died was not entirely and invariably the fault of their owners, however. In the eighteenth century, communications were often disrupted by warfare (see Chapter 8). Supplies were often expensive or even unobtainable, especially during the War of American Independence, when the English islands found it difficult to obtain foodstuffs from north America and the rations of the slaves had to be cut down. In such times of crisis, the slaves would be the first to suffer.

In spite of the high death-rate, however, the sugar islands were overwhelmingly black by 1800. In St Domingue, the Africans were able to use this superiority to seize their freedom and their country's independence (see pages 102–3). Elsewhere, the whites were able to keep them in subjection though the pressures for change were building up. The slave trade and slavery itself were facing mounting criticism. Sugar was beginning to lose its pre-eminence in the economies of the European states, and the early nineteenth century was to see an irresistible movement towards emancipation and free trade. At the same time, it seemed that the returns from sugar no longer justified the expenditure on new slaves. The time was fast coming, then, when it would be necessary fundamentally to re-examine the societies and economies, and eventually the politics, of the West Indian islands. But such a re-examination could never put back the clock. Except in the Spanish islands, the West Indian population was predominantly African and even the Spanish islands had substantial African communities. Future developments were bound to take account of this.

* *From Columbus to Castro*, p. 146. Others have argued, however, that slave economies in the Americas were efficient and humane, at least in north America. See R. Fogel and S. Engerman, *Time on the Cross: The Economics of American Negro Slavery*.

Exercises

1 What do you understand by *each* of the following terms: the labour supply; the indenture system; deficiency laws? Why was slave labour used more extensively than indentured labour in the English islands in the seventeenth century?

2 Identify the principal economic and social developments which took place in the West Indies arranging your answer under the following four headings: (a) The English and French islands in the seventeenth century; (b) The Spanish islands in the seventeenth century; (c) The English and French islands in the eighteenth century; (d) The Spanish islands in the eighteenth century.

3 Show what parts were played in the slave trade by the European national companies. Why did the companies object so strongly to interlopers, and why were they unable to keep interlopers out of the trade?

4 Making use of the information in this chapter and Figure 6.1, construct the story of the life of an African slave which he might have handed on to his children. The story should deal with the slave's experiences from the time that he was free in Africa to his arrival on a sugar plantation in the West Indies. (This story can be continued, after reading Chapter 7, up to the time of the slave's death.)

5 For *each* leg of 'the triangular trade' (page 71 and Figure 5.1), list the factors which would help to determine whether the voyage would be (a) profitable or (b) unprofitable, for those who invested money in the venture.

7 The West Indies in the Eighteenth Century

I KING SUGAR

The Sugar Estate

As early as 1645, it was claimed in Barbados that in a year and a half an African slave could earn for his master what it had cost to buy him. But the slave would be likely to have to go on earning for his master for the rest of his life. The newly arrived slave was usually allowed a period of seasoning before he began his labours on the sugar estate. During this seasoning time, a couple of months or so, he would become familiar with the routine of the estate, and with what was expected of the Africans who supplied its insatiable demand for work. He would realize quickly that Africans such as himself, though of a variety of tribes, were the most numerous people on the estate. Several hundreds might well be living in the area set aside as their quarters, living either in barracks or in small thatched huts. Each slave would have a minimum number of personal belongings such as working-clothes, a general-purpose knife and a hat to protect against the sun. After the working-day, devoted entirely to the service of the owner of the plantation, there would be a few precious hours for work on the slaves' provision grounds (on which they grew small crops for themselves), for recreation, and for sleep. Only in the brief moments of recreation, in singing and dancing, was the slave likely to be reminded of his homeland in Africa. For the rest, his new life was probably totally different. He had lost his freedom and independence, and he had been separated from his tribe and its traditions. In exchange, there was unrelenting labour geared to the output of sugar and the pursuit of profits from which he was unlikely to secure any benefit at all, unless a benevolent master chose to dole out, in charity, some simple reward.

Sugar estates varied, of course, according to their location, the temper of the masters and the quality of the management. But the majority bore remarkable similarities to one another. Bryan Edwards, a Jamaican planter writing in the late eighteenth century, described a typical Jamaican estate as consisting of 900 acres, a third of them growing sugar-cane, with woodlands and pasture where possible. Such an estate would need a couple of mills to grind the cane, preferably water-powered, and an extensive collection of buildings, from the great house of the owner (or his agent) to the quarters of the officials and the housing of the slaves, and including the factory close by the mills. It would need cattle and mules, and above all it would need about 250 slaves. In the smaller islands, estates were likely to be smaller. In the French islands, an account left by Moreau de St Méry suggests that a rather higher proportion of the estate was taken up by cane fields. But all the estates needed a large African labour force and eighteenth-century technology was invariably primitive. Steam power was being applied to industry in Europe at this time, but more traditional sources of power, those of wind and water, animals and human beings, continued to be most common in the West Indies.

Figure 7.2 on page 80 illustrates a typical eighteenth-century estate. It was the aim that the estate should be self-sufficient as far as possible. Apart from the main crop of sugar, food would be grown for the great house, the slaves and the animals. The possession of woodlands would provide timber for buildings, fences and equipment, and fuel for the factory, where the boiling process called for great quantities of wood, supplemented by cane trash or *megasse*. A few additional cash-crops might also be grown, such as tobacco and ginger. The sugar-cane did not need to be replaced annually. Newly planted cane usually yielded a better sugar-content, but ratooning allowed further crops to be grown from roots which were left in the soil after reaping. Newly planted cane took some fifteen months to mature,

Figure 7.1 Jamaica: Economic Maps

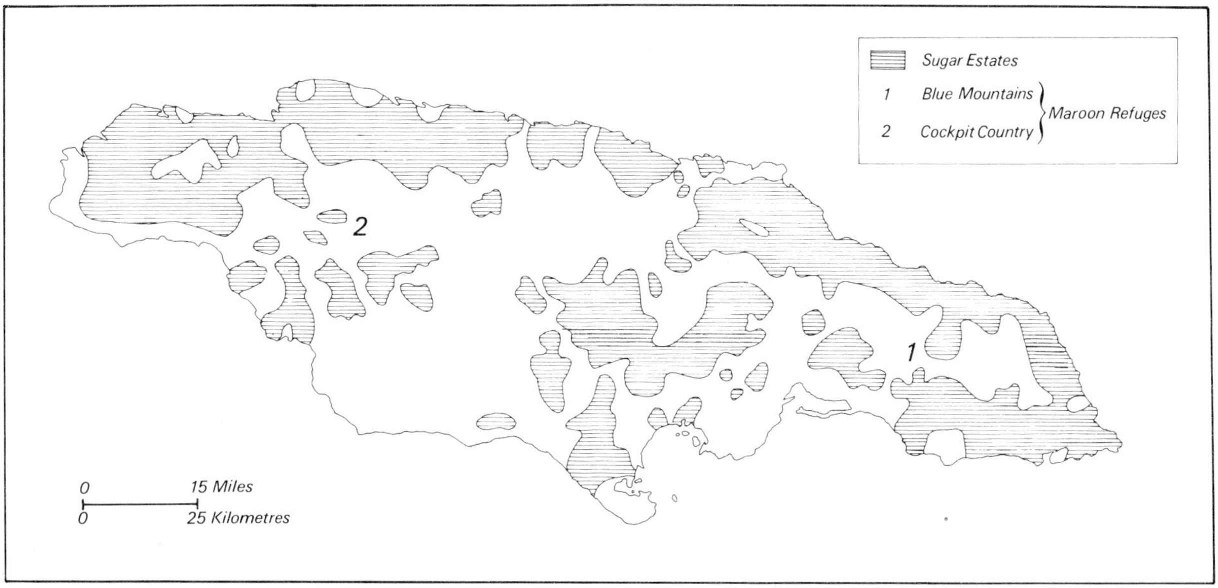

(a) Sugar Production

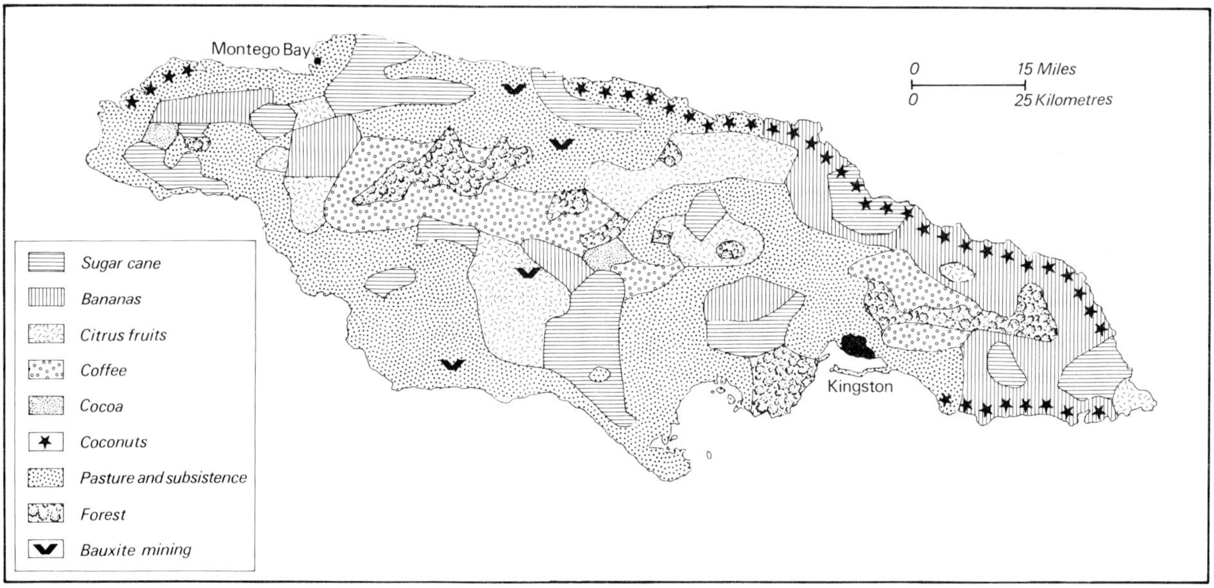

(b) Economic Diversification

but ratoons grew more quickly and could be harvested in twelve months; and ratooning could be continued for perhaps as long as twenty years.

Even so, sugar estates worked on rather small profit margins. They required considerable capital to start them, as much as £30 000 in Jamaica, and much of the yearly return was taken up in the expenses of the estate and in new investment. New cane plants and new slaves might have to be bought, the wages of the free workers paid

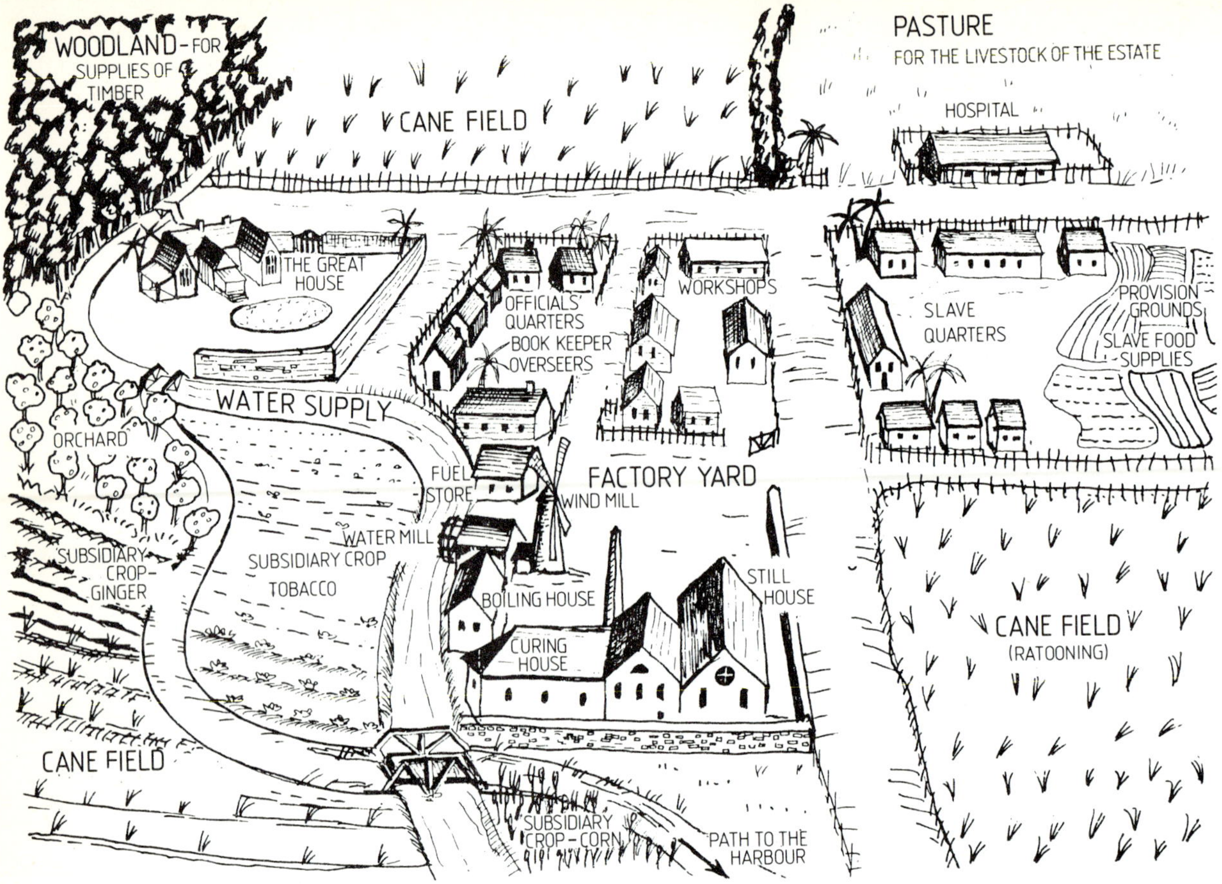

Figure 7.2 A Typical Sugar Plantation in the Eighteenth Century

and, since the yield from the provision grounds alone was seldom adequate, foodstuffs imported. A profit of 10 per cent on the year's operations was unusually high, and was likely to be achieved only in the French colony of St Domingue, where the large area available to the planter and the quality of the soil formed a particularly favourable combination. Elsewhere, a profit of 5 per cent was more usual and even that could be wiped out in times of war or other adversity. The bankrupt plantation owner was no less common than the one who retired in luxury.

Sugar Production and Slavery

The main activity of the estate revolved around only a small number of processes: sugar-cane was grown; the grinding-process extracted the juice from the cane; the juice was boiled to produce a syrup and sugar crystals remained as liquid dripped from the syrup. However these crystals were unrefined—brown sugar. The refining process, which would turn the brown sugar into the finer grains of white sugar, was usually reserved by the English and French for refineries in Europe. In 1753, there were eighty refineries in London and twenty in Bristol. In 1774, Liverpool had eight. In 1789, there were twenty-six in Bordeaux, in France.

In the eighteenth century, the production of the unrefined sugar in the West Indies called at every stage for the labour of the African slave. De St Méry described a French-owned estate where fifty-eight slaves worked in the fields and thirty-nine in the factory, with another twelve acting as domestic servants to the master. But since work on the estate depended on the seasons such an arrangement was likely to be flexible. Much of the year was taken up with the rearing of the cane plants. The field-worker was particularly employed to clear the ground, plant new roots in orderly rows, bank soil round the plants as they grew, remove weeds and dried trash from the fields and generally ensure the health of the crop. Without modern equipment, it was tedious, back-straining labour. The social structure of the estate could be clearly seen in this work. The slaves worked in the fields in gangs, watched over by drivers who were themselves usually slaves. The drivers were in turn responsible to minor white officials, the overseers and book-keepers. They in turn reported to the owner of the estate or his agent whose principal concern was that of the general manager for whom growing the crop was only part of the production process.

Crop time was a time of crisis. The cane had to be cut and delivered to the mill as quickly as possible before it could deteriorate. During this period there was more than enough work for all. Brute strength and endurance were required of the cutters who used machetes and similar primitive hand-tools. While daylight lasted, the cane was cut at an unrelenting pace. Getting the crop to the mill was the job of another large force of Africans, loading and unloading the carts, ensuring a supply of animals to pull them and gathering up whatever might be spilled. At the mill, there were slaves to feed in the cane and to take away the trash. Since a maximum harvest gathered at speed was the aim, all hands were enlisted to the work. The drivers, overseers and the owner himself were likely to be especially demanding at this time.

The early sugar factories in the West Indies employed only primitive technology in grinding the cane and boiling the liquid—a late seventeenth-century print

From the mill, the juice was usually channelled to the boiling-house to begin the first of the heating processes. Some slaves were responsible for adding lime to assist the clarification of the liquid, but the main task for the factory-workers was to feed the fires. The juice was boiled in a succession of copper pans. As evaporation and the removing of impurities reduced the volume of the liquid, the coppers became smaller and the heat more fierce. The final boiling in the teache produced a syrup, the end-product of the work in the boiling-house. To decide when this syrup had reached the right consistency required skilled knowledge, though in hogsheads was raw sugar, now ready for export when the trading-ships arrived. Inevitably, many of the casks were shipped before the molasses had finished leaking, making a sticky mess of the ships' holds and also reducing the weight of sugar which actually reached Europe. A hogshead of fourteen hundredweights could well be reduced to twelve or even ten by the time it reached the market. Moving such casks at all was, of course, work which required strength and once again the African slave was invaluable.

The factory and its out-buildings also required the services of a team of craftsmen, not only to

Figure 7.3 The Social Structure and Economic Features of an Eighteenth-Century Sugar Estate

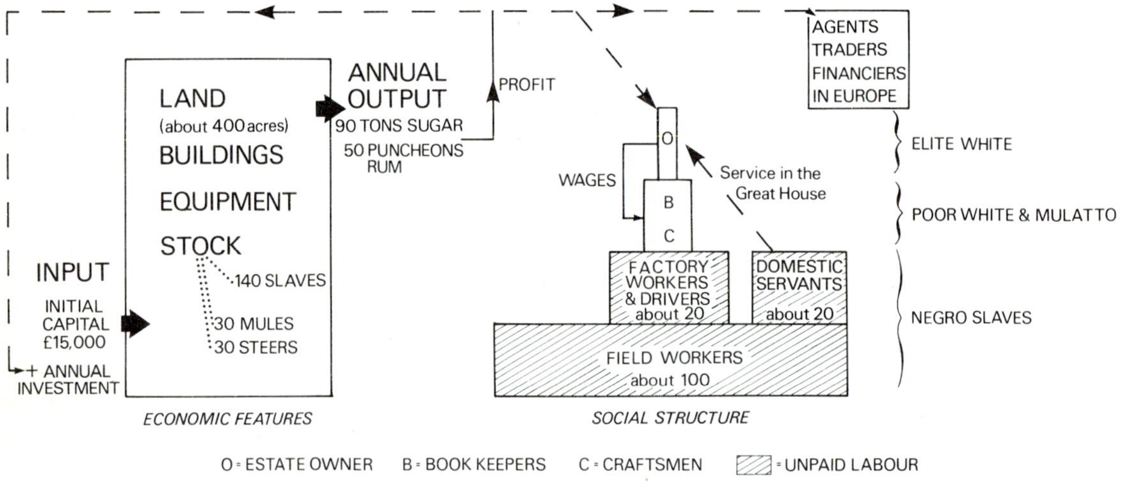

Note Sugar estates varied considerably but the general principles were similar on all estates. They varied in size from *c.* 100 acres to well over 1000 acres. They required heavy capital investment and many were under-capitalized. Productivity was lower in Barbados than in Jamaica and the French colonies: Barbados had large African labour forces but output was low

the primitive technology of the eighteenth century the test was often to stretch the sticky substance between the hardened thumb and forefinger of an experienced slave. The syrup could now be transferred to the hogsheads and taken to the curing-house.

The hogsheads were large casks with perforated bottoms which allowed the excess liquid which still remained to drain off. This liquid, known as *molasses*, could be collected from beneath the hogsheads and sent back to the boiling-house. Thus, for many weeks after the cutting-time, the factory was kept busy. What was left in the process the sugar but to keep in good repair all the equipment of the estate. Such work might involve both blacks and whites. The proper functioning of the estate thus required not only a large labour force but also a varied one. The newly arrived African slave would be fitted into the system according to his physique and aptitudes. Once he had seen the whole process through, it would begin again. On a well-run estate with the crop time spread out over several months, the cane maturing at different times in different fields, the factory busy both day and night for many months of the year, the slaves would be left with little time for the idleness and gossip which all the masters feared. An idle slave was assumed to be a conspirator, for few masters cherished the illusion that the Africans enjoyed plantation work or felt a commitment to its success. A master's agent and perhaps senior officials might be paid a commission. Six per cent of the sale-price of the sugar was not uncommon for an attorney, an agent who acted on behalf of an absentee owner. But hardly anyone else had such a vested interest in the output. The whites would be indentured servants or lowly paid wage-labourers. The Africans received no payment at all.

These circumstances made it questionable whether the slave-based plantation was an efficient economic unit, and doubts multiply when one recalls the low profit margins and primitive technology of the estates. William Miller, an attorney in Jamaica, boasted that he was the agent for forty-eight estates with 10 000 labourers. Even if one makes allowance for the fact that this was in the 1830s, the decade of emancipation when many estates had passed their peak, such a spread of responsibilities would not lead to efficient management. The ever-present problem, however, was that of the African labour force which had nothing to look forward to but a life of toil. The slaves were often unco-operative, and the brutal lashes of the driver's whip were not much of a solution to the problem. Rebellious slaves would sometimes set fire to the cane fields and their masters' buildings, and even murder their tormentors. Fray Alonso de Sandoval had warned the Spaniards as early as 1627 that 'slaves live as dying men and die as living men', and that the practice of slavery brought with it the risk of 'disturbances and revolts'. The successful revolution in Haiti at the end of the eighteenth century was preceded by storm-warnings over more than 150 years. There were slave rebellions in Barbados in 1649 and in Guadeloupe in 1656. In the eighteenth century, there were various outbreaks in the smaller islands, in Surinam and in Jamaica, amongst which was Tacky's rebellion (see page 68). At this time, Cuba was not primarily a sugar island yet Cuba had serious uprisings in 1729 and 1731. But these major outbreaks took place against a continuous backcloth of murders, sabotage and lesser disturbances.

The flight of Africans from the plantations was no less serious for the estate owners. Such escape was difficult in the smaller islands, but in St Domingue and Jamaica there was space enough to hide. Runaway slaves in Jamaica, referred to by the English as *maroons*, established communities in the hills and lived as outlaws and desperadoes. The violence of the slave trade and of much of the life on the plantations inevitably produced violent retaliation, and yet what is perhaps most remarkable is how passive vast numbers of slaves remained. Most of them endured their lot, and died from it. The majority who protested got no further than passive resistance. Some turned to witchcraft, and committed isolated acts of destruction and murder. But mass-revolt was comparatively rare, given the vast numbers of slaves. On the other hand, Jamaica alone had a dozen serious revolts in the eighteenth century.

Regulations for Slave Societies

It was in the *Spanish islands* that mass-revolt occurred least often. Of the European nations, only Spain made a serious effort to check the influx of African slaves. The *Asiento* (see page 19) was granted only to favoured slave traders, and it was official policy to keep down the number of imported Africans. But at the end of the seventeenth century, the Spanish crown passed to a French prince, who promptly allowed French traders to secure the *Asiento* and they imported nearly 50 000 slaves into the Spanish empire. This inheritance of the Spanish throne was disputed in Europe and the War of the Spanish Succession occurred (see Chapter 8). When this War ended in the Treaty of Utrecht, in 1713, the British demanded the *Asiento*. They were permitted to import into the Spanish colonies 5000 slaves a year for thirty years. Britain's contract was renewed in 1748 in the Treaty of Aix-la-Chapelle, but interlopers were by that time so numerous that the *Asiento* no longer carried much weight. The British thought it good business to surrender it in 1750 in exchange for a lump sum of £100 000, paid as compensation by the Spanish government. Spain itself abandoned the *Asiento* system in 1789, and gave up the struggle to maintain over the supply of slaves a control which had never been entirely watertight.

But the number of slaves in the Spanish islands had also been kept down by Spain's avoidance of a massive concentration on sugar production. The Spaniards had had long experience of captive labour forces and, learning some lessons from the extermination of the Amerindians, they drafted regulations which gave at least some small protection to African slaves. As with the Indians, emphasis was placed on the teaching of Christianity, and slave owners were required to provide adequate food and clothing for their Africans and to care for them in sickness and old age. Perhaps most important, the regulations also made provision for Africans to gain their freedom, either by purchase or by the verdict of a court where a master disobeyed the law. Enforcing regulations was always a different matter from issuing them, but the Spaniards persistently tried to see that their laws were obeyed. Compared with the English and French sugar islands, the Spanish islands, therefore, had fewer Africans in relation to other ethnic groups and amongst the Africans many were freemen. There were 30 000 free non-whites in Cuba in 1787 alongside a slave population of 50 000. In Puerto Rico, there were 130 000 free non-whites in 1827 alongside a slave population of only 34 000. In Jamaica, on the other hand, shortly before the end of the eighteenth century, there were only 4000 free non-whites alongside 250 000 slaves.* The figures in Guadeloupe at this time showed a similar imbalance to those of Jamaica.

Guadeloupe, of course, was one of the *French sugar islands*. To deal with the problem of the massive slave populations demanded by sugar, the French had introduced their own code of laws, similar to the earlier Spanish laws except with regard to manumission (that is, the freeing of slaves). Colbert, who was said to have had 'a mania for regulation', had made a start on the codification of French law in the *Code Louis*, and on the codification of the laws of the French empire in the *Code Noir*. The *Code Noir* was issued shortly after Colbert's death, in the reign of Louis XIV in 1685. It was designed, in particular, to meet the needs of the French West Indian colonies. Its aims were far-reaching: partly religious (to ensure that the slaves were Christianized); partly humanitarian (to provide the slaves with a measure of protection against inhuman treatment); partly economic (to ensure that the slaves were productive); and partly political (to produce stability in the slavery-based societies).

The *Code Noir* provided some limited protection for the slaves in the French islands (Guadeloupe, 1947)

The *Code* strongly reflected the religious enthusiasm of the King and declared that only Roman Catholics could be slave owners and that Catholicism should be the form of Christianity taught to the slaves. Jews were banned from the French islands, and Sundays were to be observed as holy days. An attempt was made to deal with the problems arising from sexual intercourse between free white and slave black. A married slave owner who fathered the child of a slave was to forfeit both the slave mother and the child; and an unmarried owner was to marry the slave mother and make her free. If the white father was not a master, fines were imposed; and the general principle was laid down that children were to take the social status of the mother. Amongst themselves, the slaves were to be encouraged to marry, subject to their owner's consent, but a Christian marriage ceremony was not made compulsory. The Code also tried to provide for the problem of intermarriage between slaves from different estates, and the regulations thus became highly complicated on the subject of intermarriage and parenthood. Not surprisingly, the regulations often remained unenforced.

The regulations which concerned the slaves' entitlements and the punishment of their misdemeanours were similarly thorough. Owners

* Figure 7.1a shows how sugar dominated Jamaica in the 1790s.

were forbidden to leave their slaves to feed themselves from their provision grounds, but were required to issue fixed quantities of food (cassava, beef and fish) and clothing. Sick and old slaves were also made the responsibility of their owners. Freedom could be granted after twenty years' service. Casual and brutal punishment was forbidden and, if sold, slave families were not to be split up. Unfortunately, little was done to ensure that these regulations were obeyed.

What the *Code Noir* made clear, however, was that a slave was the property of his master and possessed hardly any rights. On no account could he sell sugar, acquire property, hold public office or even, without his master's permission, dispose of the produce of his provision grounds. Although protected from torture and mutilation at the whim of his master, the slave could be chained and flogged for disobedience and could be punished savagely by the courts for listed offences. A slave who ran away could lose his ears and suffer branding. If he persisted in running away, he could be put to death. Death was also the penalty for striking his owner or the owner's wife. Flogging and branding were laid down for those guilty of stealing. And since a dead slave was a loss to his master a fine could be levied, in certain circumstances, whereby living Africans would compensate the owners for their fellow-slaves who had been killed.

The *Code Noir* remained the basis of French law for dealing with the slave population although it was added to in points of detail from time to time during the eighteenth century. The additional regulations almost invariably worked against the African, for example by restricting further what he could plant and sell. The French authorities also kept up a stream of ordinances forbidding intermarriage between white and non-white, and limiting the opportunities for advancement in wealth and social status of those who, though free, were not white. The mulattoes were thus held down, while at the same time the number of Africans who gained their freedom in the French islands remained pitifully small. This no doubt served the interests of King Sugar, but in St Domingue at least it laid all the foundations for a violent explosion in the 1790s (see pages 102–3).

The *English islands* had no comprehensive *Code Noir*, but hundreds of fragmentary regulations added up to a treatment of Africans on the sugar estates which was similar to the French system. The (Protestant) Church of England was now the established religion in Britain and was thus the official religion of the empire. Otherwise, like the French, the British regulations were designed to achieve social stability and the success of sugar production, with some small protection of the African against the worst brutality of his master. The details of the regulations varied from island to island, but the most common laws were those dealing with restricting and punishing the slaves. They were forbidden to grow and to sell certain listed produce. They were forbidden, in eighteenth-century Jamaica for example, to rear certain livestock. For various offences, like the slaves in the French islands, they could be punished—flogged for minor misdemeanours,

A tread-wheel in Jamaica for the punishment of slaves. The first duty of the slave was to obey and work for his master

killed for more serious crimes. In Barbados in the late seventeenth century, death was the punishment for stealing property valued at a shilling. Slave owners, however, could often interpret the laws to suit themselves. William Wilberforce collected a great deal of evidence about the ill-treatment of Africans and he found that the official regulations (including the *Code Noir*) were frequently ignored in both the French and English islands. In Barbados, flogging was limited by law to thirty-nine lashes. Evidence was given to Wilberforce by eye-witnesses that a Barbadian planter flogged a young African girl throughout the night—thirty-nine lashes followed by another thirty-nine, and so on.

Towards the end of the eighteenth century, the volume of protest about the cruelties of the slave trade and slavery began to grow (see pages 104–8). In some of the British islands, the criticism was met by the passing of ameliorative laws to try to improve the lot of the African. Jamaica produced the Consolidated Slave Law in 1784, a code similar to the French *Code Noir*, which regulated the slave's food and clothing, his hours of work and his liability to punishment. It forbade excessive brutality and the splitting up of slave families, but the same problem of enforcement remained. All these regulations were based on the acceptance of slavery as a necessity and the acceptance of a huge social gulf between the superior white and inferior black which stemmed from slavery. As long as slavery remained, therefore, regulations could, at best, do little more than provide for the slave a minimum of material comfort; and even that depended less on the laws than on the good nature of a kindly master. Some slaves were fortunate in falling into the hands of owners who treated them as well as the system allowed, who obeyed the laws and even went further in providing a civilized environment in which the slave could live. But, by definition, a slave was always denied elementary human rights, and good treatment by his master could never be much more than a sort of kindness-to-animals.

II METROPOLITAN CONTROL

Centralization

It was taken for granted in the eighteenth century that the interests of the mother countries were of greater importance than the local interests of the West Indian islands. But the West Indies are over 4000 miles from Europe and each mother country faced the problem of how to control its colonies. In general, each tended to import into the islands the political and social systems which existed at home. Thus, Spain's system of government was highly centralized (see Chapter 2). It also tended to be autocratic, although the governors of the islands were supervised by the Audiencia and they had also to respect the rights of the cabildos. The governor of Trinidad, for example, had to respect the rights of the cabildo of Port of Spain, for the authority of the cabildos was based on the Spanish institution of the municipality which Spaniards respected. Rights and privileges were also extended to the Catholic Church and, according to their rank, to those who were Spanish-born. Nevertheless, the whole system was geared to metropolitan supervision and to the preservation of social distinctions, especially amongst the upper classes. A considerable bureaucracy, civilian and military, was required, and the system tended to be inflexible and to produce a society which was static rather than dynamic, just as in Spain itself.

The French too favoured a centralized system which was consolidated in the time of Louis XIV and Colbert. The French did not follow the English example of allowing the West Indian islands to have their own assemblies until 1787. Laws, for example the *Code Noir*, were made in France and, even after 1787, the assemblies were only permitted to approve the laws made in Europe: they were not permitted to make new laws. Responsibility for ruling the French islands rested with royal officials, especially the governors and the intendants. In theory, general oversight was exercised by a governor-general based in Martinique. Each governor was assisted by a council of advisers drawn from the officials and the more important landowners. The whole system was supervised from France.

Sugar produced its own social hierarchy and class distinction was probably even stronger than in the Spanish islands. Plantation owners, especially in Martinique and Guadeloupe where most of them took personal charge of their estates, were the *grands blancs*, men often powerful enough to influence the governor and his council. The poor whites were the *petits blancs*, a class above the mulattoes if only on account of their colour. In spite of guarantees in the *Code Noir* that the mulattoes should be treated as freemen, steps were taken towards the end of the eighteenth century to restrict their wealth and influence. Free blacks were comparatively few in the French islands and the mass of Africans were, of course, without effective rights.

By the end of the eighteenth century, therefore, the French had created a system which was under severe strain. The *grands blancs* resented what they regarded as too much control from France; the *petits blancs* feared the rise of more prosperous mulattoes; and the non-whites resented the well-entrenched privileges of the whites.

The British system for controlling the West Indian islands produced results similar to those of Spain and France but it bore traces of traditional British institutions. Even the Elizabethan system of poor relief was introduced into the British colonies along with the institution of the parish as a unit of local government.* Parish authorities, for example, were to levy a poor rate and repair roads. But the most important distinguishing feature in the British system was the assembly, a sort of colonial parliament modelled on that at Westminster in London.

Assemblies in the British Islands

Like the Spanish and French islands, the British colonies were ruled by governors sent out from Europe, assisted by councils of advisers. Part of the governor's job was to enforce the laws which had been passed in Britain, for example the Navigation Acts. But each island also had an assembly, members of which were locally elected by men of property. These assemblies could pass laws, subject to confirmation in London, and they passed revenue bills to authorize the taxes from which the governor was able to finance the administration of the island. The members of the assemblies were mainly concerned with the interests of the planters, whereas the governors owed their first loyalty to Britain. Frequent conflicts were, therefore, inevitable and they naturally tended to centre on the subject of money. Governors often found it difficult to persuade an assembly to pass the annual revenue bill to meet the expenses of government. On the other hand, the assemblies sometimes wanted to introduce laws to which the governor, on behalf of Britain, objected. Such laws were sometimes tacked on to the revenue bill, giving the governor no choice but to accept them or to lose his taxes. Thus the assembly system made the business of administering the British islands more complicated, although it undoubtedly safeguarded for the plantation owners what they thought were the traditional liberties of Englishmen.

So jealously did the planters insist on their traditional liberties that each small island demanded its assembly. An attempt to create a single assembly for the English Leeward Islands came to little and was abandoned in 1711; a similar attempt ended in a similar failure in 1876,

The Assembly in Jamaica dated from 1664 in the reign of Charles II (Jamaica, 1945)

when the British proposed an assembly for the Windward Islands where additional colonies were acquired in the eighteenth century. Throughout the eighteenth century, therefore, the British government and its governors fought a running battle with the West Indian colonial assemblies and the plantation owners whom the assemblies represented. The assembly in Jamaica was particularly troublesome. Jamaican estate owners, in the late seventeenth and eighteenth centuries, constantly sought to make the granting of revenue conditional upon the acceptance of their own laws. The British gave in, in 1728, and confirmed all the Jamaican laws up to that date in return for an agreement that £8000 would be paid each year

* See Glossary.

without the need to obtain an annual vote. But there were still squabbles about whatever additional revenue might be needed and about the new laws which Jamaican planters wished to pass, many of which concerned their rights over the slaves. The assembly became expert in passing short-term laws, which might already have expired before the British government could consider them. And there was increasing exasperation in London with the assembly system which so clearly protected the vested interests of the estate owners but was not always in the best interests of the people of the colonies as a whole.

Matters came to a head when the British took possession first of Grenada and then of Trinidad. Grenada was added permanently to the British empire in 1783, having been taken from the French. The usual assembly was granted and the usual $4\frac{1}{2}$ per cent levy was imposed on exports (see page 42). But the levy was challenged in the courts by a plantation owner who claimed that, without the consent of Grenada's assembly, it was illegal. To the dismay of the British government, Lord Chief Justice Mansfield upheld this claim. When Trinidad was seized from the Spaniards in 1797, no assembly was granted.

Trinidad, it was declared, would be ruled as a crown colony with a governor appointed in London and a nominated council to advise him—'a council of advice, not of control'. Elections would not be held in Trinidad, and British laws would require no local approval. Britain had thus moved towards the French system of more centralized control in Trinidad, and would do the same later in the older British colonies. It was argued that Trinidad had a population of which a substantial proportion was not British, and which would therefore be unfamiliar with the practices of the British constitution. The whites were also outnumbered by free non-whites, for the island had not, under Spanish rule, been committed to producing sugar. It was, indeed, extremely sparsely populated and it seemed to the British to present an excellent opportunity to break away from the assembly system. When further additions were made to the empire at the end of the Napoleonic Wars in 1815, these territories too came under crown colony government without assemblies. Later in the nineteenth century, the assemblies were abolished in most of the other West Indian islands (see pages 150–1). Although the assemblies had never represented more than the most privileged section of the white community, they were nevertheless the first parliamentary institutions in the West Indies. Before parliamentary institutions were to blossom again in the twentieth century, the British apparently thought it necessary to move to a less sophisticated system of government.

Meanwhile, the social structure in the British islands was in many ways similar to that in the French islands, described on pages 86–7, the product of the sugar economy. But while the French colony of St Domingue was poised on the edge of a mass-rebellion by the non-whites towards the end of the eighteenth century, the British estate owner was threatened much more by the quickening campaign against the slave trade and the institution of slavery.

Exercises

1 See No. 4 of the Exercises on page 77.

2 'Sugar estates worked on rather small profit margins' (page 79). Explain what this statement means, and account for the fact that eighteenth-century estates did not make more substantial profits.

3 Describe how sugar was processed on an estate in the eighteenth century from the cutting of the cane to the loading of the ships.

4 In what ways did African slaves on West Indian sugar estates respond to the slavery-based society in which they lived in the eighteenth century? Suggest reasons why organized large-scale rebellions occurred comparatively rarely.

5 Write two letters to the British government, dated 1800, *the first* from a British governor who argues that the assemblies in Britain's older West Indian colonies should be abolished, *the second* from an estate owner who argues that these assemblies should be preserved. *In each case*, arguments should be stated clearly and supported with historical information.

6 To what extent did 'Metropolitan Control' lead to major differences between the Spanish islands, French islands and British islands in the ways that the islands were governed in the eighteenth century?

7 Explain what particular hardships in the eighteenth century faced West Indians who were (a) non-white but free and (b) white but poor.

8 The Anglo-French Imperial Conflict in the Caribbean

Wars and More Wars

In 1661, Louis XIV came of age, taking personal control of France at the death of Cardinal Mazarin. In 1815, Napoleon I, the Emperor of France, was defeated at Waterloo and was sent into exile. The period between 1661 and 1815 was one in which wars occurred frequently between France and England (Britain, see Glossary). The causes of these wars were many and varied, but colonial and economic rivalry almost always played a major part. In the middle of the eighteenth century, when the wars were at their height, France and Britain were struggling for the mastery of both north America and India and, inevitably, French and British islands in the West Indies were caught up in the struggle. Other European nations were also involved in the conflicts. During this period, Spain declined as a major power and the Dutch lost their commercial supremacy. Britain made colonial gains at the expense both of Spain and the Netherlands, and the Spanish empire in the Americas began to move rapidly towards its extinction. France had also suffered major setbacks by 1815, losing its colonies in north America and India to the British, and St Domingue to the first successful independence movement in the West Indies.

Mention has already been made in Chapter 5 of the late seventeenth-century wars which helped to undermine the Dutch. The eighteenth century began with the War of the Spanish Succession (1702–13). In 1739, the War of Jenkins' Ear began, merging into the War of the Austrian Succession from 1740 to 1748. Since, in 1748, this War was inconclusive in its outcome, it was continued in the Seven Years War (1756–63). France had been defeated when the Seven Years War ended, but the British colonies in north America rebelled in 1776 and declared their independence and France then seized the opportunity to resume hostilities against Britain, assisting the Americans in their War of Independence (1776–83). The French Revolutionary Wars began in 1792, and Britain became involved in them within a year. There was a brief lull with the Treaty of Amiens in 1802, but the fighting began again almost immediately and the conflict, now known as the Napoleonic Wars, lasted until 1815, by which time the French had suffered a major defeat.

Time and again, the West Indies were caught up in these struggles. The importance of the wars for the West Indian colonies lay partly in the naval and military operations which took place in the Caribbean, partly in the changes of ownership which affected islands such as Grenada and Trinidad, but mainly in the economic and social dislocation which was caused by the wars. Dependent on the export of their produce and the import of their supplies, the West Indians were vulnerable to all interruptions of trade.

The Decline of Spain

Throughout the second half of the seventeenth century, once-mighty Spain lingered and then died as a great power; as the last Habsburg ruler of Spain, Charles II, lingered, a chronic invalid, and died in 1700, leaving Europe in turmoil over the succession to Spain and its empire. Europe had waited a long time for the sickly Charles II to die. For years it had seemed unlikely that he would produce an heir and his vast possessions riveted the attention of Europe, making bulletins on the King's health a matter of constant international interest. In Spain itself, economic stagnation and religious bigotry produced a suitably gloomy environment for the dying ruler. Shortly before Charles had become king, the English had snatched Jamaica. While he reigned, Spain was forced to recognize the English and French West Indian islands in the Treaties of Madrid and Ryswick. When he died, he vainly hoped to write the last chapter in the long series of intrigues about the Spanish succession by leaving everything in his will to the French prince, Philip of Anjou. But, in fact, Charles was writing only the opening paragraph to the War of the Spanish Succession.

The major European countries, among them Britain, were simply unwilling to risk the possibility that Prince Philip or one of his descendants might one day inherit not only all the possessions of the Habsburg rulers of Spain but also all the possessions of the Bourbon rulers of France. Louis XIV of France, however, would not give up such a tempting prospect without a struggle, and the issue was settled in the War of the Spanish Succession and the Treaty of Utrecht which ended it. Peace came largely as a result of exhaustion—neither side won an outright victory. With few allies, France and Spain had resisted the onslaughts of the British, the Dutch and much of Europe, but had been quite unable to overwhelm their enemies. At Utrecht, Louis XIV had to agree that the French and Spanish thrones should never be merged and to accept the partitioning of the Spanish possessions in Europe. But he was able to ensure that Philip kept Spain itself together with the overseas Spanish empire. Britain concentrated on obtaining colonial rewards which included full possession of St Kitts, no longer to be shared with the French, territories such as Newfoundland in north America, and European bases such as Gibraltar. Britain also obtained the *Asiento* (see page 83), which conferred the right to supply slaves to the Spanish empire, together with the privilege of sending one ship a year to trade at Porto Bello, the most important market in central America. For the first time, therefore, Spain was forced to accept and legalize British trade with Spanish America.

Strict conditions were laid down under which this trade could take place. The *Asiento* was granted for only thirty years, and the size of the one vessel to Porto Bello was strictly limited. But there was recurring trouble when the British tried to cheat. The 'one ship' became a sort of off-shore depot. When its cargoes were landed to be sold at the fair, they were replaced by new cargoes, brought by other vessels; and these, in turn, could be unloaded the next day. Angry Spaniards tried to hunt down the smugglers, and recriminations about the alleged cruelties of Spaniards and Englishmen echoed around the Caribbean as they had once done in the days of Drake. It is easy to exaggerate the importance of the trading concessions made to the British at Utrecht and the affairs off Porto Bello which resulted from them. The trade was handled by the British South Sea Company, and the Company thought Porto Bello important enough to warrant only eight voyages in the thirty years of the contract; after 1733, no voyage was made at all. But by that time, it appears that the Spaniards had sliced off an ear from Robert Jenkins, the captain of a British ship in the Caribbean. The ear, pickled and preserved, turned up some years later in the British House of Commons, and Britain declared war on Spain in 1739 in a storm of national indignation. Dubbed the War of Jenkins' Ear, it was simply the outcome of national jealousies, fed by stories of wrongs, real and imagined.

The war took on more importance in 1740 when it became part of a major European war in which Britain fought against France. France was by now a more worthwhile enemy for the British than was Spain. But on a variety of occasions when France was at war with Britain in the eighteenth century, Spain was involved as a French ally; and this sequence of wars weakened Spain still further. The Spanish monopoly of trade with their American empire crumbled and the *Asiento* system was in due course abandoned. Eventually, the empire itself collapsed.

In part, the empire was eaten away by foreign conquest. The British seized Trinidad in 1797 and consolidated their hold on part of Honduras. Part of Hispaniola had already been ceded to the French in the Treaty of Ryswick in 1697 and the rest of the island was lost in 1795 when the French named the whole of Hispaniola, St Domingue. Spain regained the Spanish part of the island, Santo Domingo, in 1808, but the recovery was short-lived. The inhabitants of Santo Domingo wanted independence and they secured it in 1821. The Spaniards kept Puerto Rico and Cuba until 1898 (see pages 131–3), but the rest of the empire on the mainland became independent at about the same time as Santo Domingo.

Independence first came to the Americas when Britain's north American colonies blazed the trail in 1776, immortalizing their principles in the

Declaration of Independence. The rebellion of St Domingue against the French and the proclamation of the independent non-white state of Haiti in 1804 provided the Spanish colonies with a second example to follow. Nationalist ideas were beginning to spread like wildfire at the beginning of the nineteenth century, both in the Americas and in Europe, and the Portuguese and Spanish empires were both beginning to totter. Portugal and Spain were beset with problems in Europe. During the Napoleonic Wars, both were invaded by the French, and Napoleon placed his brother Joseph on the Spanish throne for a time. When the Wars ended, the people of Portugal and Spain demanded more liberal government than that which had been practised in the past and their rulers were preoccupied with the problem of keeping their thrones: they had few resources to spare for the business of preserving their American empires where nationalists were clamouring for independence.

It seemed possible, however, that other European monarchies would send armed forces to the Americas to restore the authority of the kings of Portugal and Spain. But they were delayed by rebellions in Europe and obstructed by the British. Finally, President Monroe of the USA forced them to abandon their ambitions. It would be advantageous for Britain if the Portuguese and Spanish colonies could make good their claims to independence. During the wars which ended in 1815, Britain had used its naval supremacy to strengthen its trading links with the Americas, and British merchants had no wish to see the restoration of the old trading monopolies which Portugal and Spain had always claimed. Castlereagh and Canning, the British Foreign Secretaries after 1815, both defended the right of the Portuguese and Spanish colonies to be independent and to choose their own partners in trade. But the most decisive event was probably the issuing of the Monroe Doctrine in 1823. The essence of the Monroe Doctrine was that,

> 'the American continents are henceforth not to be considered as subjects for future colonization by any European powers.'

European powers who refused to accept this principle would be guilty of

> 'the manifestation of an unfriendly disposition towards the United States.'

It was argued that the mainland colonies had successfully rejected European government during the recent European wars and their disturbed aftermath, and it was now clear that the USA would not tolerate an attempt to restore European control. On the other hand, Monroe indicated that the USA would not interfere with existing colonies nor with Europe itself. Without allies, neither Portugal nor Spain had the strength or the determination to challenge Monroe's declaration; and the monarchies of Europe faced too many problems of their own to risk a conflict with the USA and perhaps with Britain too. One after another, the mainland colonies and Santo Domingo asserted that they were, indeed, independent. The Portuguese and Spanish empires on the mainland disappeared to be replaced by new states such as Brazil, Mexico and Colombia. These were virtually guaranteed by Monroe and quickly recognized by Canning. With some pardonable exaggeration, Canning boasted that *he* had 'called a New World into existence to redress the balance of the Old'.

The USA itself took over parts of the Spanish empire, eventually absorbing Florida and much more into the Union. There were those in the United States who had visions of extending the influence of Washington further southwards, into the formerly Spanish territories, and here were the seeds of a new imperialism (see pages 127–8). But for the moment, the USA was more interested in expanding westwards and in extending the Union to the Pacific Ocean. The Monroe Doctrine, therefore, provided an opportunity for the new countries of central and south America to begin to develop their individual identities as free nations. For Spain, all that was left of the vast empire was Cuba and Puerto Rico.

The Eclipse of France

When the War of the Spanish Succession ended and when Louis XIV died in 1715, the French West Indian possessions were still intact except for the loss of their share of St Kitts. But the long reign of Louis XV, who died in 1774, saw a more determined Anglo-French struggle for colonial supremacy. Warfare from 1740 to 1748 was largely indecisive, and the Treaty of Aix-la-Chapelle which ended it settled nothing. But in 1763, at the end of the Seven Years War, France had to make extensive concessions.

St Lucia was in French hands after the War of American Independence. It often changed hands during the eighteenth century (St Lucia, 1974)

It was during these years that interest developed in the *neutral islands* which the Treaty of Aix-la-Chapelle listed as Dominica, St Lucia, St Vincent and Tobago. These islands had been generally neglected before the eighteenth century, because they were comparatively small and waspish Caribs made them inhospitable. Migrants from the French and English islands sometimes settled on them in small numbers and, following the example of the Dutch, used them as trading posts where provisions, timber and even slaves were on sale. Deals could be done without worrying about nationality and national monopolies and without the meddling of government officials. But eighteenth-century wars focused attention on the neutral islands. They had strategic possibilities and could become useful bases, for harrying the enemy or supporting a nation's own colonies. The French showed more interest in them than the British in the early years. France had taken control of Grenada in the middle of the seventeenth century, and St Vincent and St Lucia then seemed to be natural stepping-stones from Grenada to Martinique, as Dominica could be a stepping-stone from Martinique to Guadeloupe. The French reoccupied St Lucia in 1744, but this was not to Britain's liking and, since the Treaty of Aix-la-Chapelle was based on restoring the *status quo*, Britain and France then agreed that the neutral islands should belong to neither of them.

The Treaty of Paris, in 1763, reached a quite different conclusion. By that time, France had been soundly defeated in the Seven Years War and St Domingue was the only French colony in the West Indies which had escaped capture. Fortunately for the French, Britain was prepared to bargain. The British thought trophies on the north American mainland more important than West Indian islands, whose output of sugar might flood the English market and alarm the producers in the English islands. France was thus allowed to regain Guadeloupe, Martinique and St Lucia in return for concessions elsewhere. On the other hand, Britain took Grenada, and added the neutral islands of Dominica, St Vincent and Tobago to its empire.

In 1778, France joined the Americans in their War of Independence. The new war seemed to offer a splendid opportunity to regain lost ground in the West Indies and to take revenge on Britain. For a few years, naval guns thundered again across the Caribbean while national flags were run up and down the flag-poles of the smaller islands. The British were defeated in north America and were content to emerge from the Treaty of Versailles (1783) with the loss to the French of nothing more than Tobago. France had had the better of it during much of the fighting,

Admiral Rodney, the victor in the Battle of the Saints. A British naval squadron was based in Antigua (Antigua, 1970)

Figure 8.1 The Guianas after 1815

but a late victory by Admiral Rodney in the Battle of the Saints saved Jamaica from surrendering to the French and enabled the British to preserve almost all of their West Indian empire.

Six years after the Treaty of Versailles, the French Revolution began. Inflamed by exciting slogans about Liberty and Equality, St Domingue flared into rebellion which the French were powerless to contain. The European wars which followed the French Revolution again came to the West Indies, and once again islands changed hands. There were early French successes in the smaller islands, but more sweeping British victories in the later stages of the conflict. In 1810, Britain held almost all of the West Indies except for the two largest islands—Cuba and what had once been Hispaniola. When peace was made, France was allowed to take back only Guadeloupe and Martinique and the tiny islands of Marie Galante, St Bartholomew and St Martin.

The general peace settlement in London, Paris and Vienna in 1814–15 also sorted out the problems of ownership in Guiana. France was allowed to keep French Guiana, the colony which dated from 1674 and centred on Cayenne. The Dutch had, on occasions, helped the French in the recent wars and so Britain now took its pick of the Dutch overseas possessions. The Dutch settlements on the Rivers Demerara, Berbice and Essequibo had been overrun by British forces and Britain decided to keep them, merging them to form the colony of British Guiana in 1831. Elsewhere, Britain took Ceylon and the Cape of Good Hope from the Dutch. But the Dutch were allowed to keep Surinam (Dutch Guiana), and to recover islands such as Curaçao which had also been lost during the fighting.

The year 1815 marked the end of the wars of empire for the West Indies. The lines of demarcation had now been drawn and, in some ways, it was Britain which emerged from the centuries of struggle as the most forceful colonizing power in the West Indies. The British held mainland territories in Guiana and Honduras, the islands of Jamaica and Trinidad, most of the Lesser Antilles and a miscellany of small islands from the Caymans to the Bahamas and the Bermudas. Future struggles in the West Indies would not be about the national rivalries of European powers. What mattered now was whether slavery should continue; how the islands were to be developed; and, ultimately, when and how they were to follow in the footsteps of the USA and Haiti and achieve their independence.

Table 8.1 The Eighteenth-Century Wars of Empire: the Possession of West Indian Colonies

		Ryswick 1697		*Utrecht 1713*		*Aix-la-Chapelle 1748*		*Paris 1763*		*Versailles 1783*		*Amiens 1802*		*Paris, London 1815*	
	Treaties														
	Wars		*Spanish Succession 1702–13*		*Jenkins' Ear Austrian Succession 1739–48*		*Seven Years 1756–63*		*American Independence 1776–83*		*Revolutionary 1792–1802*		*Napoleonic 1803–15*		*After 1815*
	Cuba	Spanish	Spanish	Spanish	Spanish	Spanish	★ part	Spanish	Spanish	Spanish	Spanish	Spanish	Spanish	Spanish	Independent 1898
	Puerto Rico	Spanish	Spanish	Spanish	Spanish	Spanish	Spanish	Spanish	Spanish	Spanish	Spanish	Spanish	Spanish	Spanish	To the USA 1899
Hispaniola	Santo Domingo	Spanish	Spanish	Spanish	Spanish	Spanish	Spanish	Spanish	Spanish	Spanish	★	French	★	Spanish	Independent 1821
Hispaniola	St Domingue	French	French	French	French	French	French	French	French	French	Revolution Haiti (Independent 1804)				
	Trinidad	Spanish	Spanish	Spanish	Spanish	Spanish	Spanish	Spanish	Spanish	Spanish	★	British	British	British	Independent 1962
	Guadeloupe	French	French	French	French	French	★	French	French	French	★	French	★	French	French Département 1946
	Martinique	French	French	French	French	French	★	French	French	French	★	French	★	French	French Département 1946
	Grenada	French	French	French	French	French	★	British	★	British	★	British	British	British	Independent 1974
	St Kitts	French British	★ British	British	British	British	British	British	★	British	British	British	British	British	Associated State 1967
	Barbados	British	British	British	British	British	British	British	British	British	British	British	British	British	Independent 1966
	Jamaica	British	British	British	British	British	British	British	British	British	British	British	British	British	Independent 1962
Neutral Islands	Dominica					Neutral	British	British	★	British	★	British	British	British	Associated State 1967
Neutral Islands	St Lucia				French	Neutral	British	French	★	French	★	French	★	British	Associated State 1967
Neutral Islands	St Vincent					Neutral	British	British	★	British	★	British	British	British	Associated State 1969
Neutral Islands	Tobago					Neutral	British	British	★	French	★	French	★	British	Linked with Trinidad
	Surinam	Dutch	Dutch	Dutch	Dutch	Dutch	Dutch	Dutch	★	Dutch	★	Dutch	★	Dutch	Independent 1975
	Berbice, Demerara and Essequibo	Dutch	Dutch	Dutch	Dutch	Dutch	Dutch	Dutch	★	Dutch	★	Dutch	★	British	Independent (Guyana) 1966

Spanish ▣ French ☰ British Dutch ○ Neutral

★ Captured in wartime: change of ownership temporary or permanent

Meanwhile, for West Indians, the wars which ended in 1815 had other results beyond that of changing the allegiances of many of the Caribbean territories (see Table 8.1).

The Effects of the Conflicts on the West Indies

The Scars of Battle

The most spectacular events in the West Indies of the eighteenth-century wars were the large-scale expeditions, which European governments occasionally mounted, and the naval engagements between rival fleets. An example of the former was the British expedition under Admiral Vernon which was mounted during the War of Jenkins' Ear. The most outstanding example of the latter was the Battle of the Saints in 1782.

West Indians, especially those on the British islands, argued vigorously that defence was the responsibility of the mother country, and that their own part in it went no further than amateur service in a local militia for the defence of their own properties. It was, therefore, the job of the mother country to provide professional troops. This immediately gave rise to disputes about how these troops were to be paid for, and whether they

Figure 8.2 The West Indies in 1815: the End of the Wars of Empire

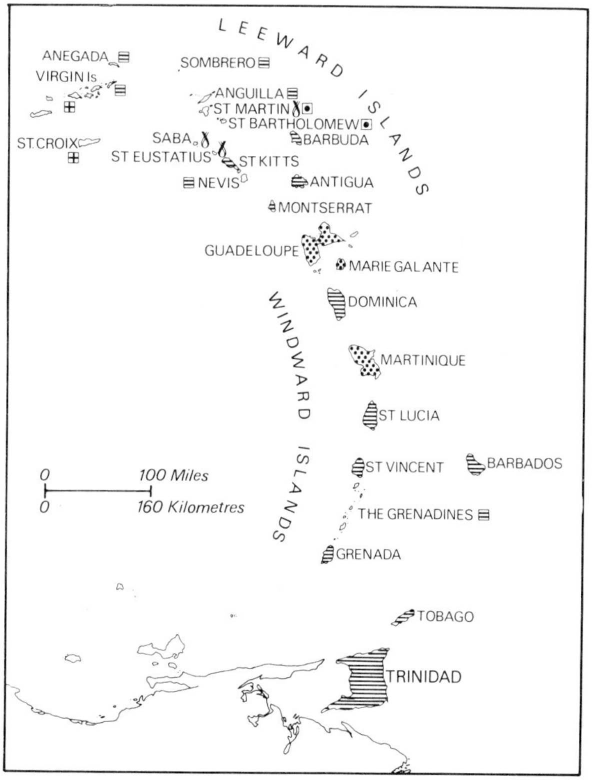

should be billeted on the settlers. One result of the wars was an increase in taxation in the colonies: the British increased the export duty on sugar before 1783, which plunged some estate owners into bankruptcy. The professional troops, for which the increased taxes helped to pay, also brought their own commanders to the West Indies, and another result of the wars was a conflict of authority between these commanders and the colonial governors.

But the professional troops were seldom effective. Most of them were new to the tropical climate and the expeditions were always ravaged by disease. Vernon's expedition had some success in 1739, doing damage to Porto Bello, but when some 15 000 men assaulted Cartagena two years later they failed dismally. Only a fraction of the force was killed in battle, but malaria and yellow fever wiped out more than 10 000 of them, leaving the disease-ridden remnant to limp back to their base in Jamaica. A year later, in 1742, Vernon made an unsuccessful attempt to plunder

Santiago de Cuba and then turned again to Porto Bello where he had at least had some success. This time, disease struck again and once more the expedition met only failure. Even the buccaneers had seldom been so uniformly ineffectual, but they had had the advantage of being hardened to the climate.

In the Anglo-French struggle, expeditions were more concerned with seizing islands than with ravaging mainland fortresses. Naval supremacy usually determined the outcome of such expeditions, for with the possible exceptions of St Domingue and Jamaica, the white populations of the islands were too small for successful defence, even where professional garrisons manned the forts. At first, the British stationed two naval squadrons in the West Indies, one at Port Royal in Jamaica, the other at English Harbour in Antigua. The French relied on annual fleets sent out from Europe. But both retreated from the Caribbean in the hurricane season, usually departing in July for the waters of north America. Not surprisingly, these fleets provided only patchy protection and both sides continued the practice of employing privateers. In any case, the naval forces were thinly stretched, concerned as much with the protection of shipping as with the defence of the islands.

The skirmishing of the early eighteenth century, when the outright capture of islands was rare, gave way to more determined operations in the second half of the century. In the Seven Years War, Britain gained naval supremacy and, by co-ordinating naval and military forces more effectively, captured all the French islands except St Domingue. When Spain joined the war in a vain attempt to remove British log-cutters from Honduras, even parts of Cuba fell to British raids, though Cuba was among the territories restored at the Treaty of Paris. The importance of sea power was now self-evident and during the American War of Independence, the French showed that they had learned the lesson. Count D'Estaing quickly collected for France such trophies as Dominica. In the later stages of this War the French aimed for a greater prize, the capture of Jamaica. The British Admiral Rodney hastened to Jamaica's defence against the French expedition under Admiral de Grasse. The scene was set for the Battle of the Saints, a tiny group of islands north of Dominica, where the rival fleets met. The British victory in this battle once again tilted the balance of power in the West Indies against the French.

Sea power was decisive again in the wars of 1793 to 1815. Islands changed hands rapidly in the early stages. 1794 was a good year for the British when almost nothing remained in French hands. 1795 brought French successes; but almost immediately, the tide turned again in Britain's favour. Sea power gave Britain a marked advantage and Martinique, for example, was continuously in British hands from 1794 to 1802. It was then restored to France at the Treaty of Amiens. The most important naval battles at this time were fought in European waters. The Battle of Trafalgar, in 1805, proved the most decisive, and this British victory effectively settled the fate of the West Indies. French naval power had now been destroyed and thereafter, almost at will, the British were able to prey on enemy shipping and to overrun every one of the French islands.

The Caribbean islands were thus trapped in this web of international conflict. Physical damage in the West Indies should not be exaggerated.

The Battle of the Saints: the British close with the *Ville de Paris*, flagship of Admiral de Grasse

Forts, settlements and harbours were sacked from time to time and plantations laid waste; casualties could be heavy, but the heaviest toll was that taken by tropical fevers of the forces fresh from Europe. The worst scars which were left in the West Indies, however, resulted less from destructive battles and the depredations of raiding parties, than from the regular dislocation of the economies and societies. Service in the militias diverted manpower from more constructive work. More seriously, the wars frequently disrupted shipping and this, with the changes of ownership in individual islands, played havoc with established markets and patterns of trade. The sugar islands were not dynamic societies and constructive development was slow at the best of times, based as they were on a slave economy. But the wars created great uncertainty: they discouraged investment and hampered the development of a settled and forward-looking population which could feel a commitment to a secure future in the West Indies. Thus, it was in its economic and social effects that this period of turbulence was at its most damaging.

The Economic Effects

In wartime, sometimes even between the wars, trading ships were seriously at risk of being sunk or captured, so it sometimes seemed wise not to sail at all. This had two disastrous consequences for the West Indies: one was that vital services were interrupted; the other was that prices moved in adverse directions. These consequences had their effect on both imports and exports. The interruption of imports usually meant hunger, a shortage of estate equipment and a shortage of slaves; and when food, equipment and slaves did become available, they were likely to be more expensive. The interruption of exports meant the accumulation of unsold sugar and other produce, and from this followed a shortage of money which their sale would have brought; and when the produce was exported and it successfully crossed the Atlantic, the market was likely to be glutted and the prices depressed accordingly. This was especially likely to be the case if enemy sugar islands had been captured and their output was added to the produce on the market. Even when the wars gave the plantation owners a momentary advantage by making sugar scarce in Europe so that prices were high, there was a counter-balancing disadvantage in that this only stimulated the Europeans to seek supplies elsewhere—from the East and, later, from sugar-beet which could be grown in Europe itself. There was the further special difficulty for the British islands that the declaration of independence by the USA meant that there was no longer a protected market for British produce on the eastern seaboard of north America, nor a reliable supply-source for cheap foodstuffs and timber.

It was largely due to the independence of the USA and the turbulence caused by the wars that, after about 1775, the sugar estates in the British islands began to lose their profitability. In the 1770s and 1780s almost 200 estates in Jamaica were either abandoned, or sold, to pay off their owners' debts. The planters usually relied upon the sale of their sugar crop to meet their commitments. Indeed, most of the money which came from the sale of the crop in Europe tended to remain there, repaying loans, paying off duties and transport charges, purchasing new supplies, and perhaps discharging the personal obligations of a planter to his relatives. The non-arrival of the crop or depressed prices could quickly involve the estate owner in a spiral of debt. The wars, therefore, played havoc with what had become the normal trading routine of the West Indies.

But the wars took place against a background of other factors which should not be ignored. One was that French sugar production was becoming more competitive than British production. St Domingue gave the French the advantage both of space and an extremely fertile soil. They could not sell their sugar on the British market, but by the 1780s they supplied most of the needs of continental Europe and left little opportunity for the British producers to sell anywhere but in Britain. In this connection, Britain's loss of the American colonies was vital because, having successfully achieved independence, the USA preferred to buy French sugar. Yet the treaties of 1763 and 1783 had added sugar-growing islands to the British empire, producing the combination of an increased crop and a shrinking market. The revolution in St Domingue in the 1790s, and the capture by the British of yet more sugar-growing areas, including those of the Dutch settlements in Guiana, might have been expected to bring the British planters some relief. The revolution ruined sugar production in St Domingue, destroying the principal competitor; and as Britain had now

Bligh's belly-filling breadfruit. Present-day harvesting of the breadfruit which Captain Bligh brought from Tahiti to Jamaica in 1789

come near to having a monopoly of West Indian sugar islands, buyers might have been expected to come to the British for their sugar. But it was precisely at this time that Cuba turned more seriously to sugar production, making considerable inroads into the American market. Moreover, the Napoleonic Wars at the beginning of the nineteenth century disrupted the established patterns of Europe's trade, causing the development of new commercial links which included links with the East, where additional supplies of sugar could be obtained. France itself, blockaded by the British, at this time encouraged the widespread planting of sugar-beet.

Another problem which harassed the plantation owner in the late eighteenth century was that of rising costs. The demand for slaves throughout the Americas was growing, and the demand drove up the price. By 1750, there were about 300 000 slaves in the British colonies in north America. Thirty years later, the number had doubled and it went on rising as 'King Cotton' prospered in the southern states. The high mortality rate of slaves in the West Indies and the constant need to replace them faced the planter with an expense which was now beginning to soar. Other supplies also became more expensive, partly because of wartime scarcities and partly because of the loss to the British West Indies of much north American trade after 1776. In the last quarter of the eighteenth century, the cost of timber, cattle, horses, salted beef and salted fish rose sharply, sometimes by 100 per cent. In these circumstances, feeding the slave labour force and adequately equipping the estate imposed a formidable strain on the plantation economies. Planters were forced to re-examine old practices, to become more self-sufficient where possible, and perhaps even to treat their slaves better. One breakthrough was made, however. Having found the breadfruit growing wild on the islands of the South Seas, the British fitted out the *Bounty* to bring such plants to the West Indies. Under the notorious Captain William Bligh, the *Bounty* sailed from Tahiti for Jamaica in 1789. Bligh himself was cast adrift when the crew mutinied, but the breadfruit survived to become a staple food on many a plantation.

At this time, whatever the difficulties, it was still taken for granted that the function of the West Indian islands was to produce sugar. By 1815, there was a greater emphasis on by-products such as rum, which might help to improve profitability, but progress towards any diversification of the crops was strictly limited. Where the tradition already existed for the growing of, for example, tobacco, ginger, coffee and cocoa, these crops continued. Occasionally, there was a slight change of emphasis: for instance in Jamaica coffee-growing was taken more seriously at the end of the eighteenth century, but sugar remained dominant. Therefore, until well into the nineteenth century, though patches were applied where necessary, the economic fabric of the West Indies changed little.

War and Society

Why, when the British in north America rebelled against European control in 1776, did the whites in the West Indies remain loyal? The answer to this question lies, largely, in certain essential differences between the society in America and that in the West Indies at this time. The West Indian white, far from radiating self-confidence about his destiny, often seemed to be beleaguered amidst a variety of perils. After the Treaty of Paris in 1763, the French threat to the British colonies in north America had been removed, but in the West Indies the British islands still felt the need for a defence which only the mother country could supply. Whites in the West Indies were also few in number and geographically scattered. They had little sense of any West Indian unity compared with that which was developing in the colonies of north America. Far from feeling a yearning for independence, the most prosperous West Indian whites tended to look forward to a time when, having built up a fortune, they could return to Europe. Like the north Americans they were annoyed by the taxes, the trade restrictions and the meddling of the colonial governors. But, unlike the north Americans, they felt they had neither the strength nor the self-sufficiency to be able to sever their ties with Britain. They were, for example, utterly dependent on the British sugar market, the loss of which would be disastrous.

The confidence of West Indian whites was also undermined by the huge slave communities over which they presided. The garrisons of British troops gave some protection against the French but they also seemed to offer a comforting support against rebellious Africans. To talk of independence could itself be dangerous: it could be the match which set fire to the powder keg of slave resentment. In Nevis, the assembly insisted that if British soldiers were billeted on the planters they

A mass rising of African slaves erupted in St Domingue in 1791 and eventually brought independence to Haiti—a French print

should earn their keep by working in the fields alongside the Africans. But at the same time, they were grateful for the added security of the presence of the soldiers. Poor whites, for their part, were fearful of the mulattoes, and of a political change which could trigger off a social revolution in which colour might no longer determine social status. So when the Americans rebelled, the West Indians remained loyal, albeit with a grumbling reluctance. The assemblies of Jamaica and Barbados fired darts to sting the British government by expressing their sympathies with the Americans. Beyond that, they did not dare to go.

The independence of the USA had one beneficial result for the West Indies. Empire Loyalists, who wished to remain under British rule, left the States for areas such as Canada and the West Indies which remained British. For the first time, the Bahamas secured a substantial influx of settlers. Other settlers helped to increase the white populations of British islands such as Jamaica where there was still land to be had.

From War to Peace

The closing stages of the wars to which this chapter has referred coincided with a ferment of new and often exciting ideas. The second half of the eighteenth century in Europe was an age of Reason, an age of Enlightenment. New ideas stirred; many old ideas were challenged. Soldiers from France fought alongside the Americans in their War of Independence, and returned to France to add fuel to the criticisms of privilege and inefficiency. In 1789, Revolution broke out in France itself. In 1776, Adam Smith had published *The Wealth of Nations,* and vigorously attacked mercantilism. Ten years later, Thomas Clarkson published his *Essay on Slavery,* and helped to found the Society for Effecting the Abolition of the Slave Trade, in 1787. This was a time when the missionary societies were becoming increasingly active in the West Indies and, not infrequently, the missionaries appeared to challenge the very basis of the plantation societies. Some of the Loyalists who came to the West Indies from north America brought their slaves, and among these slaves were Moses Baker and George Lisle who founded the Baptist Church in Jamaica, and inspired Christianity in the island with a new evangelical spirit.

When the wars of empire ended in 1815, the foundations of the slavery-based sugar economies were beginning to crumble. The British had declared the slave trade illegal in 1807, and slavery was tottering but not yet extinct. Mercantilism was dying but not yet dead. Independence had come to the whites in the USA and the blacks in Haiti, and was sweeping across the mainland of central and south America. In Europe, the old order was being attacked on all sides. There were movements towards more liberal political systems in many European countries. And, beginning in Britain, there spread a wave of industrialization which was bringing in its wake fundamental social and economic changes. Inevitably, changes were imminent too in the West Indies. Chapter 9 will consider one of the first and most important of these changes, the gaining of freedom by the Africans.

Exercises

1 Name the chief neutral islands at the beginning of the eighteenth century. Why had these islands been left largely unsettled by Europeans? What were the changes which took place in their political ownership during the eighteenth century?

2 What developments, in the century from 1715 to 1815 and in relation to the West Indies, made it possible to speak of (a) the decline of Spain and (b) the eclipse of France?

3 'The Caribbean islands were ... trapped in a web of international conflict' (page 96). Illustrate the truth of this statement for the years 1701 to 1815, and show how it affected the well-being of the islands which the British already held at the beginning of the eighteenth century.

4 Compare the attitudes towards Britain in the second half of the eighteenth century of the colonists in north America and the settlers in the West Indies. What were the eighteenth-century effects on the West Indies of the establishment of the USA?

5 'Almost 200 estates in Jamaica were either abandoned or sold ... in the 1770s and 1780s' (page 97). Imagine yourself to have been the owner of one of these estates, and list and explain the reasons why you decided to abandon your estate.

6 Find out as much as you can by further reading about *one* of the eighteenth-century wars mentioned in this chapter in so far as it affected the West Indies. Write an account of the war from the West Indian point of view, illustrating your account with a detailed map.

9 Freedom

I PROTEST AND REFORM

In the 1790s, rebellions in the West Indies were almost as much a part of the wars as were military operations against enemy territories. Insurrection was infectious. The Revolution in France and that which followed it in St Domingue provided inspiration for all who were discontented. The Europeans also found it useful to stir up insurrections against their enemies, a tactic which the French often employed in the islands which the British took from them. The Caribs joined in the fray in St Vincent and struck at their new masters. About the same time, in 1795, revolutionary emissaries from St Domingue unsettled the maroons in Jamaica where a maroon rebellion broke out. Tension was present in most West Indian societies and many in the lower classes felt a deep sense of grievance. But the danger which was feared most by those in authority was that of a mass-rising of African slaves. This danger was especially terrifying in the sugar islands and the Guianas where the white populations were perilously small.

The French Revolution had begun in 1789, and slogans about 'liberty, equality and fraternity' quickly reached the West Indies. In 1794, French Republicans declared that slavery was at an end in the colonies of the French empire (see page 102). However, they may have been more concerned to enlist the goodwill and help of the Africans against the British forces which were then invading St Domingue, than genuinely to spread the brotherhood of man. Certainly the declaration proved a false dawn, for the Republicans were overthrown and slavery was reaffirmed. But change and reform were clearly no longer impossible.

The maroon rebellion in Jamaica alarmed the British in case too much change should happen too quickly, and in case the rebellion should spread to the slaves. Europeans had learned to live with the fact that maroons and bush Negroes existed. Wherever the sugar estates were surrounded by large expanses of land, for example in the Guianas, that land was likely to shelter runaway slaves and other refugees from eighteenth-century society. Slaves were too valuable to be allowed to run free, but recapture was sometimes impossible and the authorities had no alternative but to tolerate the unofficial societies which developed in the more remote parts of the larger colonies. One such society was that of the Jamaican maroons. They had been peaceful since an earlier uprising in 1734, when the governor of the island had confirmed their possession of land and agreed to leave them unmolested. In return, Jamaican maroons usually sent newly runaway slaves back to the plantations. The maroon communities were well run on co-operative lines and, as long as they kept themselves to themselves, the Europeans were inclined to leave them alone. In 1795, however, the Jamaican maroons attacked the plantations. Military units were at hand because of the war against France, and retribution was swift and thorough. The maroons were routed. Then they were hunted down with bloodhounds, and shipped out of the island, to be dumped—at a safe distance—on the chilly shores of Nova Scotia.

Except in St Domingue, the mass-rising of Africans which was feared did not occur. The independence movements which shortly afterwards swept across the Spanish mainland were the protests not of African slaves but of creoles and mulattoes. And the abolition of, first, the slave trade and then of slavery itself was the work of the more enlightened and humanitarian of the Europeans. Denmark was the first European country to renounce the slave trade, three years after the French Revolution proclaimed its ideals of liberty and equality. The British followed suit in 1807, and then the USA, Sweden and the Netherlands in swift succession. France delayed until 1818. The Revolution had been followed by the Consulate in 1799, when Napoleon Bonaparte was the

First Consul; Napoleon made himself the Emperor in 1804, and it was not until the monarchy was restored, on Napoleon's defeat, that France gave up the slave trade. Spain and Portugal renounced the trade in 1820 and 1836 respectively. The traffic in Africans across the Atlantic declined rapidly as the result of these renunciations, but slavery itself had still to be abolished.

Britain took the lead in this. In 1838, slavery came to an end throughout the British empire. Other countries again followed the lead only at intervals. Sweden was the first to act, but the Swedes had very few slaves anyway. France waited until 1848, when slavery was abolished by a new set of successful revolutionaries who overthrew the government of Louis Philippe. The Netherlands delayed until 1863, the USA until 1865. In the Spanish colonies, slavery continued even longer and slaves were only emancipated in Puerto Rico in 1873 and in Cuba in 1880.

II THE FRENCH EMPIRE

The Birth of Haiti

The first effect of the French Revolution in St Domingue was to trigger off a scramble among various vested interests. *Grands blancs* tried to get representation in the National Assembly, the new French parliament, and in the government of France. *Petits blancs* tried to improve their status, aiming to get a voice in the government of the colony if not in the National Assembly in Paris. Taking seriously what they heard about equality, the mulattoes aimed to achieve at least as much as the *petits blancs*. Laws had been passed only recently to exclude the mulattoes from certain appointments, to forbid them to carry firearms, and even to subject them to a curfew. Assemblies had been allowed in the French islands in 1787, and the whites had squabbled vigorously amongst themselves about who should be allowed to vote. They had generally agreed that mulattoes would not have the vote, but the mulattoes were now determined to get it and to repeal the laws which discriminated against them. The *petits blancs* were panic-stricken when the French National Assembly seemed to be about to grant the vote to free non-whites. The all-white Assembly in St Domingue argued fiercely that the government in France had no authority to decide the qualifications for voting in the colonies, and the whites of St Domingue struck at the mulattoes by eliminating their leaders. Vincent Ogé was seized and broken on the wheel, a martyr to the cause of the mulattoes.

St Domingue, at this time, had a white population of some 40 000 compared with a free non-white population of fewer than 30 000. Neither group gave much thought to the much vaster population of slaves, of whom there were well over 400 000. In 1791, the French National Assembly tried to solve the problem of voting qualifications by enfranchising only those non-whites who were free-born. The decision merely led to dissatisfaction, and skirmishing occurred between St Domingue's whites and the mulattoes. It was at this point that the slaves erupted, rampaging across the north of the island in the late summer of 1791, murdering their white tormentors and setting fire to the cane fields. They too had heard the heady slogans about liberty and equality.

The next few years in the colony were years of chaos. Revolutionaries arrived from France, bent upon enforcing equality between whites and free non-whites. The enemies of France, especially the British, welcomed the confusion as an opportunity to try to take control of St Domingue. But for all of them the slaves complicated the issue. The British were not able to take effective action against St Domingue because of the maroon rebellion in Jamaica and because of uncertainties about the loyalty of their own slaves. A new revolutionary commission arrived from France, led by Victor Hugues, and he brought a declaration that the French slaves were to be free. He also made certain that news of this would reach the slaves in the British colonies. The British successes of 1794, therefore, gave way to French victories in 1795, only for the tide to turn again in 1796 (see page 96).

A variety of conflicts were inter-twined in and around St Domingue. There were the national struggles, between the French and the British and between the French and the Spaniards—until Spain withdrew from the war in 1795 and at that time surrendered Santo Domingo to France. There were slave rebellions in search of freedom, and the slaves were assisted by revolutionaries from France and by the maroons who were numerous in St Domingue. There were conflicts between the various classes, each in pursuit of self-interest; and there was an ideological

Toussaint and Dessalines, the founders of Haiti, and Magloire, a twentieth-century ruler of the country (Haiti, 1954)

struggle, between those who wished to preserve the old order and those who were spreading the ideals of liberty and equality. Moreover, the ground shifted in 1795 when political events in France took a turn to the right: much more conservative forces came to power and they were hostile both to Victor Hugues and to the ending of slavery. French troops restored order in Guadeloupe, subdued the Africans and brought back the old order, reviving slavery in the island in 1802. Other French islands were seized by the British, and they too restored order and the traditional slavery-based economies and societies. The British commander, Ralph Abercromby, had many such successes among the small islands in spite of the constant toll taken of his troops by yellow fever. But he could not subdue St Domingue and, by 1798, the British had abandoned their ambitions there. St Domingue was defended by a resolute force of over 20 000 non-whites who were united in their determination that slavery should never be reintroduced into the colony. The British had only 1000 men in a fit condition to campaign. But the British were little perturbed: they had crushed the Jamaican maroons and seized most of the French West Indian possessions and, above all, their own slave populations showed little inclination to burst into open rebellion. The uprising in St Domingue had been virtually isolated.

Power in St Domingue was firmly in the hands of the Africans in 1798. Overall authority rested with Toussaint L'Ouverture, a former slave who was now a victorious general. Toussaint was willing to allow the colony to remain French, but he was not prepared to see any form of slavery restored there. The Africans had already created a black state and ruthlessly purged it of whites and mulattoes who clung to ideas of superiority. They had also driven away the British who would not have hesitated to restore slavery. At the time of the uprising in 1791, Toussaint had been a domestic slave, a coachman who had learned to read and write. He was now virtually the ruler of the colony. The French were powerless for the moment and, by 1801, Toussaint liberated Santo Domingo and was ready to embark on the construction of a new state in which the economy and the society would be very different from the old. Immense tasks lay ahead. The sugar plantations were in ruins and hardly anyone on the island had experience of government. Whether Toussaint would have been equal to the tasks he faced was not to be put to the test.

A new constitution was drafted in which Toussaint was named governor for life. The island would have an assembly, but Toussaint's powers were almost dictatorial. Although he recognized the overlordship of France, St Domingue/Santo Domingo would be well-nigh independent, for the laws which Toussaint and the assembly made would not need to be confirmed in Paris. Continued links with France were thought, however, to be valuable. The island might well need to rely on France for much of its trade, and the influence of France could clearly be seen in the constitution in such matters as the system of local government. But slavery was outlawed and the constitution also sought to ban racial discrimination in many aspects of life. The constitution was not democratic but, on paper, it seemed to provide the basis for an orderly future.

The French reply to the constitution of 1801 came in the form of an expedition, commanded by Charles Leclerc and sent by Napoleon Bonaparte. Leclerc had the support of Alexandre Pétion, an influential mulatto. Divide-and-rule tactics won Leclerc some early successes. He was able to take Toussaint prisoner and to despatch him to France, where a cold jail and too little food quickly killed the African leader. Before the end of the same year, 1803, Leclerc himself was also dead, the victim of yellow fever. Yellow fever also decimated the ranks of Leclerc's troops until they were no match for the Africans of St Domingue. New leaders took Toussaint's place: Jean Dessalines, Henri Christophe, and Pétion who had changed sides. In November, 1803, the French expedition was abandoned. On New Year's Day, 1804, Dessalines declared Haiti independent, and French rule never returned.

The subsequent history of Haiti was no success story, however. Dessalines survived for only two years. He proclaimed himself the Emperor Jacques, savaged the whites who remained in Haiti, and showed a ruthless intolerance towards all his opponents. Dessalines was assassinated in 1806 at the height of a conflict with the mulattoes. The island then became fragmented: Christophe and the Africans took control of the north and Pétion and the mulattoes took control of the south. The division was a stark demonstration of the fierce rivalry between the Africans and the mulattoes, and civil war inevitably followed. In the meantime, Spain regained control of Santo Domingo.

Pétion died in 1818 and was succeeded as leader of the mulatto part of Haiti by Jean Boyer. Christophe suffered a stroke and committed suicide in 1820. The result of these changes was that the mulattoes were able to overwhelm the Africans and to conquer the north. They also took over Santo Domingo again, after that state had renounced Spanish rule in 1821. This unification of the island was not to last, and Santo Domingo broke away in 1844 to become the independent Dominican Republic. Meanwhile, Boyer's rule had achieved very little of the constructive work which was desperately needed. Sugar production all but ceased and, as the plantations decayed, the economy stagnated. At the root of Haiti's troubles was the feud between the mulattoes and the Africans, a racial conflict which wasted the talents of the inhabitants in intrigue, political disruption and periods of civil war. The history of Haiti was one of dictatorship, corruption and disorder, which lasted well into the twentieth century and led eventually to the dismal rule of François Duvalier from 1957 to 1971. This was a sad outcome of the pioneering work of Toussaint and, although the blacks had eventually triumphed at the expense of the mulattoes, it was a triumph not of the African race but of the political thugs of the Tonton Macoute (see page 138).

Guadeloupe and Martinique

France regained Guadeloupe and Martinique from the British in 1815. The subsequent history of these French islands differed from that of the British sugar islands in two principal ways: the slaves had to wait longer for emancipation; and France preferred *assimilation* to the granting of independence in the twentieth century. Colonial empires were everywhere questioned after the Second World War and many new nations achieved their independence. But the French preferred a different arrangement for their overseas possessions in the West Indies, and they made Guadeloupe, Martinique and French Guiana into departments of metropolitan France. They are, therefore, politically, economically and socially, part of France—detached, as it were, by the accident of geography. Such an arrangement, as in the case of the Netherlands Antilles, presupposes that in certain pockets of the Caribbean European rule will continue for some indefinite time into the future.

III THE BRITISH EMPIRE

The Long Struggle

The years 1772 to 1838 were the years of the long struggle to end slavery in the British empire. It took place mainly in and around the British parliament, where the abolitionists fought to secure the passage of the necessary laws. But at the same time, many were at work in the West Indies, struggling to improve the conditions of the Africans until such time as they would be free people. The missionaries were especially prominent in this work. 1772 was the year in which Lord Chief Justice Mansfield delivered a judgment as to whether slaves in Britain must be returned to their masters and the plantations, a judgment which was widely believed to have brought about the end of slavery in Britain itself and to have emancipated the 15 000 slaves then in the country.* 1838 was the year in which slavery was abolished completely in the British empire under the terms of the Act of Emancipation which had been passed in 1833.

The Mansfield Judgment arose out of a case which was brought by Granville Sharp, a Quaker. The Quakers, the Society of Friends, were a protestant sect which had been founded in the seventeenth century by George Fox. Even at that time, Fox had condemned slavery, and the Quakers were among its most outspoken critics. Sharp came across a Jamaican slave, James Somerset, who had been brought to England by his master and then abandoned. The master was now reclaiming his property and intended to send Somerset back to the plantations. Somerset was not the first such slave Sharp had encountered in England, and he was already horrified at the extent to which these Africans were exposed to the whims and brutalities of their owners—moved around, beaten, sometimes sold, and sometimes abandoned to fend for themselves in a strange land. Sharp appealed to the courts to save Somerset from deportation. The case eventually reached Mansfield, and the Chief Justice ruled that he could see no basis in law for slave owners to enforce their right of 'property in slaves' in England. This Judgment saved Somerset, and it certainly called into question the legality of slavery on English soil. It did nothing, of course, to restrict the slave trade or to curtail slavery in the West Indies, but it gave an incentive to Sharp and to all those who hated slavery to widen and intensify their campaign against it. Two years later, the Quakers agreed to expel from the British Society of Friends any Quaker who was involved in the slave trade. The Quakers in Britain were only a small minority, however, and they faced a long uphill struggle if they were to persuade the government to interfere with colonial slavery.

In particular, they would have to contend with the West Indian Lobby. West Indian planters were well-organized in Britain. Retired planters and the agents and friends of West Indian estate owners formed a powerful pressure group. They also had social connections with many members of the British government and parliament. It could be said of them, therefore, that they had friends in high places; and they constantly argued that the slave trade and slavery were essential to the well-being of the West Indies, by which they meant the profitability of the sugar industry. This was a time when many of the seats in the House of Commons could be bought by bribing the handful of those who were entitled to vote. The West Indian Lobby considered it money well spent to ensure that they were represented in parliament. When David Hartley proposed in the House of Commons, in 1776, that slavery was against the law of God and the rights of man, his motion was quickly rejected.

For a time, therefore, the Lobby successfully frustrated all abolitionist legislation in Britain. Meanwhile, in the West Indies, the plantation owners struck back against the missionaries.

Missionary Activity

By the eighteenth century, the Protestant Church of England was firmly established in England as the official church. It was taken for granted that this was also the official church of the empire, but both in England and the colonies it was often lethargic, more popular with the upper classes than with the lower, to whose sufferings it often seemed to show an unchristian indifference. More radical groups, the sects, sometimes known in Britain as Dissenters, wanted a more active religion—one more responsive to social injustices. Several of these groups began to show a particular interest in the welfare of African slaves. Their first concern was to teach the Christianity which the Church of England often seemed to neglect. But contact with the slaves inevitably made them sympathetic to the African's defencelessness, and this inspired a deep suspicion in the planters that the missionaries were trying to undermine the system of slavery.

Before 1815, however, missionary activity in the West Indies was on only a small scale. The Society for the Propagation of the Gospel in Foreign Parts was founded in 1701 to spread Church of England teaching, but it had little impact on the West Indies except in Barbados where a bequest by Christopher Codrington, once Governor of the Leeward Islands, enabled the Society to set up Codrington College. At the end of the eighteenth

* This view has been challenged by F. O. Shyllon, *Black Slaves in Britain* (Oxford University Press, 1974), who argues that Mansfield did no more than rule on the case of James Somerset.

Pocomania in modern Jamaica: an evangelical religious movement which takes its inspiration from a fusion of Christian and African culture

century, the Church of England set up another Society for the Conversion of Negro Slaves. By this time, however, other groups were in the field, especially the Moravians, who sought to teach Christian morality by example. They carried on their work in the Dutch and Danish islands and became strong for a time in Antigua, Jamaica and St Kitts; and where they led, others followed.

John Wesley founded a movement in England which came to be known as Methodism and which was particularly concerned in bringing Christianity to the poor. It was associated with open-air preaching, and by the end of the eighteenth century Methodist missionaries were at work among the slaves of the West Indies. About the same time, Baker and Lisle brought the Baptist Church to Jamaica (see page 100), and the Baptist Missionary Society was founded in 1792. Congregationalists founded the London Missionary Society three years later and, in 1799, the Church Missionary Society was created by the Clapham Sect, which soon became prominent in the campaign to end slavery and of which William Wilberforce was a member. The Clapham Sect was made up of Evangelicals who shared with the Methodists a concern for the under-privileged, but who, unlike the Methodists, remained within the Church of England. When the Napoleonic Wars ended, all these societies were poised to expand their work in the West Indies. Apart from their work among the slaves before the granting of emancipation, many came to be closely connected with education and schools, and they contributed to the diversity of Protestant religions to be found in the West Indies in the twentieth century. The Church of England, the Methodists and the Baptists all claim large numbers of followers today but there also exist many smaller groups such as the Moravians, Seventh Day Adventists, Congregationalists and Presbyterians.

Before 1833, when the British decided to end slavery, the missionaries were in a difficult position. They were hindered by the planters and liable to be accused of spreading sedition among the slaves; but they were liable to be accused by the slaves of supporting white power if they kept within the law. The colonial assemblies hampered them with new laws, making them obtain licences and forbidding preaching in the only hours the slaves were free to hear them. Fresh from Europe, many missionaries caught tropical fevers. Planters were reluctant to offer them hospitality and shelter. To make contact with even a fraction of the vast population of slaves, extensive travel was necessary, and being few in number and handicapped by barriers of language between themselves and the Africans, the missionaries were up against overwhelming odds. Even when the British and Foreign Bible Society was founded in 1804 to supply Bibles to the colonies, the missionaries often had little to bring to the slaves but their own voices. But something of the message of Christianity was spread and a small number of slaves learned to read and write, while, perhaps just as important, the reports of the missionaries helped to add fuel to the campaign for abolition in Britain.

Martyrdom helped the cause of abolition. In 1823, there was a slave rebellion in Demerara which the planters blamed on the missionary, John Smith. After a biased trial, the authorities in Demerara condemned him to death and, although the sentence would almost certainly have been revoked by higher authorities in Britain, Smith died in prison while awaiting the outcome. In Barbados, Thomas Shrewsbury met a similar vindictiveness on the part of the planters, though he escaped with exile from the island after the destruction of his church. In Jamaica, the Christmas Rebellion of the slaves in 1831 was blamed on the missionaries and many were arrested and their churches destroyed. But the ownership of slaves was in its death throes. The Tory government in Britain in the 1820s had favoured laws of amelioration to protect slaves against ill-treatment. The Whig government which came to power in 1830 was inclined towards emancipation. In the West Indies, the air was filled with rumours and the slaves grew increasingly restless. It was such rumours that caused the Jamaican rebellion in 1831, as they had caused that in Demerara in 1823. To blame the missionaries and to take revenge on their churches was the last desperate refuge left to the planters, but their own violent conduct only added to the growing conviction in Britain that slavery must be ended.

The Abolitionist Crusade

The *Christian Directory,* which Robert Baxter published in 1673, was one of the earliest printed condemnations of the slave trade, but it was not until 1787 that the voices raised in protest began to cry in unison. In that year, the Society for Effecting the Abolition of the Slave Trade was founded, bringing together Granville Sharp, Clarkson (see page 100), Wilberforce, the clergyman James Ramsey, the industrialist Josiah Wedgwood and the supporters of the earlier Quaker abolitionist movement. Within a year, they persuaded the government to set up a committee to inquire into the slave trade. But that was as far as it would go. The Prime Minister, William Pitt the Younger, sympathized with the abolitionists but his cabinet was divided and the West Indian Lobby had powerful friends. The inquiry produced useful evidence of the atrocities of the slave trade, but parliament would accept nothing but a feeble law to restrict over-crowding on the slave ships. Pitt was not prepared to endanger his government by insisting on more. In 1792, the House of Commons did agree on a phased abolition of the trade but the proposal was vetoed in the House of Lords, and a year later war broke out with revolutionary France. Pitt became even more convinced that the time was not ripe for change. From 1793 to his death in 1806, he lost his reputation as a reformer, and his main objectives now were order and stability in Britain and the empire, and victory over the French.

The abolitionists were not deterred. Their first target was the slave trade and later they would aim higher, at slavery itself. Parliament was bombarded with petitions. Public opinion was wooed with sermons, pamphlets, newspaper articles and letters and, as far as repressive wartime legislation allowed, public meetings. Clarkson followed up his *Essay* with the collection of a mass of evidence about the slave ships, which was gathered, often at considerable personal risk, in ports such as Liverpool and Lancaster, Bristol and Plymouth. Every effort was made to spread the information he collected about the inhuman, brutal and insanitary conditions of the Middle Passage and to display the typical equipment of the slave trader—shackles, thumb-screws, mouth-openers (to force-feed stubborn slaves who preferred to starve to death) and the implements for beating. One of Clarkson's most valuable informants was John

Newton, captain of the *Duke of Argyll*, who had been nine years in the slave trade until he retired in 1754. He too had become an abolitionist. Having once thought of the business of the slave trader as 'genteel', he ended his days as the Reverend John Newton, preaching against it. Wilberforce sat in the House of Commons for Yorkshire. He was an effective parliamentarian, eloquent and persuasive; he was also well-connected and a friend of William Pitt. He thus became the chief spokesman of the movement, ever ready to argue with the West Indian Lobby. Ramsey had spent many years in St Kitts and his sermons provided first-hand accounts of the evils of slavery until he died in 1789, sufficiently feared by the planters to cause them to launch a campaign to blacken his character.

William Wilberforce, English abolitionist (St Vincent, 1973)

The End of the Slave Trade

The French Revolution, the French wars and the bloodshed which attended the birth of Haiti, all reinforced the resistance of those who defended the slave trade and helped to brand the abolitionists as dangerous radicals and a threat to the existing social organization. At regular intervals, Wilberforce's proposal to end the trade was rejected. In 1806, however, Pitt was succeeded as Prime Minister by Charles James Fox, whose commitment to abolition had long been known. At the same time, the West Indian Lobby was in confusion. Britain had captured many French and Dutch possessions in the West Indies and Guiana, and British planters feared that the market for sugar would be glutted. Some of them were, therefore, in favour of suspending the slave trade in the hope of denying an adequate labour supply to the new conquests. This was the abolitionists' opportunity.

In 1807, both the House of Commons and the House of Lords accepted the Act of Abolition, which made slave trading illegal though punishable only by a fine. The last legal trade ship was the *Kitty's Amelia*, which sailed under the captaincy of Hugh Crow from Liverpool to Bonny, near the mouth of the Niger. But illicit trading continued for some years. Penalties were stiffened in 1811 and, first faced with the threat of transportation for life and then with execution, British captains withdrew from the Slave Coast. At the end of the Napoleonic Wars, Castlereagh got a general European agreement that the trade in Africans should be ended.

For years, British patrols off the African coast tried to ensure that the trade had indeed ceased. But while slavery itself remained legal anywhere in the Americas there were still men who were prepared to ignore the law, and many of those who persisted flew the flag of the USA. It was clear that the trade could not totally be suppressed until slavery itself was abolished. After 1815, however, slaves were transported in little more than a trickle, compared with the previous flood. Meanwhile, British abolitionists had begun a new campaign, seeking the end of slavery itself throughout the empire.

The Arguments

The most forceful arguments against the slave trade had been based on humanitarianism, and such was the demonstrated cruelty of the business that these arguments were difficult to counter. Rather, the trade was defended on grounds of economic necessity by those who had vested interests to protect—both in sugar and in shipping. By 1807, however, the British economy and society were undergoing change. A new wave of industrialization was beginning to transform areas of England such as Lancashire. It brought to the fore a new group of industrialists and businessmen with interests, not in sugar and slaves, but in textiles, iron, coal and—like Wedgwood—pottery. Few of these men could be classed as humanitarians. They exploited the British working classes and cried out for the raw cotton grown by slaves in the USA, but they had little in common with the old, dominant land-owning class and with the West Indian Lobby. Moreover, many merchants were now beginning to see the possibilities of trade patterns which no longer centred on the triangular trade and its dreadful Middle Passage. It has been calculated that from 1761 to 1807 the average return on British slave-trading ventures was just under 10 per cent, a useful profit but below the exaggerated claims for the trade which have sometimes been made.* Trading in slaves could, therefore, still be worthwhile financially, but there were now many shifts of emphasis in Britain's economic activities. The port of Liverpool, for example, was increasingly importing raw cotton to supply the cotton-manufacturing industry of Lancashire, and exporting Lancashire's industrial products. The ending of the slave trade would threaten one lot of profits, but others could take their place.

The merchants and the new industrialists were often jealous of the political power and influence of the old landowners. Many of them were Methodists; a few, like the Bright family in Rochdale, were Quakers. They were inclined to favour free trade rather than mercantilism, and they were not afraid of change. Although it was not until after the Parliamentary Reform Act was passed in 1832 that they began to be more adequately represented in the House of Commons, they had already begun to undermine the security and pre-eminence of the landed interests: and the British landed interests were the traditional allies of the West Indian estate owners. Against this background, humanitarian arguments in favour of stopping the slave trade met a weakening resistance. The abolitionists triumphed, but it would take them another twenty-six years of argument before they could remove the institution of slavery itself.

The abolitionists persisted with humanitarian arguments. They combed the Christian scriptures for evidence that slavery was contrary to the will of God, and preachers and poets, orators and journalists joined in the condemnation of the ownership of one man by another. A valuable recruit was gained in James Stephen, who could speak with first-hand knowledge of the West Indies and the sufferings of the Africans. The missionaries supplied further information, adding to the formidable files about the iniquities of plantation life. Those who defended slavery quoted passages from the scriptures which seemed to allow it. They argued that the slaves were well treated, that they were happy, that they were being taught Christianity and a civilized way of life they had not known in Africa. They claimed that many of the Africans were slaves before they came to the West Indies and that they now had a better life, with medical care and organized housing. If they were set free, they would be helpless. Amidst such generalizations, there was plenty of room for arguments in detail and each side found examples with which to try to prove its case. In the dispute about the morality of slavery, however, the balance inevitably tilted in favour of the abolitionists.

The supporters of slavery constantly fell back on the argument of economic necessity. Without slaves, the plantations would not function. Without plantations, there would be no sugar. Britain would not be able to compete with those countries which still permitted slavery. The bogey of instability was also paraded. Free slaves in Haiti had produced a holocaust of murder, pillage and economic breakdown, and once one embarked on change there was no way of knowing where it would stop. With well over half a million slaves in the British West Indian colonies, the social upheaval of emancipation was sure to be enormous.

It was easier for the abolitionists to show that slavery was cruel and immoral than to show that it was economically unnecessary. They pointed to the fact that the slavery-based plantations were already often unprofitable and that as an economic unit such a plantation was not very efficient (see page 83). A parliamentary inquiry of 1832 reported widespread distress in the West Indies, fuel to the abolitionist flames. It also seemed logical to argue that a free worker would work more willingly than an unfree one, and the frequent disturbances and sabotage in the islands were taken to show that the system had grave faults. Against this, however, it was maintained that the Africans were undisciplined and needed the strict control of the slave system.

For every argument there was a counter-argument, but what was perhaps decisive was the declining importance of sugar and of the West Indies in the British economy. In the 1820s, British exports to the islands fell by about 25 per

* R. Anstey, *The Atlantic Slave Trade and British Abolition, 1760–1810* (Macmillan, 1975) is one of the most recent and most exhaustive studies of the trade.

cent, and the British imports of West Indian sugar were a shrinking proportion of Britain's total trade. In any case, there were alternative sources of supply, often cheaper. As British shipping now carried many more cargoes, it no longer depended on the West Indian trade to train sailors and stimulate ship-building. Moreover, West Indian sugar sometimes glutted the market, for while mercantilism lasted, it still had to be sent to Britain. Its arrival was no longer awaited with the same greedy enthusiasm for the profits its sale would bring, since merchants sometimes had problems in disposing of it. Re-export was difficult because of competition in Europe from the sugar produced in Cuba and Brazil. Mercantilism, like slavery, was a legacy from the past and both began to seem out of place in the fast-changing times of the early nineteenth century. In the event, slavery was abolished by the Whigs in the 1830s and mercantilism was finally destroyed by the Conservatives (Tories) in the 1840s.

Amelioration

After 1807, there had been a lull in the activities of the abolitionists but they took on a new lease of life with the foundation, in 1823, of the Society for the Mitigation and Gradual Abolition of Slavery. The first target was some improvement (*amelioration*) of the conditions in which slaves lived and worked. Then would follow a phased abolition of the system, during which time the slaves could prepare for their freedom. There were those among the West Indian planters who saw amelioration as a last chance to save slavery by making it respectable with a veneer of humanitarianism. There were other planters whose lack of foresight was such that even amelioration seemed dangerously radical.

The Society of 1823 had powerful friends. It was supported by George Canning, Britain's Foreign Secretary who was briefly Prime Minister in 1827. It attracted clear-sighted civil servants such as the younger James Stephen of the Colonial Office who later drafted the Bill of Emancipation almost overnight. It won the allegiance of Elizabeth Fry, the outstanding Quaker prison-reformer. Additional voices were raised in parliament on behalf of abolition, among them that of William Huskisson who, at the Board of Trade in the 1820s, began to modify the Navigation Acts, preparing the way for their complete abolition in 1849. The campaign got into its stride when Thomas Buxton initiated a debate in the House of Commons in 1823. With the guidance of Canning, it was agreed that 'measures for ameliorating the condition of the slave population' should be introduced as soon as possible.

Notice of a slave for sale in Jamaica, 1826

PHŒBE.

Jamaica Royal Gazette, Oct. 7, 1826.

35—42 **Spanish-Town Workhouse.**

Notice is hereby given, that unless the undermentioned Slave is taken out of this Workhouse, prior to Monday the 30th day of October next, she will on that day, between the hours of 10 and 12 o'Clock in the forenoon, be put up to Public Sale, and sold to the highest and best bidder, at the Cross-Keys Tavern, in this Town, agreeably to the Workhouse Law now in force, for payment of her fees.

PHŒBE, a Creole, 5 feet 4½ inches, marked NELSON on breasts, and I O on right shoulder, first said to one Miss Roberts, **a free Black, in Vere, secondly, to Thomas Oliver, Esq. St. John's, but it is very lately ascertained that her right name is Quasheba, and she belongs to Salisbury-Plain plantation, in St. Andrew's; Mr. John Smith is proprietor. May 11**

Ordered, that the above be published in the Newspapers appointed by Law, for Eight Weeks.

By order of the Commissioners,

T. RENNALLS, Sup.

In Britain's new West Indian possessions where, as in Trinidad, no colonial assembly had been permitted (see page 88), this could be done at once under the authority of the British government. In the older colonies, the assemblies were urged to adopt similar reforms. Some of the regulations which were suggested were similar to the French *Code Noir* of 1685. Religious education was thought to be essential, and the planters were requested not to split up slave families but to encourage the slaves to marry, in the European fashion. The flogging of female slaves should cease and that of male slaves should be limited and properly documented. It should be easier for the slaves to negotiate their freedom, and they were to be allowed to give evidence in court in the way of other British subjects.

The West Indian Lobby in Britain had seen the sense of these proposals and recommended them, but planters in the West Indies often took a different view. Amelioration worked reasonably well in Trinidad, where sugar had not achieved its stranglehold, but in Guiana and St Lucia the authorities had an uphill struggle to enforce obedience. In the older colonies the assemblies were stubbornly obstructive, accepting only a few minor changes and, even then, doing little to enforce them. By 1830, the conditions of the majority of slaves had changed hardly at all and the slaves became increasingly restless, aware, perhaps because of the activities of the missionaries, that in some undefined way their conditions should have changed. Nowhere were the slaves more restless than in Jamaica and the outcome was the Christmas Rebellion at the end of 1831.

The Jamaican planters had no doubts that the blame for the Christmas Rebellion lay with William Knibb, an energetic Baptist missionary. His offence was that he preached the word of God and worked to better the lot of the slaves. There was no evidence that he preached rebellion—on the contrary, he counselled obedience. But the slaves were inflamed by rumours of a 'freedom paper' which had been secured for them by 'Saint Wilforce' in England, and their patience was exhausted. After Christmas, they went on strike on the plantations around Montego Bay and Falmouth. Hotheads set fire to the cane fields and damaged property, and a handful of whites were murdered. The estate owners were furious. In revenge for each dead European, a hundred Africans lost their lives, some killed by bullets and over 300 hanged when the Rebellion was over. The whites convinced themselves that the African ringleader was a domestic slave known as Daddy Sharp, who was among those hanged. William Knibb was exiled from Jamaica and promptly devoted himself to the cause of abolitionism in Britain.

By this time, the Whigs were in power in Britain. They introduced a new urgency into the policy of amelioration in 1831, issuing new regulations about food, clothing and housing for the slaves, limiting the hours of work and re-defining the legal punishments. The colonial assemblies were instructed to adopt these regulations forthwith or to be excluded from the financial assistance to the colonies which Britain was now offering. Once again, common sense came up against the blind stupidity of the planters. Not much was achieved, and exasperation with the estate owners undoubtedly helped to move British opinion further towards an Act of Emancipation. James Stephen summed up the shortcomings of the West Indian plantation owners:

> 'Their lives are passed in a contracted circle amidst petty feuds and pecuniary embarrassments. There is no civilized society on earth so entirely destitute of learned leisure, of literary and scientific intercourse and even of liberal recreations.'

Amelioration had proved a very damp squib.

Emancipation and Apprenticeship

Events moved swiftly from 1831 to 1833. The abolitionists launched a vigorous new campaign. The British government was displeased with the Christmas Rebellion and its outcome, and even more displeased with reports of wild talk among the West Indian planters of rejecting British rule and joining with the USA. Earlier in 1831, an election in Britain had confirmed the Whigs in power and, in 1832, they passed the Parliamentary Reform Act which struck a blow at the landed interests formerly so powerful. The moment was ripe for the freeing of the slaves and Buxton introduced the Emancipation Bill. It was passed in August, 1833, with the provision that it should take effect throughout the British empire from 1 August, 1834.

The terms of the Emancipation Act were straightforward. On 1 August, 1834, all slave

Kingston, Jamaica, in the 1830s

children under six would be free. All other slaves would serve an apprenticeship to prepare them for total freedom. For field workers, the apprenticeship would last for six years; for domestic slaves, four years. During this time, the Africans were to remain on their plantations and to give their masters forty-and-a-half hours of unpaid work each week, with the right to be paid for additional work. Sundays were to be free of work, and regulations were laid down about the duty of the masters to provide food, clothing and shelter. Recognizing that the emancipation would lead to severe labour problems on the plantations, the British government set aside £20 million as compensation to the owners, in effect valuing a slave at about £28.* Recognizing also that slave owners had a far from blameless record in caring for their slaves, up to a hundred special magistrates were to be appointed, at a salary of £300 a year, to act as watchdogs during the years of the apprenticeship. The Act was passed just in time to crown the lifetime's work of Wilberforce as he lay on his death-bed.

It was one thing to pass the Act through the British parliament, another thing to see that it was applied in the West Indies. Here, the situation varied from colony to colony. In Antigua, freedom was virtually instantaneous and apprenticeship was ignored. In the larger colonies such as Jamaica and Guiana, many slaves took the law into their own hands and fled from the plantations. In smaller islands, such as St Kitts, there were head-on conflicts between Africans who felt cheated by six years of apprenticeship and planters who felt cheated by the coming loss of their

* The British government thought at first of collecting this money from the Africans, but abandoned the idea. The government calculated the compensation as being £37½ for each slave.

labour force. The magistrates were too few to do their job properly and were often caught up in a tug-of-war between planters, intent on squeezing as much from their slaves as possible before complete freedom, and slaves, reluctant to give any further service at all to the plantations they detested.

In the newer colonies, British law could be enforced by zealous British officials. In the older colonies, the assemblies were cowed into agreeing to emancipation by the threat that shares in the compensation money would otherwise be forfeited. But that did not buy the goodwill of the planters and obstructiveness was common, especially in Jamaica. The magistrates were overwhelmed by the volume of complaints about the hours of work, the degrees of punishment, food and living conditions, and Africans who refused to serve. Most of the magistrates, many of them former army officers, were sent out from Britain and they brought to the West Indies new standards of professional and impartial justice which survived long after the 1830s. The local magistrates, who already existed in the West Indies, like their counterparts in England, were unpaid justices of the peace who secured their appointments mainly in recognition of their social standing. As in the England of the sixteenth century, they were often renowned for their self-interest and loyalty to their own class. The new special magistrates were paid, *stipendiaries* whose first concern was to serve the law and uphold justice. They reported to higher authorities in Britain, not to the planters and their assemblies. In general they were well-spoken of by the British officials, such as Lord Sligo who was Governor in Jamaica in the difficult years from 1834 to 1836, but they were much obstructed and disliked by the estate owners.

The magistrates, of course, faced all the problems of the European newcomer to the West Indies. Disease took its toll, and they had to do the best they could with makeshift arrangements about lodgings and transport. They had to learn quickly in order to understand the mysteries of plantation life, the fine social distinctions of the West Indies and the economics of sugar production. They had then to administer the law to the best of their abilities in an atmosphere of distrust, where the planters suspected them of being interfering busy-bodies and the Africans suspected them of being in league with white power. It was to their credit that they had considerable success in overcoming the suspicions of the Africans. But their reports only confirmed what others were also discovering. Apprenticeship was well-intentioned and it sometimes worked well, but too many planters merely went on exploiting their labourers, and tensions too often resulted from it, rather than constructive preparations for full freedom.

The period of apprenticeship ended prematurely in August, 1838. The British Colonial Office ruled that 'domestic slaves' should include those who worked in the sugar factories; and the four-year apprenticeship was about to expire for the domestic slaves. The assemblies in the Leeward Islands such as St Kitts and Montserrat promptly decided to follow the example of Antigua and to end slavery completely. It seemed impracticable to manage plantations on which some Africans were already free while others were unfree. The assemblies in the larger colonies, therefore, chose to follow suit rather than add these new difficulties to the already-intolerable strains of the apprenticeship system. Unfortunately, though the magistrates had done much to protect the apprentices from injustice, valuable time had been lost in arguing about the details of the present instead of planning for the future. The West Indian islands were now woefully unprepared to cope with the economic and social problems of full freedom. The gesture of 1838 was dramatic. It was of historic importance as the first renunciation of slavery by a colonial power; but it was also the beginning of a period of readjustment for which few of those involved had made adequate preparation. Where the labour force had little alternative but to work on the plantations, in

Slavery ended in the British islands in 1838 (Jamaica, 1955)

Figure 9.1 The Ending of Slavery

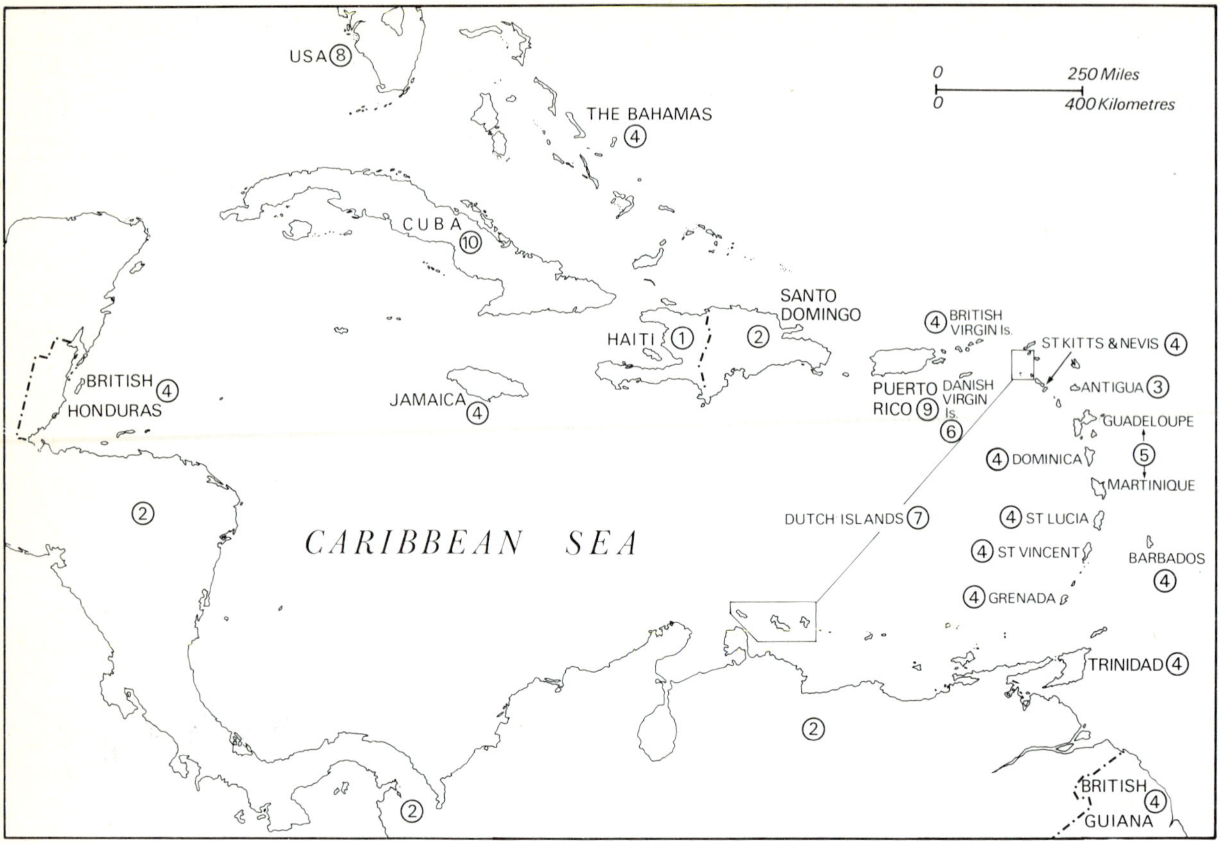

Antigua and St Kitts for example, the planters could expect to pay small wages and to some extent offset them against what was saved by no longer paying for the workers' food, clothing and shelter. But in the larger colonies such as Jamaica, the future would be less simple: manning the plantations was likely to prove difficult. The biggest problem, however, was that faced by the African who was now forced to undertake responsibilities for which his recent life had done almost nothing to fit him. Emancipation also revived the anxieties of poor whites and mulattoes in an even more acute form, for they were now no longer divided from the Africans by the legal barrier between free and unfree. They too were unprepared—unready for a society which would value a man for his abilities and services to the community rather than for his colour.

IV OTHER EUROPEAN EMPIRES

When the French slaves were emancipated in 1848, the British example of awarding compensation to the owners was followed, but not the example of apprenticeship. Freedom in the British islands had fired the ambitions of the slaves in the French colonies. Following serious disturbances in Guadeloupe and Martinique and mass desertion of the plantations in French Guiana, both the new republican government in Paris and the planters themselves agreed that emancipation should be immediate. A quarter of a million Africans became not only free but entitled to the rights of full citizenship which were still denied in the class-conscious British territories.

In 1848, Danish slaves were also freed. Led by an African known as Buddoe, who had carried the torch of emancipation from the British islands, the slaves rebelled in the Danish Virgin Islands. They did extensive damage to property but avoided murder, and the Danish authorities responded with a grant of freedom tied to an apprenticeship system. But the Danes would not grant political independence and, when the rebellion continued, Spanish and British help was enlisted to enforce Danish rule. Slavery was not brought back, but

Table 9.1 The Ending of Slavery

Country	Abolition of Slavery Completed in	Abolition Brought About by	Apprenticeship System	Owners Compensated	Slaves Freed
① Haiti	1791	Revolution	No	No	450 000
② Santo Domingo	1821	Independence	No	No	
Spanish Mainland	early 1800s	Independence	(Arrangements varied)		
③ Antigua	1834	British legislation and local decision	No	Yes	23 000
④ British Empire	1838	British legislation	Yes	Yes[3]	540 000
⑤ French Empire	1848	French legislation	No	Yes	259 000
⑥ Danish Virgin Islands	1879	Rebellion and Danish legislation	Yes	Yes	
⑦ Dutch Empire	1863[1]	Dutch legislation	Yes	Yes[2]	
⑧ USA	1865	Civil War and Federal legislation	No	No	almost 4 000 000
⑨ Puerto Rico	1876	Puerto Rican protest and Spanish legislation	Yes	Yes	31 000
⑩ Cuba	1886	Cuban protest and Spanish legislation	Yes	No	350 000

Portugal declared the end of slavery in 1858 but the slaves were to remain with their masters for a further twenty years

[1] The gradual abolition of Dutch slavery *began* in 1863
[2] The slaves were, in effect, required to buy their freedom
[3] Compensation in the British West Indies amounted to over £15 million. Payments to the owners of slaves were as follows:

(Million £s)	(Thousand £s)	
Jamaica: almost 6	Trinidad: 973	Nevis: 145
Guiana: over 4	Grenada: 570	Bahamas: 118
Barbados: over 1.6	St Vincent: 554	Montserrat: 100
	Antigua: 415	
	St Kitts: 309	*less than £100 000*
	St Lucia: 309	Honduras
	Dominica: 265	Virgin Islands
	Tobago: 226	Bermuda

(Compensation figures from E. Williams, *From Columbus to Castro* (Deutsch) p. 332)

Denmark kept possession of the western Virgin Islands until they were sold to the USA in 1917.

The Portuguese undertook to end slavery over a period of twenty years starting in 1858, but Portuguese colonial possessions were now in the eastern hemisphere, not the western. In the West Indies, it was the Dutch and the Spaniards who held out against the tide, encouraged by the persistence of slavery in the cotton states of the USA. The Dutch favoured a policy of gradual abolition with compensation for the owners on the British pattern. They added the condition, which the British had dropped, that required the slaves to contribute to the compensation. Dutch slaves were not apprenticed until 1863, two years before the outcome of the American Civil War ended slavery in the USA.

In Puerto Rico and Cuba, slavery continued because that was the policy of the Spanish government and the Spanish government, in spite of the loss of its mainland colonies and Santo Domingo, was still too short-sighted to give much consideration to West Indian opinion. In Puerto Rico, slaves were only a small minority of the population, not much more than 10 per cent. Sugar was only one of many crops and sugar plantations occupied only about an eighth of the cultivated lands. There was no shortage of free labour and slavery seemed to have no justification. In vain, the planters argued with Spain that free labour was not only more efficient but actually cheaper. But neither common sense nor arguments about social justice could move the Spanish government, until 1873. By that time, there was civil war in Cuba and the Spaniards at last gave way to the pressures on them from the Puerto Ricans. But they insisted on a final foolishness, decreeing that there should be a period of apprenticeship to be supervised by officials similar to the British magistrates of the 1830s. This merely added to the renown Spain already had in Europe for being far behind the times, and added a few more years of restriction to the lives of Puerto Rico's 30 000 slaves.

Only in Cuba was slavery ended without compensation for the owners. In 1868, Carlos de Céspedes led a rebellion against the Spanish government, to free the island from European meddling and the slaves from their bondage. At that time, slaves made up about 25 per cent of the island's population and whites more than 50 per cent. White opinion was divided on the subject of independence from Spain but there was little enthusiasm for continuing slavery. By 1878, the rebellion was defeated and Spanish authority restored, with Spanish promises that the Cubans would be allowed a greater part in the government of their island. In 1880, making a concession to Cuban opinion, Spain belatedly agreed to the emancipation of the slaves. Once again, however, the emancipation was accompanied by regulations about apprenticeship and slavery was not completely ended until 1886. In punishment for the Cubans' ten-year rebellion, no compensation was paid. But the last group of slaves in the West Indies were now free, almost 350 000 of them, who had been made to wait almost fifty years after their brothers in the British islands had been emancipated and who were still subjected to apprenticeship more than thirty years after the French had shown it to be unnecessary. Spain was thus the last colonizing power to free its slaves. It was also the first, in the post-emancipation period, to be booted out of its West Indian possessions (see Chapter 11).

Exercises

1 Describe the achievements of Toussaint L'Ouverture and Jean Dessalines, and explain why theirs are honoured names in the history of Haiti.

2 Study the various arguments in favour of ending slavery in the British empire (pages 108–10) and the various events (pages 110–11) which led to the introduction of the Emancipation Bill by Buxton. Which, in your opinion, were the *three* most convincing arguments, and the *three* most influential events?

3 Write two accounts, dated 1832, concerning the recent activities of missionaries in Jamaica, *the first* from the point of view of a typical plantation owner, *the second* from the point of view of an African slave.

4 What were the main terms of the Emancipation Act of 1833? Compare the difficulties faced by special magistrates during the period of apprenticeship with the difficulties faced by missionaries during the period of slavery.

5 Write an imaginative essay to express the feelings of an African slave who was freed after a lifetime of service on a sugar plantation.

6 Study Figure 9.1 and Table 9.1. Name (a) the British island where slaves were set free earlier than in other British colonies, (b) the three British colonies which were the producers of the largest amounts of sugar at the time of emancipation, and (c) the British and French islands where no system of apprenticeship was imposed. Why was Haiti the first West Indian state to abolish slavery, and why was Cuba the last?

7 Make a list of six Europeans who worked for the ending of the slave trade and/or slavery. Find out more about each of these humanitarians and make biographical notes. Then arrange your list in what you consider to have been the order of the importance of the contributions these humanitarians made to the cause of the African slaves.

10 Economic and Social Changes in the Post-Emancipation Period

I FREE TRADE

The estate owners in the British West Indies had lost their slaves in 1838 and they lost what remained of their protected market in Britain in 1852. Like the Spaniards and French before them, the British became increasingly disenchanted with the principles of mercantilism. Support was won for the argument that, as a rapidly growing industrial nation, Britain had everything to gain if trade were unrestricted: British purchases could be made wherever goods were cheapest, and British goods could be sold wherever customers could be found. British goods were in great demand by the middle of the nineteenth century, and it seemed foolish to impose tariffs and restrictions on the produce which foreigners might offer in exchange. The Navigation Acts were modified in the 1820s, mainly by Huskisson, and a cautious beginning was made to the admission of foreigners into Britain's colonial trade. In 1849, the Navigation Acts were abolished completely. Meanwhile, extensive reductions had been made in the tariffs on foreign goods, especially by Peel's government in the early 1840s. Peel's work culminated in the abolition of the Corn Laws which protected Britain's farmers against foreign grain, and the Repeal of the Corn Laws in 1846 was a vitally important milestone in Britain's movement towards free trade.

Amidst changes of such magnitude in Britain's trading policies, it was only to be expected that the continued protection of West Indian sugar interests should be questioned. Huskisson admitted sugar from Mauritius into Britain on the same terms as West Indian sugar in 1825, and Indian sugar was similarly admitted in 1836. The only protection which remained for the West Indian producers was that against the output of the non-British territories, especially Brazil and Cuba; but the general lifting of restrictions suggested that even this safeguard was unlikely to survive for much longer. In the meantime, the West Indies had gained only one major advantage from the changes in Britain's trading policies: the USA was being encouraged to trade with the British islands almost without hindrance, restoring something of the position which had been normal before the War of American Independence. But West Indian sugar was finding it difficult to be competitive. The emancipation of the slaves upset the plantation economies, and supplies of British West Indian sugar dwindled. Compared with the 1830s, prices in the 1840s rose steeply, and the British began to look enviously on other Europeans who were obtaining sugar at only about 60 per cent of what the British consumer had to pay. Politically, 'dear food' was a dangerous slogan. Peel, Britain's Prime Minister, began to doubt the wisdom of protecting both British grain farmers and colonial sugar producers. In 1844, he cut the duties on foreign sugar, and in 1845 he cut them again. If West Indian sugar was in short supply, it would now be possible to buy foreign produce with only a small duty. In 1846, West Indian sugar *was* in short supply. That was the year in which the Corn Laws were repealed, and West Indian producers were exposed to the full blast of the free traders' attack. By the Sugar Duties Equalization Act, all protection for West Indian sugar was withdrawn. To cushion the blow, this Act of 1846 would be applied gradually and it was 1852 before the last shreds of protection were finally removed, but from then until 1932 the sugar of the British West Indies enjoyed no privileges in the British market. It would sell only if it were competitive in price and quality. Defeated on the issues of both slavery and a protected market, and weakened by the Parliamentary Reform Act of 1832 which made it more difficult for its members to gain seats in the House of Commons, the West Indian Lobby was now no longer a force in British politics.

In the West Indies, plantation owners faced an uphill struggle to survive. Compensation for the loss of their slaves, some £15¾ million, was quickly spent in the settlement of debts, and one major problem was an acute shortage of capital. To be competitive, the estates in the British islands needed technological improvement but, throughout the nineteenth century, capital investment lagged far behind that of the sugar estates in Cuba. Highest levels of British investment were obtained in British Guiana, but even there the level was much lower than in Cuba. Absenteeism continued to be high amongst British plantation owners and the absentee planters were reluctant to export their capital to their West Indian properties. Other British investors preferred to put their money into Britain's industrial developments such as railways and cotton mills. Legislation in 1849 began the practice of assisting West Indian planters with government loans, but too little of this money found its way into new machinery and more scientific sugar production. The British West Indian estates were, therefore, often both small and comparatively inefficient. A Royal Commission, sent out in 1896, condemned both the continuing concentration on sugar and the general lack of enterprise.

Slow to introduce major new technology and slow to diversify his crops, the British estate owner tried to reduce his labour costs to the minimum. Ex-slaves had little choice but to remain on the sugar estates in Barbados, Antigua, St Kitts and the Leeward Islands, and their labour could be had for a shilling a day or less in the 1840s. But wherever there was an alternative, the Africans were eager to avoid the sugar plantations. Many migrated from the Windward Islands to Trinidad and Guiana where, as in Jamaica, there was unused land to be found. In Guiana, for example, refugees from the plantations founded co-operative settlements and cultivated tobacco and a variety of foodstuffs. They pooled their resources and bought land, either from the crown or from bankrupt estate owners. Extensive settlements developed along the Demerara and Berbice Rivers shortly after emancipation, mainly as the result of co-operation and self-help. By 1852, there were perhaps as many as 70 000 people living on such smallholdings in British Guiana. Even if Africans could be tempted back to the estates in these larger colonies, it was usually necessary to pay them double the wages which could be obtained in places such as Antigua, and many ex-slaves now looked on plantation work as merely temporary or even part-time employment.

In these circumstances, the cry soon went up for a new labour force which, the planters insisted, must be cheap and reliable. From 1838 until well into the twentieth century, there was a new influx into the West Indies. Some newcomers came from Europe and Africa, but they came in vast numbers from Asia; and they did not come only to the British territories, for the Spaniards, French and Dutch needed labourers too. Their main task was to supply the labour on sugar plantations—many of which were now denuded of their former African slaves—and to produce as much cheap sugar as possible to compete in markets which were now only rarely protected.

II THE OLD LABOUR FORCE AND THE NEW

The Former Slaves

There is little evidence to suggest that the Europeans gave any deep thought to organizing their Caribbean colonies in the post-emancipation period except on the basis of a new imported labour force. With almost indecent haste, they rushed to bring in new workers without fully exploring how the colonies could be developed without them. Ex-slaves were assumed to be unhelpful and, except in special cases such as Antigua, little real effort was made to adapt the plantations to the use of free African labour once apprenticeship ceased. The Africans, for their part, had miserable memories of plantation life and, not unnaturally, they tended to drift away from masters who offered them little incentive to stay.

Land was obviously the key to the problem. Planters in Barbados, Dominica, Antigua and elsewhere could often keep their African workers by allowing them to occupy a house and a small plot of ground—tied cottages, whose occupiers were tied to working on the estate, the tenancy of the cottage being part of the wage. In other places such as St Kitts, land was sometimes leased to the Africans by the estate owners under certain conditions: the tenant could be required to share his produce with the estate owner and to grow a specific crop, usually sugar. An ex-slave with sufficient money could do better: he could probably buy the freehold of a smallholding and be his own master, if he were able to find an estate owner who was willing (or desperate enough) to sell. In the larger colonies, *squatting* occurred—that is, the occupation of crown land or unoccupied land without any legal right. But it was only with a *freehold* that an ex-slave could enjoy complete security and independence: the freehold was a full legal title to land, free from obligations to any landlord. Such a freehold had almost always to be bought, and the poor African had little opportunity to acquire one. Therefore, the number of independent peasant proprietors among the ex-slaves grew only slowly. The African's most powerful allies in the period of resettlement were the missionaries, especially the Baptists and, to a lesser degree, the Methodists and Moravians. These missionaries organized the purchasing of lands for the setting-up of *free villages*, similar to those already described in Guiana. John Clark was a Baptist missionary in Jamaica who, for £700, acquired over a hundred acres to be sub-divided into freeholds which ex-slaves might then purchase. The ex-slaves could then develop their own village-communities. Within a short time of emancipation, there were about 200 such communities in Jamaica. Much of their effort was organized on co-operative lines. They grew maize, fruits and vegetables and generated local trade, and so other ex-slaves could be employed as shopkeepers and general handymen. The free-village movement made even more progress in Guiana. As early as 1842, nearly 5000 ex-slaves in Berbice were living on freehold lands in about 1200 family units.

Although the free-village movement was active for some ten years after emancipation in the British colonies, the authorities gave it little encouragement. What the Africans achieved was largely by their own efforts and that of the missionaries. Official attitudes were sceptical. In 1850, Governor Barkly of Guiana praised the Africans who still worked on the sugar plantations but thought the freeholders, now a quarter of the ex-slaves in the colony, 'far less industrious'. Official policy was still to encourage the sugar estates. Smallholders, producing other crops, did not seem to fit in with the expected pattern. Nevertheless, they grew slowly in number, even outside the larger colonies of Guiana, Trinidad and Jamaica. About 1860, Antigua had sixty-seven villages and Barbados over 3500 freeholders. They also helped to diversify the exports from the British West Indies, albeit on a small scale. In St Vincent, they increased the production of arrowroot, in Jamaica that of arrowroot, coconuts, honey and timber. Elsewhere, they exported coffee and ginger. But still the authorities could think of little but sugar, until in 1897 the Commission which then examined the British West Indies recorded of the colonial administrations that

> 'the settlement of the labouring population on the land, and the encouragement of the products and forms of cultivation suitable for a class of peasant proprietors formed no part of their policy.'

What was part of their policy was to bring in new labourers for the sugar estates, and to pay little heed at all to those African labourers who had now left the estates.

Not all of the ex-slaves, of course, remained on the land either as labourers or as smallholders. Some settled in the towns and made their way into the professional classes as lawyers, doctors, teachers and businessmen. Some gained seats in the assemblies, preparing for the time when black men would have a more effective voice in the affairs of the colonies. For others, emancipation was merely the beginning of a miserable poverty-stricken existence and a period of readjustment with which they could not cope. In the nineteenth century, even in Europe, governments rarely did much to help such unfortunates and the poor were often blamed for their own poverty. Once given their freedom, the ex-slaves too were simply expected to fend for themselves. In the West Indies, it was considered far more important that the sugar estates should be restored to prosperity than that the Africans should be cushioned against misfortune. That the majority of the ex-slaves survived and that some even prospered was evidence not of enlightened official policy but of their own resilience.

Contract Labour

Indentured labour had not been markedly successful in the seventeenth century (see pages 66–8). Nevertheless, it was to this idea that the estate owners returned when the Emancipation

Act was passed in Britain. The idea of a contract, to bring workers to the plantation and keep them there for a number of years, exercised a magnetic appeal. Details as to the terms of the contract could vary but the system differed little, in its basic pattern, from the indentured labour of two centuries earlier. The new contracts were usually for a period of five years, and they included provision for the labourer's wages, medical care, food and clothing, and for his return to his own country when the contract expired. Towards the end of the nineteenth century, such a return came to be discouraged, and as an alternative to assistance with a passage home it became customary to offer smallholdings when the term of the contract had been completed. In this way, the West Indies came to have a substantial population of Asian descent.

The ships which brought the labourers in the 1830s were often little better than the slave ships had been. Squalor, disease and death took a heavy toll of the newcomers. In Britain, the Anti-Slavery Society began to fear that a new slavery would develop and that estate owners would over-work and neglect the welfare of their new labour force. Uncontrolled private enterprise in recruiting the workers quickly provoked an outcry and, in 1838, the British suspended the new traffic. But the case for labourers who could make West Indian sugar competitive in an age of free trade seemed a strong one, and the suspension was short-lived. Instead, the British and colonial governments turned their attention to supervising the traffic. Those who recruited the workers had to be licensed, and the labourers themselves were registered so that it would be possible to monitor the extent to which both sides kept to the terms of their contracts. Government also helped to finance the traffic from the end of the 1840s, since, even with low wage rates and contracts heavily weighted towards giving maximum value to the employer, the transportation of such a vast army of workers was bound to be expensive. By the end of the nineteenth century, in Guiana and Trinidad, about 8 per cent of public expenditure went on the financing of immigration.

The Newcomers

Contract labour was not confined to the British colonies. Almost every West Indian colony was involved in it except British Barbados, which already had too much labour, and Spanish Puerto Rico. The French recruited labour in their own Asian colonies, including what is now Vietnam, and they also gained a special concession to recruit labour in British India until they were

Chinese immigrants were imported into Guadeloupe to supply labour to the estates in the mid-nineteenth century—a French print based on a photograph

East Indian immigrants in Trinidad, from a painting by Cazabon (Trinidad and Tobago, 1970)

Figure 10.1 Immigration into the West Indies, 1838–1917

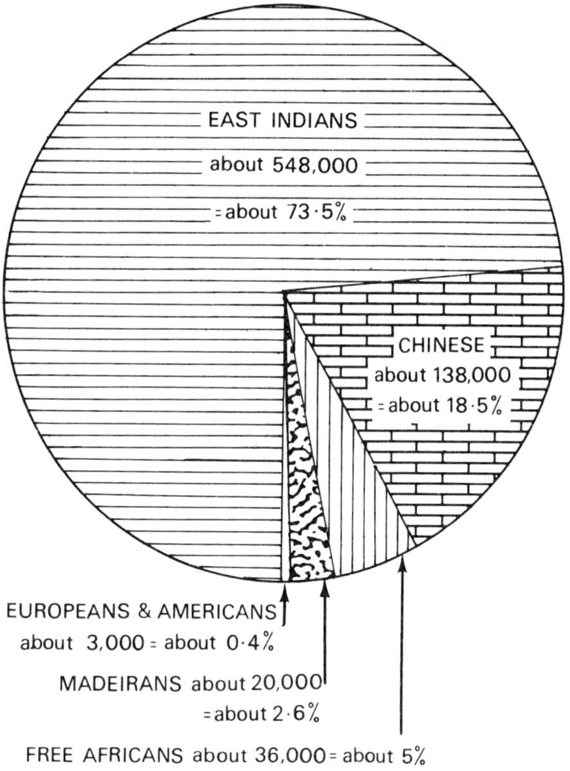

The subject of the Exporting of Indian Labour has been studied by H. Tinker, *A New System of Slavery* (Oxford University Press, 1974). The traffic to the West Indies began in earnest when the *Lord Hungerford* cleared Calcutta, bound for British Guiana, in 1845.

Emigrants in 1845: to Trinidad, 1332; to British Guiana, 816; to Jamaica, 261; (compare, to Mauritius, 10 972).

Emigrants in 1846: to British Guiana, 4019; to Trinidad, 2264; to Jamaica, 1890 (to Mauritius, 7339).

Mortality on the transport ships was high in the 1850s. In 1856–7, it averaged 17.27 per cent on passages to the West Indies, and reached over 28 per cent on the *Roman Emperor*. By 1890, the mortality rate on the passages to British Guiana had fallen to around 1.5 per cent.

banned in 1886. The Dutch were also allowed to recruit in British India to add to the labourers from their own East Indies, especially Java; and they thus sought to supply the needs of Surinam. Spanish Cuba made extensive use of Chinese contract labour, in spite of the fact that African slavery lasted longer in the island than elsewhere in the West Indies. Wherever sugar was grown, there seemed to be an insatiable demand for more labourers. Indeed, the new recruitment of contract labour had first begun in British Mauritius, where the sugar planters were looking towards India as early as 1830.

It was India which provided the bulk of the new labour force (see Figure 10.1), but East Indian immigration was to some extent the result of trial and error, as so often in West Indian history. After the emancipation of the slaves, labour was reshuffled in the Caribbean as Africans moved from one territory to another, especially from the Windward Islands. About the same time, efforts were renewed to attract indentured labour from Europe, and Jamaicans in particular tried to recruit in Scotland and in continental Europe. The mid-1830s brought an influx of Portuguese subjects from the Madeira Islands, the majority of whom, some 30 000, settled in British Guiana. Africa and China were also tapped. But Africans associated the West Indies with the slave trade and neither British Guiana nor the French colonies could persuade Africans to come in large numbers. The British Navy helped, however, by intercepting the ships of those nations which still traded in slaves and casually depositing the luckless Africans, albeit as free labourers, in the British West Indies. The Chinese arrived in a steady flow in the middle of the nineteenth century in Cuba, the French colonies and the ever-demanding British Guiana, but like the Indonesians and Indochinese their numbers were not sufficient to satisfy the estates.

The real answer to the alleged needs of the West

Indies was provided, from 1845 onwards, by the East Indians. By the time that the British government of India banned further contracts and emigration in 1916, well over 500 000 Indians had made the long journey to the Caribbean. However, more than 100 000 of them had also made the return journey when their contracts expired. British Guiana took in the largest number of Indians, about 250 000, while nearly 150 000 entered Trinidad. Indians remained in large numbers in both countries, so that today they form a majority group in Guyana and run the Africans a close second in Trinidad. The French colonies, Guadeloupe, Martinique and French Guiana, also took nearly 100 000 East Indians. India attracted the West Indian planters on two counts: it had a very large population; and vast numbers of its people were so desperately poor that they were willing to travel half-way across the world for a job and a wage, however small.

The early newcomers from Asia were often sickly. Many died, and many others produced inadequate work. Of those who survived, large numbers returned home as soon as their contracts expired. Nevertheless, after some interruptions to the traffic which were caused because the British government was still inclined to hesitate, the flow of Indians became steady in the 1850s and continuous from the 1860s. It was ended in 1916, not because the demands of West Indian estate owners had finally been met, but because the authorities in India, prodded by the Indian National Congress, refused to permit the further shipment of the Indian people.

The Advantages and Disadvantages of the Influx

Throughout the period of Indian migration, European and West Indian authorities made spasmodic efforts to protect the newcomers against injustice. No doubt, Indians were well satisfied with the deal they obtained, for they were rewarded far beyond what they could have hoped for in India itself. But the whole system of contract labour was cumbersome, costly and undignified. It inevitably involved much personal hardship as the rate of illness among the immigrants testified. Although the West Indian sugar estates were becoming profitable again by the mid-1860s, it is arguable whether contract labour was the cause. Even if contract labour did create the profitability, it is questionable whether it justified the sufferings of the labourers. Barbados doubled its exports of sugar in the second half of the nineteenth century without contract labour, while British Guiana, with the greatest influx of labour of all the West Indian colonies, gained no appreciable advantages in proportion to the labourers admitted. Perhaps it was only the Trinidadian sugar output which seemed to gain extensively as the result of Indian immigration (see Table 10.1).

The system was certainly wasteful. Most of the Asians, even if they remained in the West Indies, served the sugar estates only briefly. The Chinese were renowned for their determination to exchange plantation life for business and the towns. Indians followed the Chinese, or sought their own smallholdings; they preferred to cultivate their own crops and some crops, such as rice, became more firmly established in Guiana and Trinidad. Even on the plantations, many of the Asians were helping to produce bananas and cocoa, rather than sugar, by the end of the nineteenth century.

The system also wasted away the wealth of the West Indies. Money was spent in recruiting labourers which could have been invested more positively in developing the amenities which were available to the Caribbean societies. The Asians themselves, of course, often sent or took much of what they earned back to India. But the recruitment of labour was the product of the concentration on the sugar estates, which led inevitably to the neglect of other sections of the West Indian society and economy. The concentration on a large labour force, in its turn, delayed the day

The Hindu Festival of Phagwah. The Asian newcomers enriched West Indian societies (Guyana, 1969)

Table 10.1 Nineteenth-Century Immigration and Sugar Production

Country	Area (1 square=500 square miles)	Indian Immigration (thousands) 1838–1917	Sugar Exports (thousand tons) 1828	1894	(% change) 1828–94
British					
Guiana	(almost) 90 000	238	40.1	102.5	+156
Jamaica	4411	21.5	72.2	20	−72
Trinidad	1864	145	13.3	46.9	+253
Dominica	290		2.5	1.1	−56
St Lucia	238	1.55	4.2	4.5	+7
Barbados	166	nil	16.9	60	+255
St Vincent	150	1.82	14.4	2.7	−81
Grenada	120	2.57	13.5	nil	−100
St Kitts-Nevis	68 50	0.3	8.4	16.9	+101
Tobago	116		6.2	0.6	−90
Antigua	108		8.8	12.4	+41†
Montserrat	38	nil	1.3	1.8	+38
French					
Guadeloupe	657	39	35.2	43	+22
Martinique	420	39	32.8	36.4	+11
Dutch					
Surinam	70 000	34	11.7 (1825)	8 (1895)	−32 (1825–95)
Spanish					
Cuba	44 200	125 (Chinese)*	113.4 (1840)	1054‡	+c.800
Puerto Rico	3435	nil	112 (1853)	48.5 (1893–4)	−57 (1853–94)

* 1852–74. By 1877, c. 44 000 Chinese in Cuba † Antigua exported only 7219 tons in 1895—less than in 1828
‡ Output

when sugar technology would be revolutionized and less labour-intensive methods of production introduced.

Nor could it be argued that Asian immigration dramatically increased the population of the West Indies. As Asians moved in, Africans were often moving out, many of them to the mainland. The population of the British West Indies stood at about half a million in the 1870s, but population changes differed from island to island. Trinidad was expanding at about 3 per cent a year, Jamaica more slowly and some of the smaller islands not at all. Immigration made little difference to the overall population compared with the great increases which resulted later in the nineteenth century from improved medical standards. These improvements at last began to reduce the high death rate and, in less than a century, many of the West Indian islands became over-populated, with too many people who were heavily dependent on the land and its produce.

Yet investment in the newcomers was an investment in people, in human resources. The Asians brought further enrichment to the already varied society and culture of the West Indies. They brought with them the art forms, customs and religions of Asia, the business sense of the Chinese and the thriftiness of the Indians. Again, the impact differed from one territory to another. Jamaica remained overwhelmingly African and

Grinding the cane and boiling the juice: Cuba was a major producer of sugar by 1877 and was making use of more modern technology

took in little more than 20 000 Indians, whereas in Trinidad the Asians were almost as numerous as the Africans. In Cuba, both Africans and Asians remained no more than minorities. To the old problem of how to develop societies which contained whites, blacks and mulattoes was now added the further problem of integrating newcomers who were mostly brown. This was perhaps the most important result of the Asian immigration: it was a lasting result.

III SUGAR, THE NINETEENTH-CENTURY KING

Cuba

At the beginning of the nineteenth century, Cuban sugar output was less than half that of Jamaica. At the end of the century, Cuba's output was almost four times the total produce of the British West Indies including British Guiana. At first, the Cuban expansion was based on virgin soil and slave labour. Later in the century, Cuba was faster than the British colonies in introducing new technology and more modern methods of production. It is also true, of course, that Cuba's greater size gave it an advantage, allowing it to replace Hispaniola as the major sugar-producing island when the latter became the independent states of Haiti and the Dominican Republic.

Except for the interruptions of civil war and, at the end of the nineteenth century, the struggle for independence from Spain, Cuba was able to expand production steadily throughout the century. By earlier standards, plantations were often very large, Santa Susana topping 10 000 acres in the 1850s. The introduction of railways made the transport of the cane more efficient, and this in turn made it possible to reduce the number of factories. Meanwhile, the factories themselves were made more efficient through the use of steam power in the mills and of new equipment such as vacuum pans and centrifugal spin-driers. Such equipment was, of course, expensive and would be profitable only where great quantities of cane needed to be processed. In the British colonies, only Guiana and Trinidad had large estates where this sort of development could be introduced and made profitable. But at the same time the British were slow to realize that a group of estates could benefit from the establishment of centralized factories which worked more efficiently. In general, the British producers clung to the eighteenth-century pattern of separate factories for individual estates.

Capital was necessary for modernization of course. In Cuba, profits were often large enough for the estate owners to pay for new equipment. However, like those of the previous century, the sugar magnates all too often became absentee.

They preferred to spend their money away from the estates and many of them competed in building luxurious properties in Havana. But outside capital was forthcoming. Before the end of the nineteenth century, about 30 million dollars were invested in Cuban sugar production by the financiers of the USA, and these financiers were particularly inclined to favour large-scale enterprises with up-to-date technology.

America's financial interest in the island was one of the results of Cuba's nineteenth-century concentration on sugar. Another result, the importing of Chinese labour, has already been mentioned. A further result was the running down of alternative crops such as coffee, although the tobacco produced on the smallholdings of the mainly white farmers still accounted for 40 per cent of Cuba's exports in 1902. But the Cubans were dissatisfied with an economy dominated by large sugar estates and with the sort of society produced by this domination. They were also politically discontented, resentful of the inflexible rule of Spain. As a result, the nineteenth century ended not only in the pre-eminence of Cuban sugar but also in the Cuban War of Independence (see pages 132–3).

The British West Indies

The British islands persevered to keep King Sugar on his throne in spite of Cuban competition and competition from Brazil and the East. Guiana and Trinidad produced more than half of the sugar exported from the British West Indies in 1882. Both had considerably expanded production in recent years, together with Barbados. The Leeward Islands of St Kitts and Nevis, Antigua and Montserrat, and the Windward Islands of Dominica (for a time) and St Lucia expanded too, but at a slower rate. The French islands of Guadeloupe and Martinique matched the rate of increase in Dominica and St Lucia, but operated on a larger scale. Elsewhere, however, sugar declined. It fell dramatically in Jamaica which produced considerably less than Barbados in 1882. It fell in St Vincent and Tobago and, by 1900, it had virtually disappeared from Grenada.

Sugar still accounted for over half of the exports from the British West Indies in the 1890s. Amongst individual colonies, it accounted for over 90 per cent of the exports from St Kitts and Nevis, Antigua and Barbados, over 70 per cent of those from St Lucia and British Guiana, and over 50 per cent of those from Trinidad and Montserrat. Compared with Cuba, capital investment tended to be low, plantations small and factories out-of-date. Except in Jamaica, Trinidad and British Guiana, the principal sugar produced was muscovado. Except in these three colonies and St Kitts and Nevis, the majority of the factories still relied on mills not yet converted to steam power. Of almost a thousand factories in the British West Indies, less than half used steam.

In these circumstances, the economies of the British West Indian colonies became increasingly precarious, and the final years of the nineteenth century saw the sugar producers and all who depended on them on the verge of bankruptcy. No longer protected on the British market, they had been helped for a time by sales to the USA, but the British producers found it increasingly difficult to compete. Apart from Cuban competition in the West Indies, sugar was now produced in places as far apart as Louisiana and Java and, by the 1890s, West Indian sugar (including Cuban) was only 41 per cent of the total world production from cane. That of the British West Indies was no more than 7 per cent. But this was not the whole extent of the competition for, in the nineteenth century, great strides were made by beet sugar which Europe itself began to produce and export. In the 1890s, almost half of the sugar imported into Britain had been produced from beet, and Austria, France, Germany and Russia were now substantial producers of beet sugar. An increasing world population offered hope that an expanding market could still absorb the production, but those whose sugar was the most expensive, as that in the British West Indies threatened to become, had every reason for alarm. Over-dependence on sugar, and especially over-dependence on sugar which was inefficiently produced, was clearly a recipe for disaster. In the 1890s, cane was struck by disease almost everywhere in the British West Indies. King Sugar himself was clearly ailing and, in 1896, Joseph Chamberlain, Britain's Colonial Secretary, appointed a Commission under the chairmanship of Henry Norman to investigate the health of Britain's Caribbean colonies.

The *Norman Commission*, which reported in 1897, was particularly concerned with the sugar industry and the competition it faced from beet sugar, whose price was often artificially low (and thus competitive) because of government subsidies to exporters in the producing countries. The Commission was unable to resolve this problem. But it also reviewed the general economic and social problems of the British West Indies. It could hardly do otherwise, 'in view', as Norman put it, 'of the probable failure of the sugar industry'. The consequences of such a failure would undoubtedly be deplorable since it would leave destitute large numbers of labourers who had been fitted for no other life. In this connection, the Commission's Report criticized the extent of the influence of the sugar planters on the administration of the colonies and recommended economic diversification. Only in St Kitts, Antigua and Barbados did the Commission believe that sugar should continue to dominate the colonies' economies, and in these islands it was essential to modernize the industry, with centralized factories; and it was tentatively suggested that cane-growing could be spread out amongst more small farmers rather than being confined to great estates. The logic of developing alternative crops was also that land ownership should be more widespread and the Commission recommended that 'small peasant proprietors' should be encouraged. This would spread prosperity, develop social stability and help the colonies to become more self-sufficient. The Commission noted that, as a result of the emphasis on sugar, much food was imported which could well have been grown in the colonies.

Economic diversification and social reorganization were, therefore, the keynotes of the Report. The British Colonial Office was recommended to take active steps to promote both. This would involve agricultural education and resettlement planning and, partly to encourage the export of fruits, improved communications making use of steamships. It would also involve an injection of money into the colonies. To modernize the factories of Barbados, the sum of £120 000 was suggested, but this would be in the form of a loan. Comparatively small amounts of money were recommended as grants (gifts) and as part of a ten-year programme of development. This money would go to paying off the official debts of the administrations of the smaller islands, to settlement schemes, to improved communications and to more advanced agriculture.

The results of the Report were as modest as its recommendations. St Kitts, Antigua and Barbados clung loyally and almost exclusively to King Sugar, as they had been bidden. Elsewhere, sugar declined only slowly in its importance to the colonies' economies though the process was hastened in Trinidad by the discovery of oil. When, in 1928, another Commission, the *Olivier Sugar Commission*, went over the same ground, it found that sugar still made up 60 per cent of the exports of British Guiana and 45 per cent of those from St Lucia. Moreover, the 'small peasant proprietors' seemed to have made only limited headway, though the Olivier Commission again spoke well of them while criticizing the sugar estates with their armies of labourers.

A number of factors helped King Sugar to prolong his reign between the Commissions of 1896 and 1928. The European producers of beet sugar met in the Brussels Convention of 1898. Eventually, in 1903, they agreed to stop their subsidies, and this removed some of the pressure from the cane producers. The British West Indies also benefited from Canadian encouragement which helped to make up for the loss of the United States market when the USA imposed high tariffs on British West Indian sugar. Canada favoured a system of Imperial Preferences, which departed from free trade by imposing duties on foreign produce but smaller duties on the produce of 'preferred' partners. Joseph Chamberlain wanted Britain to adopt a similar system and to give Preferences to the produce of the British colonies, but the idea was decisively rejected by the British public in the general election of 1906. Britain did not adopt Imperial Preferences until 1932. Meanwhile, Canada's Preferences enabled the British West Indies to increase their sugar exports to that country by a thousand per cent in the ten years after 1897, and the Canadians helped to save the industry. Modernization also helped. The operations of the British West Indian sugar producers remained small and rather primitive by the standards of the vast new enterprises supported in the West Indies by the USA at this time (see page 127)—enterprises which showed that the Commission of 1896 had been wrong to assume that it would no longer be profitable to produce sugar on vast estates—but progress did take place. Centralized factories were introduced, St Kitts making use of financial assistance from Britain to follow the example of Jamaica, Antigua and Barbados in 1912. An Imperial Department of Agriculture was set up, with headquarters in Barbados under the direction of Dr Daniel Morris. Chamberlain launched this Department in 1898 in response to the recommendations of the Norman Commission. It received an annual grant from the British government and was intended to encourage the more scientific selection of cane plants, the use of fertilizers and generally improved methods of cultivation. But West Indian planters still thought of low wages rather than streamlined technology and scientific farming, as the best way to cut their costs and become competitive. It was for this reason that the Olivier Commission still spoke disparagingly of the demoralized labourers employed on so many British estates in 1928.

1928 was the year in which the beginnings of a new and general trade recession could be detected. Widespread over-production, tariffs which hindered sales, and a general shortage of purchasing-power began to diminish the markets. Since 1897, it had been a hard struggle for British West Indian sugar to survive except when, during the First World War from 1914 to 1918, wartime dislocation caused a minor boom and pushed up sugar prices. Now, with the Great Depression looming, the industry was again about to be put to the test.

IV SUGAR, THE TWENTIETH-CENTURY BUSINESSMAN

American Capital

The Spanish–American War which ended in 1898 (see page 133) resulted in the independence of Cuba and the cession to the USA of Puerto Rico and the Philippines. It paved the way, in the West Indies, for the massive sugar-producing operations of large American companies such as the Eastern Sugar Associates and the United Fruit Company, whose empire also embraced bananas. Against such companies, with their interests in growing, manufacturing and marketing, the European colonies in the West Indies could not hope to compete, and the American market was lost. The American companies operated in Cuba and the Dominican Republic as well as in Puerto Rico. By the 1930s, they controlled three-quarters of the sugar output of the Dominican Republic and more than half that of Cuba. They owned land, property, equipment and railways, and they employed vast armies of wage-labourers. One consequence of this was the migration of labour from other West Indian islands. Cuba, for example, acted as a powerful magnet for labour from Haiti and Jamaica until about the mid-1920s.

Another consequence was that King Sugar increased his grip on the islands where American influence was strong. In the early twentieth century, sugar accounted for some 80 per cent of Cuba's exports, nearly 70 per cent of those of the Dominican Republic and almost 50 per cent of those of Puerto Rico. In Cuba, tobacco had a correspondingly diminishing importance, shrinking from 40 per cent to 10 per cent of the exports between the beginning of the century and the outbreak of the Second World War in 1939. In Puerto Rico, tobacco and coffee showed a similar declining importance. As had happened so often in the past in the West Indies, economies were distorted to serve King Sugar. But King Sugar was now a Businessman. His many labourers were seldom well-paid and this set the pattern for commonly low standards of living. His demand for lands led to overcrowding on the smallholdings which escaped his clutches and which, with their somewhat primitive agricultural methods, yielded little more than mere subsistence to their occupiers.

Instead of the diversification which had seemed so necessary to West Indian development, the new influx of capital produced, in the largest islands, a new emphasis on sugar. It also encouraged larger-scale operations elsewhere. Already, Guadeloupe and Martinique had followed the nineteenth-century Cuban example and that of European producers of beet sugar, in centralizing their factories. These islands were too small for operations on a massive scale, but the American example seemed to dictate that operations should be as extensive as possible. Thus, although bananas were also introduced into Martinique, the French islands continued to concentrate to the best of their abilities on the production of sugar and its by-products.

Big business was also interested in minerals. Outside the British islands, bauxite was discovered in Surinam and was worked by the Surinam Bauxite Company. Oil was found in Venezuela, and one result of this was the establishment of refineries in the Dutch islands of Curaçao and Aruba. Thus West Indians began to confront some of the economic difficulties of the twentieth century: the difficulty of obtaining capital to facilitate development and the difficulty of retaining independence in the face of powerful pressures from large companies. Many of these companies became increasingly international as the twentieth century went on. They naturally served the interests of their shareholders rather than the interests of small nations. Just as absentee planters had often exported their profits from the West Indies, so there now existed the danger that foreign companies would do the same. The companies provided employment and West Indian governments could collect royalties and taxes from them; but dependence on foreign capital made it difficult for West Indians to achieve prosperity and even to achieve genuine political independence, as the case of early twentieth-century Cuba demonstrated.

Diversification in the British West Indies

Almost with satisfaction, the Olivier Commission noted that some sugar estates had died since the Norman Commission of 1896. Their unfortunate owners often rented out parcels of estate land in return for a share of the crops grown on them. Gradually, in many of the British West Indian colonies, the new crops began to eat into the pre-eminence of sugar. By 1928, fruit, especially bananas, was far more important than sugar to Jamaica, and other islands had begun their search for an ideal alternative crop. In St Vincent, arrowroot was important; in British Guiana, rice. Nevis was turning to sea-island cotton and coconuts, while Trinidad discovered the advantages of exploiting asphalt and oil.

Research and experiment were encouraged by the British government. The Department of Agriculture provided general assistance to the islands, and each colony had its own Botanic Department. Scholarships in agricultural studies were awarded to young West Indians, and a regular journal was circulated, *The Agricultural News*. Dr Morris put in ten years of energetic work at the Department of Agriculture before his retirement, and useful foundations were laid for progress. The Department went on until 1922, when it was replaced by the Imperial College of Tropical Agriculture, located in Trinidad. This College became the Agricultural Faculty of the University College of the West Indies in 1960. In the meantime, each of the larger colonies was encouraged to set up its own agricultural department to co-ordinate research and development.

Some islands abandoned sugar almost completely. Grenada turned to nutmegs, and eventually to bananas. As the new crops spread, so too did the small proprietors. Change seldom occurred with dramatic suddenness, but few of the British territories were still dominated by sugar in the 1960s. The table on pages 168–9 shows that although sugar remained important in the economies of states such as Barbados and Guyana, and was still dominant in St Kitts, it had given way almost everywhere else to other principal exports. Bananas were well established in the Windward Islands and Montserrat did well with cotton. During the First World War, British Guiana began to produce bauxite, a mineral which also existed in Jamaica, and both found greater profit in extracting and exporting it than could be had by persevering with sugar. British Honduras exported timber, and chicle which was used in making chewing-gum.

Thus the produce which could be exported from the British West Indies became steadily more varied: sugar (and its by-products such as rum), bananas and citrus fruits, coffee and cocoa, timber, coconuts, oil, asphalt and bauxite.* Old-established activities such as cattle-rearing for hides took on a new lease of life, and new experiments were made, in an attempt to grow rubber trees for example. West Indians were no

* See Figure 7.1b on page 79, for diversification in Jamaica.

William Wrigley's multinational chewing-gum industry provides an outlet for chicle from Belize, formerly British Honduras (Belize, 1976)

longer handicapped as the early settlers had been by the problems of a Transatlantic voyage. The Canadian market was near at hand and, in any case, modern shipping could offer greater space and speed and also, when necessary, refrigeration. Manufactured goods, however, remained more expensive than agricultural produce, and industrial development in the West Indies was very slow indeed.

The extraction of minerals produced one level of industrial development. The pitch lake at La Brea in Trinidad yielded asphalt and the island also had oil. Both needed to be worked on a large scale. The Trinidad Oilfields Company dated from 1910 and the Trinidad Lake and Asphalt Company from the 1920s. In Guiana, the Demerara Bauxite Company began in 1916. These companies, like the American sugar

The *Geestland*, built in 1972, regularly brings general cargo to the Windward Islands and carries for export the vital cargoes of bananas (Grenada, 1976)

Bananas and coconuts helped to diversify the economy of Jamaica, but they did not eliminate poverty and squalid living conditions

companies, introduced foreign capital and the economies of large-scale enterprise into the West Indies.

The banana trade also involved some large-scale organization. Banana-growing in Jamaica began with the smallholders. In 1870, Lorenzo Baker carried a cargo of their bananas to New York. He was quick to spot the potential demand for the fruit, and had soon set up the Boston Fruit Company to supply the markets of the USA with bananas from several West Indian islands. At the end of the nineteenth century, the Company merged with another and became the United Fruit Company, which soon dominated the production of bananas in both the West Indies and central America and also extended its operations into sugar. But big business did not go unchallenged. In the early 1930s, Jamaican banana growers regained something of their independence with a co-operative of smallholders known as the Jamaica Banana Producers' Association, which was strong enough to compete with the United Fruit Company. Such co-operatives spread to other areas and came to include the West Indies Citrus Growers' Association and the Windward Islands Banana Growers' Association. In this kind of union, small producers often found it possible to survive against large-scale enterprises, but they could only operate in businesses where the need for capital was not extensive.

For many West Indians, smallholdings were not obtainable and even the operations of the large organizations in sugar and mineral-extraction did not provide enough work. Such West Indians often had to emigrate. The twentieth century has become keenly aware of the scourge of unemployment: most countries now keep careful records of the numbers out of work. Unemployment was an old problem in the West Indies, in spite of the demands of the sugar estates, but with the growth of population in the twentieth century—about 2 million people lived in the British West Indies in the 1920s—it became a great social evil. Until restrictions were imposed in 1924, many West Indians emigrated to the USA and many more moved about the Caribbean in search of work. The mainland naturally attracted them. Before the First World War, there was work to be had in building the Panama Canal. These migrant workers were able to send their earnings home to their families in the islands, just as the earlier Asian migrants had sent their earnings home to India. But, just as was true of India, the fact that it was necessary to do this was a clear indication that many West Indian territories still had serious economic difficulties. They neither produced enough wealth to support all their people nor provided enough work to give them all employment. When the Great Depression of the early 1930s struck, the West Indies were bound to suffer even more. The diversification of crops, the extension of smallholdings and the coming of modern extraction-industries had done something to strengthen the old sugar-based economies, but prosperity eluded the masses; and this was a problem which was still unsolved thirty years later when, from the British West Indies, a new wave of emigrants moved into Britain (see pages 181–2).

Exercises

1 How do you explain the setting up of free villages in certain countries in the West Indies in the 1840s? Why did they receive little encouragement from the authorities?

2 Assess the effects on sugar production in the British West Indies in the nineteenth century of *each* of the following: the emancipation of the slaves; Britain's free-trade policies; the cultivation of sugar-beet; the arrival of new immigrants.

3 'The whole system of contract labour (in the nineteenth century) was cumbersome, costly and undignified' (page 122). Illustrate the truth of this statement.

4 Compare and contrast the ways in which attempts were made to solve the labour problems of the West Indies by importing indentured servants in the seventeenth century and contract labour in the nineteenth century.

5 Why did the Norman Commission (1896–7) criticize the extent to which sugar was dominant in the British West Indian colonies? Why, at this time, was Cuba showing an increasing enthusiasm for sugar production?

6 Describe and explain, in the case of a typical East Indian migrant to the West Indies in the nineteenth century, (a) the reasons why he was attracted to the West Indies, (b) his feelings about his work on a plantation and (c) the choice he made about staying or returning when his contract expired.

11 Exit Spain. Enter the USA

I THE END OF THE SPANISH EMPIRE

Cuba and Puerto Rico

Spanish rule survived in Cuba and Puerto Rico when the mainland and Santo Domingo had been lost (see pages 90–1), but Spain was fighting a losing battle to retain these last remnants of the empire in the second half of the nineteenth century. Spain faced two challenges: one was the demand for independence, the other the demand that the islands should be incorporated into the USA. Opinion in the colonies themselves was divided on both issues. Simon Bolivar, the Liberator of south America, had proposed freeing the Spanish islands before his death in 1830, but Cubans and Puerto Ricans hesitated to encourage such a move. Each racial group in the islands considered without enthusiasm the strife and turbulence which independence had brought to Haiti. On the other hand, the USA gave very limited encouragement to the suggestion that the islands should join the Union. President Polk offered to buy Cuba in the 1840s, if Spain were willing to sell, but nothing came of his offer.

Spain was not willing to sell; but the Spanish government was equally unwilling to exert itself to introduce the reforms which might make its government more palatable to its West Indian subjects. The Spaniards clung to the tradition of rigid metropolitan control, blind to the fury of the creoles and the mulattoes at the arrogance of the peninsulares. The Captain-General of Cuba exercised dictatorial control as the representative of the Spanish crown: his job was to exact obedience, collect taxes and suppress every manifestation of liberal and nationalist thinking. Miguel de Tacón, who governed Cuba from 1834 to 1838, suppressed the new Spanish constitution of 1834 almost as soon as it was proclaimed in the island, and ruled with the zeal and iron hand of a medieval despot. Few of his successors had more sense than to try to imitate him.

Spain itself was the source of this blindness. In theory, Spain had a constitutional monarchy after 1834; in practice, it had a series of military dictatorships. Liberal protest tended to favour republicanism and a short-lived republic was actually set up in 1873. But it was soon overcome by the powerful forces which tied Spain firmly to the middle ages. Cuban liberals made similarly little headway in spite of several revolts in the years before 1855. A more serious outbreak began in 1868. Liberals and nationalists, under the leadership of Manuel de Céspedes and later that of Estrada Palma, embarked on an armed resistance which was to last for ten years and to claim many thousand Cuban lives. For all that, it did not seriously imperil Spanish rule and Havana was almost untouched. De Céspedes issued a declaration of independence and Máximo Gómez came from Santo Domingo to lead the military operations. The rebels wanted liberal government, fewer taxes and the abolition of slavery, but they were not entirely united as to what the political future of Cuba should be. De Céspedes himself lost his life in the struggle, but not before he had been deserted by many of his earlier supporters. The rebellion was an example of determined resistance to European misgovernment but it failed to develop into a mass movement for national liberation. In 1878, the Cubans were bought off with the Treaty of El Zanjón which contained a string of Spanish promises, many of which proved empty. Slavery was ended soon afterwards in the island (see page 116), but when order was restored, basic liberties and democratic government remained conspicuously absent.

The USA gave no help to the Cubans in their ten-years struggle, and Washington continued to be inactive during the sporadic outbreaks which followed in the 1880s. Cubans in exile did their best to whip up American indignation about Spanish inflexibility. In 1850, Narciso López had led a private expedition from New Orleans in a vain attempt to liberate Cuba, but the policy of the

Cuban liberators: Martí and Gómez, the champions of West Indian independence (Cuba, 1964)

government of the USA still went no further than the offer to buy the island, an offer renewed by Presidents Pierce and Buchanan in the 1850s. On the other hand, American businessmen were beginning to show an interest in Cuba's prosperous estates and to contemplate the possibilities of unrestricted Cuban–American trade. The moral appeal of freeing reluctant subjects from foreign tyranny, added to the prospect of financial gain, could not forever be ignored by the politicians in Washington.

The War of Independence and the Spanish–American War

José Martí became the outstanding champion of Cuban independence. It was he who laid the foundations for the new invasion of Cuba by Cuban exiles in 1895. Martí had at one time been a supporter of de Céspedes, but exile to Spain and wanderings in central and south America culminated in his arrival in New York. There he won fame as a poet, essayist and journalist and, above all, as the voice of free Cuba. In 1892, he was elected *delegado* of the Partido Revolucionario Cubano and preparations were made for a new attempt to drive the Spaniards from the island. When Martí himself went to join the War of Independence, he had already done much to influence United States opinion and also to inspire in innumerable Latin Americans a self-respect and a love of liberty, justice and the rights of their fellow-men. It was not merely a tragedy for Cuba when, arriving there with Máximo Gómez, Martí was killed in one of the first skirmishes, while still in his early forties.

The War of Independence went on. It was continued by Gómez and by Antonio Maceo, a mulatto leader who also lost his life in 1896. A republican constitution was proclaimed, and Martí's political work was continued by Palma. The moment to strike had been well chosen: Cuba was in the grip of a trade recession brought on by the difficulty of selling sugar to the USA. Discontent was widespread and the cane plantations were soon ablaze. The Spaniards could think of little in reply but repression, executions and curfews. The Cubans hastened to publicize every Spanish atrocity and to inform the Americans in particular that the Spaniards were herding their prisoners into barbed-wire encampments. There was already concern in the USA about the damage to American property and about the disruption of trade. There was also sympathy for the insurgents, and anti-Spanish sentiment burst into anger when the US battleship, *Maine*, blew up in the harbour of Havana. President McKinley was still willing to let Spain settle the matter with reforms and the Spaniards did make hesitant moves in that direction, but the Cubans were determined to have independence. A century of misgovernment and repression had in any case left Spain unfitted to introduce sweeping reforms, and two months after the destruction of the *Maine*, in

April, 1898, the USA declared war. As ill-equipped for battle as for modern government, Spain put up only feeble resistance and a peace agreement was signed in Paris at the end of the year. Cuba was to be independent but would have an American army of occupation until stability was restored. The USA took outright possession of other Spanish territories: the Philippines and Guam in the Pacific, and Puerto Rico in the West Indies. The brief Spanish–American War thus brought to an end Spain's once vast empire in the Americas.

The American military rule of Cuba lasted until 1902. During that time, a new constitution was drawn up and Palma became the first President of the independent Cuban Republic. The Americans busied themselves with getting the Republic off to a good start. They organized efficient administrative machinery and a more advanced educational system, and they instituted public works and new standards in sanitation. Almost overnight, yellow fever was wiped out in the island. Sugar was restored to prosperity and favourable access arranged to the American markets. But the USA also exacted its price. Guantánamo had to be ceded to the USA, for use as a military base, and Cuba was forced to agree to the Platt Amendment. This Amendment authorized the Americans to keep a watchful eye on the financial management of the Cuban government. The Cubans had independence, but the independence had strings (see page 135).

II THE AMERICAN EMPIRE

Puerto Rico

After almost four centuries of Spanish rule, Puerto Rico became the property of the USA by the Treaty of Paris. Spain had belatedly granted self-government to Puerto Ricans in 1897, but whether this would have proved successful was not to be tested. Almost at once, the island exchanged its old Spanish and Catholic master for a new American and mainly Protestant one. Spanish rule left the Puerto Ricans very poor.

Their history had not been dramatic. More often than not, it had been a story of neglect. Even the slavery-based sugar plantations had been slow to develop in Puerto Rico, and its population was more Spanish in character than that of the other islands which Spain had owned. This population had now to begin again to win the right of self-government, and it took half a century to achieve it. The first civilian government was instituted by the Foraker Act of 1900, but the first Puerto Rican to become the governor of the island was Muñoz Marin who did not take office until 1949. At that time, Puerto Rico was still a Territory of the USA, a status conferred on it in 1917 by the Jones Act which granted American citizenship to Puerto Ricans. In 1952, the island was declared to be an *Estrado Libre Asociado*, or Commonwealth, and its citizens were given self-government at last. It was not a State within the American Union and it was rather ambiguous to what extent it was still a colony of the USA. But ambiguous or not, 60 per cent of the Puerto Ricans who voted in the plebiscite of 1967 supported its existing status. Of the rest, the vote was in favour of Statehood within the USA, but the plebiscite was boycotted by a third group, those who wanted the island to be completely independent.

One advantage of Puerto Rico's status after 1917 was that its inhabitants were freely admitted into the USA and many, therefore, emigrated.* Puerto Rican exports also had free access to the USA. But the transition from Spanish to American control produced changes in the island's economy. United States capital flowed into the Territory and produced a far more intensive concentration on sugar (see page 127). By 1930, Puerto Rico was producing almost a million tons of sugar a year, compared with the mere 50 000 tons under Spanish rule. The Brookings Institute estimated that 120 million dollars had then been spent in developing the economy of the island, but it is likely that the development was of greater benefit to the USA, and especially to the great sugar corporations, than to the people of Puerto Rico. The Territory was now over-dependent on sugar, and the Great Depression of the early 1930s showed how vulnerable it was to a recession in trade.

The American connection did, however, bring improvements in communications, education and the public utilities. Banking was encouraged and, after the Second World War, efforts were made to diversify the island's economy. Under Marin,

* 'Everyone there will have moved here.' Bernstein's *West Side Story*. There is a particularly large Puerto Rican community in New York.

Operation Bootstrap was launched, to develop industry, expand the social services and tackle the problem of unemployment. Tourism was promoted, to provide work and to boost the island's income. Cattle-rearing and dairy-farming began to rival sugar production as the principal source of wealth. But a rising population meant that Puerto Rico had to struggle to maintain its forward momentum. In general, the ties with the USA brought a greater prosperity to the island than that achieved by other West Indian islands, but they also brought a change in Puerto Rico's way of life. The pursuit of efficiency to serve the interests of American capital led to an Americanization far removed from the traditionalist Spanish rule of the nineteenth century. Marin's government, until his retirement in 1964, was dynamic, efficient and honest. He was succeeded by Sánchez Vilella and the rule of the Popular Democrats, Marin's party, continued for a further four years, when the New Progressive Party secured control. But although the economy was shaped on the lines of the USA, political self-government helped to retain something of Puerto Rico's Latin heritage and allowed its inhabitants to keep their own identity. For a minority of resolute opponents, it was not enough and agitation continued at sporadic intervals for the total separation and independence of Puerto Rico.

The Watch on the Caribbean

Following the failure of Ferdinand de Lesseps and the French to build the Panama Canal in the 1880s, the task was undertaken by the USA. Work commenced during the Presidency of Theodore Roosevelt at the beginning of the twentieth century, and the Canal was opened for traffic in 1914. The Republic of Panama was forced to lease in perpetuity to the USA strips of land on both sides of the Canal, known as the Panama Canal Zone.* The Spanish–American War and the building of the Panama Canal symbolized the deep and developing interest of the USA in central America and in the Caribbean. Puerto Rico and the Canal Zone were the largest properties under direct US control, but in the twentieth century, American influence became dominant throughout the entire area. Much of the influence was economic (see page 127) but the USA also took a strong political interest, of which the Platt Amendment concerning Cuba was an outstanding example.

One manifestation of the USA's interest in the West Indies was the spread of American bases. The West Indies controlled the approaches to the Panama Canal. To Guantánamo in Cuba and to the island of Puerto Rico, the USA added the harbour of St Thomas by buying the Danish Virgin Islands in 1917. The outbreak of the Second World War offered a further opportunity to the Americans and, in 1940, Britain agreed to lease naval bases to the USA throughout the West Indies. These were in the British islands as far apart as Trinidad, Antigua and the Bahamas (see Figure 11.1). In exchange, Britain borrowed fifty reconditioned but antiquated destroyers. The bases were leased for ninety-nine years and several became the targets of nationalist criticism when Britain began freeing her West Indian colonies. Eric Williams of Trinidad led the criticism, and he considered it a triumph when he persuaded the USA to surrender the Trinidadian base at Chaguaramas in 1961. At that time Washington agreed to a number of withdrawals, no longer convinced that the bases were vital, and anxious to secure goodwill amongst West Indian nationalist movements.

An interest in the good government of West Indian islands was another feature of the USA's Caribbean policy. 'Good government' tended to mean stability, security for American investments and the exclusion of hostile influences. The Monroe Doctrine of 1823 had warned Europeans not to attempt further colonization in the Americas, but after the Second World War 'hostile influences' often meant communism, and it seemed a tragedy to the USA when Castro planted communism in Cuba (see page 144). Although Washington could appreciate the desirability of social and economic progress as a foundation for political stability, it often seemed that the USA was prepared to settle for less. There was little or no direct US intervention in the remaining colonies of Britain, France and the Netherlands, but independent West Indian states found themselves closely supervised by the USA and American intervention was by no means always on the side of progress.

Before 1933, US policy was often high handed. In 1904, Theodore Roosevelt considered that

---

* In 1978, President Carter of the USA signed new Panama Canal Treaties, to transfer the Canal to the government of Panama in year 2000.

there were circumstances in which the USA should exercise 'an international police power'. Woodrow Wilson felt that he had a mission to teach America's republican neighbours 'to elect good men'. Thus the USA took it upon itself to guide the footsteps not only of Cuba but also of Haiti and the Dominican Republic. Franklin D. Roosevelt, the US President from 1933, proposed as a variant a Good Neighbor Policy. The Platt Amendment was cancelled, thus giving Cuba more effective independence, and the USA sought to be less of a policeman and more of a helpful friend. But with the onset of the American–Russian Cold War after 1945, the policeman re-emerged. The West Indies were simply too close to the United States to be left to their own devices, although President Carter, who took office in the USA in 1977, showed readiness to pursue a new liberalism.

The Independent Republics

In the early twentieth century, therefore, the independent republics were not entirely independent. In *Cuba*, Palma was soon in difficulty. There was an uprising in 1906 and when the USA could not restore order with mediation, American troops and an American administration took control. Cuban rule was restored in 1909 but it led to an African uprising in 1912, and the USA intervened again. There were renewed disturbances in 1917, but this time order was restored without American troops and the USA was, in any case, more concerned with the war in Europe. In 1919, however, the USA was called upon to draw up new electoral laws for Cuba and then to help deal with a financial crisis which lasted from 1920 to 1923. Cuba's troubles stemmed from a variety of causes. Governments were often financially inept and corrupt; there were racial tensions; and politicians tended to look to US intervention to further their own causes. Cuba needed to learn the arts of self-government and to learn from its own mistakes, but with extensive foreign investment in the island, British, French and German as well as American, and the USA's watching role, it had a limited opportunity to do so.

After the political confusion of its early years, Cuba drifted into dictatorship. General Gerardo Machado came to power in 1925 and retained power by methods which were increasingly repressive. He proved unable to deal with the Depression, however, and in 1933 he was forced to flee. Cuba was again torn by strife, and again American troops were sent to the island. The outcome was a succession of presidents who thinly disguised the fact that real power rested with Fulgencio Batista, a sergeant self-promoted to colonel who had succeeded Machado as the effective controller of the army. The cancellation of the Platt Amendment in 1934 gave Batista an even freer hand. As the policeman of Cuban affairs, all that the USA had achieved was to leave the island in the hands of a dictator who aspired to emulate the fascists in Europe.

For a brief interval, from 1944 to 1952, Cuba broke free from Batista's grip. Under Grau San Martin a start was made on political and social reform. The new government gave some indication of moving towards socialist principles, but San Martin was in power only until 1948 and in 1952 Batista was able to seize control again. His new regime was not entirely illiberal and some

Cuba was not annexed by the USA after the war of 1898, but Washington kept a close watch on Cuba's affairs

"FLOR DE CUBA!"

(WITH THE BLOOM OFF.)

UNCLE SAM (TO CUBA). "SEE HERE! IF I'D KNOWN WHAT A DURN'D, WORTHLESS, ILL-CONDITIONED SKUNK YOU ARE, I WOULDN'T HA' LIFTED A HAND FOR YOU! BUT—NOW I'M HERE—GUESS I'M GOIN' TO STAY, AND *LICK YOU INTO SHAPE!*"

attempt was made to observe constitutional conventions. But there were two essential facts about Batista's Cuba: the first was that the vast majority of its people, especially those in the rural areas, were sadly neglected and had little share in the country's wealth; the second was that it was heavily dependent on foreign capital and on the fluctuating price of its exports, especially of sugar, in foreign markets. Although by general standards in the West Indies, Cuba was quite an advanced country, a quarter of the Cuban labour force suffered from chronic unemployment, and United States investment dominated many Cuban enterprises from sugar growing to the telephone service. As early as 1953, Fidel Castro made an attempt to overthrow Batista. He tried again in 1956 and secured a base in the Sierra Maestra. In January, 1959, he occupied Havana and Batista fled. Castro's appeal to the Cubans was based on anti-Americanism and the promise of sweeping social reform. In American eyes, he represented the dangerous 'hostile influence' of communism. In the eyes of many Cubans, he was a nationalist and a liberator (see page 144).

Neither nineteenth-century independence nor twentieth-century American supervision did much to lead the *Dominican Republic* to tranquillity and prosperity. Fraud and corruption led the USA to take over the Republic's customs revenue in 1907, to protect the interests of foreign creditors. In 1911 and again in 1916, US troops were sent to quell disorders. They remained from 1916 to 1924 and, much as in Cuba, the Americans attempted to lay the foundations for 'good government' and to initiate some material progress. One of the legacies of American intervention, however, was a trained

Fulgencio Batista: a dictator who aspired to emulate the fascists in Europe as the Mussolini-like trappings in this photograph show

A stamp to celebrate the twenty-fifth year of the rule of Trujillo, the self-styled Benefactor—and a stamp to celebrate the first anniversary of the assassination of Trujillo (Dominican Republic, 1955 and 1962)

constabulary with a zeal for law and order. The head of the constabulary was Rafael Trujillo, who became the effective ruler of the Dominican Republic in 1930. Like Batista in Cuba, Trujillo sometimes ruled behind a façade of puppet presidents.

Trujillo's regime was dictatorial and corrupt. Its methods were ruthless and there was little to justify the title of 'Benefactor' which Trujillo conferred on himself. Superficially, the Republic was improved by a programme of public works, and after more than fifty revolutions between 1844 and 1930 there was certainly a need for the stability which Trujillo achieved. But the economy remained mainly agricultural, heavily dependent on American investment, and the mass of the Republic's people had little for which to thank their 'Benefactor'. He was assassinated in 1961 and at last free elections could be held. Although more than half the electors were illiterate—itself a comment on Trujillo's long years in power—they chose wisely and made Juan Bosch their President to implement a reforming programme based on 'Land and Dignity', which promised reduced dependence on sugar and an attack on corruption. This was too radical for the army and Bosch was overthrown by a military coup to the accompaniment of an orchestrated chorus alleging that Bosch might be a communist, a Dominican Castro. Pro-Bosch forces led a counter-attack and in 1965 there was civil war. The USA decided once more that the time had come to play the policeman. In due course however, US troops were disguised as part of an Inter-American Peace Force, sponsored by the Organization of American States in which Cuba had conveniently been silenced. The Peace Force clearly took the same view as President Johnson of the USA, that communism was not consistent with 'good government'. Order was restored and new elections held in which Bosch was defeated and Joaquin Balaguer, an anti-socialist, became President.

Balaguer's administration lasted. During the next ten years, benefiting from active government, the Dominican Republic began to make progress. Although still primarily agricultural, the economy was helped by the working of bauxite and the encouragement of tourism. A programme to help small farmers and an emphasis on diversified and modern cultivation suggested that, at last, the Republic was moving towards the fulfilment of its potential.

In neighbouring *Haiti*, events took a course not dissimilar from those in the Dominican Republic but with fewer reasons for optimism. Coffee continued to be the principal export with too little industry for economic strength. The underlying friction between mulattoes and Africans (see page 104), which had been a problem in the nineteenth century, continued to plague the state.

The twentieth century began with factious intrigue, civil war and scandals about French

Table 11.1 The USA and the West Indies in the 1970s

Country	Population (millions: 1977 est.)	Ethnic groups %	Economically active population % Industry	Agriculture	Services	Per capita income (US dollars)
USA	216.8	White 87* Negro 11.5	29.7	3.8	66.5	7860 (1976)
Cuba	9.4	White 73 Mulatto 14.5 Negro 12.5	26.3	30	43.7	1000 (1975)
Haiti	4.7	Negro 95 Mulatto 5	5.9	61.5	32.6	158 (1974)
Dominican Republic	5.0	Mulatto 73 White 16 Negro 11	10.5	44.3	45.2	700 (1975)
Puerto Rico	3.3	White 82* Negro 18	29.3	7.7	63	2730 (1976)
US Virgin Islands	0.1	Negro 65 Mixed 19 White 16	25.5	1.2	73.3	—
Jamaica	2.1	†	16.9	29	54.1	1200 (1975)
Trinidad and Tobago	1.2	†	28.1	13.9	58	1400 (1974)
Guyana	0.8	†	23.1	29.6	47.3	588 (1975)

* Mulattoes classed as white.
† See page 185.

Immigration into the USA from the West Indies (1975): 386 194
including, from Cuba: 25 995
from Dominican Republic: 14 066
from Jamaica: 11 076
from Trinidad and Tobago: 5 982

loans. They culminated in 1915 when, in an outbreak of mob fury, Guillaume Sam, the most recent self-appointed President, was torn to pieces in the street. Concerned about the comparatively small US investments in Haiti and about gross financial mismanagement, the USA took control of Haiti's finances in an agreement of 1916. The USA also undertook the restoration of the rule of law and sent in troops. Troublesome Haitians were shot and a constabulary, similar to that in the Dominican Republic, was set up. American troops remained in Haiti until 1934 and financial supervision was not ended until 1947. The USA effected some material improvements in the country but it did nothing to set Haiti on the road to responsible and democratic government. Of the succession of politicians who came to the fore, Elie Lescot was one of Haiti's most successful presidents, ruling from 1941 to 1946, but he was a mulatto and the army ousted him in favour of the African, Dumarsais Estimé. The army then ousted him too, in favour of Paul Magloire who was the President from 1950 to 1956. Magloire showed some ability to govern, but his rule also terminated in disorder amidst rumours that he was seeking illegally to extend it.

The way was now clear for Francois Duvalier who, from 1957, ruled with an iron fist against the mulattoes. He was supported by a sinister private army known as the Tonton Macoute, and he relied on something of an appeal to Voodooism and the apparent agreement of the African masses. The army was purged in order to curb its capacity to intervene further in political affairs, and Haiti succumbed to one of the grimmest political dictatorships of the twentieth century. Although at first inclined to encourage Duvalier as a bulwark against Castro, his neighbour in Cuba, even the USA found it difficult to justify the stability he achieved in the light of the thuggery he employed in its achievement. American aid still trickled into Haiti, but even that was misused and Duvalier's stability was not much more than stagnation. Able and educated Haitians, especially

Figure 11.1 United States Influence in the West Indies: Twentieth Century

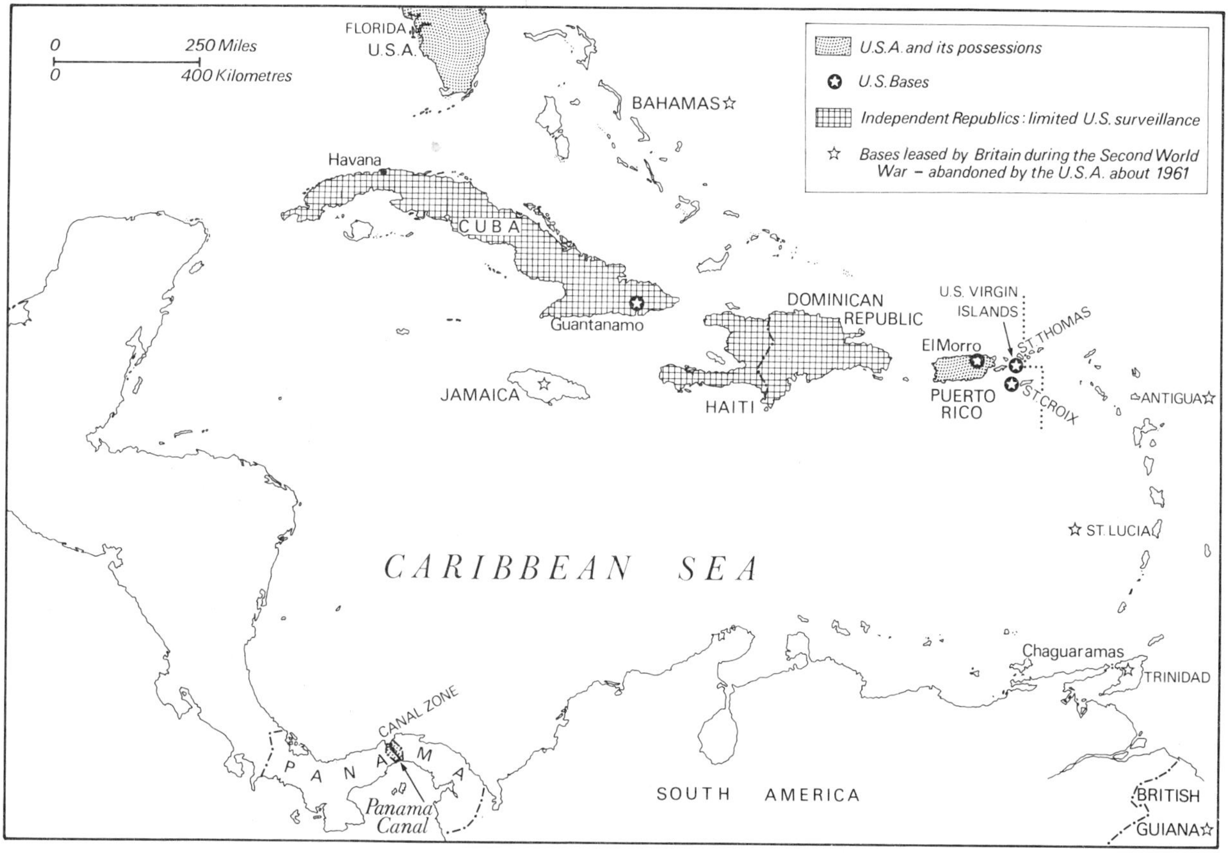

After the father, the son. Jean-Claude Duvalier (left) succeeded his father as ruler of Haiti in 1971. After Papadoc, Babydoc the mulattoes, were often driven to emigrate. The regime quarrelled with Venezuela and the Dominican Republic and upset the Catholic Church, causing Duvalier himself to be excommunicated. But although Magloire and other exiles tried to trigger off a revolution and overturn the dictator, he remained firmly in control and became President-for-Life in a national plebiscite. Duvalier, originally a country doctor, came to be known as Papadoc and his regime circulated a prayer for his people to offer to whatever god protects the political thug: 'Our Doc, who art in the National Palace of Life, hallowed be thy name ...' it began. There was little hallowing of the name of Papadoc outside Haiti. His rule seemed to have no major objective other than to prolong itself. Duvalier's Haiti provided a dismal sequel to the pioneering efforts of Toussaint L'Ouverture. Illiteracy was almost universal. The economy was moribund, and, barely touched by western civilization, Haiti was African in only the most primitive sense.

Duvalier died in April, 1971, having rewritten the Haitian constitution to allow his son, Jean-Claude, to succeed him as another President-for-Life.* There was suddenly talk of liberalization, economic development and an attack on corruption; and the hope was held out that there might be a new flow of aid from the USA. The Tonton Macoute was reduced in importance, while a new security force, The Leopards, came to the fore to combat sedition and communism. There was obviously a good deal for Jean-Claude to do to make up for his father's wasted years. By the mid-1970s, he had done much to consolidate his power, something to develop the economy, but almost nothing to improve the lot of the masses who worked the land in Haiti's crowded valleys and on eroded mountain slopes. It needed considerable economic advancement simply to keep pace with the expanding population, and such advancement required capital. By 1975, Haiti was borrowing heavily—from the World Bank, the International Monetary Fund, the Inter-American Development Bank, the government of France and the government of the USA. The increased production of bauxite offered some prospect of a step towards prosperity, and there was hope that Haiti would prove to have workable reserves of copper. But, in 1977, famine occurred in northern Haiti and there were extensive failures in the country's electricity supply owing to inadequate maintenance of a hydro-electric dam. It was also necessary to resort to emergency imports of foodstuffs at a time when Duvalier himself was alleged to be in the process of purchasing a luxury yacht. 77 per cent of Haitians were still dependent on agriculture, the highest proportion in the Caribbean; and little or no industry existed in the country. The annual growth rate of the economy had jumped to 6 per cent in 1971, having been stuck at a dismal 1 per cent for the previous decade, but the *per capita* income of Haitians was only 110 US dollars, less than a third of that in the Dominican Republic and a mere fraction of that in Puerto Rico.

* The arrangement was approved, it was claimed, in a national referendum in which 2 391 916 voted in favour of Jean-Claude's title; one person voted against; two Haitians abstained.

Exercises

1 Why did Spanish rule continue longer in Cuba and Puerto Rico than it did in Santo Domingo and on the American mainland? Why, on the other hand, did Spanish rule in Cuba and Puerto Rico not last as long as the rule of other European powers in the Caribbean?

2 'An interest in the good government of West Indian islands was a feature of the USA's Caribbean policy' (page 134). Explain some of the ways in which this 'interest' showed itself, and discuss the extent to which the USA brought about results which were (a) beneficial and (b) harmful to the West Indian islands in the years before the Second World War.

3 Trace the history since independence of (a) Haiti and (b) the Dominican Republic. Why has progress in these independent states been slow and difficult?

4 Find out more about the lives of José Martí and Muñoz Marin. For what reasons should they be remembered as outstanding West Indians? Select one other West Indian who is referred to in this chapter whose career seems to have similarities with those of Martí and Marin, and make similar investigations into his life.

5 (a) Study Figure 11.1 and Table 11.1. What information do they provide about United States influence in the West Indies in the twentieth century, and what conclusions can you draw about this influence? (Your conclusions should be based *only* on the map and the table.) (b) In what ways, other than those shown on the map and in the table, may the United States exercise influence in the West Indies at the present time? How could this influence be measured and documented?

12 Contrasts in the Non-British Islands

I THE FRENCH EMPIRE

Guadeloupe and Martinique

It was a logical step for the French to declare, in 1946, that Guadeloupe, Martinique and Guyane (French Guiana) were overseas departments of the French Republic. The slaves who were freed in 1848 had gained the rights of free men in the French Caribbean colonies, and that meant that they were regarded as French citizens. Moreover, the colonies were allowed direct representation in the French parliament. The French system bore some similarities to the centralized control of Spain, but it avoided the rigid Spanish distinction between Europeans and creoles. At the same time, the French colonies were more closely linked with France than were the British islands with Britain. Overseas-department status, in effect, confirmed that the territories were part of France and that their citizens possessed the same rights as Frenchmen, including the right of free movement into France itself. The population of the French departments was mainly African and mulatto, the culture a blending of French and African. But, at least in theory, French West Indians were Frenchmen.

In some ways, this was a privileged position. French West Indians enjoyed a greater equality with their fellow-Frenchmen than did Puerto Ricans in their ambiguous relationship with the USA. The French government was prepared to spend money on raising the standards of Guadeloupe and Martinique to the normal French levels, for example in education. The French did not contemplate abandoning their overseas departments, so that it seemed natural to make them as much like the rest of France as possible. Efficient European administration was applied to them. Progress was slow at first, for the Second World War left the European countries with many problems of reconstruction which could not be solved overnight. The economies of Guadeloupe and Martinique were also mainly agricultural with an emphasis on bananas, sugar and coffee, and over-population and unemployment handicapped development. Nevertheless, by 1963, *per capita* income in Martinique had risen to 420 US dollars a year and was rising at an annual rate of about 6 per cent (compare the table on page 138).

Election results in the 1960s and 1970s seemed to show that in Guadeloupe and Martinique there was general satisfaction with the French connection. On the other hand, serious rioting occurred in Martinique in 1959. It was impossible to ignore the facts of geography. The islands were remote from France and the real seat of power was in Paris. Many of the administrators came from Europe, and the economies were developed primarily for what they could contribute to the French economy as a whole. The role of the islands was chiefly to provide foodstuffs and not much encouragement was given to industry until the late 1960s. Being French had other disadvantages as well. French West Indians, like all Frenchmen, were required to undergo a period of military service, often in Europe. Young West Indians were inclined to be more critical of the ties with France than their elders were. Some of the critics preferred a looser system, similar to that which existed in Puerto Rico. Others wanted outright independence such as was being granted to the British West Indies in the 1960s, but the majority seemed to want neither. Charles de Gaulle, the President of France from 1958 to 1969, granted independence to most of the French empire, but in the Caribbean he merely stepped up the efforts to make the departments truly part of France, and he enjoyed considerable popularity in the West Indies. France had helped to found the European Economic Community in 1957, and, as overseas departments, Guadeloupe and Martinique automatically became integral members of the Community. They were thus able to benefit from EEC aid as well as from French financial assistance; but, in return, they were tied even more closely to Europe.

Guyane

Similar attempts were made to integrate Guyane into France. The problem here was very different from that in the French islands, for the department was seriously under-populated with fewer than 50 000 inhabitants. Development was slower, but de Gaulle received an enthusiastic welcome when he visited Guyane in 1964 and again he expressed the French determination to promote the department's prosperity. Until 1946, however, Guyane had been used as a French penal colony, and its association with the notorious Devil's Island left a stigma which was difficult to escape. The inhabitants of Guadeloupe and Martinique were particularly reluctant to abandon their overcrowded islands for the almost empty forests and swamps of Guyane. The French respected the free choice of the individual, and sought to encourage settlement and investment in Guyane by indirect methods, such as tax incentives.

II THE DUTCH EMPIRE

Surinam

Surinam took the plunge into independence in 1975 and was admitted to the United Nations Organization as the 144th member. Surinam's history under Dutch rule had been similar in many ways to that of the larger colonies under British rule (see Chapter 13). During the nineteenth century, the system of administration resembled that in a British crown colony, but the Dutch allowed Surinam to have elected representatives earlier than they allowed similar concessions to the Dutch islands and, in 1950, Surinam moved on to self-government. At that time, this was perhaps as far as the Dutch intended to go. They had already lost the Dutch East Indies, and they now experimented with a Tripartite Kingdom made up of all that was left of the Dutch empire: the Netherlands, Surinam and the Netherlands Antilles. The people of Surinam, in effect, ruled themselves but the Dutch looked after their defence and foreign policy.

The continuing Dutch connection was helpful to Surinam. It brought various forms of expertise which were much needed after years of comparative neglect, and Dutch membership of the EEC enabled Surinam to secure aid from the European Community. Bauxite provided a valuable export commodity, and some hope was offered that substantial reserves of oil might exist. British Guiana, Surinam's western neighbour, became independent in 1966, and total independence now began to appeal to the people of Surinam too. The Dutch gave way gracefully, and Surinam was launched into independence with a parting gift. There were some doubts as to whether Surinam's frail economy could cope with the strains of complete independence, and, immediately after independence, there was an emigration of many skilled Surinamese, especially the descendants of Indian immigrants, who preferred the greater security of the Netherlands and Europe. Like Guyana, Surinam had a mixture of races, and nation-building seemed sure to be difficult both socially and economically. Nevertheless, the majority of Surinamese had shown the confidence to add yet another new nation to the growing total in and around the Caribbean.

The refining of oil on Curaçao began in 1915, a source of prosperity but perhaps a precarious one (Netherlands Antilles, 1965)

The Netherlands Antilles

The Dutch West Indian islands were granted little in the way of representation and self-government before 1948, but events then moved swiftly. Within a few years, like Surinam, they became almost wholly self-ruling in all but foreign affairs.

Figure 12.1 Trade Table: French and Dutch Territories

	Population (1976 est.)	Main Exports		Trade (1975)* Exports to		Imports from	
French							
Guadeloupe	360 000	Sugar Bananas Rum	41% 37% 7%	France	73%	France	74%
Martinique	369 000	Bananas Petroleum products Rum	48% 20% 13%	France	69%	France	65%
Guyane	62 000	Shrimps Timber	44% 14%	USA France	46% 25%	France	71%
Dutch							
Netherlands Antilles	241 000	Petroleum products and crude oil	96%†	USA	62%	Venezuela Saudi Arabia	57% 17%
Independent (formerly Dutch)							
Surinam	435 000 (Indian 37%; Creole 31%; Indonesian 15%; Bush Negro 10%; Amerindian 2.5%)	Alumina Bauxite	43%† 18%†	USA W. Germany Netherlands	19%† 8%† 7%†	USA Netherlands Trinidad and Tobago	24% 10%† 6%†

* Percentages of whole.
† Figures for 1974.

They had a single parliament for Curaçao, Aruba and the smaller, more northern islands such as St Eustatius. A Prime Minister and cabinet were responsible to this parliament. They ruled two groups of islands almost 600 miles apart, and, since the islands were also a part of the Tripartite Kingdom, complicated constitutional links with the Netherlands were also necessary. When Surinam chose to become independent, the Netherlands Antilles remained within the Kingdom. There was perhaps no really practicable alternative. The widely scattered islands had been united by historical accident under Dutch rule. In the age of decolonization, they were an unlikely collection from which to build a single new nation.

But the Netherlands Antilles were amongst the most prosperous territories in the West Indies. Well over 90 per cent of the population lived in Curaçao and Aruba. Their *per capita* income in the mid-1960s was higher than that in Puerto Rico and second only, in the Caribbean, to that of the United States Virgin Islands. But the economy was lop-sidedly based on the refining of oil imported from Venezuela and elsewhere, and on the employment which was provided by the great oil companies. The latter were continually searching for labour-saving technology, so that there was reason to question whether the prosperity was firmly based. The Netherlands Antilles may also illustrate another West Indian problem, that of language. The fragmentation of the West Indies amongst the European powers in the seventeenth and eighteenth centuries meant that the islands became divided by language. Yet the division was not absolute. Dutch was the official language of the Netherlands Antilles, but English was more commonly spoken in the Leeward Islands under the influence of neighbouring islands. The southern group of the Netherlands Antilles, however, contained many who were Papiamento-speaking. Dutch and a high level of literacy helped to bind the Netherlands Antilles together, but it also divided at least some parts of the Antilles from their neighbours.

III CASTROISM

Cuba's Revolution

The comparative ease with which Castro chased out Batista at the end of 1958 and occupied Havana in January, 1959 (see page 136), showed clearly the rottenness of the Batista regime. What Castro stood for was far less clear. The story has become something of a legend of how twelve men in the Sierra Maestra prepared for the revolution and then, with the help of 'illiterate, uneducated and technically untrained' peasants, defeated a 'regular, disciplined army'. The 'man of the Sierra Maestra' was represented by Castro himself as one who could say,

> 'I have lived all my life without fuel, without electric light, without transport, without medicines, without everything.'

The Revolution was, therefore, a rising of the under-privileged, the have-nots. Castro claimed to be acting as one who was 'democratic, nationalist' and a supporter of 'social justice'. His reforming programme promised the distribution of unused lands, faster industrialization (to create wealth and work), the preservation of political and civil liberties, and an attack on corruption and illiteracy. It seemed likely that he would favour state control of the Cuban economy, or at least state intervention in it, as the leaders of many developing countries did. And he was likely to lean towards the principles and policies of socialism which encouraged the more equal sharing out of wealth. These were aims which almost every West Indian nationalist would have applauded. But Castro and his followers had little experience of government and little training in economics. Fidel Castro himself had been a lawyer; Ernesto ('Che') Guevara, his chief supporter, a doctor. They were now soon to find themselves involved in a bitter confrontation with the whole apparatus of the government of the USA.

Che Guevara was a Marxist who shared a belief in the revolutionary peasantry with Mao Tse-tung of China. Castro himself did not declare a commitment to Marxism until 1961. Much of Castro's early reading had been of the works of José Martí, and at first it was possible to regard him as a liberator of Cuba, perhaps Martí's disciple. The governing party was the Popular Socialist Party, but it became the United Party of the Socialist Revolution and, in 1965, the Cuban Communist Party. Elections had been promised but they were not held. Censorship of the press and forced-labour camps took the place of the promised democracy. On the other hand,

Che Guevara (centre) at Peking Airport, leading a Cuban economic delegation in 1960

Contrasting leaders: Batista with a favourite horse, and Castro cutting sugar-cane

considerable changes were made in Cuba's economy and society, many of them for the better. The changes were accompanied by a head-on collision with the USA, and Castro's admirers can argue with some force, that this collision helped to push Castro towards Marxism and to push Cuba towards the Soviet Union.

Guevara did not remain long in Cuba. His first work was concerned with agricultural programmes and the setting up of co-operatives. In 1961, he became the Minister for Industries. But he found administration dull and he set off for south America in 1965, to wage a guerilla struggle against the social and political systems which kept the peasants in poverty and misery. He was ambushed and killed two years later in Bolivia. By that time, Cuba had become a centre for revolutionary activity throughout Latin America and the Caribbean. With Castro's support, the Latin American Solidarity Organization was founded in 1966 to encourage peasant revolutions and to attack the influence of the USA. The American interference in the affairs of the Dominican Republic in 1965 (see page 137) had seemed to the supporters of Castroism to be yet another example of the ever-present meddlesomeness of the United States policeman. Whatever other views he held, Castro was violently anti-American. As early as 1958, he had prophesied that when the struggle for power in Cuba was over there would be a new struggle, against the USA. He wrote in a letter, referring to an attack on the house of a peasant in the Sierra Maestra by a Batista plane carrying American-made weapons,

> 'When I saw rockets firing at Mario's house, I swore to myself that the Americans were going to pay dearly for what they were doing. When this war is over, a much wider and bigger war will begin for me: the war that I am going to launch against them.'

Castro certainly proved himself to be a revolutionary, a radical and a nationalist; and he has proclaimed his attachment to Marxism–Leninism. He provided a focus in the West Indies for a new disruptiveness which threatened all kinds of imperialism and empires, and which, he hoped, would help to overthrow neighbouring dictatorships such as that in Haiti. Castroism had its origins in an intense desire to rid Cuba of foreign influences and to befriend the poor, but circumstances aligned Cuba with the communist world. United States influence in Cuba gave way to Russian influence, though it was never Castro's intention that Cuba should be the puppet of any foreign power. To what extent Cuba has become subordinate to Russia is a matter of fierce controversy. But Castro was born on a West Indian sugar plantation, the son of an immigrant farm labourer from Spain who had become a prosperous landowner. First and foremost, he was a West Indian; for better or for worse, his intention was to develop a new independence and a new kind of society in and around the Caribbean. His enemies branded him, simply, as a communist, but Castroism was a West Indian product and it differed in a variety of ways from the communism of the Soviet Union and that of China.

Cuba's Internal Changes

The National Institute for Agrarian Reform was set up almost as soon as Castro came to power. It aimed to curtail the vast estates and to encourage peasant co-operatives. At the same time, public utilities were to be brought under state control so that their development would be in the interests of the people. The Ministry for Industries was created in 1961 to expand industrial production. A clash with United States business interests came quickly, for the Cuban government began seizing their properties in exchange for government bonds. Washington tried to take advantage of the fact that more than 60 per cent of Cuba's exports were sold to the USA, and an American boycott was imposed on Cuban sugar. The Cuban seizure of about a thousand million dollars worth of US investments and Castro's approaches to the Soviet Union persuaded Washington to go further in teaching him a lesson, and the USA broke off diplomatic relations with Cuba in 1961. During the next few years, economic pressures were stepped up with the result that Castro came to rely increasingly on the communist world for markets and supplies.

Rapid industrialization was not successful. Complete factories were imported from Russia, but Cuba lacked the technical skills and even the raw materials to make them competitive. By the mid-1960s, it seemed that Cuba would have to rely on a basically agricultural economy for some considerable time to come. The first agricultural developments in Castro's Cuba had seen the introduction of state farms and peasant co-operatives. The former were often large, similar to those in Russia, and it was intended that they would take advantage of mechanization. But they strengthened rather than weakened Cuba's dependence on sugar, while the co-operatives were often inefficient. Rationing of foodstuffs had to be introduced in 1962, and by the end of the 1960s state control became dominant in both agriculture and industry. Perhaps the greatest disappointment for Castro was that the annual target for sugar production had had to be raised to 10 million tons. A revolution which had set out to destroy sugar's stranglehold was proceeding only to intensify it. But, as Castro himself admitted, sugar was what Cuba could produce best. He could at least claim that sugar production was now in the hands of Cubans and not of Americans.

One reason why the development of the Cuban economy was disappointing in the first ten years of the revolution was that resources were often used for social improvement rather than for economic investment. Batista left behind a legacy of squalor, vice and corruption. Gambling casinos and an army of prostitutes in Havana were evidence of Cuba's demoralization. A huge gap existed between the rich and the poor. The new government intended to make fundamental changes. It was estimated that a million Cubans were illiterate and a successful crash-programme was launched to change this. Almost all learned to read and write, concluding their learning with the exercise of writing a letter to Fidel himself. Road-building, housing and medical programmes were given high priority with an emphasis on rural health centres, drains and piped water. Every effort was made to stamp out vice. Castro aimed to achieve honest government and a dignified society in which the status of the lowly, and especially of women, was raised. The literacy campaign was only the start of a revolution in education on which the government was prepared to spend generously. The government also attacked unemployment, again with considerable success.

Critics, on the other hand, argued that the educational system produced too few technicians and that manpower was often used wastefully to achieve only a low level of productivity. More superficially, some Americans lamented that Havana was no longer what it had been: the rumba bands had been conscripted to work in the fields, drink was expensive and even the bright lights were dimmed for reasons of economy. Such criticisms and academic arguments about the state of Cuba's finances counted for far less among the peasants, the Africans, women and the poor generally, than the fact that tens of thousands could now see tangible benefits from Castro's rule. That his rule was near to being a dictatorship, in some ways even an inefficient one, was a price that many were probably willing to pay.

A celebration of Cuban–Soviet friendship: the Lenin Hospital (Cuba, 1966)

Cuba's External Relations

Cuba's faltering economy was much sustained by economic aid from the Soviet Union, and from other communist states. There were invaluable trade agreements, credit facilities and outright grants, but Russia's enthusiasm for a somewhat expensive ally in the West Indies was beginning to wane by the late 1960s. Cuba's exports were not vital to the welfare of the Soviet Union any more than were Russian sales to Cuba. By that time, it had begun to seem unlikely that Cuba was going to be an effective apostle in spreading communism into the rest of the Caribbean and Latin America. The influence of the USA in these areas remained very strong. The long-term advantages to Cuba of the connection with the communist world may not be extensive.

Meanwhile, 1961 and 1962 were years of bitter confrontation between Cuba and the USA. The breaking-off of diplomatic relations in January, 1961, was followed by the fiasco of the Bay of Pigs in April. Cuban exiles, prodded by the American CIA, launched an invasion of southern Cuba with the intention of overthrowing Castro in favour of Miro Cardona. President Eisenhower encouraged the enterprise and John F. Kennedy, his successor, allowed it to go ahead. The invasion was launched from Nicaragua with considerable ineptitude. Kennedy's support was half-hearted and there was far too much advance publicity. The expedition was soundly defeated by Castro's forces. The prisoners that the Cubans took were eventually released for a ransom of United States medical supplies.

A more serious crisis occurred in 1962 when American spy-'planes detected rocket sites on Cuban soil. By this time, Castro had seized even more American investments, 3000 million dollars worth in all, and the US economic boycott was intensive so that Cuba drew ever closer to the Soviet Union. A combination of genuine Cuban fears that the USA might attack and of Russian ambitions to embarrass the USA resulted in the installation of rocket-launching sites at San Cristobal and Guanajay. The rockets would be a breakthrough for Khrushchev, the effective ruler of Russia, in the East–West struggle for power. They were the first such weapons west of Europe, and Kennedy reacted vigorously. Cuba was blockaded and the USA insisted that the missiles should be withdrawn from the island. Russian ships which tried to reinforce them would be stopped by the American fleet. It was not so much a Caribbean problem as a confrontation between the super powers. Castro seemed to be almost irrelevant to the crisis and the key decision was taken in Moscow: Khrushchev decided to have the weapons crated and returned to the Russia. He claimed, however, that,

> 'it was a great victory for us . . . that we had been able to extract from Kennedy a promise that neither America nor any of her allies would invade Cuba.'*

---

* *Khrushchev Remembers* (Deutsch, 1971).

Figure 12.1 Cuba after 1959

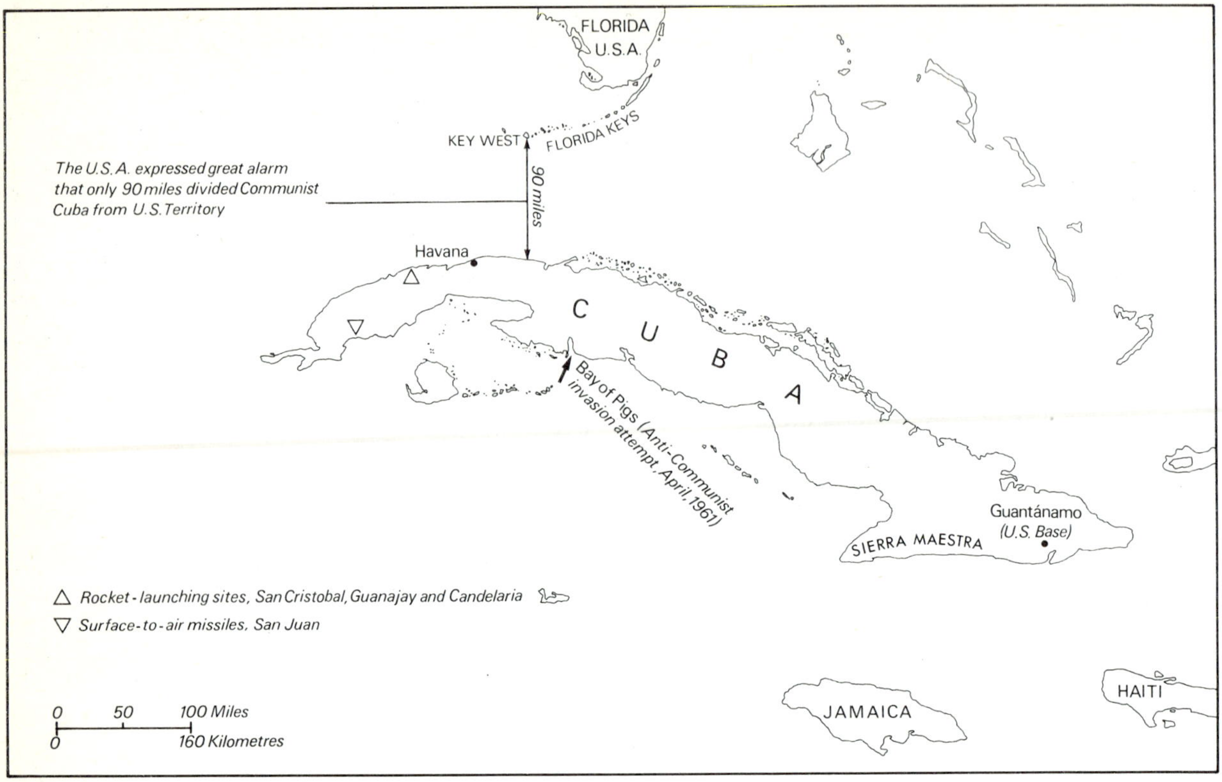

Table 12.2 Cuban Trade (percentages of whole)

Year	Main Exports		Imports from		Exports to	
1950s	Sugar	over 80%	USA	74%	USA	63%
1966	Sugar products	85%	Russia	61%	Russia	44%
			China	7%	China	9%
			France	6%	Spain	6%
1971	Sugar	74%	Russia	53%	Russia	35%
	Non-ferrous metals	16%	East Germany	5%	Japan	12%
					East Germany	6%
1974	Sugar	86%	Russia	47%	Russia	36%
	Nickel and Copper Ores	6%	Japan	8%	Japan	17%
			Britain	5%	Spain	7%

(Cuban Society and Economy: see also Figure 11.1)

In this sense, Cuba seemed to have been saved from any future American attempt to attack Castro openly, though there was no evidence that such an attack was envisaged. Rumours persistently circulated, however, that the CIA would have been pleased if Castro had been assassinated.

Cuba was isolated from the Organization of American States in 1962 and the members of the Organization voted in favour of boycotting trade with the island. This decision owed a good deal to Castro's efforts to promote subversion in Venezuela. By 1964, Cuba's isolation was almost complete and only Mexico stubbornly refused to break off diplomatic relations with Castro. Cuba then became a fashionable destination for hijacked aircraft: it was the symbol of defiance for all those who hated the USA and the capitalist system. For a time, Castro explored the advantages of links with communist China, disillusioned perhaps with Russia's capitulation in the Missiles Crisis; but, in the end, it was on the Soviet Union that Cuba relied most heavily and, in 1972, Cuba became a full member of Comecon, a communist and mainly east European association for mutual economic assistance.

Cuba's involvement in the politics of the great powers thus made for some strange alignments in its relations with the outside world. It had few contacts with its immediate neighbours and was barred from membership of Caribbean and

Latin American associations. Castro was a turbulent neighbour and several Latin American governments had their own good reasons for resenting his passion for revolution. His isolation, however, owed a great deal to the pressures from the USA, and they too were often resented. The cry of 'Yankee imperialism' was as likely to be raised by Latin American nationalists as by communists. It was not surprising, therefore, that in 1972 moves began to renew contacts with Cuba. The initiative came from Guyana and Trinidad and was taken up by Jamaica and Barbados. Their lifting of the boycott was followed, three years later, by the lifting of the boycott imposed by the Organization of American States. The USA continued to ban direct trade between Cuba and the United States, but the way was being cleared for the restoration of more normal trade patterns in the Caribbean. Tentatively, Washington and Havana reached an agreement to discourage hijacking, and it seemed possible that Castro might eventually achieve a degree of respectability in American eyes.

Angola, in Africa, then provided evidence that Castro was still full of revolutionary enthusiasm. Cuban troops were sent to Angola in 1976 to support a Marxist party in the struggle for control of that newly independent state. The Marxists were successful, and the outcome was widely considered to be a triumph for Russia and its allies and a setback for the USA in the international power conflict. Cuban involvement in Angola and, soon afterwards, in other parts of Africa such as Ethiopia, revived the arguments about the extent to which Castro was manipulated from Moscow, and it certainly did nothing to endear the Cuban leader to Washington. When Castro made a flying-visit to Africa in 1977 and another in 1978, he was often accorded a warm welcome and seemed clearly to have become a figure of some international importance; but his Caribbean neighbours must have had mixed feelings about his crusading zeal. Anti-Americanism was not unfashionable, although it could be economically inconvenient. Pro-Marxism was more disturbing to governments which were themselves not Marxist.

By 1978, however, Castro's regime was beginning to make economic progress. Sugar still made up three-quarters of Cuba's exports but nickel production was expanding, with Russia's help, and growth rates were substantial. The rise of world sugar prices in the mid-1970s, combined with some generosity in the price the Russians were willing to pay, produced a healthy balance-of-payments surplus for the island. A third of Cuban land was now owned by small farmers, and development plans held out the prospect of ambitious progress in industry, agriculture and the public services. The Cuban economy had begun to settle down after the upheavals of the early 1960s, and there were a growing number of useful commercial agreements with Mexico and other countries outside the communist bloc. Tourism was also beginning to revive. The economy remained fragile, nevertheless. Many of the problems which face all developing nations remained, but Cuba, perhaps, had achieved more genuine independence than many of them under the man whom almost all Cubans referred to as Fidel.

Exercises

1 'General satisfaction.' 'Serious rioting' (page 141). Explain why mixed feelings exist in Guadeloupe and Martinique concerning the continued links between the islands and France.

2 Which West Indian islands still belong to (a) France and (b) the Netherlands? *In each case,* account for these remaining ties.

3 Show how Cuba, in the course of the last hundred years, has been dominated in turn by (a) Spain, (b) the USA and (c) the Soviet Union. What evidence is there that Cuban national ideals have managed to outlast all these influences?

4 'Writing a letter to Fidel himself' (page 146). Summarize the points which would have been likely to have been made in two such letters in the mid-1970s by (a) a poor Cuban peasant and (b) a well-to-do Cuban who admired the political and economic systems of the USA.

5 Summarize the points which could be made to support, and the arguments, if any, which could be put forward in opposition to *each* of the following descriptions of Castro: a West Indian nationalist; a radical reformer; a dedicated Marxist; a ruthless dictator.

13 Towards Independence: the British West Indies

I THE NINETEENTH CENTURY

Four major developments in the British West Indies have already been considered. Britain's Caribbean empire was enlarged for the last time during the wars which ended in 1815 (see Chapter 8); slavery was abolished (see Chapter 9); so too was the mercantilist system (see Chapter 10); and there began the new influx of immigrants from Asia (see Chapter 10). It now remained to face the question of how best this changing West Indian empire should be governed. The decision had already been taken that newly conquered territories such as Trinidad should not be granted assemblies of the old sort (see page 88), but these assemblies still existed in colonies of longer standing such as Jamaica. The assemblies jealously preserved the privileges of the narrow social group which they represented. Sometimes they obstructed the imperial government, as the particularly obstinate Jamaican assembly did when, in 1839, it refused to agree to direct imperial control of the island's squalid prisons. These same assemblies had often obstructed efforts to improve the lot of the slaves in the years before emancipation. It seemed to the British Colonial Office that they were much too biased in favour of the estate owners, and an obstacle rather than a help to fair and efficient government. And so the Colonial Office looked for an opportunity to abolish them. Consequently, most of the older colonies took one step backwards in the second half of the nineteenth century before they could take one step forwards, and direct British control was applied to them by means of crown colony government. Only then was a new move permitted towards representative government, which would represent not one class but wider sections of West Indian opinion. Under the representative system, West Indians could begin to play a part in governing themselves, but progress towards representative government was a twentieth-century rather than a nineteenth-century feature of the British West Indies.* Meanwhile, the British began to consider the problem of how best to govern the small islands, and to experiment with federations which grouped them into larger political units.

Crown Colony Government

Under the system of crown colony government, the governor was all-powerful, subject only to the ultimate control of the imperial government in London. He could make laws, administer them, and appoint the judges to interpret them. He chose for himself those who would assist him, including the members of a legislative council (to discuss new laws) and of an executive council (to carry them out). Thus, the extent to which local opinion was consulted depended on the will of the governor. In theory, well-chosen governors would bring to the colonies up-to-date ideas, impartiality and expertise. The system seemed particularly suited to colonies in which there was little expertise and where vested interests were likely to undermine good government in their own self-interest. In time, it was bound to become inappropriate as the inhabitants of the colonies became educated and eager to take part in their own government. At this stage, it would be wise to adapt the system towards representative government, allowing elections to the councils and eventually handing over power to the elected representatives of the people. This was the theory on which British colonial government came to be based in the nineteenth and twentieth centuries.

---

* Details of the constitutional changes in this chapter and Chapter 14 will better be understood if reference is also made to Appendix I on page 195.

Of course, there were always those who argued that representative government should have come earlier than it did. In Trinidad, for example, a Reform Association was founded in 1856 to demand early self-government through elected representatives. But although, in the nineteenth century, Britain was prepared to move in this direction in Canada, Australia and New Zealand, its attitude to the West Indies was different. In the West Indies, non-whites were in a majority and whites, in the old assemblies, had often been selfish and sometimes obstructive. Not until well into the twentieth century did the British seriously contemplate West Indian self-government. Meanwhile, crown colony government seemed likely to be fairer than the oligarchy of the old assemblies, and more efficient and stable than the premature granting of democratic representative government. From Britain's point of view, it had the advantage of being tidy and comparatively free from the friction between the old assemblies and their governors. From the West Indian's point of view, it could easily appear paternalistic, even arrogant, and it was still based on rule by the whites.

By the end of the nineteenth century, crown colony government had been established everywhere in the British West Indies except in *Barbados* which was allowed to retain its old assembly. Barbados was comparatively free from racial antagonism and class feuds. Its assembly was constructive and, partly through the campaigning of men like Conrad Reeves, a coloured lawyer, the vote was extended to the elite amongst the free coloureds. Throughout its history, Barbados thus had uninterrupted representative government. With the gradual extension of the right to vote and, in the twentieth century, the transfer of greater powers to the people's representatives, the island moved on to eventual independence in 1966.

Rather curiously, *Guiana* too kept a small measure of representation throughout the nineteenth century. When the British took control of the Dutch territories in 1803 and unified them later into British Guiana in 1831, no assembly was granted but guarantees were given that the inhabitants could keep the rights they had enjoyed under Dutch rule. The result was that Guiana kept a legislature of two chambers: the Court of Policy and the Combined Court. Some members of this legislature were elected and, by 1909, the number of those entitled to vote had grown to 11 000 out of a total population of 300 000. When the constitution was changed in 1928, and a more typically British legislative council was introduced, a majority of its members were elected. Thus, British Guiana had always had some elected representatives with its unorthodox Anglo-Dutch form of crown colony government.

Elsewhere, crown colony government followed a more uniform pattern. *Trinidad* was allowed no elected representation until 1924. The same was true of *St Lucia*. The other British colonies all possessed assemblies which were abolished at various times in the years 1854 to 1875 in favour of the legislative councils which assisted the governors. With the removal of their assemblies, West Indians hoped that they might be allowed to elect at least some of the members of these councils, and thus secure a measure of representative government. In fact, governors expressed dissatisfaction with the quality of those who were elected and, in island after island, all elected representation was removed, leaving only Barbados and Guiana, as has been seen, with uninterrupted representation. The changes were made at different times in different colonies. In *Jamaica*, the abolition of the assembly in 1865 was followed immediately with a legislative council no member of which was elected, although the principle of election and restricted representation were reintroduced in 1884. *Montserrat* lost its assembly in 1861, but was allowed to elect representatives to the council until 1866. *Grenada* kept its assembly until 1875 and election to the council ceased two years later. *Dominica* and *Antigua* went on electing council representatives until 1898, more than thirty years after they lost their assemblies.

The basic pattern was clear in spite of these apparently untidy local differences. The old assemblies were abolished wherever they existed, excepting only those in Barbados and Guiana. There followed a period in every colony during which the governor ruled with a council whose members were all nominated by himself. At varying times, West Indians were then allowed to begin electing some members of the council as the first step on the long road to independence. Jamaica set out on this road in 1884, but the start was delayed in Trinidad until 1924. Gradually, however, the elected members grew in number and in importance until the British eventually handed over power to the West Indians.

The example of nineteenth-century Jamaica will serve to illustrate the first part of this process.

Jamaica

The British colonies which possessed assemblies were, in effect, required to make a choice in the nineteenth century between their old system of government and crown colony government. The British expected that, sooner or later, they would choose crown colony government. The old system had serious shortcomings. In Jamaica, for example, the sugar planters were still dominant in the assembly and this gave them control over finance. Executive power, on the other hand, rested with the governor who had in some way to bridge the gap between what was thought best in London and what the members of the assembly thought best, usually for their own self-interests. This was a recipe for achieving very little. In Jamaica, there was a sort of three-cornered tug-of-war between the governor and two distinct factions in the assembly, that of the planters and that of a rising coloured elite. At that time, the population of the island was about 450 000, but in 1864 fewer than 2000 were entitled to elect the members of the assembly and fewer than 1500 bothered to cast their votes. In general, there was great political apathy among the masses.

When Edward Eyre became the Governor of Jamaica in 1862, conditions in the island were deplorable. Poverty, high prices, maladministration and social divisions embittered the poor and alarmed the propertied. There was a lack of public utilities such as roads and of social services such as hospitals. The population was growing and there was a demand for more land to be made available for smallholdings, but the planters relied on the shortage of such land to drive cheap labour to their estates. An injection of money from Britain was badly needed, but there was no hope of such imperial funds while the governor was denied really effective control of the island by the assembly. Meanwhile, the American Civil War made supplies scarce and drove up prices, and three years of drought added to the miseries of the poor and hungry. The misery produced a violent outbreak of protest at Morant Bay in 1865. Years of hardship in the post-emancipation period had already disheartened the estate owners, and now they were near to panic. Crown colony government seemed to be the only way out. Jamaica desperately needed rule which was efficient and well-financed and, since the existing system failed to produce it, the assembly voted itself out of existence. A year later, in 1866, elections too were abolished and the power of the governor became virtually absolute.

The rising at Morant Bay, which produced these constitutional changes, was not entirely the fault of the assembly's obstructiveness. Governor Eyre was hardly better fitted to rule than most of the estate owners. When George William Gordon, a coloured landowner and a magistrate, pressed him to make changes, he simply cancelled Gordon's appointment to the magistracy. Indeed, most of Eyre's energies were directed into a witch-hunt for troublemakers rather than into any programme of reform. This was the kind of governor the planters liked, but the imperial government in London also seemed to be satisfied with him.

Edward Underhill, the Secretary to the Baptist Missionary Society, took up the matter of the reforms which were urgently needed in Jamaica, and addressed the 'Underhill Letter' to the British Colonial Office. He had been persuaded by the reports of Baptist missionaries that much was amiss. At the same time, poor Jamaicans were encouraged by the Baptists to petition for crown lands to be made available for smallholdings. But apart from referring the matter to Eyre, the British government made no effort to find out what was wrong in Jamaica. Instead, it preferred to blame agitators for trying to stir up trouble, and offered

Paul Bogle and George William Gordon both fell victims to the vengeance of Governor Eyre (Jamaica, 1965)

Temporary court house after that at Morant Bay had been burned down in 1865

the 'Queen's Advice' to Jamaicans. In the name of Queen Victoria, this grandly suggested that Jamaicans could improve their lot by 'their own industry and prudence'. By 'industry' appeared to be meant, working for wages on the plantations. By 'prudence', Victoria was appealing to thrift and the self-help then popular in Britain. Her 'Advice' showed little understanding of, or relevance to, the conditions of Jamaican Africans. A Baptist preacher, Paul Bogle, led a demonstration to the Morant Bay court-house in October, 1865. Eyre called out the militia and, when shots were exchanged, the demonstration became a riot. Twenty-one whites and nine Africans were killed, and the court-house was burned down.

Eyre insisted on regarding this outbreak of misery and frustration as an African uprising. Although it may only have been his intention to browbeat the assembly, his attitude caused such panic that the assembly disbanded itself before the end of the year. In the meantime, savage punishment was inflicted on the 'rebels'. Over 400 were killed and 600 flogged. A thousand African houses were burned. Ringleaders, real and imagined, were seized and executed, many without trial. Amongst them was Gordon, whose alibi was simply ignored in the general reign of injustice and terror. Only now did the British Colonial Office send a commission of inquiry, as a result of which Eyre was recalled to London but was half-rewarded for his sternness with a pension. The blinder elements in British politics regarded him as a hero who had saved Jamaica from following in the footsteps of Haiti.

More sensible opinion saw to it that he was replaced by John Peter Grant, a Governor prepared to use the authority of the crown colony system to make improvements in Jamaica. He improved the judicial system to make the courts faster and fairer. He began the development of a Jamaican civil service with an emphasis on efficient administration. Roads were built and irrigation schemes extended. Similar reforms to those being introduced in England and Ireland at this time were brought to Jamaica: an official savings bank was started; education was overhauled in a search for competence; the Anglican Church was disestablished and some of its income used for educational expansion and improvements in medical services. With no need to consider the vested interests of the planters and no assembly to argue about money, it was at last possible to begin the modernization of Jamaica. Bananas and economic diversification (see page 130) helped to put Jamaica on a firmer economic footing and, between 1881 and 1911, the number of smallholdings increased almost threefold. Grant retired from Jamaica in 1874 but his was one of the island's outstanding governorships.

The reforms which Grant began did not, however, produce prosperity in Jamaica. Improvements in medicine and hygiene had the effect of prolonging life, and that had the effect of increasing the population. The majority of Jamaicans continued to live near the poverty-line in the twentieth century, many of them in deplorable conditions. Poverty existed in Britain too, and late nineteenth-century social surveys, such as that undertaken in London by Charles Booth, showed just how widespread the problem was: hundreds of thousands of Englishmen lived in hideous slums. But if conditions were bad in Britain, they were worse in the colonies, for the colonies inevitably had less claim to whatever money the British government could spare for improvements. What Jamaica, like all colonies, needed was a government which would give the highest priority to the interests of the people of the island. This was something crown colony government could never do, however well-intentioned it was. Britain would almost always come first. But to be self-governing required certain preliminary levels of development, economic, social and political, if self-government were to be successful. An elected element was introduced into Jamaica's legislative council in 1884 and the

THE JAMAICA QUESTION.

WHITE PLANTER. "AM NOT *I* A MAN AND BROTHER, TOO, MR. STIGGINS?"

Official concern for the African majority in Jamaica after the rising at Morant Bay resulted in the abolition of the Assembly which the planters had dominated. *Punch* spared a thought for the white planters

right to vote was gradually extended over the next thirty years. An educated middle class began to grow, and from this developed a new protest movement and then, eventually, a nationalist movement for the independence which would enable Jamaicans themselves to tackle Jamaican problems (see page 161).

The founding of the Jamaican Constabulary was one of the reforms of Governor Grant (Jamaica, 1967)

Experiments in Federation

Jamaica, like Trinidad, was large enough to stand as a separate colony. For other Caribbean islands, the British thought that federal rule was likely to be more efficient and less expensive. This meant grouping the islands under a central administration and one governor. Individually, many islands had very small populations. *The Leeward Islands*, for example, had a population even in the

Figure 13.1 Constitutional Change in the British West Indies: Nineteenth Century

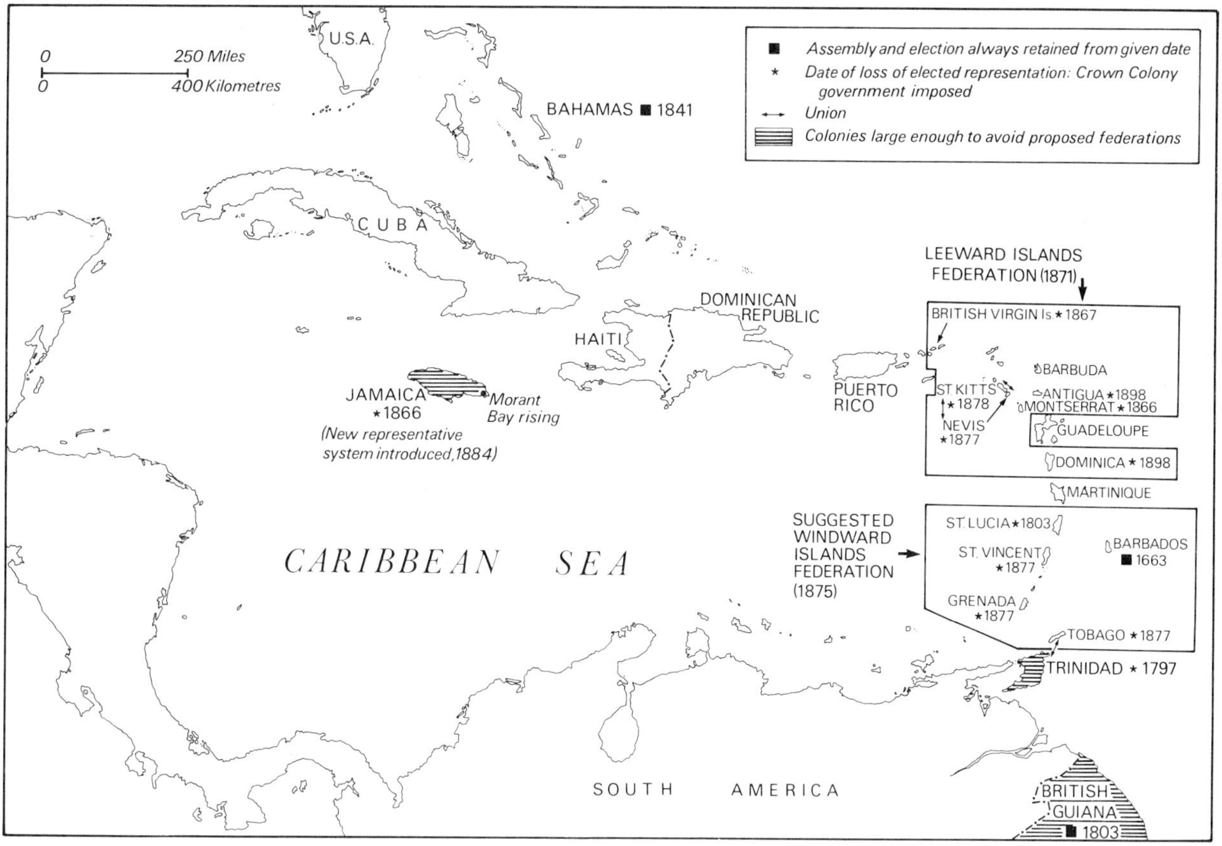

1970s no bigger than that of a single large English town such as Wolverhampton, though it was scattered across a variety of islands. The idea of a federation of the Leeward Islands came up in the 1670s, and William Stapleton summoned a common assembly to make laws for all of them. It was not a popular idea, and the assembly did not meet again after 1711 except for one isolated occasion in 1798.

Separatist interests and fierce local jealousies killed this first attempt at a federation, but the idea was revived in 1871. This time, the common administration for the Leeward Islands lasted until 1956. There was one governor for the British Virgin Islands, Anguilla, Barbuda, St Kitts, Nevis, Antigua and Montserrat; and he also governed Dominica until 1940, when Dominica was associated with the Windward Islands. The common legislative council provided the basis for a Leeward Islands parliament to which elected representatives could eventually be admitted. The union aroused little enthusiasm, however. It made it possible to devise common solutions to common problems, but the individual islands cherished their individual identities and always feared that these might be submerged in a federal arrangement. In any case, the Leeward Islands Federation was somewhat artificial for it could include only British islands. Ownership by various European powers sometimes ruled out more logical associations. British Dominica, for example, was cut off from Guadeloupe and Martinique, its immediate neighbours, because they were French properties.

There were other reasons why federation was not popular. A federal government meant federal taxes to pay for federal programmes. Moreover, a man might enjoy local importance which would be lost in a federation, and local vested interests might less easily be protected. Some whites also feared that non-whites might less easily be kept out of power in a Leeward Islands Federation. But, above all, the small islands had not yet developed close contacts amongst themselves. Communications between the islands were poor and inter-island trade was very limited. West

Indians lacked a strong sense of regional cohesion and thought mainly in terms of their individual islands and their ties with the mother country. Anguilla and Montserrat competed to sell their cotton, and their only binding connection was that both were under British overlordship.

Attempts to federate *the Windward Islands* were even less successful. John Pope-Hennessy, as the Governor of Barbados, was entrusted with the task in 1875. A federation was planned which would include Barbados, St Lucia, St Vincent, Grenada and Tobago. Barbadians at once suspected that it was a British plot to rob them of their assembly, and to burden them with responsibilities for the other, less-developed, islands. The Barbadian elite formed a Defence Association to resist the federal proposals, but the poorer classes in Barbados rioted. The poor were in favour of a federation which they hoped would bring about their betterment. Pope-Hennessy decided that his first duty was to suppress disorder, and eight Africans were killed in the skirmishes and then more than 400 arrested. By the end of 1876, the plan for the federation was dead. Barbados kept its assembly, and the plantocracy kept the island free from federal entanglements. When the estate owners had talked of some sort of union with Canada, partly for commercial reasons but also to preserve the assembly and steer clear of federation, the British had decided not to annoy them further. With their usual capacity for compromising, however, the British invented a new system whereby there was a single executive committee to help to govern the Windward Islands but each island had its own separate legislative council.

In 1888, Tobago was amalgamated with Trinidad, and the British now tried to bring about other such small-scale unions. St Vincent rejected a plan to amalgamate it with Grenada, but, in the Leeward Islands, Nevis was persuaded to join with St Kitts and could therefore take

Gordon Town, Jamaica, towards the end of the nineteenth century

advantage of a centralized sugar factory which was established at Basseterre in 1911. Until well into the twentieth century, however, almost every island in the British West Indies remained deeply suspicious of enforced links with others, and was slow to appreciate the advantages of co-operation and of joint programmes for development (see Chapter 15).

II THE EARLY TWENTIETH CENTURY

Representative Government

Perhaps more by accident than by design, Britain established a pattern for the constitutional development of its colonies which may be summarized and simplified as follows.* The first modification to *crown colony government* was to admit elected members to the legislative council. As their numbers grew, so would their influence. This system can be termed *representative government*. The next stage was that of *ministerial government*. At this point, elected members would be admitted to the governor's executive council and given ministerial duties for which they would be answerable to the legislative council as well as to the governor. At first, these duties were likely to be carefully selected and limited, concerning perhaps only those areas of administration which were thought to be least important. Ministerial government was rather like an apprenticeship for *self-government* (sometimes called responsible government): the whole government would now be made up of ministers who were chosen by and were responsible to a fully elected legislative council. The legislative council would now have the full status of a parliament, and it might, as happened in Jamaica in 1944, be a newly created House of Representatives. During the first stages of self-government it was usual for Britain to keep control of external relations (matters such as defence and foreign policy). The surrender of all such remaining control marked the point at which full *independence* was achieved.

Although self-government had been granted to Canada by the North America Act of 1867, the most that West Indians could hope for in the early twentieth century was representative government. West Indian voices began to be heard through the elected members of the legislative councils. But further privileges and responsibilities were not granted before the Second World War, and West Indians themselves were not at this time pressing hard for self-government. The age of popular nationalism took longer to arrive in the West Indies than it did, for example, in India. After the Second World War, however, progress became steady and even rapid.

It is, of course, relevant to ask whom did the elected members of the legislative councils represent. Members of the old assemblies had almost invariably represented the plantocracy. At first, members of the legislative councils were, in the main, the representatives of the middle classes. But the right to vote was gradually extended in the twentieth century. Universal suffrage was adopted in Britain in 1928, and in due course it was applied in the colonies, for example in Barbados in 1951. The early nationalist movements were usually elitist and middle-class, but by the 1930s the West Indian working classes were beginning to make themselves heard. After the Second World War, therefore, it was a mass nationalist movement which demanded ministerial government, self-government and independence in rapid succession.

Jamaica's first elected representatives having been won in 1884 (see page 154), the middle classes in other British colonies formed reform groups known as representative associations and they agitated for similar representation. David Lloyd George was the Prime Minister in Britain when the First World War ended in 1918, and his government was taking a new look at the constitutions of the empire, especially in India and Ireland. Lloyd George sent Charles Wood (who later became Lord Halifax) to investigate the situation in the West Indies. The representative associations pressed him to recommend the election of members to the legislative councils on a broad, but limited, franchise. The elected members were likely, therefore, to speak for moderate and mainly middle-class opinion. Precedent for this already existed in India as well as in Jamaica, and it seemed to be a reasonable request. Wood reported in 1921 that such a concession was 'ultimately inevitable' anyway.

The British government responded extremely cautiously. Trinidad and the Windward Islands were allowed elected members from 1924, but they were to be few in number. They would be

* See also Appendix I.

A flourish of imperial grandeur in the early twentieth century (Jamaica, 1920)

able to do little but offer advice, and the governors' powers would not be reduced in any way. The Leeward Islands were not to have any elected representatives, since the merchants and estate owners there argued that it would be far too dangerous a step towards democracy to hold even limited elections. In Jamaica and British Guiana, things were simply left as they were. But another commission visited Guiana in 1927 and recommended changes which brought that colony more into line with the rest of the British West Indies (see page 151). Guiana's legislative council kept the elected members it had had under the earlier Anglo-Dutch system, but the governor's powers were strengthened and Britain took a more firm control of the colony's finances. The qualifications for the right to vote confined the franchise to those who were literate and who either owned property or had a substantial income. Before 1939, it was clear that the British were thinking only in terms of allowing a small advisory role to the West Indian middle classes and well-to-do.

Popular Nationalism

In India, Mahatma Gandhi did much in the years after 1918 to turn the elitist Indian National Congress into a movement of popular nationalism. He realized that, unless the Congress had the support of the masses, it was unlikely to force the British to grant early self-government; and he recognized that it was amongst the masses, not the Europeanized middle classes, that the real traditions and culture of India were to be found. The West Indies had nothing like the long history, traditions and distinctive culture of India behind them, but many West Indians also began to realize, like Gandhi, the importance of developing the political consciousness of the masses. In the early twentieth century, West Indians had a background of many cultures of which the European was only one but, under colonial rule, it was European values which almost always counted most highly. The problem was to work out a West Indian identity, a task all the more difficult because of the often-conflicting interests of the many racial groups. In the end, West Indians would have to rule themselves but Haiti stood as an example and a warning of the confusion into which it would be easy to fall. On the other hand, the West Indies were only a very small part of the British empire and neglect was often a characteristic of British rule. The creation of a Colonial Development Fund in 1929 showed some willingness in Britain to try to promote prosperity in the empire, but economic conditions in the West Indies in the 1930s showed that an enormous amount remained to be done.

Popular nationalism was the product of a variety of forces. Education steadily increased the number of West Indians who were aware of the world in which they lived. Leaders emerged, some of whom like Marcus Garvey aimed to make the Africans aware of their heritage and proud of their race, some of whom like Hubert Critchlow aimed to develop trade unions. The Depression of the 1930s brought to the West Indies acute distress and protest, and out of these grew political consciousness and a demand for self-government. In 1939, the West Indies became involved in the Second World War and were thus made even more aware of the world around them. That war triggered off enormous changes. When it ended, in 1945, colonial empires were no longer fashionable and Europeans could no longer claim their almost mystical right to rule the non-white world. Britain withdrew from the Indian sub-continent in 1947, and India and Pakistan became independent. West Indian demands for a similar independence suddenly grew more urgent, and by now they were the demands not of a few but of the many. Nationalism had become a people's movement. The masses demanded both the right to vote and independent power for those whom they elected. Many factors had combined to help to bring this about, amongst which it will be appropriate to consider the expansion of education, the inspiration of Marcus Garvey, and the development of trade unions.

Education

The development of schools in the British West Indies followed a pattern similar to that in Britain. The earliest schools were run by religious bodies and were often financed from legacies. They were mainly for white children but, after 1815, the missionaries began to take a keen interest in the education of the slaves. In 1833, the same year that the Act of Emancipation was passed, the British government took its first interest in schools in Britain, granting £20 000 to them to help meet their costs. Two years later, a grant of £25 000 was made towards the education of Africans in the West Indies, rising to £30 000 in 1836 and continuing to rise thereafter. The grants were always totally inadequate both in the West Indies and in Britain, and in 1883 only one in ten of the Africans in Jamaica was able to write. The education was often poor in quality, and for large numbers of children no education was available at all. The churches did their best, but they lacked both money and trained teachers. Religious funds, private contributions, legacies* and the British grant were sometimes supplemented by grants made by the West Indian assemblies, but it was still impossible to educate the masses to even the lowest level of literacy. The extent of what was achieved varied, of course, from one colony to another, since education was so dependent on private gifts and the willingness of the assemblies to add to the educational resources.

In England, a national system of state schools, paid for out of public funds, was introduced in 1870. Soon afterwards, education became compulsory and free and, in the early twentieth century, it was extended to include secondary education. In the colonies, such a system was likely to be far too expensive. The British government tried to make West Indian schools efficient, to increase their number, to train teachers and encourage some secondary education. But it stopped short of making education universal; and it did not make it West Indian. The education was European in character: English was its language, and English history, culture and traditions formed the core of the curriculum. The aims, in so far as they were given definition, were to equip the masses with basic skills in literacy and numeracy which was in keeping with liberal ideals, and to give further education to a small Europeanized elite. Some of the latter might go on from secondary school, perhaps with a scholarship, to a British university. In general, the system served the whites best, and the browns better than the blacks. It fitted West Indian society as it then existed and, like almost all educational systems, sought to preserve that society. It also compared favourably with the education which then existed in the non-British islands. The fact that it was sadly defective, and that in Jamaica, for example, only one child in eighty reached secondary school in the 1930s, was not due to British wickedness but to the low level of wealth in the West Indies. Both under British rule and then under independent governments, massive efforts were made after 1945 to improve and expand educational standards and to build on the foundations which had been laid.

Imperfect as it was, however, this early educational system produced many of the future leaders of the West Indies. It taught the leaders to see the shortcomings of colonial government and it began to equip the masses to understand the appeal of popular nationalism. Moreover, Britain set up the Imperial College of Tropical Agriculture in Trinidad in 1924 to further the study of West Indian agricultural problems, and established the University College of the West Indies in Jamaica in 1949. From this College grew the University of the West Indies which eventually developed campuses in Barbados and Trinidad.

The Universal Negro Improvement Association

Slavery left the West Indies with a large population of Africans and a serious social problem. Dr

* The Lady Mico Trust provided a windfall for the educationists. Lady Mico had left £1000 in the seventeenth century 'for the redemption of poor Christian slaves in Barbary'. While the number of such slaves dwindled to nothing, Lady Mico's legacy was invested and accumulated more money until it stood at £120 000. The Abolitionists succeeded in having the money converted to the purpose of educating West Indian non-whites. Schools were opened in Guiana, Trinidad, St Lucia and the Bahamas, and colleges for training teachers in Jamaica and Antigua.

Sherlock has referred to the latter as 'the doctrine of black badness and white virtue'. Until well into the twentieth century, it seemed that whiteness meant superiority and privilege, and that blackness meant inferiority and indignity. The Africans themselves accepted this: it seemed to be a fact of the society and the life they knew. This was something which Marcus Garvey set out to change.

Garvey was a Jamaican African, born in 1887. In material terms, he achieved little. In 1914, he founded the Universal Negro Improvement Association which, with the Negro Progress Convention in Guiana and the Negro Welfare and Cultural Association in Trinidad, aimed to uplift the African race, to unite it and to create an independent Negro nation in Africa. From 1916 to 1927, he campaigned in the USA, launching a newspaper, the *Negro World*, a shipping line for Negro trade and a Negro Factories Corporation. He appointed himself provisional president of the nation to be born in Africa, but his enterprises landed him in prison and eventually the Americans deported him. Returning to Jamaica, he again fell foul of the authorities and again went to prison. His was one of the many voices raised in protest against unemployment and poverty in the 1930s, but his last years which he spent in England, before his death in 1940, suggested that his energy had been used up. He had little that was concrete to show for his life's work and he had quarrelled with many of his colleagues. He was criticized for what some considered to be narrow and racial interests since his concern was with the African rather than with the under-privileged in general. But he helped to change social attitudes and to make others, as well as the Africans themselves, look on the black man with a greater respect.

Marcus Garvey, champion of the Africans and founder of the Universal Negro Improvement Association (Jamaica, 1970)

Trade Unionism

Industrial workers in the early twentieth century were turning to trade unionism. It took a century of effort in England for trade unions to become powerful there. Before 1914, they were constantly harassed by unsympathetic employers and hostile laws and it was not until after 1945, partly in alliance with the Labour Party, that they became really forceful. Trade Unionism in the West Indies followed a pattern similar to that in Britain, but its development began much later. The first working-class associations were friendly societies and burial clubs which aimed to help their members in sickness and in paying for funerals. Slowly, they then turned to industrial activities and agitated for better wages and conditions. The associations sometimes organized strikes, as the dockers in Guiana did in 1906 under Hubert Critchlow's leadership. Work in industry brought men together in large numbers and encouraged them to seek strength by uniting, but it was more difficult for the agricultural workers to become organized.

The law, however, was often hostile to any active trade unionism. Like their British counterparts, West Indian unions had to struggle—for the legal right to exist and possess funds, and for the right to picket and make strikes effective. In 1919, picketing was forbidden in Jamaica as it had been in Britain until 1875. And twenty years later the Moyne Commission reported that only in Guiana did West Indian unions have protection against an employer's claim for his loss of profits and for damages caused by a strike, protection which British workers had won in 1906.

The early West Indian unions were, therefore, seldom effective. Trinidad had a Working Men's Association before 1900. About the same time, Jamaica had a craft union, for Carpenters, Bricklayers and Painters, and a more general association in 1907, the Jamaica Trades and Labour Union. Critchlow founded a similar Labour Union in Guiana in 1919. But these organizations tended to mushroom and collapse, perhaps then to be re-born. It was not until the late 1930s that they came to stay. At that time, they were able to cash in on the great discontent of the workers, and to organize strikes and extract concessions from the authorities as the oil workers were able to do in Trinidad in 1937. Such concessions were few, but workers could now see the likely usefulness of unions. The Bustamente Industrial Trade Union sprang into being in Jamaica, for example, and by 1948 its membership numbered more than 46 000, 80 per cent of the island's organized labour force. The Orde Brown Report on labour conditions had found unionism virtually non-existent in many islands in 1937, but within the next few years unions took root in islands such as Barbados, St Kitts and Antigua. Many union leaders became politicians, leading the demand for self-government; and political parties developed alongside the unions, both of them giving expression to popular nationalism.

The 1930s

The 1930s were important formative years in the British West Indies. The economy was already vulnerable (see page 127), and the Depression added greatly to the hardship. After years of over-production, markets were glutted at a time when there was a serious lack of purchasing-power in the USA, Canada and Europe. Everywhere, production was cut back and millions became unemployed. West Indian produce was difficult to sell and the price of sugar fell lower than at any time since the 1890s. Wages were reduced and jobs terminated throughout the Caribbean as they were elsewhere in the world. But wages in the West Indies had already been low and jobs hard to find, and whereas, after the bleak depressed years of 1929 to 1933, there was slow recovery in the advanced countries, the effects of the Depression lingered tenaciously in the Caribbean throughout the decade. For those who had lost their jobs in Britain, there had been unemployment benefit, the dole and public assistance, but in the West Indies there was hardly any money available for relief schemes. The governors appeared to be helpless and crown colony government was much discredited. In their poverty and frustration, West Indians turned to strikes, demonstrations and riots.

The disturbances of 1934 and 1935 were little more than sporadic strikes and hunger marches with occasional flashpoints of violence. Jamaica had strikes in 1934. There were more vigorous outbreaks among sugar workers in St Kitts and Guiana in 1935, when there was also a strike of coal-heavers in St Lucia. But it was in 1937 and 1938 that the worst disorders occurred. The oil workers of Trinidad were inflamed by the violent speeches of Uriah (Buzz) Butler, who savaged the white employers and made a Garvey-like appeal for African rights. From the oil fields, strikes spread to the cane fields, and the workers were only suppressed when troops were called in and blood spilled. Clement Payne carried Butler's call for action to Barbados, where he promptly came into conflict with the authorities and was in due course deported. The workers rioted in Bridgetown and again there was bloodshed. Jamaica and Guiana also erupted. In Jamaica, industrial workers, dockers and agricultural workers demanded jobs, better wages and self-government. In Guiana, plantations were set on fire. The clashes of 1938 in various parts of the West Indies resulted in nearly fifty deaths.

In themselves, the riots were not particularly dangerous. A thousand or more troublemakers were arrested including Butler in Trinidad and Alexander Bustamente in Jamaica, but the British had a habit of arresting the future leaders of their colonies. This was the real significance of the disorders: West Indians were beginning to realize the importance of becoming organized, both in trade unions and political parties, and leaders were coming to the fore. Among them were Bustamente and Norman Manley in Jamaica, Grantley Adams in Barbados and Robert Bradshaw in St Kitts. The outbursts made it clear that the poor were no longer prepared to suffer in silence, and that blacks and browns must be given consideration. Their leaders realized, however, that there must be constructive planning for the future, for self-government and for economic and social reform. There was an immediate upsurge in trade unionism, and political parties achieved a new popularity. These included the early Trinidad Labour Party led by Arthur Cipriani, the Progressive League in Barbados led by Adams, and the People's National Party in Jamaica led by Manley, who parted company from Bustamente, the founder of the Jamaica Labour Party.

The British response was sluggish but not entirely unconstructive. The Colonial Development Act of 1929 had provided little more than token assistance to the colonies. But there were further Colonial Development and Welfare Acts in 1940, 1945 and 1949. That of 1940 earmarked £220 million for such things as public works and relief in the colonies, but the West Indies got only a fraction of this total grant and most of the money was not available until the Second World War had ended. Nevertheless, a Comptroller was sent to Barbados to set up a headquarters to administer the Fund, and in the post-war years both the British and the West Indian leaders paid far more attention to the welfare of the people.

In 1932, Britain abandoned free trade. A conference in Ottawa discussed a system of Imperial Preferences (see page 126) with the intention of making sure that goods from the empire would be taxed less heavily than foreign goods. In fact, Britain put no tariffs on the produce of those territories which, like the West Indies, were still colonies, and efforts were made to persuade the Dominions* to adopt a similar policy. From 1934, therefore, sugar from the British West Indies again enjoyed substantial protection. By 1938, production had climbed to 620 000 tons compared with only 370 000 tons in 1928. The Second World War helped the industry still further with Britain and the Commonwealth* eager to purchase all the West Indies could produce. Some years later, in 1951, the Commonwealth Sugar Agreement brought new security with a fixed agreement to buy from the West Indies and some guarantee of a maintained price. When Britain joined the European Economic Community, in 1973, some continued security for Caribbean sugar producers was one of the terms which Britain tried hardest to negotiate.

Development acts and protection for sugar were helpful, but the *Moyne Commission* revealed the extent of the problem which, sooner or later, had to be faced. Alarmed by the riots, the Colonial Office had appointed Lord Moyne in August, 1938, to make yet another study of West Indian economic and social conditions. He collected evidence for many months, but his Report coincided with the beginning of the Second World War and the bulk of it was not made public until 1945. So thoroughly had Moyne collected his evidence that he was able to describe West Indian conditions in great detail, and the Report told a sorry story. There were now more than $2\frac{1}{2}$ million people in the British West Indies and most of them suffered hardship in almost every aspect of their lives. Social conditions were wretched with inadequacies in housing, education, and health services. The statistics for infant mortality and juvenile delinquency bore witness to the islands' ill-health and malnutrition and the general lack of opportunities for the young. Suffering was not confined to any one group: hardship faced industrial and agricultural workers, town-dwellers and countrymen. Low wages were universal, unemployment chronic. Having described the existing state of affairs, Moyne had then to suggest a policy for improvement.

Some of his suggestions were far from new. Technological improvements in agriculture and some further diversification of crops were clearly needed; and more money would have to be spent on social services such as education and health facilities. In keeping with the recent movement towards protection, Moyne also emphasized the need for stable markets for sugar and other crops. About industrial development, he was cautious, recommending little in the way of new industries except a cement works in Jamaica. But he came down firmly on the side of trade unions, and recommended that West Indian unions should have the same rights and protection that unions in Britain had won. West Indian administrations should also set up labour departments to deal with the many problems of the workers.

In most cases, these were old problems for which Moyne prescribed old remedies. But he also faced two fundamental issues: how were the improvements to be paid for, and how best were the colonies to be governed. To provide finance, he suggested that Britain should put £1 million a year into a Welfare Fund for the next twenty years. To improve the government, he proposed only limited changes. He thought it desirable that West Indians should be allowed to elect the majority of the members to the legislative councils and that they should be brought more into decision-making and the carrying-out of the decisions, but under the continued control of the governors. This proposal disappointed West Indians, for it would not carry them forward even to ministerial government. Added to that, Moyne did not think the time had yet quite come for universal suffrage.

The Report lay in the Colonial Office for the duration of the war, but most of its recommendations were known and Britain began to act on them. A flood of legislation was passed to make

---

* See Appendix II.

up a new labour code, which encouraged trade unionism and tried to improve industrial relations. The Act of 1940 sanctioned the Colonial Development and Welfare Fund and, after the war, Britain spent well in excess of what Moyne had recommended to keep this Fund supplied. Protection was given to West Indian sugar, as has already been noticed. And before the war ended, the British drafted a new constitution for Jamaica which was followed shortly afterwards by rapid changes in the rest of the West Indies.

The Jamaican Constitution, 1944

The importance to Britain of the empire and of the Commonwealth, which had begun to take the place of the empire (see Appendix II), was made clear during the Second World War. The Commonwealth and the colonies gave invaluable help to Britain in withstanding and eventually defeating the Axis powers (Germany, Italy and Japan). The West Indies contributed both manpower and produce to the war effort, and the way in which Britain depended on its colonies gave a boost both to their morale and their economies. The war also enabled many West Indians to add to their experience of the outside world and to compare West Indian conditions with those elsewhere. The relationships between the colonies and their mother country were bound to move into a more mature phase when the war ended in 1945. In the colonies, nationalists were insistent that they must now be heard. In Britain, there was a greater readiness to listen and to make a constructive response.

The Jamaican constitution provided some evidence of this. Jamaicans were allowed to elect an entirely new House of Representatives, chosen by universal suffrage. A two-party system soon developed in this House with Bustamente and Manley competing for the people's support. The more successful was likely to be the future prime minister of the island. The House of Representatives had law-making power, subject to the consent of the governor and to a small delaying power which the old legislative council retained. Meanwhile, although the governor still ruled on behalf of Britain, he was now clearly in a position to hear and respond to the voice of the people. As Jamaicans became experienced in the affairs of government, it would be possible to move forward, to ministerial government and then to self-government. In Jamaica, these steps followed in 1953 and 1957, respectively.

Universal suffrage was also introduced into other West Indian colonies, for example Barbados in 1951 and Guiana in 1952. In this way, the will of the people could become known, and following a path similar to that trodden in Jamaica, the people's chosen government could eventually be brought to power. By the end of 1966, Britain had granted complete independence to Jamaica, Trinidad and Tobago, Guyana and Barbados. Chapter 14 will consider further how this came about. It was, essentially, the outcome of the growth of popular nationalism in the British West Indian colonies.

Exercises

1 What were the arguments for and against the abolition of the assemblies in the British islands in the nineteenth century?

2 'When Edward Eyre became the Governor of Jamaica in 1862, conditions in the island were deplorable' (page 152). What facts illustrate the truth of this statement? Why were conditions so bad, and how did (a) Eyre and (b) Grant respond to them?

3 What do you understand by *federation*? Why was federation not more popular in the British islands before 1939?

4 What do you understand by *popular nationalism* (page 158)? In what ways did trade unionism help to encourage popular nationalism and why, in your opinion, were trade unions slow to develop in the West Indies before the 1930s?

5 Find out more about the life of Marcus Garvey. Does the passage in this book which refers to Garvey (page 160) do justice to his achievements? Find out what George Padmore contributed to the uplifting of the African people, and compare his work with that of Garvey.

6 Find out what you can about the Reports of the Commissions of 1896 (Norman), 1928 (Olivier) and 1938 (Moyne). Tabulate the facts about conditions in the British West Indies which were described in these Reports, and the recommendations which were made. What similarities do you notice?

7 Make a written survey for the island or state in which you live of the present-day educational facilities which exist. Trace the origins of several individual elementary schools and of several individual secondary schools. In what ways are the origins of the schools you have chosen typical of the sort of schools they represent?

14 The Decolonization of the British West Indies

The Period of Preparation

The problem of how to dismantle the British empire in the West Indies was complicated by the fact that the empire consisted of scattered territories. From the introduction of the new Jamaican constitution in 1944, and especially after the ending of the Second World War and the election of a British Labour government in 1945, the British were willing to make progressive constitutional changes which would lead to independence in the West Indies. The Indian subcontinent also soon provided an example of how it might be done: in 1947–8, independence was granted to India, Pakistan, Burma and Ceylon.* But there had been lengthy preparation in India. The Indian National Congress, which ruled after independence, had been founded in 1885. Moreover, the Indian empire was dismantled so completely that, in 1948, Britain was left with no possessions whatsoever in the Indian subcontinent. In the West Indies, on the other hand, preparation began later, and there was the added complication that the British West Indies were not part of a single land-mass. British Guiana and British Honduras were mainland colonies which were likely to have to be dealt with separately. Like the individual islands in the Caribbean, each would go through a series of constitutional changes, such as those referred to in Chapter 13 and Appendix I, to transfer power by stages and to widen the franchise; and, eventually, they would reach independence, as British Guiana did in 1966 when it took the name Guyana. Such a series of changes enabled Jamaica and Trinidad to achieve independence in 1962, and Barbados four years later. But, in the meantime, the short-lived West Indies Federation had been set up which, the British had hoped, would make it possible to deal with the British West Indian islands as a single unit. The Federation collapsed in 1962, with two results. One was that it became necessary to grant independence to individual islands, and this was done on the basis of the constitutional changes already made in these islands. The other was that Britain was left with the responsibility for the small and scattered islands, for whom separate independence could perhaps bring burdens too heavy to carry. However, the years after 1945 saw British West Indians playing a major part, at last, in shaping their own futures, and in giving a positive, unique and West Indian identity to the individual states.

The history of Guyana will serve to illustrate the process by which preparation led to independence, although Guyana's road to independence was rather more bumpy than that of the larger British islands. The history of the West Indies Federation will illustrate the difficulties which stood in the way of dealing with the British Caribbean islands as a single unit.

The Independence of Guyana

Constitutional change in British Guiana in 1928 (see page 158) carried Guiana backwards rather than forwards. In 1953, however, a new constitution established a parliament of two houses, the lower of which, the House of Assembly, was largely elected by universal suffrage. Some degree of ministerial government (see page 157) was also introduced. In the following elections, the People's Progressive Party won a majority in the House of Assembly and secured some ministerial offices. Within months, the Governor declared a state of emergency, dismissed the PPP ministers and suspended the constitution. It was an unhappy beginning to the process of bringing

* Now Sri Lanka.

about self-government as the prelude to independence.

The People's Progressive Party strongly represented the forces of popular nationalism. Under the joint control of Forbes Burnham, an African barrister, and Cheddi Jagan, an Indian dentist, it appealed to electors of both African and Asian descent, and the Party campaigned for the improvement of the conditions of workers on the sugar estates and in the bauxite industry as well as for self-government. It leaned towards socialism, and its appeal to the masses was effective partly because of the efficient organization which was built up by Jagan's American-born wife, Janet. At first sight, the PPP seemed well-fitted to become the ruling party of Guiana and to lead the country to independence. The Burnham–Jagan alliance, however, was an uneasy one, to some extent because of the different races they represented; and the British were suspicious of Jagan's alleged sympathies with communism. Taking exception to an attempt to intimidate trade unions which were not linked with the PPP, the Governor took back complete power into his own hands. This was a setback to constitutional development, but there was worse to come when Burnham, Jagan and their followers split, mainly on racial lines.

A new constitution was drafted in 1956, less liberal in some respects than that of 1953. Jagan led the PPP in the elections and again secured some influence in Guiana's government, as the leader of the most popular party. Having done less well, Burnham began to create the People's National Congress as an opposition party. It was at this point that Guiana chose not to join the West Indies Federation. Guianese politics were now firmly based on race, the support for the PPP being predominantly Asian and that for the PNC largely African. The PPP was not anxious to join a Federation in which the majority were African. So Guiana continued to develop as a separate country. The constitution of 1960 introduced self-government and elections were held to choose a government and Prime Minister in 1961. Britain's role would be supervisory but with continued responsibility for foreign policy and defence.

The general election of 1961 again returned the PPP as the majority party and Jagan became Prime Minister. It seemed likely that the British would soon complete their withdrawal and that Guyana would become independent. But Britain dragged its feet. Jagan demanded swift action and spoke of 'raising hell' if necessary, whereas Burnham favoured delay. Meanwhile, Jagan produced an unpopular budget and the 'hell', when it

Cheddi and Janet Jagan in 1953. Jagan's T-shirt bears the PPP slogan. He became the Prime Minister of British Guiana, but independence was withheld

occurred, took the form of strikes and riots, which ravaged Georgetown's business centre and seemed to be aimed at Jagan's government rather than at the British. British troops restored order and independence was withheld. In 1963, however, disorder broke out again. Against the background of furious argument between Jagan and Burnham about the details of a constitution under which Guyana might achieve independence, the government of the PPP antagonized the Guiana Trades Union Council with proposed legislation about trade unions. The TUC called a general strike, which led to a state of emergency and the further intervention of British troops. When the dust had settled, the British insisted on introducing a voting system based on proportional representation, in the hope that this would help to break down the confrontation between Asians and Africans which seemed to have resulted from the split between Jagan and Burnham. New turbulence occurred in 1964. The strife resulted from confused conflicts between the races, between unions, and between town-dwellers and countrymen. But again, British troops restored order and a new election was held at the end of the year.

This election produced an almost equal balance between the PPP and the PNC. Neither Jagan nor Burnham had an overall majority in parliament. With twenty-four and twenty-two seats, respectively, a government could only be formed in alliance with the small United Force, led by Peter d'Augiar, which had won seven seats. Burnham secured d'Augiar's support and he thus became the Prime Minister of a PNC/UF government. The British were now prepared to move rapidly to the granting of independence and, although the PPP boycotted the talks, details were agreed which enabled Guyana to become independent in May, 1966. There would be universal suffrage, five-yearly elections and a single-chamber parliament elected on a single-list system of proportional representation; and Britain agreed to one further point of detail—Elizabeth II would continue to be the Queen of Guyana for the time being, but Guyana could become a republic if it so chose and elect its own head of state after 1968. This change was effected in 1970, and Guyana's only remaining political link with Britain was then its voluntary membership of the Commonwealth (see Appendix II).

The election of 1968 gave Burnham and the PNC an overall majority. Long before the election results were declared, however, Jagan was accusing the government of malpractice. He darted about the Commonwealth, trying in vain to get intervention. Jagan claimed that votes were given to people who did not exist, and he challenged the right to vote of Guyanese who were overseas. But Burnham remained in power and, throughout the first dozen years of its existence as an independent state, Guyana had only the one Prime Minister. The PNC was firmly in control, so much so that it sometimes seemed that Guyana might become a one-party state. At the same time, the PNC moved towards the policies which Jagan might have pursued—of socialist co-operation, the nationalization of foreign enterprises such as the Demerara Bauxite Company, the Demerara Sugar Company and the Booker-McConnell holdings, and the creation of links with Cuba and the communist world. Such policies helped temporarily to heal the breach between Burnham and Jagan, and this in its turn was helpful to the government's efforts to foster racial harmony to which considerable priority was given.

History had left Guyana with a divided population. About half of the Guyanese people were of Asian descent, and these provided the bulk of the labour force which was engaged in growing sugar and rice. Africans made up almost a third of the population, many of them urban industrial workers. The rivalry of Asians and Africans had been embittered by the power struggle between Jagan and Burnham and by the conflict between the PPP and the PNC. To weld the Guyanese people into one multi-racial nation was one of the main aims after independence. Guyana could not afford the continuation of racial strife. Like most emergent nations, it faced formidable economic and social problems. A united effort was essential to overcome them and the new state adopted the slogan, 'One People, One Nation, One Destiny'.

The delaying of independence in the 1950s and 1960s naturally aroused controversy. Jagan's leanings towards communism were certainly not popular with the British and with Americans who had business interests in Guiana; but how best to explain the disorders, which occurred so often when Jagan was in power, is a matter for controversy. Such disorders damaged Guiana's development and several attempts were made to mediate and restore harmony in the country. Among the would-be mediators were Eric Williams of Trinidad and Ghanaians from Africa.

Guyana became independent under the leadership of Forbes Burnham. Four years later the state became a republic (Guyana, 1970)

The British chose to believe that the turbulence showed that the colony was not ready for full independence. Jagan's opponents blamed the disturbances on the maladministration of the PPP. Jagan's supporters blamed them on the agitation of his enemies. Some blamed the British for delaying independence, and there were those who thought they detected the sinister hand of the CIA.* When independence was granted, however, Guyana was reasonably stable, and the British took this to show that the delay had been justified.

Burnham's government was able to make steady progress with policies of land settlement, electrification, the improvement of communications and the development of the social services. Exports of bauxite and sugar came near to paying for much-needed imports, though, like all emergent nations, Guyana was at the mercy of fluctuating commodity prices (see Chapter 15). The constitution produced stable government and attention could be given to healing racial divisions. It was, of course, impossible for Guyana to become rich overnight. European powers left their ex-colonies with generally low standards of living and many unsolved problems, although the British usually left at least some foundations on which to build. Three-quarters of Guyana was still forested, and industry was largely confined to processing local raw materials. The first dozen years of independence gave the new nation an encouraging start, but only long-term development can bring adequate and secure employment and a high standard of living for all.

The West Indies Federation

West Indians themselves, as well as the British, were beginning, by 1945, to consider the possible advantages of a federation of the British islands. Old prejudices were beginning to crumble (see page 156). Businessmen were among the first to see the usefulness of uniting the various islands into one state, of free trade between the islands, and of a common policy for marketing Caribbean produce, for example in Canada. Professional men recognized that the islands faced common problems, in fighting disease and extending education. West Indian agriculturalists learned common techniques in the Imperial College of Tropical Agriculture, and trade unionists formed the Caribbean Labour Congress for unity and strength in their struggle to lift up the labouring classes. At the end of the Second World War, the British called for a West Indian debate on federation, and many Caribbean organizations expressed support for a federal arrangement. A conference was held at Montego Bay, Jamaica, in 1947, to begin to translate the idea into a reality.

That did not prove easy. To hammer out the details, further conferences met, in London in 1953 and 1956, and in Jamaica in 1957. By that time, Britain was offering early independence to a Federation, once it had been established successfully. But individual islands, especially Jamaica and Trinidad, were reluctant to give the federal government too many powers, fearful lest it should interfere in their own affairs. Suspicion also grew that Britain was trying to saddle the larger islands with responsibility for the smaller ones. The larger islands feared a flood of immigrants in search of work, and Jamaica was worried that it would be federal policy to reduce import duties and thus to reduce Jamaica's revenue. Even

* See Glossary.

Table 14.1 West Indian Members of the Commonwealth

State	Population (1976 est.)	Main Exports	% of Whole	Exports mainly to	% of Whole
Jamaica	2 057 000	Alumina	43%	USA	43%
		Bauxite	23%	Britain	17%
		Sugar	9%	Norway	12%
		(1976)		(1976)	
Trinidad and Tobago	1 149 000	Petroleum products	58%	USA	69%
		Crude oil	34%	(1976)	
		(1976)			
Guyana	783 000	Sugar	50%	Britain	28%
		Bauxite	24%	USA	23%
		Rice	10%	USSR	9%
		(1975)		(1975)	
Barbados	247 000	Sugar	47%	USA	30%
		Petroleum products	13%	Britain	27%
		Clothing	12%	Trinidad/Tobago	6%
		(1975)		Canada	6%
				(1975)	
Bahamas	211 000	Crude oil	56%	USA	76%
		Petroleum products	40%	(1975)	
		(1975)			
Belize	144 000	Sugar	48%	USA	30%
		Fruits	12%	Britain	24%
		Timber	8%	Mexico	22%
		(1970)		(1970)	
St Lucia	110 000	Bananas	64%	Britain	60%
		Coconut oil	10%	Jamaica	10%
		Cardboard boxes	10%	Barbados	8%
		(1973)		(1973)	
Grenada	106 000	Cocoa	29%	Britain	33%
		Nutmegs	28%	USA	8%
		Bananas	16%	(1973)	
		(1973)			
St Vincent	94 000	Bananas	49%	Britain	61%
		Animal/veg. oils	14%	Barbados	15%
		Arrowroot	11%	(1972)	
		(1972)			
Dominica	76 000	Bananas	58%	Britain	78%
		Citrus fruits	11%	(1975)	
		(1975)			
Antigua	71 000	Petroleum products	84%	Bunkering*	37%
		(1973)		USA	21%
				Switzerland	11%
				(1973)	
St Kitts–Nevis–Anguilla	54 000	Sugar	65%	Britain	61%
		Electrical equipment	24%	Puerto Rico	22%
		(1971)		(1971)	
Montserrat	13 000	Cattle	25%	West Indies	c. 70%
		Potatoes	24%	Britain	18%
		(1975)		(1975)	

* Fuel services to shipping.

Imports mainly from % of Whole		Trade Balance (Exports as % of Imports)	Capital	Status (1978)
USA Venezuela Britain (1976)	37% 14% 11%	70% (1975) 64% (1976)	Kingston	Independent 1962
Saudi Arabia USA Indonesia (1976)	26% 20% 16%	118% (1975) 112% (1976)	Port of Spain	Independent 1962 Republic 1976
USA Britain Trinidad/Tobago (1975)	30% 22% 18%	117% (1974) 104% (1975)	Georgetown	Independent 1966 Republic 1970
Britain USA Trinidad/Tobago Venezuela (1975)	22% 19% 10% 10%	41% (1974) 50% (1975)	Bridgetown	Independent 1966
Saudi Arabia Nigeria (1975)	38% 18%	210% (1975) 90% (1976)	Nassau	Independent 1973
USA Britain Jamaica (1970)	34% 25% 7%	82% (1974) 70% (1975)	Belmopan	Self-governing Colony
Britain USA Trinidad/Tobago (1973)	30% 16% 13%	36% (1974) 34% (1975)	Castries	Associated State
Britain Trinidad/Tobago USA (1973)	27% 20% 9%	47% (1974) 51% (1975)	St George's	Independent 1974
Britain Trinidad/Tobago (1972)	28% 17%	26% (1974) 29% (1975)	Kingstown	Associated State
Britain USA Canada (1975)	30% 10% 10%	53% (1973) 56% (1975)	Roseau	Independent 1978
Venezuela Britain USA (1973)	31% 22% 16%	64% (1973) 46% (1974)	St John's	Associated State
Britain Puerto Rico (1971)	35% 14%	35% (1972) 44% (1973)	Basseterre	Associated State
Britain Trinidad/Tobago USA (1975)	29% 18% 18%	1% (1974) 6% (1975)	Plymouth	Ministerial Government in Crown Colony

Tourism helps many West Indian islands to earn foreign currency to supplement the earnings from exports. Numbers of tourists: Jamaica (1975) 396 000; Barbados (1975) 222 000; Bahamas (1975) 1 381 000; St Lucia (1974) 52 000; Grenada (1975) 21 000; Antigua (1976) 63 000.

the location of the federal capital caused problems: when Chaguaramas, in Trinidad, was chosen, Jamaicans noted glumly that it was a thousand miles away. Meanwhile, the mainland colonies of Guiana and Honduras decided not to join the federation.

The West Indies Federation came into being, in spite of arguments and misgivings, in January, 1958. It was made up of Jamaica, Trinidad and Tobago, the Windward Islands and the Leeward Islands, except for the Virgin Islands. The first elections gave a majority to the Federal Labour Party which was supported by Manley (Jamaica), Williams (Trinidad) and Adams (Barbados). But the majority was smaller than expected and the Democratic Labour Party, led by Bustamente (Jamaica) and Albert Gomes (Trinidad), came a close second. Grantley Adams became the Federal Prime Minister, partly because neither Manley nor Williams wished to put federal duties before those in their own island-politics.

From the outset, therefore, there was a less than whole-hearted commitment to the Federation by both politicians and electors. Adams presided over a government whose powers had been severely curtailed during the drafting of the constitution. Jamaican misgivings were reflected in the support given to Bustamente and his Democratic Labour Party, and in the fact that some candidates had been defeated who would have been able ministers in the Federal government. The latter was financed by a levy on the islands within the Federation, and this too was not popular. Jamaica paid 43 per cent of the Federal revenue, Trinidad 39 per cent and Barbados 9 per cent, so that, between them, the smaller islands paid only 9 per cent. Yet the small islands held thirteen of the forty-five seats in the Federal House of Representatives, and it was they who, in effect, gave the Federal Labour Party its majority. Adams found himself almost powerless, and criticism of the Federation mounted in Jamaica and Trinidad. Although Britain had requested that the Federal constitution should remain unchanged for a trial period of five years, demands for immediate change soon flooded in. Essentially, the larger islands were unwilling to be dominated by an outside authority. For the moment, Britain retained a supervisory role, but Jamaicans and Trinidadians feared that, when Britain withdrew, they would find themselves at the mercy of the government of the Federation.

Jamaica wanted to protect its developing industries with tariffs, and feared a Federal free trade policy. Trinidad feared immigration from the small islands which would worsen unemployment. Britain now seemed eager to grant independence as soon as possible and to escape the need to give financial help to the West Indies in the future, so Adams suggested that the Federal government might need to impose direct taxation throughout the islands to finance its operations. This too provoked alarm, and fear and wrangling began to dominate the Federation's short history. The Federation had little opportunity to do the constructive work which could have won friends for it. It began to appear as a millstone round the necks of the larger islands, a device to extract money from them, and an organization to force them to support the small islands, and at the same time share power with them. Williams, the leader of the People's National Movement and, since 1956, the Chief Minister of Trinidad, was not unwilling to persevere with the Federation, but it was in Jamaica that opposition to it came swiftly to a head.

Bustamente declared himself in favour of Jamaica's secession from the Federation. The ruling party in Jamaica was still Manley's People's National Party, which had won power in 1955 and so far retained it in subsequent elections. Under pressure from Bustamente's Jamaica Labour Party, however, Manley decided to hold a referendum in 1961, to allow Jamaicans to decide for themselves whether the island should remain within the West Indies Federation. The supporters of the Federation obtained British consent to several constitutional changes in a last-minute effort to meet Jamaica's criticisms, but the referendum still went ahead. The first votes to be counted, from Kingston, suggested that Jamaicans would approve of the Federal connection, but as the rural votes were counted the balance tipped the other way. In the end, 54 per cent of those who voted wanted to leave the Federation. It was, however, a low poll: only about 60 per cent of the electors voted. In these circumstances, it was possible to argue that Jamaicans had not delivered a decisive verdict. This was not Manley's view and he withdrew Jamaica from the Federation. If Manley hoped to gain popularity in this way, however, he was to be disappointed, for within a few months he was defeated in a general election.

Without Jamaica, the Federation seemed likely to be a much greater burden on Trinidad and it came as no surprise when Trinidad too withdrew from it, a few months later. In May, 1962, Britain declared the Federation at an end. The islands would now have to come to independence one by one and although this presented no great difficulties in the case of the larger islands, it left unsolved the problem of what was to be done with the smaller ones. For a time, there was an attempt to create an Eastern Caribbean Federation to unite the small islands with a federal government in Barbados. But that plan also failed, when Barbados chose to follow Jamaica and Trinidad and achieve independence on its own. The remaining islands were then offered Associate Status, and a group of them became the West Indies Associated States.

The breakdown of the West Indies Federation stemmed from various causes. There were the acute economic problems of the smaller islands, which Jamaica and Trinidad were not rich enough to cope with and which they feared. There were lingering remains of the parochialism which had long been present in the West Indies, one island distrustful of another. The Federal government was weak, its powers limited and its membership lacking in strong personalities. There was even delay in providing it with a proper headquarters, since it began in temporary buildings in Port of Spain, while efforts were made to persuade the USA to withdraw from the American base at Chaguaramas. In any case, Trinidad was not central to the Federation and the site of the capital was criticized, especially in Jamaica. All these problems could have been overcome, however, had the will to overcome them existed. Perhaps Britain could have done more to put the Federation on a firmer constitutional and financial footing. But then more could also have been done by the leading politicians of the Caribbean, to give the Federation whole-hearted support.

Norman Manley, the Prime Minister of Jamaica before independence and the father of Michael Manley who became the Prime Minister in 1972

Manley, Bustamente and Williams all gave a higher priority to their own islands than to making the Federation succeed.

The Independence of Jamaica

The Federation had always envisaged that there would be separate governments in the islands as well as the Federal government for them all, a system of government similar to that in the USA and in Canada. Progress had continued, therefore, to transfer power to West Indians in islands such as Jamaica. In 1953, Jamaica got ministerial government and, in 1957, self-government (see page 163). It was this which made Norman Manley one of the most important politicians in the West Indies because, from 1955, he had been the elected leader of the Jamaican people and, since 1957, Jamaica's Prime Minister. Manley was a man with a distinguished academic record who, in his youth, had been a sprinter. He enjoyed great popularity in Kingston. His main political opponent was Alexander Bustamente, the son of an Irish planter, imposing, turbulent, and an orator with a gift for moving the masses, especially those in Jamaica's rural areas. When the Federation collapsed, Jamaica claimed independence and Britain was ready to grant it. The final changes were made to Jamaica's constitution; a general election was held, and Jamaica became independent early in August, 1962.

The election, however, toppled Manley in favour of Bustamente and the Jamaica Labour Party. Unemployment was high in the island and the people voted for a change of government. Bustamente, therefore, was Jamaica's first leader when the island became an independent state. He was already seventy-eight, a veteran of Jamaican politics and trade unionism, and he retired shortly before the next general election, in 1967, to be succeeded by Donald Sangster. The JLP retained office but the sudden death of Sangster brought Hugh Shearer into power as Prime Minister, a prominent trade unionist. Five years later, the People's National Party won the general election. It was now under the leadership of Michael Manley, the son of the founder of the PNP, who thus became the Prime Minister of Jamaica in 1972.

For more than fifteen years after independence, the constitution worked well and Jamaica had stable government. Rather like the British system, Jamaican electors had, in effect, a choice between two parties, each of them developed in the pre-independence years by Bustamente and Norman Manley. There was some violence in the election of 1967 and there were many accusations of corruption in that of 1972, but Jamaica had little of the racial strife that plagued Guyana, and its political record compared favourably with that of many emergent nations. The main problems were the usual ones of eliminating unemployment, poverty and illiteracy, and of obtaining sufficient output to produce the wealth to make this possible.

Alexander Bustamente, veteran of the Jamaican labour movement and one of the pioneers of independence (Jamaica, 1968)

Bustamente introduced a five-year plan for development. Industrial expansion was promoted by the Jamaica Industrial Development Corporation, and bauxite, clothing-manufacture, oil-refining and cement-making contributed to Jamaica's growth. Agriculture continued to make a vital contribution too and the encouragement of tourism helped to increase the island's earnings. Nevertheless, it was not easy to pay for the imports Jamaica needed and a growing population hampered the spread of prosperity. For a time, emigration to Britain helped to ease the pressure but Britain imposed restrictions in the 1960s (see page 182). In the 1970s, therefore, Jamaica was still struggling to provide full employment, to conquer illiteracy and to balance its books. In emergent nations, independence almost always brings unrealistic expectations of imminent prosperity, with the danger that disillusionment and frustration will quickly follow. By the mid-1970s, Jamaica had an uncomfortably high level of crime and of industrial unrest, with a tendency towards political gang warfare. Inflation brought new strains and, like all primary-producers, Jamaica was too much at the mercy of fluctuating prices for produce such as sugar and bauxite. The JLP and the PNP had both a record of achievement, but it was impossible to solve all Jamaica's problems within such a short time of independence.

Sometimes, indeed, the problems seemed only to multiply. In 1968, Hugh Shearer came near to confessing himself baffled. 'We have a black government,' he said. 'We have votes for everyone; we have got rid of colour discrimination.' In spite of this, he had to face the problem of the Rodney riot which followed the expulsion from Jamaica of Walter Rodney,* a lecturer suspected of connections with the Black Power movement. Shearer found it worrying that Black Power could still make an appeal and stir up disorder with its militant racialism, in a country where more than three-quarters of the population were of African descent. Racial mixtures gave the West Indian states a character of their own with the mixture varying from one country to another. To be 'rid of colour discrimination' was the aim of most governments, and usually there was tolerance and goodwill. Beneath the surface, however, danger lurked: governments which failed to achieve a contented society through solid economic and social progress could well face racial troubles, stirred up by agitators.

Black Power seemed to spread to the West Indies from the turbulent cities of the USA. To a certain extent, it joined hands in Jamaica with some elements of the Rastafarians. Many of the latter claimed that their only intention was to turn their backs on materialism and the rat-race to secure wealth, and that they desired to live in peace. But in 1960, Rastafarians had been stirred up by a wild preacher known as Henry, and an

* Author of *How Europe Underdeveloped Africa*.

A Rasta-man—a descendant of Garvey's Back-to-Africa movement effort to overturn the government had resulted in the shooting of two white policemen. The Rastafarian movement was in some ways similar to Garvey's Back-to-Africa movement. Its supporters looked to Ethiopia as their spiritual home. They were divided into groups which differed in their dress and hair styles: the Locksmen wore their hair long like some east African tribes; the Beardsmen delicately trimmed their beards, and the Baldheads shaved industriously. The Rastafarians were an unorthodox element in Jamaican society, rejecting the more commonplace values. They caused some worry to those who sought to build racial harmony, with their apparent emphasis on the unique identity of the African. Such racial consciousness seemed to hold a threat to Jamaica's stability, particularly when it could feed on the contrast between the luxurious hotels for the tourists and the hovels and slums of the poor.

In an attempt to make radical improvements in housing, Michael Manley imported prefabricated units from Cuba in the mid-1970s. By this time, the PNP had moved to the left and forged a variety of links with Castro. In contrast, Edward Seaga, who took over the leadership of the JLP from Shearer, advocated closer ties with the USA and a stronger emphasis on private enterprise. Jamaicans had, therefore, a genuine choice to make in the election of December, 1976. They could confirm Manley and the PNP in office, in spite of the criticism that his government was becoming too much influenced by Castroism; or they could turn to the more capitalist policies of the JLP. The Cuban connection also added a new dimension to Jamaica's problems, for an anti-Castro group of Cuban exiles declared that they would apply terrorist tactics against Jamaica, in protest against Castro's spreading influence. Meanwhile, Manley was forced to introduce a state of emergency with a special Gun Court to deal with a growing wave of violence, much of it political. In 1976, such violence claimed the lives of 200 Jamaicans and did not subside until the election had been held.

The electors' verdict was clear-cut. Manley won an impressive vote of confidence, and the JLP suffered its worst electoral defeat since its foundation. For Jamaica, the result showed widespread approval of the PNP's drive towards socialism. Castro visited Jamaica in 1977, and Manley's government took steps towards taking control of the Reynold Jamaica Mines and the island's banks. It seemed likely that Jamaica, which had so far retained the (British) monarchy would soon become a republic. In the Caribbean as a whole, the Jamaican election seemed to confirm the marked trend of the 1970s towards the 'New Left' whose main concern was to rid the British West Indies of lingering external influences and to create a stronger sense of an individual West Indian identity. The movement had begun among intellectuals, but in the 1970s it was making headway amongst politicians and voters, perhaps marking the beginning of a new phase in making the West Indies truly independent.

The Independence of Trinidad and Tobago

Like Jamaica, Trinidad and Tobago went through a series of constitutional changes which led to self-government in 1961, and to independence in 1962, a few weeks after Jamaica. Eric Williams had founded the People's National Movement in 1955, and popular support made him Trinidad's first Chief Minister and then Prime Minister in 1961. He continued as Prime Minister throughout the first sixteen years of independence. At first, opposition to the PNM was provided by the Democratic Labour Party, but by the mid-1970s opposition had become fragmented. After the election of 1971, the grip of the PNM was so strong that Trinidad seemed near to being a one-party state. The government of the PNM provided continuity, but critics argued that Trinidadian politics were less healthy than the two-party system which operated in Jamaica. Williams comfortably retained power in the election of 1976.

Williams had formerly been an academic. He was a historian and a sociologist. When Trinidad became independent, he gave it the watchwords of 'Discipline, Production and Tolerance' and, during his years in power, he sought to achieve all three for the new nation. Africans made up almost half of the population of Trinidad and Tobago, Asians considerably more than a third. From the outset, Williams strove to avoid the racial divisions in politics which plagued Guyana, and the PNM was built on inter-racial lines. The emphasis on 'Tolerance' was an emphasis on the importance of racial harmony. Increases in 'Production' would bring wealth. 'Discipline' was necessary to overcome the many problems and frustrations which invariably face emergent nations.

In 1962, Trinidad was already one of the most prosperous of the British islands. Oil and asphalt gave it an advantage. Oil provided about a third of the government's revenues and it was also the basis for a variety of industries. In developing the economy, the PNM was prepared to encourage both private enterprise and state intervention. An Industrial Development Corporation already existed and five-year plans provided programmes for state-directed expansion. Sugar production, which benefited from large-scale organization and mechanization, still played a dominant part in Trinidad's agriculture and exports, but citrus-growing was also encouraged through a Growers' Cooperative Association, and cocoa and coffee made a useful contribution to the new nation's economy. Tourism was also developed as a means to earn foreign currency. By the mid-1970s, however, Trinidad's exports were based overwhelmingly on oil and petroleum, although vigorous efforts were being made to develop other industries and valuable discoveries of natural gas were being tapped.

But developing nations have an insatiable appetite for all the wealth they can produce. At the time of independence, Williams was critical of the condition in which Britain left Trinidad and of the smallness of the parting financial gift from the mother country. The British argued that, with so many colonies being brought to independence, they could not afford more. But in almost all the colonies the needs were great. Trinidad had a growing population, and a high level of unemployment was one of the stubborn problems with which the government had to grapple. Money was needed for education, housing, health services, communications and technological development, and the government would be expected to produce rapid results if discontent and disorder were to be avoided. Considerable progress was made but it was not enough to escape industrial unrest, which caused strains in Trinidadian society and threatened the PNM policy for racial harmony. Unemployment seemed to be an almost insuperable problem and, like many other countries, Trinidad found that new processes in industry and agriculture, though producing more wealth, often put men out of work and replaced them with machines. The government, therefore, had to struggle not only to solve the underlying problems but also to maintain 'Discipline' and an orderly society. Criticism of Williams and the PNM was often vicious. They were accused of being authoritarian, for example in 1965 when the Industrial Stabilization Act restricted the right to strike. By 1970, disorders were so extensive that a state of emergency was declared. The New Beginning movement was critical of outside influences, such as the billion-dollar United States investment in Trinidad, and discontent was inflamed by the Black Power movement. Even a section of the armed forces mutinied. There was another state of emergency in 1971, and in that year the opposition boycotted the elections, vigorously finding fault with the electoral arrangements, especially the use of voting-machines. The PNM secured all the seats in the House of Representatives, but on a poll of only 32 per cent.

Trinidad and Tobago became a Republic in 1976: an emphasis on togetherness (Trinidad and Tobago, 1977)

Turbulent industrial relations, crippling strikes and sometimes sabotage handicapped economic development. The increase in world oil prices brought some relief to Trinidad's economy in the mid-1970s, but wage increases tended to buy only temporary industrial peace. Black militancy and the brooding discontent of many Asian sugar workers were a disappointing outcome of the high hopes which had accompanied independence, and it seemed impossible for the government to bring down the persistent high level of unemployment. In 1973, Eric Williams contemplated retirement but he decided to struggle on in an attempt to weather the storm. He had come to power with a reputation for wisdom and integrity, qualities which new nations badly need. In office, he recognized the need to reconcile West Indian nationalism with the inter-dependence between the West Indian nations and the outside world. The price of isolation, in the twentieth century, is invariably stagnation. But post-colonial problems are many-headed and persistent and to solve them calls for outstanding statesmanship. Trinidad may yet have reason to be grateful for the leadership of Eric Williams, though in the late 1970s the nation's course was still stormy, and it was complicated still further by rising prices, and by talk of devolution, and possibly even secession, in Tobago.

Winston Scott, the Governor-General of Barbados a year after independence (Barbados, 1967)

The Independence of Barbados

Barbados secured ministerial government in 1954, self-government in 1961, and independence in 1966. Unique in preserving its assembly in the nineteenth century, the island had a long history of parliamentary institutions. Two major parties contended for power and, on the eve of independence, the general election was won by the Democratic Labour Party, led by Errol Barrow. The Barbados Labour Party was in opposition, a party founded thirty years earlier by Grantley Adams. Barrow was a lawyer and trade unionist. He was much younger than Adams, whose long and distinguished career before his death in 1971 had included pioneering work in trade unionism, the founding of the BLP and the leadership of the West Indies Federation. Barrow remained in power throughout the first ten years of independence, but he was defeated in 1976 by Tom Adams, who favoured rather more conservative policies.

At the time of independence, Barbados had a competent civil service, a respected judiciary and a comparatively well-developed educational system, judged by standards elsewhere in the West Indies in 1966. The population, some 80 per cent of it African, was politically alert and, although small to be embarking on independence (the total population being only about a quarter of a million), the new nation promised to have political stability. A greater problem was the domination of the economy by sugar. More than half of the cultivated land was given over to cane, and Barbados had little else to export. The government fought to get secure markets for the sugar crop and also to develop tourism, but these were precarious foundations on which to rest the island's well-being. In the mid-1970s, sugar and its by-products still accounted for the bulk of Barbadian exports but, with the aid of government development plans, some diversification had been achieved and clothing, electrical goods and chemicals were now exported in significant quantities. Politically and financially, Britain had prepared Barbados well for independence, and the first decade as an independent nation passed comparatively smoothly. Barbados was one of the few emergent nations which, when sugar prices were favourable, could achieve a surplus on its balance of payments. When sugar prices fell, however, the economy faltered. Worldwide inflation and cheap sugar caused problems in 1975 and 1976, and it proved impossible to banish unemployment which stood at over 10 per cent at that time, and was rising.

The Independence of the Bahamas

Self-government was granted to the Bahamas in 1964, and the colony's first African government was formed three years under Lynden Pindling. Independence was won in 1973. The first inhabitants of the islands of the Bahamas had been Arawaks, but they were carried off by the Spaniards to work in the larger West Indian islands and, for well over a hundred years, the Bahamas were then unpopulated. The English laid claim to them in the early seventeenth century, when a proprietor was appointed. The closeness of the islands to north America inevitably entangled their history in that of the mainland, but they were also caught up in the piracy of the Caribbean and in the trade in African slaves. When the USA broke away from Britain in 1776, Empire Loyalists migrated from the mainland to the Bahamas, increasing both the white and African populations there. The Loyalists also brought an enthusiasm for growing cotton, but the cotton plantations of the Bahamas hardly prospered and they died away when the slaves were emancipated in the 1830s. More so than in other islands of the West Indies, the Bahamas developed smallholdings rather than vast capitalist estates. They supplied local needs but had constantly to struggle to produce goods for export.

The rights of the proprietors in the Bahamas were not formally ended until 1787 but, by that time, the Bahamas had become a fairly typical crown colony in which a legislative council was set up in 1841. This slowly evolved into a modern parliamentary system with universal suffrage so that, at independence, the Bahamas were similar to Jamaica in having a democratic political system with a choice of parties. Pindling became the Prime Minister as the leader of the Negro Progressive Liberal Party, while the opposition was provided by the United Bahamian Party. At that time, there was a danger that politics would divide on racial lines, similar to the division in Guyana but, in this case, the division being between black and white. That was one problem with which Pindling had to grapple. But the Bahamian population was overwhelmingly African, and the whites were heavily outnumbered. When Pindling was re-elected in 1977, racial divisions were beginning to count for less and the political argument was more about economic and social policy than about race. Pindling's Progressive Liberal Party won a convincing victory over the Bahamian Democratic Party, which was more conservative and favoured private enterprise.

Like all developing nations, the Bahamas needed capital. It was necessary for Pindling to tread carefully. American investors could easily be frightened away by policies which threatened their profits, but it was also essential to generate wealth for policies of social improvement in the Bahamas, especially for the young who made up a large proportion of the islands' growing population. In 1977, unemployment was as high as about 20 per cent; the economy had an unhealthy dependence on tourism, and a year earlier the nation had experienced its first balance-of-payments deficit. The government aimed to develop profitable modern industries and services—industries such as oil-refining and petrochemicals, and services such as insurance as well as tourism. But it also sought to provide more employment by encouraging labour-intensive agriculture and fishing, and planned for further welfare programmes to assist the young and the poor. The standard of living in the Bahamas was comparatively high, however, among developing nations, and the social problems were less difficult than those of many Caribbean islands.

The Independence of Grenada

An even smaller island, with a population of only about 100 000, became independent in 1974 when Grenada too decided to go it alone. The independence ceremonies were boycotted by other West Indian leaders of the Commonwealth, and Britain granted independence in spite of protests and of petitions to defer it. The controversy centred on Grenada's Prime Minister, Eric Gairy. Gairy had formerly been a schoolmaster and a trade unionist and, at the head of the United Labour Party, he had dominated the island's politics since 1953 and been Prime Minister since 1962. But his rule was accompanied by strikes and violence, and he hit back at his opponents with the

Grenada became independent in 1974 under Eric Gairy who had solid support in the rural areas (Grenada, 1974)

Mongoose Squad, a gang of thugs who suggested that Gairy was on the way to becoming another Papadoc. Instead of being a signal for public rejoicing, independence was a signal for bitter confrontations. Gairy proclaimed himself an anti-communist, but his opponents came from ranks far wider than those of communist sympathizers. They included landowners, businessmen and religious leaders, as well as many of the working classes. But Gairy had solid support in the rural areas where many had benefited from his work as a union leader.

Grenada's economy depended heavily on the exporting of cocoa and nutmegs, and on the visits of tourists. Prosperity depended on tranquillity, but there was little sign of this in the first years of independence. One controversy followed another, but Gairy's opponents were in disarray as the Mongoose Squad and their helpmates in the Night Ambush Squad carried out a reign of terror. Many Grenadians left the island, and the economy sagged towards bankruptcy. The government had little to show for its tenure of power, although Gairy himself got an honorary doctorate from South Korea in exchange for off-shore fishing rights. He complained that the British were in part to blame by withholding aid, but the British questioned the use to which his government put the money it already had.

Amidst arguments about electoral fraud, Gairy won the election of 1976. His majority was reduced, however, and the opposition united sufficiently to gain six of the fifteen parliamentary seats. The opposition formed a People's Alliance around the New Jewel Movement which sought to educate Grenadians in political awareness. The New Jewel Movement was fiercely critical of the Prime Minister's set of values, and its members hoped to win over his supporters to a new trade union for farmworkers, and thus remove Gairy's power base. Gairy, for his part, derided his critics as 'stupid, mentally premature, wicked people who cannot smile'. There was not a lot to smile about in Grenada, but the election results were at least encouraging to the opposition.

The Independence of Dominica

Dominica achieved independence late in 1978, under the leadership of Patrick John, whose policy was one of moderate socialism. It seemed likely that other Associated States would soon follow Dominica to independence.

The Dependencies and the West Indies Associated States

After the independence of Dominica, Britain still had a variety of dependencies in the West Indies. On the mainland, there was Belize (formerly known as British Honduras). Scattered around Cuba were the Cayman Islands, and the Turks and Caicos Islands. North of the Leeward Islands were the British Virgin Islands, and there were still many dependencies in the Leewards and the Windwards.

Belize, with a population of well over 100 000, had long seemed to be on the threshold of independence. It achieved self-government in 1964 with George Price as Prime Minister. But independence was delayed because Guatemala asserted a claim to the territory. To be merged into Guatemala was not what the people of Belize wanted and so Britain continued to exercise a supervisory role. British troops remained responsible for the defence of the dependency. Price and the People's United Party were again returned to power in the election of 1974, but, by 1978, the British were negotiating with Guatemala, and the

Figure 14.1 The Modern Caribbean (Social Map)

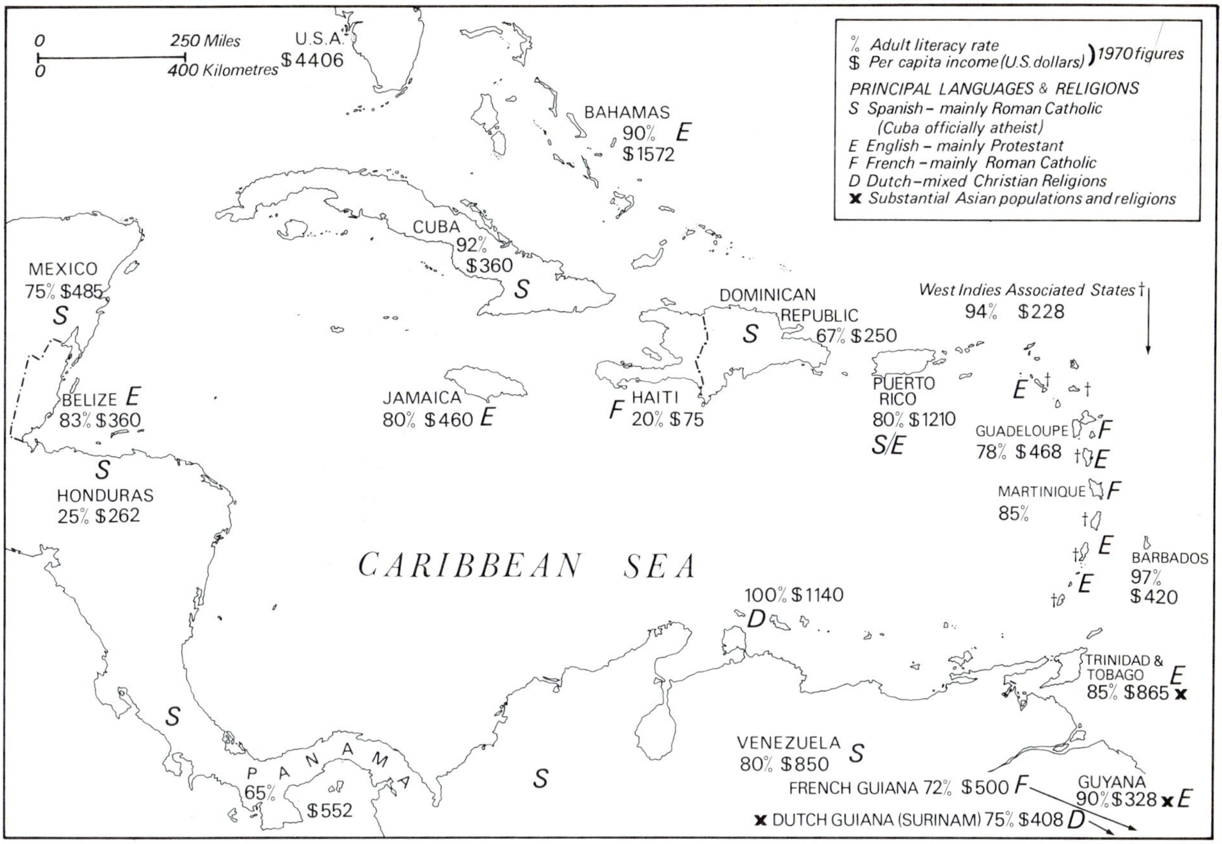

future of Belize remained in the balance despite much support for its integrity.

The *Caymans* and the *Turks and Caicos Islands* had once been administered along with Jamaica, but they remained as British colonies when Jamaica became independent. There was some talk of attaching them to Canada in the 1970s, but the Canadians rejected the idea. The Caymans had a population of about 10 000, the other islands even fewer. The Caymans exported turtles, the Turks and Caicos Islands shells, salt and crawfish. The *British Virgin Islands* were not dissimilar, a collection of thirty-six islands of which sixteen were inhabited with a total population not much above 10 000, and an economy based on cattle, fish and fruits. What, administratively, was to be done with these small islands was one of the baffling problems which remained in the aftermath of the colonial empires. In the 1970s, there seemed to be no immediate alternative but to continue colonial rule in these dependencies.

By this time, however, colonies were not fashionable. In 1967, the British had devised a new formula, *Associate Status*, for many small West Indian islands. In theory, this was somewhere between colonial status and independence. In practice, it meant little more than self-government under a protective British umbrella, but each Associated State could terminate the arrangement at any time and claim independence if it so wished. Grenada accepted Associate Status but opted for independence soon afterwards. Montserrat and St Vincent were offered the new Status but rejected it, preferring to remain colonies. In addition to Grenada, Antigua, Dominica, St Lucia and the union of St Kitts–Nevis–Anguilla became Associated States in 1967, and, with a change of mind, St Vincent followed in 1969.

Anguilla rejected the right of Robert Bradshaw

of St Kitts, the Prime Minister of the union, to take this decision and to bind Anguilla. With a village-size population of 6000, the tiny island declared itself an independent republic under the leadership of Ronald Webster. Bradshaw speculated that this act of rebellion was inspired by gangsters and, to keep the peace, Britain sent in troops in 1969, together with forty-five policemen. The policemen found Anguilla a pleasant island for swimming and playing cricket, and the army did some useful road-building. Meanwhile, the politicians struggled to find a formula which might keep the union intact. It took them a long time. From 1971 to 1976, Anguilla reverted to full colonial rule by the British—at the request of the islanders—and in 1976 the Anguillans secured extensive rights of self-government over the island's affairs when a new constitution was granted. A year later, they passed a vote of no-confidence in Webster in the island's miniature assembly and he was replaced by Emile Gumbs. By that time, it had proved impossible to revive the union with St Kitts and Nevis.

In the outer world, Britain was strongly condemned for using 'force' in Anguilla. It was an imperial problem in miniature, a tragi-comedy. The real problem was what should be done to ensure prosperous futures for these tiny islands. Many Anguillans relied on remittances from relatives who had emigrated and, although Britain spent generously on Anguilla in the 1970s, economic viability was difficult to secure. Salt and lobsters were not solid foundations on which to build. For many such small islands independence seemed likely to be too bold and too expensive a venture; but federations had failed and union with larger islands was often unpopular, even if larger islands could be persuaded to take responsibility for their poorer and smaller neighbours.

For the time being, Britain's solution was to allow as much self-government as possible but to guarantee defence, stability and some economic assistance. This continuing imperial connection sometimes infuriated the hotheads. In 1974, there was Black Power activity in Dominica which led to attacks on whites. A tourist was murdered and the island's earnings from tourism were much reduced. Patrick John, who became Prime Minister of Dominica at this time, declared his intention to suppress such extremism and racialism. This was no more than good sense and it was an attitude which most Caribbean politicians shared. John won a majority in the Dominican election of 1975, and the electorate backed his efforts to put down the Dreads, a youthful offshoot of the Black Power movement, but a product also of dismal economic and social conditions.

By this time, in large and small islands alike, West Indians had virtually complete control of their own affairs. Politicians were growing in experience, and the level of ability was often high. The problems they faced called for solutions which would emerge from deep thought, careful planning and co-operative effort. Riots, demonstrations and racial conflict would construct nothing, and much remained to be constructed in the West Indies. Popular nationalism had speeded the larger islands to independence, but it still remained to build prosperous communities, to rid the Caribbean of poverty and squalor, unemployment and widespread low standards of living. How best to achieve this, in a world which had too little sympathy to spare for the problems of others, was the problem with which West Indian leaders had to wrestle.

Milton Cato, the Prime Minister of St Vincent, turned his thoughts to tourism. Tourists brought valuable currency to the West Indies, but they could also be unsettling. They demanded luxury, which contrasted strongly with the humble living standards of most West Indians. And they required service, which readily reminded West Indians of their colour and of the former days of white supremacy and division by race. Yet the tourist industry, like sugar in its hey-day, was becoming central to many island economies, especially where productive industry seemed to be out of reach. Table 14.1 on pages 168–9 shows the difficulty many islands experienced in balancing their trade, and earnings from tourism were vital to many of them. The creation of wealth remained the dominant problem throughout the Caribbean. Crops brought a modest and fluctuating reward. Industry required capital; and only Trinidad possessed lucrative oil in quantity. The Leeward Islands, in particular, seemed to be caught in a poverty trap, from which it was extremely difficult to escape by generating sufficient wealth. Nevertheless, in 1975, George Walter of Antigua thought the island was almost ready to embark on independence; and, at the end of the year, the Caricom heads of government advocated that independence should soon be claimed by all the Associated States. By 1978, St Lucia under John

Lack of wealth is still at the root of the problems of the West Indies: a schoolroom in Jamaica in 1970 in the struggle for universal education

Compton was beginning to press for independence, like Dominica. The problem remained, however, as to whether independence should be linked with some new movement towards federation. While they carefully considered their futures, some small islands still hesitated to claim immediate independence. Even the existing unions seemed somewhat insecure: Anguilla had rebelled against rule from St Kitts, and there was some support for secession in Nevis. Barbuda sometimes showed a similar restlessness over its association with Antigua. Slowly but surely, however, the West Indian states were shaping their own destinies.

Emigration

The growth of population in the West Indies in the twentieth century—largely the result of improved standards in medicine—almost everywhere handicapped the struggle for a higher standard of living. Improved economies produced extra wealth, but there was not much per head when it was spread amongst more people. In the past, West Indians had frequently moved to the mainland or to other islands in search of work. After 1945, West Indians in the British islands emigrated in large numbers to Britain to look for employment, a more prosperous life and educational opportunities for their children. This was particularly so after 1952, when the USA restricted immigration from the West Indies. In the post-war years, Britain had a labour shortage and the newcomers were welcome. They found work in the British transport services, in the hospitals and in a variety of industries. Modern communications made the immigrants' journey to Britain possible though they often had to spend their life-savings and to get into debt to pay for the crossing.

Before the Second World War, comparatively few West Indians had reached Britain. Among them were cricketers and seamen and a handful of professional men. In the late 1950s, many totally unskilled West Indians were arriving at a rate of about 30 000 a year, about half of them from Jamaica. At this point, Britain did not even have the machinery to keep a count of the newcomers. Commonwealth citizens were simply admitted without restriction. But the immigrants needed homes and their children needed schools, and inevitably the West Indians went to those parts of Britain where they could find work and where they could join other West Indian communities. Cities like London, Manchester and Birmingham, and certain smaller industrial towns began to have noticeable West Indian settlements. In 1960, there were some 57 000 immigrants into Britain, the majority from the Caribbean. A year later, the figure was twice that number and about half of the immigrants were West Indians. But the newcomers now included large numbers from India and Pakistan, who proved valuable to Britain's textile industry but added a new dimension to the problem. Unlike the West Indians, many of the Asians were unable to speak English and, in speech, dress and religion, seemed to be very different from Englishmen.

Britain went through an agonized and ferocious debate. On the one hand, it was argued that Britain's imperial history and the existence of the Commonwealth, in which millions still lived in poverty, imposed a moral duty to admit all who wished to enter. Against this, it was argued that Britain was near the limit of the immigrants it could absorb, and that there were already serious problems in housing and in employing the newcomers. Some, including Enoch Powell, MP for part of Wolverhampton, added that the newcomers were changing the traditional nature of British society and that certain towns were becoming the centres for large non-white communities. This brought into the open the question of how far the growing criticism of unrestricted immigration was based on colour prejudice. Those who vigorously condemned the attacks on non-white immigrants pointed out that white Irishmen had long poured into Britain with hardly any objection to them.

It was true, however, that unlimited immigration was beginning to impose strains in Britain and to produce social and economic problems. In the West Indies, both Jamaica and Trinidad had recognized the difficulties of allowing immigration into these islands from their smaller neighbours. In the case of Trinidad, this had been one major reason for leaving the West Indies Federation. Britain was richer than Trinidad, but it began to appear urgent that the flow should be checked. In 1962, the Commonwealth Immigrants Act was passed, to stop all admissions except those of the close relatives of earlier newcomers and of those who had vouchers (limited to 8500 in 1965) showing that they had a job in Britain already arranged for them. Thus the number of immigrants was cut back. Later Immigration Acts were passed to deal with special problems, such as Asians who had been expelled from east Africa, but, for West Indians, immigration into Britain was now strictly controlled. One result of this was that the growing population in the West Indies could no longer be kept down simply by a mass movement to Britain.

The census of 1971 in Britain showed a population of almost 54 million, of whom just over 2 per cent had been born in the non-white areas of the Commonwealth. Of these, about 325 000 had been born in the West Indies. These people were now British citizens, and their children were born in Britain and considered themselves (and were) British. Having restricted immigration, British governments were now concerned to ensure that there should be no racial discrimination within the country on grounds of colour or anything else. From 1965 onwards, a series of Race Relations Acts were passed, to try to secure equal treatment for all in areas such as employment, housing, education and financial matters. In general, race relations were harmonious in Britain but there was no room for complacency. By the 1970s, Enoch Powell was gaining support for his suggestions that the immigrants should be repatriated to their countries of origin. More vicious and more disturbing were the growing extremist groups such as the National Front and other fascist-type organizations, which often encouraged anti-black prejudice and sought to make the immigrants the scapegoats for Britain's economic and social problems. Like the Black Power movements which plagued the West Indian islands, these hard-liners worried all those who genuinely sought racial harmony, so much so that in 1976 the British Labour Party and the TUC launched a campaign to attack all forms of racialism. So far, there had been occasional racial clashes in Britain but even mounting unemployment in the mid-1970s had not produced any massive anti-immigrant resentment. Nevertheless, the danger existed that agitators could stir up the racial strife which Powell went on predicting.

The West Indian immigrants had often been disappointed with Britain. Open resentment of them did not often show itself, but they suspected, with some justification, that many Englishmen were suspicious of them and that it was difficult to get the better jobs and the better housing. Although their standard of living was usually higher than it had been in the West Indies, they suffered similar problems of unemployment when times were difficult, and Britain sometimes seemed less liberal, less welcoming, and less prosperous than they had formerly expected it to be. Above all, the doubts lingered that to be black meant that one was regarded as a second-class citizen. Race relations legislation could only be the prelude to a massive programme of education in racial co-operation and, as in the West Indies islands themselves, the mutual respect of one people for another could grow only slowly over a long period of time. The Commonwealth Immigrants Act of 1962 had seemed like anti-black legislation, however justified it might have been. Grantley Adams had asked the question, 'Can a coloured population of less than 1 per cent destroy this great country?'. The 1 per cent grew to more than 2, and although the vast majority of British people did not view this development with great alarm, when there was competition for work and homes and hospital beds it was all too easy for whites to begin to resent black newcomers. In the 1970s, there was an even greater problem. British schools contained many black children, born in Britain. At school, they were usually treated as equals. Many worked hard and obtained excellent qualifications. Yet it was often far more difficult for a non-white school-leaver to get a good job than for his white companion. The authorities wrestled with this problem, but in the end it could be solved only with the disappearance of colour-consciousness. White Power and Black Power are equally outdated as foundations on which to build the modern world.

It is encouraging that, in the West Indies and in Britain, the vast majority of people seem to be aware of this. But there is reason for concern that, especially in times of economic hardship and social misery, hotheads and extremists can still revive only half-dead prejudices to gain support for scurrilous and irresponsible campaigns. In 1978, the National Front had still not been able to win a single seat in the British parliament, but its members were often active in the streets and, in certain British towns such as Blackburn, evidence could be found of the racial tension they provoked. Even an old nation such as Britain cannot afford such purposeless divisions between its people. New nations in the West Indies need also to strive for unity with a conscious effort, not to recall the many past injustices in order to foment future hatreds, but to remember the follies and crimes of the past as a background to the building of civilized societies, in which every man may have his dignity and may be respected for his contribution to the welfare of his community. The nations of the West Indies are fast establishing their individual identities. Their heritage is a rich one, in spite of the blood-soaked pages of Caribbean history. The diversity of the West Indian peoples is a source of strength. With a continuing high quality of leadership, the tolerance of one man for another, and a sustained attack on the real problems of economic disadvantage and social injustice, the time must surely come when it will be unthinkable to wish to emigrate from the Caribbean.

Exercises

1 'Guyana's road to independence was rather more bumpy than that of the larger British islands' (page 164). Describe the events in the years 1953 to 1966 which led to independence in Guyana. Describe the events which led to independence in *either* Jamaica *or* Trinidad and Tobago, and show how far these descriptions support the assertion that Guyana's road was 'rather more bumpy'.

2 Explain why the Federation of the West Indies was set up in 1958, and why it came to an end in 1962. In what ways do you think this Federation served the interests of the smaller islands better than it served the interests of the larger islands?

3 What parts in recent years have been played in West Indian affairs by (a) communism and (b) Black Power? In the case of *either* communism *or* Black Power, identify the principal ideas on which the movement is based and explain your own reasons for supporting or opposing these ideas.

4 What colonial territories remain in the West Indies at the present time? What reasons can you suggest for the fact that some British West Indian islands are still not fully independent?

5 Write an account of, and explain the reasons for, the migration of West Indians to Britain in the years since the Second World War, and comment on Britain's policies in controlling this immigration and on integrating the immigrants.

6 Find out details about how your own state is governed at the present time. Trace the history of the system of government and compare the pattern which emerges with that described on page 157 and in Appendix I.

7 Consider what parts can be played in promoting racial harmony among the citizens of a West Indian country by (a) the government, (b) the community, (c) the educational system and (d) the press and the radio. Which of these contributions is likely, in your opinion, to be the most valuable?

15 The Caribbean Nations in the Modern World

I THE CARIBBEAN NATIONS

Nation-Building and Bridge-Building

It is easy to show that the nations of the Caribbean differ considerably, one from another. They obviously differ in size. They may well differ in the principal language which is spoken, and in the religion which has the most popular appeal (see the map on p. 179). They differ in the structure of their economies: some more fortunate than others in the possession of mineral resources, some more dependent than others on the cultivation of this crop or that crop. They have differing political systems. The larger islands have all achieved independence, but Belize and some of the smaller islands remain under a European colonial authority. The political systems of the independent nations, moreover, are far from uniform. Trinidad and Tobago assumed republican status in 1976 while Barbados remains a monarchy. Cuba has turned towards communism, while Jamaica favours a British style of democracy. The structure of the societies and the ethnic composition of the Caribbean nations may also vary. The diagrams on page 185 show the various ethnic proportions of Guyana, Jamaica and Trinidad. Each nation is unique, but at the same time it shares with its neighbours many common problems and a common heritage—a heritage which has itself done much to produce both the unique identities of the Caribbean nations and their common problems. The ethnic proportions in Guyana, Jamaica and Trinidad differ, one from another. But they have similarities which arise from their common heritage during the years of service to King Sugar, when African slaves and then Asian labourers were imported to serve him. In the same way, these three nations face similar economic difficulties and social problems—similar, but not identical; and they face them with a similar background of many years of rule by the British, which gave them a common language and a wide variety of common attitudes towards such things as political institutions and the importance of the rule of law.

At one and the same time, therefore, each Caribbean nation is now pursuing two goals. One is to develop the unique identity and full potential of the nation itself. The second is to build not just a single nation but a Caribbean community, making use of the unifying factors already present in the West Indian heritage, and overcoming the divisive factors which were also part of that heritage. The earlier chapters in this book have attempted to show how the individual nations have developed to the present time. This chapter will concentrate more on the relationships of these nations with their neighbours and with the world at large. Nowadays, West Indian statesmen are engaged simultaneously both in nation-building and bridge-building, for no nation can prosper in isolation. The bridges which existed in colonial times were usually those between the colonies and their mother country. It is only more recently that West Indians have come to the task of building bridges between themselves.

Separation or Combination

The geography of the West Indies relieves the islands of one post-colonial problem which is not uncommon in the rest of the world. Since an island has clear-cut frontiers with the sea, the West Indian islands remain fortunately free from disputes about where boundaries should be drawn. Only the island of Haiti and the Dominican Republic is divided between two states. In Africa, however, the imperial powers often created states whose boundaries were artificial, taking little

Figure 15.1 The Ethnic Composition of Three Caribbean Nations

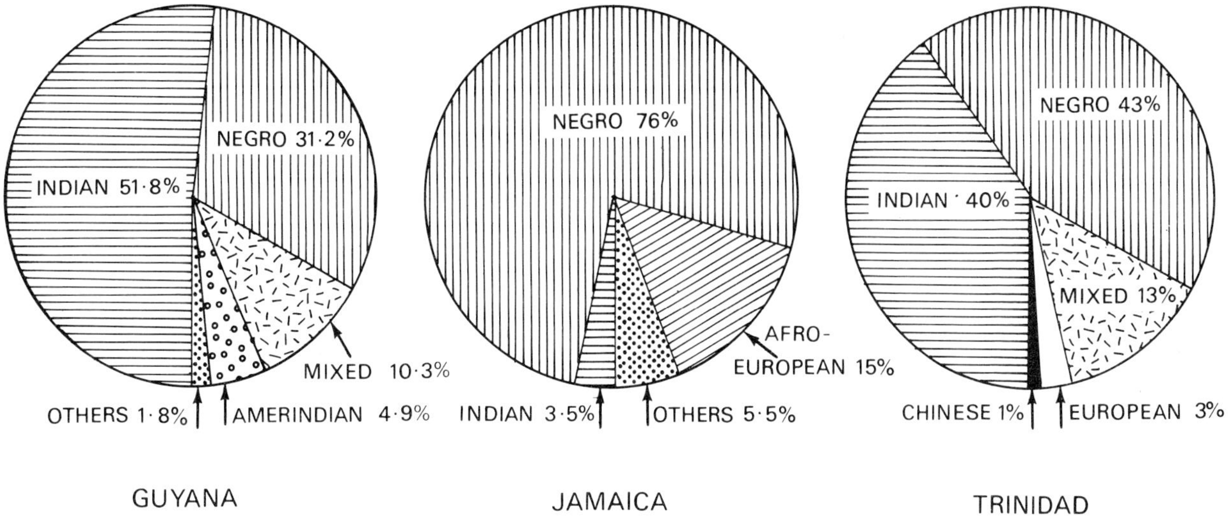

account of the tribes who already lived in the continent, so that present-day African nations face the difficult problem of building national identities within controversial frontiers. Some of these nations have sometimes threatened to fall apart: parts of the whole have demanded separation and the right to set up new smaller nations. Katanga sought unsuccessfully to break away from Zaire, and Biafra from Nigeria. It is also possible for the boundaries to be disputed between nations, for example in the way that Guyana has had border-disputes with Venezuela, and Guatemala has claimed the right to incorporate Belize. But in the West Indies, each large island can face the task of nation-building within precisely defined and undisputed boundaries. The task for each is to weld a mixture of peoples into a single harmonious nation, and there is the further advantage that almost all of these peoples are comparative newcomers. The inhuman and wasteful destruction of the Amerindians was one of the first consequences of the European invasion of the New World. Thereafter, it was necessary to people the West Indies with successive waves of immigrants, none of whom can claim an ancient right to this area or to that area and argue from this right the further right to break away as a separate nation. The diversity of peoples and cultures is part of a rich West Indian heritage, and the geography which produces fragmentation can also be a source of strength in helping to define clearly the natural boundaries of West Indian nations.

Nation-building in Guyana: many races but one people and one nation (Guyana, 1974)

But geography fragmented the Lesser Antilles to the extent that some islands may be simply too tiny to survive as independent nations. It has been seen, indeed, that some British, French and Dutch islands have been reluctant to claim independence partly because of their small size and vulnerable economies.* For such territories, union under a single government or federal grouping may eventually result in the building of a nation by the combination of islands. This is the special kind of boundaries-problem which faces the West Indies, the product of geography but sometimes made worse by the further fragmentation which resulted from occupation by more than one imperial power (see Figures 4.1 and 8.2). The growing friendship between the American and British Virgin Islands shows that, in time, bridges may well be built both across the sea and across the political divisions of the past. But the record of bridge-building in the West Indies has not so far been impressive. Early experiments in federation were unsuccessful (see page 154), and the more recent West Indies Federation collapsed after only four years of life in 1962 (see pages 170–1). Unions of islands are still comparatively few, and the resolute determination of Anguilla to resist such a union with St Kitts–Nevis (see page 180) illustrates the fierce defence of separateness which can still arise. The conditions under which a union takes place must obviously be satisfying to all parties to the union, but for unions to exist at all there must be some movement away from the parochial attitudes which have often been a characteristic of West Indian history.

It is, of course, true that there is no ideal size for a nation. Great and small may both prosper, and great size is not necessarily a guarantee of either wealth or strength. The first essential for successful nation-building is probably economic viability, that is the nation's ability to pay its way. The problem of many small West Indian islands, therefore, is not merely smallness but their lack of resources. Some kind of union or federation has the advantage that resources can be pooled, but the difficulty which arises is that the more prosperous islands are often unwilling to share their resources with their poorer neighbours. There is, nevertheless, a growing awareness in the West Indies of the fact that nations are interdependent and that all can benefit from international cooperation.

* See Chapters 12 and 14.

Commodity Prices

Almost all emergent nations in the West Indies and elsewhere in the world have to depend too much on the market prices for the commodities they produce. The prices fluctuate according to a variety of factors concerned with supply and demand. During a recession, for example, the purchasers are less likely to be willing (or perhaps even able) to pay high prices, so that both demand and prices may drop considerably. Prices are also likely to fall whenever the market is over-stocked, even if demand remains buoyant. Hardly any one single producer-nation is in a position to exert much influence over the fluctuations in the price of its commodities, unless it has a near monopoly of supply and no substitutes are available. Nations which depend heavily on monoculture (the cultivation of a single crop) are particularly vulnerable; thus it is that diversification has been a dominant theme in West Indian economic history in the twentieth century, and that almost all the islands have now moved away from a total dependence on sugar. Emergent nations, however, have an urgent need to import expensive manufactured goods, and so any loss in income from the sale of their crops and raw materials is likely to have serious effects. Diversification reduces over-dependence on one commodity but the problem of fair and stable prices remains. In the past, crops and raw materials have been subject to greater fluctuations in price than have manufactured goods. It is necessary, therefore, to pursue two objectives: to try to stabilize commodity prices, and to try to develop manufacturing industry. But an accumulation of capital is needed to develop industry and, at present, the West Indian nations possess comparatively little capital and industrial development moves forward only slowly.

The key to fair and stable commodity prices lies in international agreements, such as the Commonwealth Sugar Agreement (see page 162), which gave guarantees of purchases and of minimum prices. In recent years, the emergent nations have increasingly worked together to make their voices heard, and UNCTAD (the United Nations Conference on Trade and Development) has been set up to deal with issues of importance to the developing countries. One such issue is that of commodity prices. UNCTAD is by no means always successful, and sugar in particular has presented difficulties, but there is

The Reynold mines in Jamaica: the price of bauxite is of vital importance to the island

growing international awareness of the problems of the developing world. Some producer-nations have combined effectively to help themselves. OPEC (the Organization of Petroleum Exporting Countries) was founded in 1961 in order to influence the world price of oil. The Organization had spectacular success, for it not only maintained the price but dramatically increased it. OPEC had the advantage of marketing an indispensable commodity which was in great demand, and producers who sought to imitate the Organization achieved less success. Nevertheless, producer-associations were set up among the countries with other commodities to sell; for instance there were associations for cocoa, coffee and copper. One example will illustrate Caribbean involvement in such an association.

The International Bauxite Association was set up in 1974. Guyana, Jamaica and Surinam were among its seven founder-members, and Michael Manley of Jamaica identified one of the main problems they faced: 'the disproportionate power of the multinational corporation'. The members of the IBA hoped to strengthen their own bargaining power by co-operation, and they aimed to ensure that the companies which extracted the bauxite made adequate return to the countries from which they extracted it. Guyana favoured nationalization and had, indeed, already taken over the Demerara Bauxite Company in 1970 and now sought fair prices for the mineral. Jamaica and the Dominican Republic, a small producer, thought that increased royalties on bauxite production, rather than nationalization, would best serve the interests of West Indians by tapping the profits of the north American companies such as Alcan (the Aluminium Company of Canada). An interesting agreement was also made between Guyana, Jamaica and Trinidad. Bauxite is used for the manufacturing of aluminium, and the sale of aluminium may well be expected to bring a greater return than the sale of bauxite itself. It was agreed, therefore, to set up an aluminium smelter in Trinidad, to be paid for jointly by the three West Indian nations. Guyana and Jamaica would then provide the bauxite for the smelter, and Trinidad would supply the oil to power it. By thus pooling their resources, all three countries could be expected to benefit. But the clash of national interests soon caused the project to falter.

II THE INTERDEPENDENT WORLD

The West Indian Heritage

Each new nation must sooner or later find its own place in the world. In the past, the West Indies has been a geographical expression, and not much more. Almost all the historical links which were created in the centuries after 1492 were based on the patterns of colonization. The Spanish colonies were part of the Spanish empire, and the empire's links were with Spain; similar patterns were established by other European colonizing powers. The influence of the USA also extended into the West Indies during the last hundred years, and added new links. What almost all those links had in common was that they connected the West Indian islands with the outside world, but made comparatively few connections between the islands themselves. An important task for the new West Indian nations is to make the West Indies more than a geographical expression.

The creation of inter-Caribbean links does not necessarily mean the destruction of the old links. In themselves, the old links are not adequate for the modern West Indies but they can well provide a source of added strength. They provide the West Indies with connections with most of the countries of western Europe and, through these countries, with the European Economic Community. They provide similar connections with the USA and Canada. Fidel Castro has added Cuban links with the communist world—with the Soviet Union and Comecon and, to a lesser extent, with China. Other nations such as Guyana are now developing commercial links with the communist world—Russia bought 9 per cent of Guyana's exports in 1975. There are links too with Africa, a strong historical connection which was emphasized by Marcus Garvey and George Padmore, founder of the African Bureau, and is encouraged by the Rastafarians (see pages 173–4); and Cuban involvement in Angola and Ethiopia (see page 149) has added new African connections.

There are many advantages of such external connections. For example, they facilitate trade, the exchange of ideas and the development of goodwill. When Cuba turned to the Soviet Union after 1958, an agreement was made for the exchange of experts, Russian technicians bringing industrial expertise to Cuba and Cuban agriculturalists taking their expertise to Russia. From 1976, Cuba extended technical assistance to Jamaica and so helped to spread economic progress. The past has thus well fitted the West Indies for contact with the world at large. The individual nations bring to the area a multiplicity of overseas connections, and they are no longer, in most cases, the connections between colonies and mother countries but between free and equal nations.

The table on page 189 provides a glimpse of some of the many associations which now exist in the world and of the parts played in them by the West Indian nations. All the independent nations have joined the United Nations Organization and play their part in most of the UN Specialized Agencies which seek to improve the lot of mankind. The FAO, for example, is concerned with the development of more efficient agriculture and the production of adequate foodstuffs to feed a hungry world. The ILO aims to protect the interests of working people, the IMF to assist countries which have financial problems, and the WHO to raise the standards of health around the globe. But it will be appropriate in the rest of this chapter to consider three particular aspects of the international connections which involve West Indian nations. The first is the Commonwealth to which all the former British nations belong. The second includes the organizations which are essentially American. The third focuses on the connections between the West Indian nations themselves.

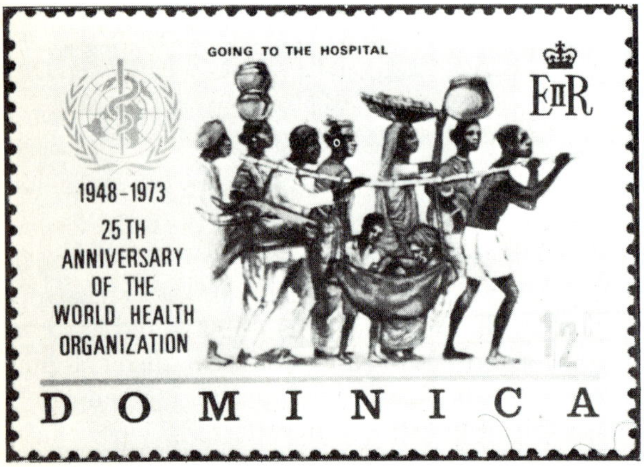

A cheerful comment on the work of the World Health Organization: Dominicans know the importance of extending medical care in developing countries (Dominica, 1973)

The Commonwealth

The twentieth meeting of the leaders of the nations within the Commonwealth was held in Kingston, Jamaica, at the end of April, 1975. Its purpose was to review matters of common interest. Such a meeting is now the almost annual practice, taking place sometimes in London and sometimes in the capitals of member-nations. The Commonwealth is a loose association of nations which were at one time British colonies (see Appendix II). The members meet as equals, and the association has very little machinery and few rules. Since 1965, it has, however, had a Secretariat. The first Secretary-General was a

Table 15.1 International Associations: West Indian Membership

Country	UNO	FAO†	ILO†	IMF†	WHO†	GATT	OAS	IDB	Common-wealth	Carifta	Caricom	WI Federation	Comecon
The Bahamas	*			*	*				*				
Barbados	*	*	*	*	*	*	*	*	*	*	*	*	
Cuba	*	*	*		*	*	*[1]						*
Dominican Republic	*	*	*	*	*	*	*	*					
Grenada	*			*	*		*		*	*	*	*	
Guyana	*	*	*	*	*	*			*	*	*		
Haiti	*	*	*	*	*	*	*	*					
Jamaica	*	*	*	*	*	*	*	*	*	*	*	*	
Trinidad and Tobago	*	*	*	*	*	*	*	*	*	*	*	*	
British Empire:									*[2]				
Antigua										*	*	*	
Belize										*	*		
Dominica[3]										*	*	*	
Montserrat										*	*		
St Kitts-Nevis										*	*	*	
St Lucia										*	*	*	
St Vincent										*	*	*	

UNO: United Nations Organization
† United Nations Specialized Agencies (examples of many):
FAO: Food and Agriculture Organization
ILO: International Labour Organization
IMF: International Monetary Fund
WHO: World Health Organization

GATT: General Agreement on Tariffs and Trade, to promote international trade by reducing tariffs

OAS: Organization of American States
[1] Since no country can technically be expelled, Cuba remained a member but was, in effect, excluded from 1962 onwards

IDB: Inter-American Development Bank

Commonwealth: See Appendix II
[2] All British colonial territories represented by Britain

Carifta: Caribbean Free Trade Area, established 1968 among West Indian Commonwealth countries. Replaced by the Caribbean Common Market (see Caricom)

Caricom: Caribbean Community and Common Market, established 1973 by Barbados, Guyana, Jamaica and Trinidad and Tobago. The other members joined in 1974

WI Federation: West Indies Federation, established 1958, dissolved 1962

Comecon: Council for Mutual Economic Assistance, a communist organization centred on eastern Europe
[3] Dominica: Independent, November 1978

Canadian who was succeeded in 1975 by the Foreign Minister of Guyana, Shridath Ramphal, on the recommendation of the leaders of Caricom.

It is not easy to quantify the advantages of membership of the Commonwealth. Its objectives are mutual assistance in almost every aspect of life. At Kingston, the members reviewed the problems of many areas of the world including the Caribbean, and they paid considerable attention to economic questions. Harold Wilson, at that time the British Prime Minister, put forward a programme for the stabilization of commodity prices, and a committee was set up under the able chairmanship of Alister McIntyre, the Secretary-General of Caricom, to work out a Commonwealth programme to be put before UNCTAD. The Kingston Conference also welcomed the Lomé Agreement which had made provision for assistance from the European Economic Community to nations in the developing world (twenty-two of them within the Commonwealth) in which the members of the EEC had a special interest. And the Commonwealth leaders also agreed to seek to ensure full equality of opportunity for women. There was not, of course, unanimous agreement on everything. But one advantage of such meetings is that every member can put forward his ideas, and Forbes Burnham was able to argue vigorously in favour of the radical reform of the world's monetary institutions. Such meetings also provide opportunities for West Indian Africans to meet with their kinsmen from Nigeria, Ghana and other African states, and for West Indian Asians to meet with their kinsmen from the Indian sub-continent.

Shridath Ramphal became the Secretary-General of the Commonwealth on the recommendation of the leaders of Caricom

Meetings between heads of government and at a great many other levels make up one aspect of the work of the Commonwealth, and from these contacts much may develop of mutual benefit. There is also the Commonwealth Development Corporation whose main aim is to help to finance development projects which will provide work and generate wealth. It was this Corporation (at that time, the Colonial Development Corporation), which built the Fort George Hotel in Belize City to attract tourists and investors. In 1965, the CDC had projects in hand throughout the Caribbean: airport construction in the Cayman Islands, electricity installations in most of the Windward Islands, housing and industrial development in Jamaica and Trinidad, and rice-growing and timber-cutting in Guyana. In 1974, the CDC was promoting nearly 250 projects in the developing nations of the Commonwealth.

A Commonwealth Fund for Technical Co-operation also exists, to bring expertise to the poorest members. The Commonwealth Foundation seeks to promote progress in medicine, planning and the training of young people. Commonwealth scholarships make it possible for some students to further their studies in the universities of the Commonwealth, and the Commonwealth Games bring together the association's athletes and sportsmen. Trade is encouraged by Commonwealth Preferences, and the bulk of the grants and loans made available by the richer members of the association go to their fellow-members of the Commonwealth.

The Commonwealth brings English-speaking West Indians into contact with other peoples as far apart as Australia and Nigeria, Canada and India. They meet in regular conferences: the Educational Conference, the Medical Conference, the Press Union, the conferences of the Parliamentary Association and many others. But it remains difficult precisely to define what the Commonwealth is. It is sometimes alleged that it is some sort of device to enable the British to re-live the days of their empire, and it is certainly a club to which only those nations can belong which were once British colonies. But it is essentially an association of equals in which Britain has no greater authority than Jamaica, and which exists for the benefit of all its members and not for the self-interest of any one member. Pandit Nehru, the Prime Minister of India, once said that it was a 'rather strange and odd collection of nations'. But he thought its strength lay in the fact that its members

> 'meet as friends, try to understand each other and try, as far as possible, to find a common way of working.'

John Strachey, a British minister, put his finger on what it was that united members of the Commonwealth:

> 'To know a no-ball from the googly and a point of order from a supplementary question is genuinely to have something in common.'

Not all the members of the Commonwealth are cricketing nations and, by 1979, not all of them scrupulously practised constitutional government, but they shared a large number of common attitudes and common aims. Barbados covered several of them with the issuing of a stamp for the Jubilee of Elizabeth II in 1977 which showed the knighting of the outstanding West Indian cricketer, Garfield Sobers, for his services to the sport and to international friendship.

(Barbados, 1977)

The American Associations

The OAS (the Organization of American States) was set up at Bogota in 1948 as the successor to the International Bureau of the American Republics. The OAS is an organization whose chief concern is the settlement of disputes between members, but it has a variety of organs to extend its work into the fields of mutual co-operation in economic matters, social problems and defence. When they became independent, most of the ex-British states, with the exception of Guyana, joined the OAS. Each member of the OAS has one vote, but to a far greater degree than is the case with the Commonwealth the suspicion exists that the OAS is dominated by one power, in this case the USA. This is perhaps inevitable since the Organization is concerned with such matters as the co-ordinating of foreign policies and the security of the Americas. Clashes between the USA and Latin American states have occurred on a variety of issues, but the domination of the USA is far from absolute. If the USA played a major part in the virtual isolation of Cuba from the OAS in the 1960s (see page 148), Latin America and the Caribbean played a major part in restoring more normal relationships with Cuba in the 1970s.

Moreover, the USA is not ungenerous in its aid to those poorer neighbours of whose political systems it approves. The Alliance for Progress began its operations in 1962 to try to increase the *per capita* incomes of Latin American states by $2\frac{1}{2}$ per cent a year, and the operations were funded by the United States Agency for International Development. A year earlier, the Inter-American Development Bank had made its first loan with objectives similar to those of the Commonwealth Development Corporation. By 1974, the Bank was able to report that Caribbean and Latin American growth rates were rising overall by more than 7 per cent a year. In 1976, the Bank made loans of over 1500 million dollars. Progress was hampered, however, by the world recession which developed in the mid-1970s.

Increasingly, the nations of Latin America looked for ways of helping themselves and reducing the influence of the USA, and this gave rise to a number of new organizations. The LAFTA (the Latin American Free Trade Association) and the CACM (the Central American Common Market) were among the first, both founded in 1960. Eight years later, the West Indian members of the Commonwealth began to move in a similar direction with the setting-up of Carifta (the Caribbean Free Trade Area).

Regional Co-operation in the Caribbean

Carifta was the result of agreements which were signed in May, July and August, 1968.* There was to be immediate free trade between the members in all but certain enumerated goods. The tariffs and restrictions on these enumerated goods

* For membership, see Table 15.1 on page 189.

Carifta, the start of a new unity among the English-speaking Caribbean nations (Montserrat, 1969)

would be removed within five years by the more developed members and within ten years by the poorer members. The principal aim of Carifta was to encourage trade between the English-speaking islands, and between the islands and Guyana. Existing inter-island trade averaged only about 6 per cent of the total trade of the West Indies and it was unlikely that the trade could become voluminous in the short term, since the members were often seeking to sell similar products. But any increase in trade would be likely to stimulate output and to increase employment, and Carifta would provide a basis for further regional co-operation. By 1973, 10 per cent of Guyana's exports were going to Trinidad and Tobago and 6 per cent to Jamaica, and by 1974, Guyana was making 23 per cent of its purchases in Trinidad and Tobago. Barbados made 12 per cent of its purchases from the Trinidadians and sold 6 per cent of its exports to them in 1974, selling a further 7 per cent in the Windward Islands. Table 14.1 on pages 168–9 shows how inter-island trade is beginning to grow slowly. It is a measure of the size of the problem, however, that there were still six separate currencies in 1978 even within the Commonwealth Caribbean.

A further step towards regional co-operation came when the Caribbean Development Bank was set up in 1969 to assist development projects. Caricom (the Caribbean Community and Common Market) came into existence in 1973 and, shortly afterwards, Eric Williams made an important declaration that the surplus funds of Trinidad and Tobago would be used in future for promoting the welfare of the Community as a whole. Oil made Trinidad the richest of the members of the Community, and the unselfish declaration of a willingness to share (even though, in the world as a whole, Trinidad and Tobago was by no means a wealthy nation) marked a distinct departure from the parochial attitudes all too often evident in the West Indies in the past. Inter-island help took a practical and effective form in 1976 when the Jamaican economy was assisted by a generous loan from Jamaica's partners in the Caribbean Community, which gave valuable support to Jamaica's foreign exchange reserves. At the same time, along with Britain, Caricom was giving support to Grenada's tottering financial position. Such co-operation, combined with the declaration by Eric Williams, may ultimately provide a solution to the teasing question of what is to become of the Lesser Antilles, drawing them into a Caribbean Community of West Indian nations who work together for the welfare and prosperity of all.

The Caribbean Community and Common Market may well be the key to such future

Trinidad's pitch lake is the source of the pitch on these trucks and, along with oil, a source of comparative wealth to the island

Figure 15.2 The Caribbean Today (Political Map)

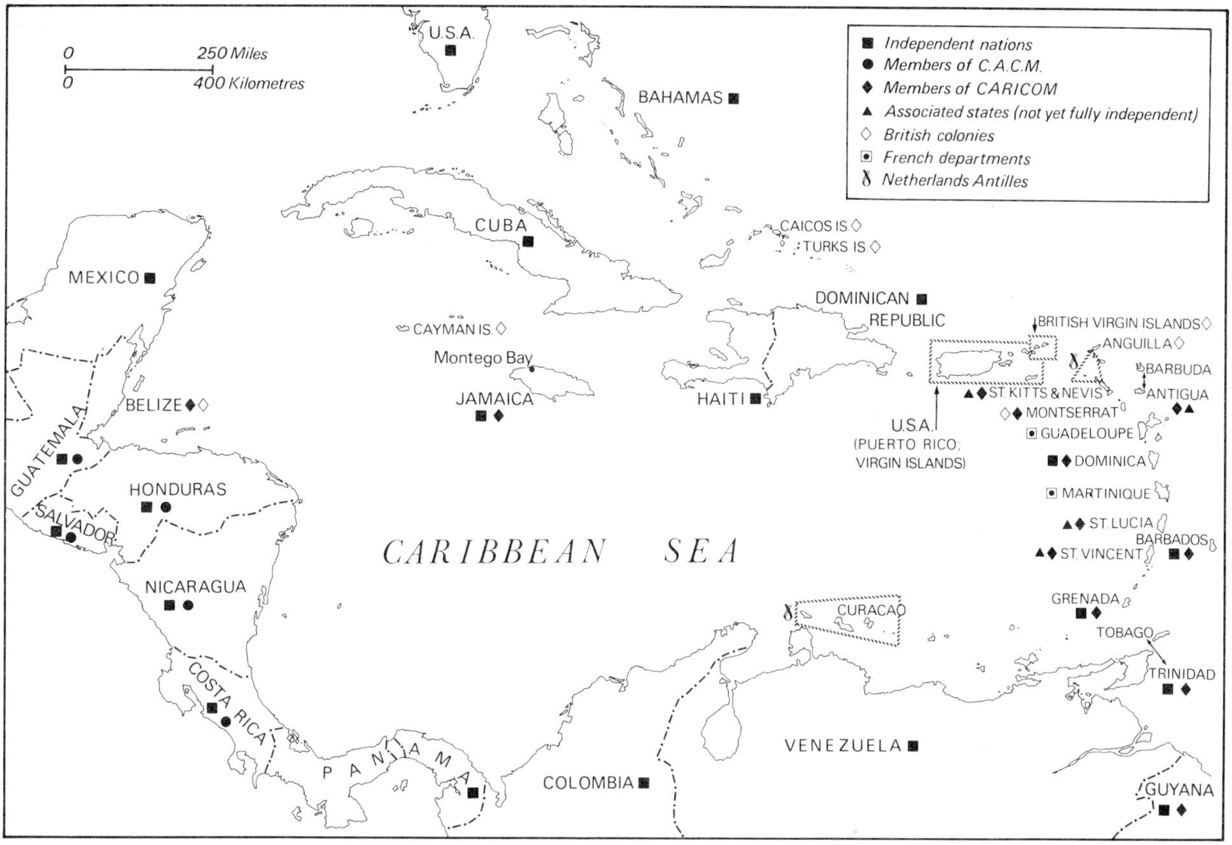

developments. The first articles of agreement for Caricom were signed in August, 1973, by Barbados, Guyana, Jamaica and Trinidad and Tobago. Belize and many of the smaller English-speaking islands joined the Community in 1974.* One aim was to build on the achievements of Carifta, to expand regional trade; and it was agreed that Caricom would co-operate with similar associations in Latin America, such as the CACM. Normal relations were also established between Caricom and Cuba, partly under the influence of Forbes Burnham. Burnham's aims were positive and often radical. Within Guyana, he wanted 'to make the small man a real man' and he believed strongly in co-operative self-reliance. He also wanted to make the small nation a real nation, and was prepared to build bridges to whichever parts of the outside world seemed to offer advantageous contacts. By 1977, he was seeking to make Guyana an associate (but not a full member) of Comecon, for he recognized that links with the communist world could bring benefits to Guyana. At the same time, Guyana had connections with the capitalist and western European Economic Community, partly through membership of the Commonwealth and ties with Britain, and partly through Guyana's association with the ACP group (African, Caribbean and Pacific). Within the Americas, Guyana belonged to SELA (the Latin American Economic System), and Burnham now put his energetic radicalism at the service of Caricom. He wanted to make Caricom a real Community.

The celebration of Community Day helps West Indians to adopt a new, dual attitude, taking pride in their nationality—Barbadian, Jamaican or whatever—but at the same time taking pride in their membership of the Caribbean Community. At an early stage, Caricom moved towards the principle of dual nationality by making it possible for the nationals of member states to travel on common Community documents. It is too early to say where Caricom will eventually lead nor even if it will survive. A United States of the West Indies or a new Federation may not be impossible, but

* For membership, see Table 15.1 on page 189.

for the present the Community aims to promote the welfare of its members in a variety of ways and to break down the old suspicions and local self-interests which have been an obstacle in the West Indies in the past. As the example of Guyana shows clearly, many contacts remain with the outside world, some of them old, some new. But since 1968, Carifta, the Development Bank, the Caribbean Investment Corporation and Caricom have encouraged important changes within the Caribbean itself, multiplying the contacts between the English-speaking nations and islands, and tackling common problems with common action.

Unfortunately, the strains which the soaring price of oil imposed on the weak economies of Guyana and Jamaica threatened to undermine Caricom at the end of 1977. Inter-island trade slumped and inter-island jealousies were reawakened. There were also ideological differences within the Community, between the socialist governments of Guyana and Jamaica and the more conservative government of Trinidad and Tobago. The early successes of Caricom had led Haiti and Surinam to apply for membership, the one formerly French, the other formerly Dutch. Had such applications been accepted, West Indians would have begun to break down the barriers erected in colonial days, but a decision was postponed lest the Community should be enlarged prematurely and its resources overstretched. By the end of 1978, however, the worrying question was not about new members but about the survival of Caricom. Without vigorous and united action by its three principal members, it seemed at least possible that the Community could break up, as the West Indies Federation had broken up.

Since 1945, great strides have been made in developing and, in some ways, transforming the West Indies. But the development of nations is a continuing story. Throughout the world, the late twentieth century is a period of rapid change, and by the end of the century the West Indies may well have changed again, radically. Recent times have been dominated by nationalism, as earlier times were dominated by colonialism. The foundation of Caricom suggested that a new internationalism was developing with a growing awareness that the West Indies is no mere geographical expression but a distinctive region. Yet there are still pressures towards fragmentation in the Caribbean, as was seen in 1977 when the people of Aruba voted to break away from the Netherlands Antilles, and began to seek independence. West Indian states share a heritage, many elements of which were common to all, and they share problems whose solutions may best be achieved by common actions. But a united West Indies, prosperous enough to resist the meddling of external forces and self-confident of its own Caribbean identity, has yet to be constructed. This book has been concerned with the West Indian heritage and its bearing on the present. The past and present will in turn have a bearing on the future, and West Indians have never been better placed than they are now to determine what the future of the West Indies will be.

Exercises

1 What are the problems which have to be faced (a) in building West Indian nations and (b) in building bridges between the West Indian nations?

2 What industries exist at the present time in the countries of the Caribbean? Which islands are seriously lacking in industries? Why has industrial development in the West Indies not been more extensive, and what arguments can be put forward in favour of more industrial development?

3 Make a list of the international organizations of which your own country is a member. *In each case*, summarize the advantages of this membership (a) to your own country and (b) to the organization itself.

4 Make a study of the Caribbean Community and Common Market, arranging your material under the following headings: the history of the Community; the rules of the Community; the achievements of the Community; discussion concerning the future of the Community.

5 Build up a factual dossier on the country in which you live, collecting the available geographical, economic and social statistics into reference tables for the most recent years for which this information is available. Collect similar information for a previous year in the early 1960s, and compare the tables. What conclusions can you draw from this comparison?

6 Undertake a survey of the attitudes of people in your community towards neighbouring islands. Does the survey support or refute the suggestion that the old parochialism of West Indian islands is no longer strong?

7 In what ways do you consider that life in your country is now better than it was a generation ago? What further improvements would you like to see by the end of the twentieth century?

Appendix I Constitutional Change in the British Empire

Colonies of Settlement and Colonies of Administration

Colonies of settlement, such as Australia, were essentially empty or near-empty lands in which British settlements were made. Colonies of administration, such as Nigeria, were areas which already had substantial native populations. The British West Indies, which originally fitted into the first category, came increasingly closer to the second as time went on. In colonies of settlement, the main purpose of government was often considered to be to secure the proper treatment and protect the interests of the settlers. In colonies of administration, the function of government was to safeguard the interests of all those who were under the British flag.

The British Colonial Office and Crown Colony Government

A British government department known as the Colonial Office was, in the course of time, set up to deal with the affairs of the empire. This Office had a staff of permanent civil servants, and it was nominally under the control of the Colonial Secretary, a minister in the British government. Although of cabinet rank, the Colonial Secretary was seldom considered to be a particularly important government minister before the appointment of Joseph Chamberlain in 1895. Chamberlain had a special interest in the empire and in that part of it in the West Indies. Amongst the duties of the Colonial Secretary was the appointment of governors for the British colonies. The first responsibility of each governor was to the British government, which might be called upon at any time to pay for his extravagance or mistakes and might even have to send troops to sort out difficult situations. The further responsibilities of the governor depended on the nature of the colony he governed. In colonies of settlement, he had a duty to the settlers. In colonies of administration he had a wider concern, for the well-being of all of the subjects of the British Crown. Crown colony government, which gave the governor almost dictatorial powers, subject to ultimate control from Britain, was usually seen to be the most effective system for the government of colonies of administration. With their large numbers of people who were not British settlers, West Indian colonies in the nineteenth century seemed to be best fitted for this system of crown colony government. In earlier days, however, when the British population was a greater proportion of the whole, it had been usual for the West Indian islands to have assemblies which represented the interests of the settlers. These assemblies were abolished before the end of the nineteenth century. Under crown colony government, the colonies were then ruled by governors who were appointed in Britain, and paid by the British government. Each governor appointed an executive council and a legislative council, the function of these councils being to advise and assist him.

Representative Government

The settlers in colonies of settlement had often demanded the same political rights as they would have expected in Britain itself. This is why assemblies had been set up in the early British colonies in the West Indies. Many governors found it prudent to listen to the advice of these assemblies even though, as in the case of George Grey in New Zealand, it might involve them in trouble with the native populations. In areas of mixed race, it eventually came to seem sensible that the assemblies should be able to offer advice on behalf of all the races and not merely of one. In the early twentieth century, the election of spokesmen to represent the inhabitants of the colonies in the governor's councils (usually the legislative council before the executive council), began to change crown colony government into representative government. The governor was now advised by elected representatives and not merely by people of his own choosing.

Ministerial Government

Colonial governors would eventually admit elected representatives to their executive councils, which were in charge of the day-to-day running of the colonies. This first happened in the nineteenth century, in the colonies of settlement such as Canada and Australia; and the elected representatives were white. The purpose of admitting such representatives was two-fold: it broadened the power-base of the governor by keeping him in closer touch with the needs and wishes of the inhabitants; and it provided the inhabitants' representatives with experience of the responsibilities of government. In the twentieth century, this system of ministerial government, where some of the members of the executive council (ministers) were elected, was extended to the colonies of administration where the elected members were often non-white. This point was reached in the West Indies shortly after the Second World War, at about the same time that it was reached in Britain's African colonies such as the Gold Coast (Ghana) and Nigeria.

Self-Government (Responsible Government)

Self-government was reached when all the ministers of the colony's government were elected and when they were responsible to an elected assembly. Such a system bore a resemblance to the system of government in Britain, with its elected parliament and a government formed by the political party which wins a majority of the seats in the House of Commons in a general election. The governor continued to act on behalf of the British Crown and to be answerable to the British Colonial Office. If the Colonial Office thought it necessary, he could veto the colony's legislation and, in theory (for it was done very seldom), remove elected ministers from office. Britain meanwhile kept control of the colony's external affairs which included certain matters such as defence and the protection of merchant shipping.

Independence

In the early twentieth century, some of the white-dominated colonies of settlement insisted that self-government was not enough. Self-government was often referred to at this time simply as 'a system like Canada's' or as 'Dominion Status'. Dominion Status was re-defined shortly after the First World War (see page 197) and, for practical purposes, came to mean something very closely akin to 'Independence'. Britain ceased to exercise control over the affairs of the former colony. The first West Indian state to reach this position was Jamaica, on 6 August, 1962.

Monarchies and Republics

When the white-dominated colonies of settlement re-defined Dominion Status to mean virtual independence, they continued to be monarchies, and they remained in association with Britain and with one another in the Commonwealth (see Appendix II). The British Crown was still the Crown of nations such as Australia and Canada and was represented in each of these nations by a governor-general; but, just as was the case in Britain itself, the powers of the Crown were very small. The Crown, and each governor-general, had certain administrative duties and judicial functions, but real power lay with the elected government in every case. India became independent in 1947 and decided to drop the monarchy, and thus become a republic, in 1950. This meant that the British king was no longer the king-emperor of India and that, in future, the head of state in India would be an elected president. Some independent states in the West Indies have followed India's example—Guyana and, more recently, Trinidad and Tobago in 1976. Queen Elizabeth II, on the other hand, remains Queen of Barbados. Elizabeth II has yet another role: she is the Head of the Commonwealth, a symbolic office without power. Guyana and Barbados are both members of the Commonwealth, for republics as well as monarchies both belong to it.

Appendix II The Commonwealth

The Commonwealth is a voluntary association of independent nations, all of which in earlier times were within the British empire. Almost all of Britain's former colonies applied for and received admission to the Commonwealth at the time they became independent. All the former-British West Indian nations are members of the association.

Before the Second World War, the Commonwealth was known as the British Commonwealth of Nations. At that time, it was rather like a white man's club since its members were the former colonies of settlement such as Canada. After the Second World War, many new nations were born and the white member-nations came to be outnumbered by the non-white member-nations after 1960. One principle which is fundamental to the Commonwealth is that of racial equality. All forms of racialism are condemned by the association. For this reason, South Africa was persuaded to resign in 1961 because of the policies of racial discrimination practised by its government.

Another fundamental principle is that all members are equal. Each independent nation, large or small, is entitled to put its point of view and play as great or as little a part in Commonwealth affairs as it wishes. Britain has no special privileges in the Commonwealth, although the British Crown is accepted as the nominal head of the association, an office which is little more than symbolic. The basis of the association was laid down in the 1920s when Canada and the other White Dominions were seeking to establish that Dominion Status truly meant Independence. The British politician Arthur Balfour, a man who was skilful in juggling with words, came up with the Balfour Formula in 1926 to explain what the Dominions were

> 'Autonomous communities within the British Empire, equal in status, in no way subordinate one to another in any aspect of their domestic or external affairs, though united by a common allegiance to the Crown and freely associated as members of the British Commonwealth of Nations.'

The British then passed the Statute of Westminster in 1931 to give legal force to the declaration that the Dominions were fully independent. The Commonwealth of Nations then went on with its members 'freely associated'. Since they were also equal members, it seemed inappropriate to call it a British Commonwealth, and after the Second World War the title was simplified to *The Commonwealth.*

In 1979, the Commonwealth has almost forty members. Regular meetings are held between the Prime Ministers and Presidents of the member-states, but there are also innumerable contacts between the members at other levels. Government ministers discuss matters of trade, education, finance, defence and almost every question of common interest. In addition to the contacts between governments, there are also numerous contacts between groups of professional men such as lawyers, teachers and journalists. The Commonwealth exists essentially to bring together the peoples of many races from all corners of the world, so that they may learn mutual respect and promote their common interests in every way. It has some similarities to the United Nations Organization, but it is much less highly-organized and possesses much less machinery. Contacts are often informal and depend for their effectiveness less on what is written down than on the personal bonds of friendship which develop between peoples.

Reference to the Index of this book will make it possible to see some of the ways in which the work of the Commonwealth brings material advantages to its members. The Commonwealth Development Corporation and the Commonwealth Sugar Agreement, for example, have brought benefits to West Indian members. But it is not easy to measure the value of the Commonwealth in specific terms. Trade preferences are certainly important, and so too are grants and loans to the members of the Commonwealth who are comparatively poorer than members such as Canada and Britain. Sometimes, the Commonwealth shows itself capable of united action, as it did during the Second World War. Sometimes, it can take a moral stand as it has done over apartheid in South Africa and white supremacy in Rhodesia. But the Commonwealth possesses no magic wand with which to eliminate the problems of the world or even the problems of its members. It simply represents an honest attempt to bring together many of the peoples of the world, not for the purpose of demonstrating superiority and winning political advantages, but for the purpose of promoting understanding and of seeking ways to improve the lot of mankind through co-operation.

Appendix III The First European Settlements in the West Indies

[1] Hispaniola	1492	Spanish (Columbus)
[2] Puerto Rico	1508	Spanish (de León)
[3] Jamaica	1509	Spanish (Esquivel)
Cuba	1511	Spanish (Velásquez)
Trinidad	1532	Spanish, first governor appointed
The Guianas	c.1616	Dutch
St Kitts	1624	English (Warner)
Barbados	1627	English (Powell)
Nevis	1628	English, from St Kitts
Barbuda	1628	English
Antigua	1632	English
Montserrat	1632	English, Irish Catholics from St Kitts
* Tobago	1632	Dutch
Curaçao	1634	Dutch
Guadeloupe	1635	French
Martinique	1635	French
Bahamas	1648	English, settlement on Eleuthera from Bermuda; and on New Providence, 1656
Anguilla	1650	English
Grenada	1650	French, after Caribs drove off English settlers of 1609
* St Lucia	1650	French, from Martinique, after Caribs drove off English settlers of 1605 and 1638. Subsequently changed hands fourteen times between the French and English
Belize	1662	English, from Jamaica
British Virgin Islands	1666	English, occupation of Tortola
Cayman Islands	1670	English, ceded in Treaty of Madrid. Earlier a pirate base. Effective colonization from Jamaica in eighteenth century
Turks and Caicos Islands	1678	English, from Bermuda
* Dominica	1750s	French, after Caribs drove off French settlers of 1632
* St Vincent	1750s	French, after Caribs drove off earlier Dutch, English and French settlers

Amerindian names

[1] Quisqueya
[2] Boriquen
[3] Xaymaca

* Declared neutral islands in 1748 (see Table 8.1 on page 94)

Glossary

Authoritarian Not liberal; usually applied to a government which imposes strict discipline and represses its opponents.

Britain The British Isles consist of Great Britain, Ireland and various small islands such as the Isle of Man. The largest island is Great Britain. It is often referred to simply as Britain and it incorporates England, Scotland and Wales. At present, England, Scotland and Wales are linked with Northern Ireland in the United Kingdom. England came to control Wales at the end of the thirteenth century, but Scotland was at that time a separate kingdom. From 1603, England and Scotland were under the same king; but they were not united until 1707. In this book, England is referred to before 1707 and Britain thereafter, since the activity in the West Indies was first undertaken by the English government and this did not become a British government until 1707.

Bull A letter, decree or other pronouncement originating from the Pope and bearing the Papal seal (Latin, *bulla*).

Charter A legal document usually issued by a sovereign or government setting out the rights of an individual person or a group of persons. Charters were often granted to commercial companies. Those to whom they were granted might well have to pay handsomely for their privileges.

CIA Central Intelligence Agency. A national security body of the United States Federal Government operating secretly for the gathering of strategical and political information. Because of the secrecy in which it operates and the sometimes dubious methods which it employs, its operations are often regarded with suspicion by the left-wing governments of neighbouring states.

Democracy Rule by the people: a system of government which permits some effective control to the masses.

Department (*Département*, French). A unit-area of local government, chiefly in France. It enjoys extensive rights of self-government but in major matters remains subject to the overriding control of the central government.

Dictatorship Rule by a dictator who exercises absolute authority, e.g. the rule of Adolf Hitler in Nazi Germany.

Enfranchisement A citizen is said to enjoy enfranchisement when he possesses civil rights, and to *enfranchise* a citizen is to confer civil rights on him. The commonest right referred to in this connection is the right to take part in democratic political processes and to vote. See *Franchise*.

Evangelicals Evangelicals believed that man's love of God should be reflected in his love of, and his care for, his fellow-men. Instead of the tame acceptance of social problems shown by many churchmen, Evangelicals brought a fierce concern to bear on social evils and did much good work to improve the lot of paupers, criminals and, of course, slaves.

Franchise A particular right, often of citizenship. Commonly, the right to vote.

Indenture Any sealed agreement or contract, especially of the type which binds an apprentice to his master and thus a workman to his employer. The indenture specifies the conditions of the agreement.

Intendants French royal officials. Cardinal Richelieu revived the practice of appointing such officials to supervise the actions of local governors, and he placed in their hands the whole judicial and police administration in 1637. Intendants were usually of middle-class origin and generally had legal training. The king preferred them to the haughty nobility whom he never really trusted.

Knighthood Originally an honour awarded as a token of military attainment, but given for a variety of other services in modern times. In Britain, a knight is entitled to call himself 'Sir'.

Labour-intensive Methods of production which make great use of labour are called *labour-intensive*. Such methods make comparatively little use of machinery but employ a great many workers especially when their labour is cheap. These methods are common in primitive economies.

Lobby A pressure group, representing the interests of a particular association of people to members of parliament and pressing its advice or its claims on parliament. Thus, the West Indian Lobby pressed its advice and claims on the British parliament; it represented the estate owners of the West Indies.

Methodists The teaching of *Methodists* stressed the moral virtue of accepting one's lot with the prospect of a rich reward in Heaven. Its basic stress was on the spiritual relationship between an individual and his God. Methodists were generally less concerned than Evangelicals with the need for action on earth, but their emphasis on individual moral responsibility often resulted in a desire to make social improvements.

Metropolitan Belonging to the centre and controlled by the centre. The centre of the early activity of Europeans in the West Indies was in the mother country, to which West Indian territories belonged and by which they were controlled. *Metropolitan control* is thus control by the European mother country.

Mulattoes The offspring of a European parent (usually the father) and an African parent (usually the mother). Also applied to succeeding generations who descend from such a union. Reference to Table 11.1 on page 138 shows that no distinction is made in the USA between mulattoes and whites.

Multinational Company A company operating in a number of countries and having production or service facilities in more countries than its country of origin. Such companies have grown rapidly in recent times; they are often very powerful and sometimes come into conflict with governments in the countries in which they operate.

Nationalization The placing of an enterprise under state ownership, making it national property; e.g. the nationalization of a bauxite company makes that company the property of the nation instead of the property of private owners.

Nationalism Pride in one's country, enthusiasm for the country's success. Nationalism may take various forms, e.g. a campaign to free one's country from foreign control; a campaign to make one's country united and strong; a campaign to make one's country supreme over others.

One-party State A state in which only one political party is permitted. This is the ruling party and no opposition party is allowed to exist. Such a system is sometimes favoured where opposition parties are particularly obstructive and make government difficult without offering a constructive alternative.

Papiamento A *lingua franca* which has evolved out of Spanish, Dutch and some other languages.

Parish The smallest unit of local government in England which was also introduced into the West Indies as part of the English administrative system. The affairs of the parish were administered by a *vestry*, which was elected by the local freeholders. See *Poor Relief*.

Parochialism A word derived from *parish* to describe narrow-mindedness, the inability to see things except in the context of a very small environment.

Poor Relief Assistance to those in poverty. The Elizabethan Poor Law made each parish responsible for its own poor, and movement of the poor from one place to another was discouraged. Overseers were authorized to charge a poor rate on the propertied people of the parish, the money to be used to create work for the able-bodied and to provide alms for the aged and sick. This Poor Law was applied in parishes in the West Indies. See *Parish*.

Protection A system of *tariffs* (see below) to protect home industries against foreign competition. The opposite to *free trade*.

Radical Enthusiastic for major change, for reform.

Reactionary Backward-looking, desiring to put back the clock; opposed to change.

Secession Separation, breaking away. Within any union of states (or races), one part may favour secession.

Separatism A movement in favour of breaking-away, usually of *secession*.

Status Quo The Latin expression *status quo ante bellum* is translated as 'the situation as it was before the war'. The abbreviated form, *status quo*, is often used to mean the situation as it was or the situation as it is. Thus, *to restore the status quo* means to put back the balance where it was formerly.

Suffrage The right to vote. *Manhood suffrage*, the right of all males to vote. *Adult suffrage* or *universal suffrage*, the right of all adults to vote.

Tariffs Duties (taxes) on imports. See *Protection*.

Suggestions for Further Reading

General

Augier, F. R., Gordon, Hall and Reckord, *The Making of the West Indies* (Longmans, 1964)
Burns, A. C., *History of the British West Indies* (Allen & Unwin, 1954)
Emeruwa, L., *The West Indies* (Longmans, 1962)
Garcia, A., *History of the West Indies* (Harrap, 1965)
Mitchell, H., *Caribbean Patterns* (Chambers, 1967)
Parry, J. H. and Sherlock, P. M., *A Short History of the West Indies* (Macmillan, 1971)
Sherlock, P. M., *West Indian Nations* (Macmillan, 1973)
Waddell, D. A. G., *The West Indies and the Guianas* (Prentice-Hall, 1967)
Williams, E., *From Columbus to Castro* (Deutsch, 1970)
Wiseman, H. V., *A Short History of the British West Indies* (ULP, 1950)

Collected Documents

Augier, F. R. and Gordon, S. C., *Sources of West Indian History* (Longmans, 1962)
Williams, E., *Documents of West Indian History 1492–1655* (PNM, 1963)

Contemporary Accounts

Columbus, C. (ed. Cohen, J. M.), *The Four Voyages of Christopher Columbus* (Penguin, 1969)
Edwards, B., *History, Civil and Commercial, of the British Colonies in the West Indies* (1794)
Las Casas, B. de, *Historia de las Indias* (1559)
Ligon, R., *A True and Exact History of the Island of Barbados* (Published 1657, n.e. Cass, 1970)
Long, E., *History of Jamaica* (Published 1774, n.e. Cass, 1970)

National Histories

Black, C. V., *The Story of Jamaica* (Collins, 1965)
Carmichael, G., *The History of the West Indian Islands of Trinidad and Tobago* (Redman, 1961)
Craton, M., *A History of the Bahamas* (Collins, 1962)
Cundall, F., *The Governors of Jamaica* (West India Committee, 1936)
Daly, V. T., *The Making of Guyana* (Macmillan, 1974)
Dobson, N., *A History of Belize* (Longmans, 1973)
Eisner, G., *Jamaica, 1830–1930, A Study in Economic Growth* (Manchester UP, 1961)
Hoyos, F. A., *Barbados, Our Island Home* (Macmillan, 1961)
Hoyos, F. A., *Our Common Heritage* (Advocate Press, 1952)
Jesse, C., *Outlines of St. Lucia's History* (Castries, 1956)
Logan, R. W., *Haiti and the Dominican Republic* (OUP, 1968)
Nath, D., *A History of Indians in British Guiana* (D. Nath, 1970)
Newman, P., *British Guiana* (OUP, 1962)
Ottley, C. R., *Spanish Trinidad* (College Press, 1955)
Roberts, A., *The French in the West Indies* (Bobs-Merrill, 1942)
Roberts, A., *Six Great Jamaicans* (Pioneer Press, 1952)
Smith, R. T., *British Guiana* (OUP, 1962)
Swan, M., *British Guiana: A Land of Six Peoples* (HMSO, 1957)
Thomas, H., *Cuba or the Pursuit of Freedom* (Eyre & Spottiswoode, 1970)
Waddell, D. A. G., *British Honduras* (OUP, 1961)
Williams, E., *History of the People of Trinidad and Tobago* (Deutsch, 1964)

Further Reading for Individual Chapters

Chapter 1

Ballard, M., *Sails and Guns, the Era of Discovery, 1491–1534* (Methuen, 1970)
Berger, J., *Discoverers of the New World* (Cassell, 1969)
Burland, C. A., *The Ancient Maya* (Weidenfeld, 1967)
'Columbus and the Discovery of America' (Jackdaw Wallet No. 4), Cape
Cundall, F. and Sherlock, P. M., *The Aborigines of Jamaica* (Institute of Jamaica, 1939)
Gallenkamp, C., *Finding out about the Maya* (Muller, 1963)
Hagen, V. von, *Search for the Maya* (Saxon House, 1973)
Kendall, A., *Everyday Life of the Incas* (Batsford, 1973)
Landstrom, B., *Columbus* (Allen & Unwin, 1967)
Richardson, P. R., *The Expansion of Europe, 1400–1600* (Longmans, 1966)

Chapter 2

Baumann, H., *Gold and Gods of Peru* (OUP, 1963)
Blacker, I. R., *Cortes and the Aztec Empire* (Cassell, 1966)
Bray, W., *Everyday Life of the Aztecs* (Batsford, 1968)
'Conquest of Mexico, The' (Jackdaw Wallet No. 51), Cape
Cubitt, H., *Spain and Her Empire under Philip II* (Longmans *Then and There*)

Diaz, B. (trans. Cohen, J. M.), *The Conquest of New Spain* (Penguin, 1963)
Francis, P., *Spanish Conquest in America* (Wheaton, 1964)
Gibson, C., *Spain in America* (Harper, 1967)
Góngora, M. (trans. Southern, R.), *Studies in the Colonial History of Spanish America* (CUP, 1975)
Jones, E., *Protector of the Indians: Las Casas* (Longmans, 1973)
McKendrick, M., *Ferdinand and Isabella* (Cassell, 1969)
Parry, J. H., *The Spanish Seaborne Empire* (Hutchinson, 1966)
'Spanish Inquisition, The' (Jackdaw Wallet No. 44), Cape

Chapter 3

Clapp, H. H., *With Sir Walter Raleigh in British Guiana* (Muller, 1965)
Cowie, L. W., *The Reformation* (Hart-Davis, 1974)
Foss, M., *Undreamed Shores* (Harrap, 1974)
Lloyd, C., *Sir Francis Drake* (Faber, 1957)
Quinn, D. B., *Raleigh and the British Empire* (EUP, 1970)
Robinson, G., *The Elizabethan Ship* (Longmans *Then and There*, 1956)
Sellman, R., *The Elizabethan Seamen* (Methuen, 1957)
Williams, N., *The Sea Dogs: Privateers, Pirates and Plunder in the Elizabethan Age* (Weidenfeld, 1975)
Williamson, J. A., *The Age of Drake* (Black, 1965)

Chapter 4

Allen, H. R., *Buccaneer, Admiral Sir Henry Morgan* (Barker, 1976)
Burney, J., *History of the Buccaneers of America* (Norton Co., 1950)
Crouse, N. M., *The French Struggle for the West Indies, 1665–1713* (Cass, 1967)
Kemp, P. K. and Lloyd, C., *The Brethren of the Coast* (Heinemann, 1960)
Roberts, A., *Sir Henry Morgan* (Pioneer Press, 1952)
Williamson, J. A., *The Caribbee Islands under the Proprietary Patents* (OUP, 1926)
Winston, A., *Pirates and Privateers* (Arrow, 1972)

Chapter 5

Boxer, C. R., *The Dutch Seaborne Empire 1600–1800* (Hutchinson, 1965)
Cole, C. W., *Colbert and French Mercantilism* (Cass, 1965)
Deerr, N., *The History of Sugar* (Chapman and Hall, 1949—2 vols.)
Mims, S. L., *Colbert's West India Policy* (New Haven, 1912)
Pares, R., *Planters and Merchants* (CUP, 1963)
Sheridan, R. B., *The Development of Plantations to 1750* (Caribbean UP, 1970)

Chapter 6

Curtin, P. D., *The Atlantic Slave Trade* (Wisconsin UP, 1972)
Davidson, B., *Black Mother: The African Slave Trade* (Gollancz, 1968)
Davies, K. G., *The Royal Africa Company* (Longmans, 1957)
Hair, P. E. H., *The Atlantic Slave Trade and Black Africa* (Historical Association, 1978)
Killingray, D., *The Slave Trade* (Harrap World History, 1974)
Mannix, D. P. and Cowley, M., *Black Cargoes* (Longmans, 1963)
Martin, B., *John Newton and the Slave Trade* (Longmans *Then and There*, 1961)
Martin, B., *The Journal of a Slave Trader 1750–54* (Epworth Press, 1962)
Mountfield, A., *The Slave Trade* (Wayland Eyewitness, 1973)
Pope-Hennessy, J., *Sons of the Fathers, Atlantic Slave Trade 1441–1807* (Weidenfeld, 1967)
'Slade Trade and its Abolition, The' (Jackdaw Wallet No. 12), Cape
Williams, E., *Capitalism and Slavery* (Deutsch, 1964)

Chapter 7

Barnes, A. C., *The Sugar Cane* (Leonard Hill, 1964)
Beer, G. L., *The Old Colonial System, 1660–1754* (Smith, New York, 1933)
Beer, G. L., *The Old Colonial System, 1660–88* (Peter Smith reprint, 1968)
Braithwaite, E., *Folk Culture of the Slaves in Jamaica* (New Beacon Books, 1970)
Hodgart, A., *The Economics of European Imperialism* (Arnold, 1977)
Montejo, E., *The Autobiography of a Runaway Slave* (The Bodley Head, 1968)
Pares, R., *A West India Fortune* (Longmans, 1950)

Chapter 8

Anderson, M. S., *Europe in the Eighteenth Century, 1713–1783* (Longmans, 1961)
Haswell, J., *The Battle for Empire, A Century of Anglo-French Conflict*—covers c.1650–1763 (Cassell, 1975)
Johnson, D. (ed.), *The World of Empires* (Benn, 1973)
Lloyd, C., *Nelson and Sea Power* (ULP, 1973)
Pares, R., *War and Trade in the West Indies, 1739–1763* (Cass, 1963)
Price, R., *Maroon Societies* (Doubleday, 1973)

Chapter 9

Alexis, S., *The Black Liberator, the Life of Toussaint L'Ouverture* (London, 1949)

Bentley, J. D., *Toussaint L'Ouverture* (Hulton, 1969)
James, G. R. L., *The Black Jacobins* (Random House, 1963)
Lawson, A. H., *The Man Who Freed the Slaves, William Wilberforce* (Faber, 1962)
Miers, S., *Britain and the Ending of the Slave Trade* (Longmans, 1975)
Ott, T. O., *The Haitian Revolution, 1789–1804* (Tennessee UP, 1973)
Pollock, J., *Wilberforce* (Constable, 1977)
Ward, W. E. F., *The Royal Navy and the Slavers* (Allen & Unwin, 1969)

Chapter 10

Beachey, R. W., *The British West Indies Sugar Industry in the Late Nineteenth Century* (OUP, 1957)
Cumpston, I. M., *Indians Overseas in British Territories, 1835–1865* (OUP, 1953)
Curtin, P. D., *The Two Jamaicans, the Role of Ideas in a Tropical Colony, 1830–1865* (OUP, 1955)
Green, W. A., *British Slave Emancipation: The Sugar Colonies and the Great Experiment, 1830–1865* (OUP, 1976)
Lawrence, K., *Immigration into the West Indies in the Nineteenth Century* (CUP, 1971)
Mathieson, M. L., *British Slave Emancipation, 1838–1849* (Longmans, 1932)
Wood, D., *Trinidad in Transition, the Years after Slavery* (OUP, 1968)

Chapter 11

Bartlett, C. J., *A New Balance of Power* (Caribbean UP, 1970)
Blakemore, H., *Latin America* (Blond, 1967)
Corwin, A. F., *Spain and the Abolition of Slavery in Cuba, 1817–1886* (Texas UP, 1968)
Guyatt, J., *Bolivar* (Harrap World History, 1974)
Mecham, J. L., *The United States and Inter-American Security, 1889–1960* (Texas UP, 1961)
Perkins, D., *The US and the Caribbean* (CUP, 1966)
Savelle, M., *Empires to Nations: Expansion in America, 1713–1824* (OUP, 1975)
Smith, R. F., *United States and Cuba* (Connecticut UP, 1960)

Chapter 12

Abel, E., *The Missile Crisis* (J. B. Lippincott, 1966)
Beggs, R., *The Cuban Missiles Crisis* (Longmans, 1971)
Draper, T., *Castroism, Theory and Practice* (Pall Mall, 1965)
Matthews, H. L., *Castro* (Penguin, 1969)
Matthews, H. L., *The Cuban Story* (Braziller, 1961)
Roberts, W. A., *The French in the West Indies* (Cooper Square Publishers, 1971)

Chapter 13

Chase, A., *A History of Trade Unionism in Guyana, 1900–61* (New Guyana Co., 1964)
Clarke, J. H., *Marcus Garvey and the Vision of Africa* (Random House, 1974)
Drummond, I. M., *Imperial Economic Policy 1917–1939* (Allen & Unwin, 1974)
Gordon, S., *A Century of West Indian Education* (Longmans, 1968)
Hamilton, B., *Barbados and the Confederation Question* (Crown Agents, 1956)
Hart, A., *The Life of George William Gordon* (Institute of Jamaica, 1972)
Knowles, W. H., *Trade Union Development and Industrial Relations in the British West Indies* (California UP, 1959)
Mathieson, W. L., *The Sugar Colonies and Governor Eyre, 1849–1866* (Longmans, 1936)
Morrell, W. P., *British Colonial Policy in the Mid-Victorian Age* (OUP, 1969)

Chapter 14

Bell, W., *Jamaican Leaders* (California UP, 1964)
Bolton, G. C., *Britain's Legacy Overseas* (OUP, 1973)
Craig, H., *The Legislative Council of Trinidad and Tobago* (London, 1952)
Davison, R. B., *West Indian Migrants* (OUP, 1962)
Eaton, G., *Bustamente and Modern Jamaica* (Kingston Publishers, 1975)
Glass, R., *Newcomers, the West Indians in London* (Allen & Unwin, 1960)
Lowenthal, D., *The West Indies Federation* (Columbia UP, 1961)
Vincent, T. G., *Black Power and the Garvey Movement* (Ramparts Press, 1971)
Watson, J. B., *Empire to Commonwealth, 1919–1970* (Dent, 1971)

Chapter 15

Bailey, R., *Promoting Commonwealth Development* (Hutchinson, 1970)
'Commonwealth Today, The' (Wallett), Commonwealth Institute
Hill, J., *The Disinherited* (Benn, 1970)
Ingram, D., *Commonwealth for a Colour-blind World* (Allen & Unwin, 1965)
Ingram, D., *The Commonwealth at Work* (Pergamon, 1969)
Lowenthal, D., *West Indian Societies* (OUP, 1973)
'Third World File' (Wallet), Third World First Group
'United Nations, The' (Jackdaw Wallet No. 100), Cape
Watson, J. B., *Success in Twentieth Century World Affairs Since 1919* (Murray 1974)
Wheare, K. C., *The Constitutional Structure of the Commonwealth* (OUP, 1966)

Index

Note: Bold numbers indicate principal references. Italic numbers indicate figures, tables and illustrations.